Architecture for Housing

Understanding the value of design through 14 case studies

Architecture for Housing

Understanding the value of design through 14 case studies

Djordje Stojanović

Birkhäuser
Basel

Contents

Projects

Foreword

Architecture versus Housing
If the System Is Broken, Design a New System

Alan Pert

As the origins of this book stem from a series of talks hosted by the Melbourne School of Design (MSD) over the last few years, I will reflect on Melbourne's contested public housing context and the debates that have run in parallel to the presentation of the fourteen case studies. Although not featured through a selected architectural case study, Melbourne becomes the twelfth city, and the fourteen case studies become important repositories of knowledge for where Melbourne's housing futures might lie.

The first case study was presented in August 2020, and in November 2020 Richard Wynne, then Victoria's Planning and Housing minister, announced the $5.4 billion "Big Housing Build," with the aim to create more than 12,000 homes in four years. Of these, 9,300 were estimated to be social housing. Fast-forward three years, and more than 7,600 homes have been completed or are under way, and more than 1,700 households have either moved into or are getting ready to move into new homes.

For an architectural profession that only ten years ago had no submissions in the multiresidential category at the annual Australian Institute of Architects National Architecture Awards, we are now seeing a fundamental shift in attitudes and alternative models being championed beyond the narrow confines of our current housing system. The Nightingale model and Assemble Communities represent two obvious additions to any case study repository—like the selected case studies in this book, they have turned our attention to the role of architecture and architects and how they navigate the system and recast new possibilities for how the built environment can better answer fundamental questions about how we might live.

Within a short few months of the last case study's being presented at MSD in April 2023, Victoria's outgoing Premier, Daniel Andrews, announced details of the state's long-awaited housing statement. On Wednesday, September 20, 2023, he made a commitment to deliver 80,000 new homes every year for the next 10 years; in addition, the government pledged to speed up approval times for developers who agree to deliver social and affordable homes. Government surplus land would be rezoned at 45 sites across the state with an expectation to deliver at least 9,000 new homes. Planning processes would also be streamlined for significant housing developments, worth at least $50 million in Melbourne and $15 million in regional Victoria, if they delivered at least 10 percent affordable housing, including build-to-rent projects. The Property Council of Australia also identified nearly 80 office buildings that are underused, and the government committed to working with them to convert these into residential and mixed-use properties, creating up to 12,000 homes.

Premier Andrews said the statement was the most significant shake-up of housing policy in decades, but the fallout from the announcement was the plan to demolish Melbourne's 44 landmark public housing towers that were built in the middle of the last century. The statement suggested they would be knocked down and redeveloped within three decades. Home to some 10,000 people, the plan is to tear them down and replace them over three decades with higher-density developments in a public-private partnership. These are the most visible legacy of the Housing Commission of Victoria and the Commonwealth Government's Nation-Building program, which provided tens of thousands of houses and flats in Melbourne and many country towns between the late 1940s and the early 1970s, providing low-rent housing for low-income families. All built using the same precast concrete panel technology, these public housing estates remain a powerful symbol of the social, racial, and architectural tensions that have dogged our cities since the mid-twentieth century.

Two days after the release of the Victorian government's housing statement, researchers from Royal Melbourne Institute of Technology's Centre for Urban Research released a statement arguing that the government had failed to justify its claim that the towers were no longer fit for purpose. Researchers from the University of Melbourne and key voices from the architectural community pointed to numerous case studies from around the world that have turned to "retrofit first." Take, for example, the Tower Blocks Project, a UK Heritage Lottery–funded initiative which ran from Edinburgh College of Art between 2014 and 2019, completing on October 31, 2019. The project emphasized the social and architectural importance of tower blocks and framed multistory social housing as a coherent and accessible nationwide heritage: "As multistory blocks increasingly vanish from our horizons, this project answered to the need to document and create an engagement with the history of multistory social housing at a local and national level." In reevaluating the historical, architectural, and social importance of high-rise living, the Tower Blocks Project aimed to provide a forum for the sharing of images, experiences, and memories. By providing a searchable image archive in tandem with various public engagement activities, the project has brought together both tangible and intangible sources for thinking about recent social history. In other words, in response to these widespread demolitions, we are also seeing a countermovement emerge which attempts to banish the negative assumptions surrounding life in multistory social housing.

The troubled existence of these estates around the world are reflective of the complexity and contradictions of the housing system in each nation. For example, a comparative study of social housing programs across the globe would suggest that they vary substantially—in their histories of origin, who they serve, where housing is located, the means of financing new housing, and even how their housing subsidies work. What is similar though is the generic architectural forms. The physical nature of the housing stock seen in the images of Flemington and North Melbourne circulating across media platforms could have been from Chicago, Glasgow (a quarter of Glasgow's high-rises have been demolished in less than ten years), London, Paris, Toronto, or any number of Eastern European cities that adopted the tower as a way of replacing postwar inner-city slums.

Martin Pawley's 1971 publication, *Architecture versus Housing*, explained that housing is a system—it is an assemblage of different actors, financial imperatives, policy goals, social conditions, architectural ideologies, planning legislation, and construction costs—in the postwar period it also had a lot to do with population growth, car ownership, a rejection of the medieval city, and an optimism for all things future-oriented! Fifty years on, the system is well and truly broken. We seem to have lost our way in the production of the built environment—our cities and suburbs are built for profit, not for people, and we have a crisis of affordability. The market for new housing is dominated by freestanding tracts on the fringes and real estate extrusions in the city. There are limited alternatives or innovative models available on the market.

"Modern architecture's social mission—the effort to establish a decent standard of living for all—seems a thing of the past. Architecture is now a tool of capital, complicit in a purpose antithetical to its erstwhile ideological endeavor."

March 2022 marked the fiftieth anniversary of the demolition of Pruitt-Igoe. The architectural historian Charles Jencks once cited this televised demolition as the moment "modern architecture died." The racially segregated, middle-class complex of thirty-three, eleven-storey towers opened to great fanfare on the north side of St. Louis between 1954 and 1956. But within a decade, it would become a decrepit warehouse exclusively inhabited by poor, Black residents. Within two decades, it would undergo complete demolition. Pruitt-Igoe's obsolescence would trigger a wave of similar spectator sport demolitions across the globe, prompted by many public housing estates' failing to address the social and individual needs of the occupants, with disastrous results. Whether you call Pruitt-Igoe's short, troubled existence a failure of architecture, a failure of policy, or a failure of society, its fate remains bound up with, and reflective of, the fate of many cities in the mid-twentieth century.

Quote
Reinier de Graaf, *Architectural Review*, April 24, 2015

After fifty years of inaction in Victoria, the need to reframe priorities across the board in funding, procurement, design, and delivery of social and affordable housing could finally be getting the urgent attention it deserves, and this book is a timely addition to the debates about the intersection of spatial intelligence (architecture) and interdisciplinary research (housing). As Djordje Stojanović suggests in his introduction to this book, housing manifests an incredible complexity of issues, touching on social, economic, political, aesthetic, and urban questions. As such it is no surprise that the Victorian government's announcement has provoked a lot of reaction. The announcement of a renewed focus on affordability, the recent creation of Homes Victoria and the Big Housing Build all give us hope and a great deal of optimism for new architectural and spatial solutions.

There is now an opportunity to implement a progressive social agenda that redefines housing from a consumer product to an important public infrastructure, with a human touch. Affordable housing has been the problem child perpetually tugging at the sleeve of Housing Ministers, Premiers, and now the Prime Minister since he recently took office. Recent announcements are as much about creating jobs as they are about tackling the corrosive effects of social inequality, but the optimist in all of us welcomes the opportunity to recalibrate Melbourne's chronic housing crisis. While the shortfall in numbers has to be a priority, it cannot be simply a numbers game; it has to be a sociospatial agenda that is about quality and community.

As architect Neave Brown once said about housing, "We have to face it as a social problem, not as an economic problem for neoliberalism to make money out of. And if we go on doing that, we are going into a future of catastrophe with our eyes wide open." We also have to move away from a fixation on traditional family stereotypes and begin to consider the complexity of lifestyle choices in the future. The realities of life have changed. Quality of life is so much more than minimum standards and square meters. Residential buildings constructed in the 1950s and 1960s were almost exclusively conceived for small families, while models of living together are more diverse nowadays. Take Denmark for instance, where there are currently 37 different types of families registered by the government: An ever-growing group of one-person households, flat-sharing communities, life partnerships, and communities with and without children from current and previous relationships, long-distance and weekend relationships, and many other ways of living have emerged. The nuclear family made up of parents and their children is only one model out of many. This alone calls for rethinking how we design housing. This calls for radical changes in the way we build and live, considering aspects of geography, identity, demography, and local communities.

In a postpandemic context, work, leisure, and education are also increasingly merging with housing. Spatial separation by functional categories are being replaced by "living" as a whole. The world of work is no longer dictated by the 9-to-5 patterns of behavior. Working in a home office has become normalized, and the digital age has altered our lives and opened up new flexible opportunities, where boundaries are difficult to fix. Leisure and work are spatially exchangeable. Housing for too long has been defined by static ideas about rooms (one, two, and three bedrooms) and by standards, rules, and programs. The results are house types that have remained unchanged and unchallenged for many years.

Maybe Homes Victoria and the government's new agenda could adopt the principle of IBA Vienna 2016–2022, which states that "each and every Viennese resident is to be able to benefit from the fundamental right to an affordable home; with a view to successfully living in the community, manifold and suitable measures are to be developed to enable different population groups to participate; and nobody should be able to guess a person's social status or income level based on their home address." In a nutshell, the focus is on the dignity and security of people and the health of Vienna's citizens. IBA Vienna recognizes that each social need which receives no answer creates a health problem, and each health problem which remains without an appropriate answer creates a social problem.

With a new political environment, there is now an opportunity to drive and implement a progressive social agenda for housing in Victoria. With the new agency, we can redefine standards, finances, occupation, land use, acquisition, and so much more. By adopting the model of an International Building Exhibition (IBA) we have the opportunity to consider our 12,000 new homes as part of a particular instrument of urban development. IBAs serve as spaces for experimentation, as urban development labs, and as prototypes for new ways of living. IBAs should be understood as temporary laboratories, as areas of both spatial and intellectual experimentation which would seem critical for Homes Victoria, whose objective it is to generate internationally effective contributions to new social housing. We need to avoid pursuing a course of business as usual so that we will not one day find ourselves faced yet again with the ruins of social housing and the spectacle of demolishing estates.

Prof. Alan Pert is Deputy Dean of the Faculty of Architecture Building & Planning at the University of Melbourne, Chair of IBA Melbourne, and Research Director of The Hallmark Research Initiative for Affordable Housing.

Housing Research and Architecture
A Closer Look from Far Away

This book presents a selection of diverse architectural projects for multiunit residential buildings and provides a closer look into architectural design practice. A curious reader should ask: what were the criteria for selection; how are these projects presented; and why is a closer look needed? This short introduction begins to give answers and should help one understand the research scope, aims, methods, and instruments used in making the book, though not necessarily in that order.

The Scope of a Closer Look

Located in eleven cities and designed for diverse cultural and built contexts, selected projects are brought together and examined according to spatial antonyms: the individual and communal; the determined and undetermined; and the interior and exterior.

The rationale for selecting projects was twofold: contribution to design knowledge according to the three nominated antonyms capturing spatial relationships; and contribution to the diversity of housing models in this study.

At the outset, it is important to clarify that the book presents architectural projects for various housing models. The research leading to this publication includes but is not limited to self-organized housing provision outcomes. The book acknowledges the benefits of residents' involvement with housing provision and includes their voices in discussions on most projects. It also explores the specifics of design processes incorporating shared decision-making but focuses on architectural design practice. In doing so, it highlights changes to conventional architectural workflows needed to enable a more robust inclusion of inhabitants' choices.

Reasons for a Closer Look into Architectural Practice

The nominated antonyms are part of the language commonly used in architectural practice, but also the knowledge that, in my view, often escapes researchers from other disciplines and policymakers concerned with housing systems. This elusive form of knowledge is spatial. It uniquely combines social, economic, and environmental aspects with a single medium: the space.

It is evident to me that housing systems worldwide face social, economic, and environmental challenges. I also believe that even if these broad challenges are well understood and a plethora of more precise housing issues are identified in recent interdisciplinary research on housing, not enough is done on the ground level and in real life. Therefore, this book does not insist on asking *why* questions, but by taking a closer look at exemplar spatial practice, it provides insights into *how* architectural design can improve housing outcomes.

The goal is to situate architectural design knowledge in the broader interdisciplinary inquiry into housing and to inform future research and practice.

The nominated antonyms are not observed as opposites. Instead, the emphasis is placed on the continuum within the spectrum they establish. The focus is on design decision-making and the employment of architectural means impacting physical space in selected case studies. We have tried to trace the tangible values of such design decisions and not discuss the notion of spatial thresholds in abstract terms.

Instruments and Methods for a Closer Look from Far Away

The research methods leading to the making of this book include a series of semistructured interviews with architects and residents of the presented projects. In several instances, for practical reasons, the resident interview was replaced by a conversation with other individuals involved with the day-to-day life of the studied building. Still, it is safe to say that the book provides a three-way perspective, including researcher, architect, and resident views.

I wrote this book with support and contributions from the following architects: José Toral (Peris+Toral Arquitectes); Verena von Beckerath (Heide & von Beckerath); Osamu Nishida (ON design partners); Marcelo Faiden (adamo-faiden); Graham Haworth (Haworth Tompkins); Fernando Brunel and Tomás Balparda (BBOA); Marc Frohn (FAR frohn&rojas); Ramon Bosch and Bet Capdeferro (bosch.capdeferro arquitectura); Hervé Potin (Guinée*Potin); Roger Riewe (Riegler Riewe Architects); Juliane Greb and Petter Krag (Büro Juliane Greb); Verena Lindenmayer (EM2N); Luis Basabe (arenas basabe palacios arquitectos); Cristina Gamboa Masdevall and Carles Baiges Camprubí (Lacol); and residents, who have provided most valuable insights.

A primary source of information is a series of talks by architects whose work is presented here. These talks were hosted by the Melbourne School of Design between August 2020 and April 2023 and moderated by the book's author as part of the debate on the role of architectural design innovation in improving housing outcomes in urban environments.

Drawings for this book are created by Milan Katic and me based on the concept design stage information produced by the architects. The floor plans are carefully drawn to the same scale and with unified graphic conventions for consistency, enabling comparing and studying buildings of different sizes. All case studies include three perspective drawings tailored to provide insight and support the discussion into how the three nominated pairs of spatial antonyms are addressed in each project.

Findings from a Closer Look

The introduction is followed with an overview organized according to three nominated antonyms, each loosely associated with three-pronged interdisciplinary research on housing systems: social, economic, and environmental. The overview is written with the benefit of hindsight as a discussion following the findings from case studies. However, it only begins to connect the dots and is meant to guide the reader toward the review of individual projects structured across fourteen chapters. Arguments in this book are presented in layers, allowing readers to get closer and closer to the architectural practice of designing multiunit residential buildings and to create a more complete picture of each project.

Individual ↔ Communal
Determined ↔ Undetermined
Interior ↔ Exterior

Individual ↔ Communal
The Social Viability

The relationship between individual and communal in the selected architectural projects is observed as one of the critical design challenges. This book explores how this relationship is structured in multiunit residential buildings with architectural means while acknowledging that related decision-making begins and ends outside an architectural project. It therefore explores how architecture correlates with the broader understanding of housing involving financing models, the forms of tenure and ownership, and the joint use of facilities. A growing body of interdisciplinary research on housing investigates financial necessity and the desire to embrace more communal living arrangements, including the shared use of domestic spaces.[1] Recent studies presented in some of the leading peer-reviewed academic journals on critical and innovative housing research, such as *Housing Studies*, *Housing Theory and Society*, *Critical Housing Analysis*, *Urban Studies*, *International Journal of Housing Policy*, *Built Environment*, and *Urban Research and Practice*, frequently address the relationship between private and communal in multiunit residential buildings when probing the social viability of housing systems. For example, recent research efforts have provided insights into the inadequacies of the private rental sector,[2,3] barriers to homeownership,[4] the emergence of the co-living industry and short-term rentals,[5,6] and an increase of intentional housing provision involving self-organized housing groups, trusts, and cooperatives.[7–10] These studies, in different ways, at least peripherally address the relationship between communal and individual in residential buildings, but it is often with insufficient emphasis on architectural design and with a need for more interest in what architects can do to help in responding to housing challenges.

The preliminary inquiry conducted in the lead-up to selecting projects for discussion in this book shows that recently published interdisciplinary studies on housing and architectural practice dealing with the design of multiunit residential buildings may not sufficiently inform each other yet. There is a difference in scale associated with studies focusing on housing systems, policy, finance, and urban planning on one side, and architectural design projects often dealing with

1. Sue Heath, Katherine Davies, Gemma Edwards, and Rachael Scicluna, *Shared Housing, Shared Lives: Everyday Experiences across the Lifecourse* (Oxon: Routledge, 2018).
2. Richard Ronald, "'Generation Rent' and Intergenerational Relations in the Era of Housing Financialisation," *Critical Housing Analysis* 5, no. 2 (2018): 14–26.
3. Christopher Feather, "Between Homeownership and Rental Housing: Exploring the Potential for Hybrid Tenure Solutions," *International Journal of Housing Policy* 18, no. 4 (2018): 595–606.
4. Kim McKee, Adriana Mihaela Soaita, and Jennifer Hoolachan, "'Generation Rent' and the Emotions of Private Renting: Self-Worth, Status and Insecurity amongst Low-Income Renters," *Housing Studies* 35, no. 8 (2020): 1468–87.
5. Laura Crommelin, Laurence Troy, Chris Martin, and Chris Pettit, "Is Airbnb a Sharing Economy Superstar? Evidence from Five Global Cities," *Urban Policy and Research* 36, no. 4 (2018): 429–44.
6. Nicole Gurran, "Global Home-Sharing, Local Communities and the Airbnb Debate: A Planning Research Agenda," *Planning Theory & Practice* 19, no. 2 (2018): 298–304.

individual residential buildings on the other. There is also a disparity in the mode of operation. Researchers employ qualitative and quantitative methods to probe into the listed topics and architectural practitioners' work within the same issues but according to the given design brief. The gap in scale, mode of operation, and other differences make it challenging for the findings from research undertakings and knowledge gained through design innovation in architectural practice to be employed together.

A brief summary of the selected projects' determinants may help establish a backdrop for further discussion on the relationship between interdisciplinary research on housing and architectural design. Out of fourteen presented projects, four are developed by housing cooperatives, one by a self-organized building group, four are social housing subsidized by the government, and the remaining five are delivered by private developers. The largest one has more than 100 units, and the smallest one is for only four dwellings. They are all low- to mid-rise buildings. Approximately half are in inner-city areas, while the other half are located closer to the outskirts of large metropolitan areas. Eight are for rental only, four are owner-occupied, and two combine the two forms of tenancy. Most buildings are completed within the last few years, although three earlier projects have been included for their significance to the topics discussed here.

Value of Communal Spaces in Multiunit Residential Buildings

Most architectural projects for multiunit residential buildings combine individual dwellings and communal or jointly used spaces. At the minimum, this is access space, such as vertical cores with staircases and elevators and horizontal corridors or open-air galleries. However, in some buildings, access areas have multiple purposes. In others, communal spaces such as kitchens, additional living rooms, laundries, and outdoor areas are planned and incorporated as integral parts. The scenarios offer themselves to the debate on the individual and the communal as well as the discussion on the social and practical value of shared spaces in multiunit residential buildings.

In the projects presented in this book, the social value of jointly used facilities is in supporting the cohesion of the resident community. Their practical value is in adding more amenities to residential buildings, achieving more efficient use of space, and enabling cost savings through childcare, energy consumption, purchasing household appliances, and more. These concepts can be traced back to housing models that emerged in Northern Europe at the turn of the twentieth century. In Denmark, *bofaellesskab* living communities were formed to replace living within the nuclear family, while in Sweden, *kollektivhuse*

7. Ivo Balmer and Jean-David Gerber, "Why Are Housing Cooperatives Successful? Insights from Swiss Affordable Housing Policy," *Housing Studies* 33, no. 3 (2018): 361–85.
8. Darinka Czischke, "Collaborative Housing and Housing Providers: Towards an Analytical Framework of Multi-Stakeholder Collaboration in Housing Co-Production," *International Journal of Housing Policy* 18, no. 1, (2018): 55–81.
9. Richard Lang, Claire Carriou, Darinka Czischke, "Collaborative Housing Research (1990–2017): A Systematic Review and Thematic Analysis of the Field," *Housing, Theory and Society* 37, no. 1 (2020): 10–39.
10. Jasmine Samantha Palmer, "Realising Collective Self-Organised Housing: A Network Agency Perspective," *Urban Policy and Research* 38, no. 2 (2020): 101–17.

provided a way to rationalize everyday life and, in particular, to help women access the labor market.[11] The arguments for the practical and social value of shared spaces in this book come across most clearly through the conversation with Cristina Gamboa Masdevall and Carles Baiges Camprubí of Lacol, part of the chapter on the building for La Borda housing cooperative, but to a varied degree, are relevant for all presented projects.

The overview of selected projects confirms that a higher ratio of shared spaces is found in residential buildings developed collaboratively by self-organized groups such as housing cooperatives, as is expected. Still, exploring other forms of housing in this book offers insights into how design decisions addressing the relationship between individual and communal are made in architectural practice. The following comparisons are discussed from an architectural design perspective.

Expanded Role of Access Spaces

In three projects, outdoor access galleries are strategically made larger than prescribed by relevant building standards and given an additional role. In the building in Berlin designed by EM2N, they double as extensions of private dwellings and create opportunities for residents from adjacent dwellings to meet. In that project, the continuum between individual and communal is such that floor-to-ceiling glass doors separate private living rooms from the communal walkway. Similarly, the upper access gallery of the Iroko Housing in London is treated as a front yard which is shared by a cluster of units. However, the distinction between private and communal in this project is made more explicit, as private living areas are not visually connected with the access gallery doubling as a communal front yard. The expanded role of outdoor access galleries in mid-rise residential buildings is worthy of a closer look. Such access typology is becoming more prevalent in many countries, and in some, it is considered a "default solution."[12] In the project by bosch.capdeferro arquitectura in Girona, access galleries are designed slightly wider by the entrance to dwellings so that space can be used in more than one way. It is a communal space, but people are encouraged to bring out their tables and chairs to use it as an extension of their dwellings. In the building design by BBOA in Granadero Baigorria, staircases are enlarged to create ancillary space jointly used by a cluster of up to eight dwellings. A sturdier distinction between private and communal is created in the project in Aytré by Guinée*Potin, whereby small bridges separate the access gallery and entrances to individual dwellings. In the project in Cornellà by Peris+Toral Arquitectes, access galleries are minimal, and instead, dwellings are given additional private outdoor areas. Selected

11. Henrik Gutzon Larsen, "Three Phases of Danish Cohousing: Tenure and the Development of an Alternative Housing Form," *Housing Studies* 34, no. 8 (2019): 1349–71.
12. Andrew Beharrell and Rory Olcayto, *The Deck Access Housing Design Guide: A Return to Streets in the Sky* (London: Routledge, 2023).

buildings by adamo-faiden in Buenos Aires, FAR frohn&rojas in Berlin, and Riegler Riewe Architects in Graz follow the same principle in minimizing access areas in their own ways.

Overall Architectural Definition

In some projects, the overall architectural definition explicitly supports the sense of community. It is evident in buildings that are formed around joint outdoor areas. Four of the presented buildings are structured around communal courtyards. In all four, the individual units overlook the communal space, but there are differences among them, too. The courtyard of the housing cooperative La Borda, designed by Lacol, has an important social role with several communal spaces, including the kitchen and dining room, a multipurpose space, and a jointly used terrace, all connected to it. In the building by Peris+Toral, there are no such communal facilities. The communal courtyard is not necessarily meant to attract people to spend time there, but it fosters similar visual connectivity and helps create a sense of community between residents. In buildings designed by Haworth Tompkins and EM2N, the inclusion of a communal outdoor area was one of the departing design decisions and defining features of the overall built form. A different

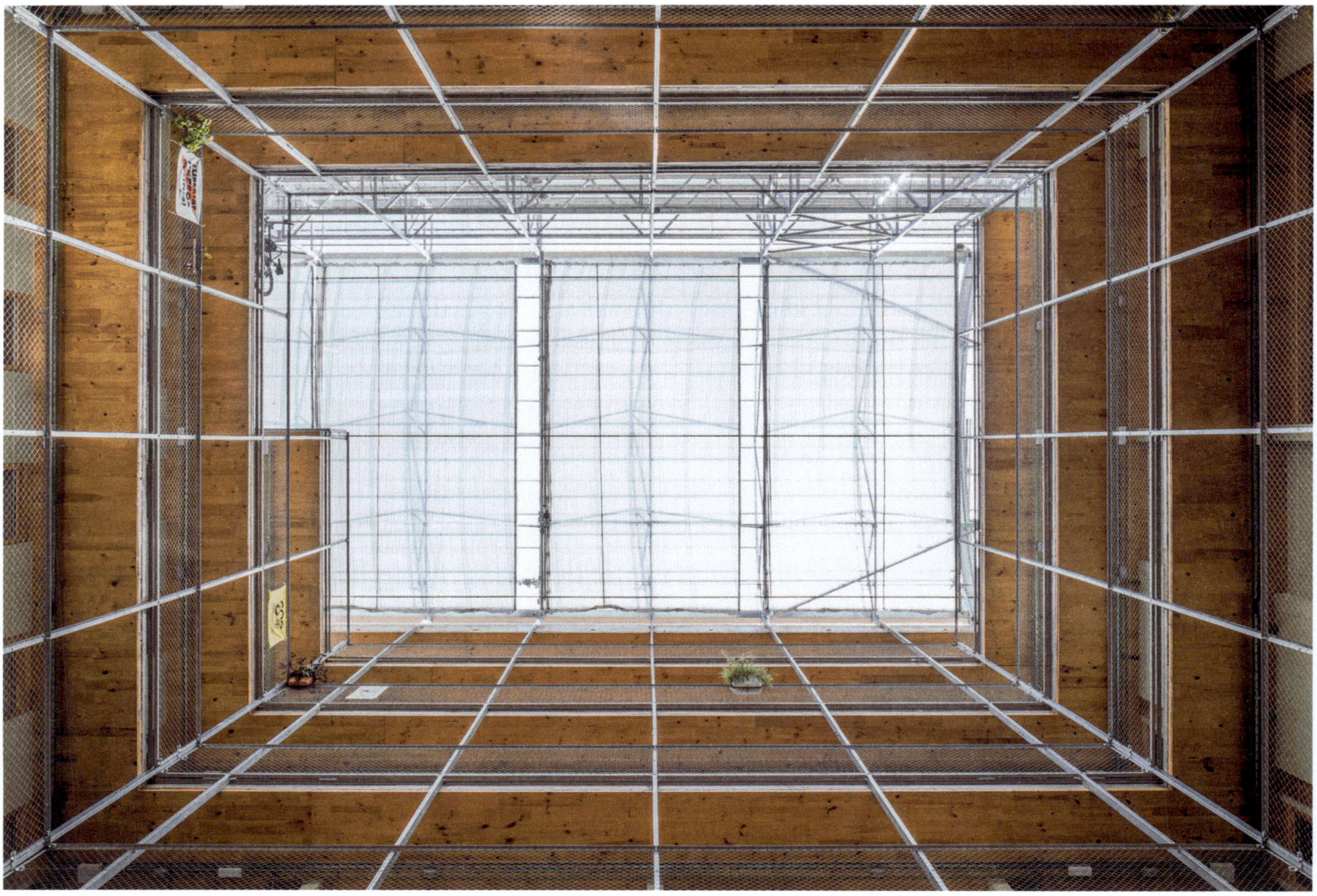

example of how overall architectural definition helps create a sense of community is the project by arenas basabe palacios in Vienna. In this project, communal outdoor areas are not enclosed but remain open and part of the larger landscaped area to facilitate social cohesion among residents from different buildings.

Joint Use of Domestic Spaces

The buildings in Yokohama—designed by ON design partners—and Munich—designed by Summacumfemmer and Büro Juliane Greb—provide additional domestic spaces shared by residents from autonomous dwellings. The R50 building, designed by ifau und Jesko Fezer with Heide & von Beckerath, includes communal outdoor areas shared by three dwellings. Like serval other projects, the design proposition for the San Riemo and R50 buildings contain spaces accessible to smaller groups of residents, in addition to those open to the entire resident community. In separate conversations with Graham Haworth, and with Fernando Brunel and Tomás Balparda of BBOA, we discuss design strategies for creating smaller communities composed of only a few households. We examine spatial means to help develop a sense of belonging and increase the likelihood of communal spaces successfully being used and cared for by residents. The excerpts from the two mentioned interviews and others in this book give more details on what architects can do to help structure the relationship between communal and individual in terms of spatial sequencing, dimensioning, and employing building materials.

Spatial Thresholds

In this book, the impact of architectural decisions is observed through the physical characteristics of space. A range of architectural means was employed to create spatial thresholds, make boundaries hard or soft, and structure the relationship between communal and individual. An example of a subtle or soft boundary is the landscape treatment employed by arenas basabe palacios in Vienna or the floor demarcation on the access gallery used by EM2N in Berlin. A different kind of threshold would be one incorporating a soil container with plants and a steel mesh used in the project by adamo-faiden in Buenos Aires to protect the privacy of dwellings on the ground floor and to separate private outdoor areas from the street. Creating limits between personal and communal in an architectural project often affects the interface between indoor and outdoor environments, and it will be discussed further in addressing the design of the building envelope. It also overlaps with spatial adaptability and will be examined again when we discuss architectural means accommodating change in the dwelling layout and size.

Figure 1
La Borda building,
Architects: Lacol

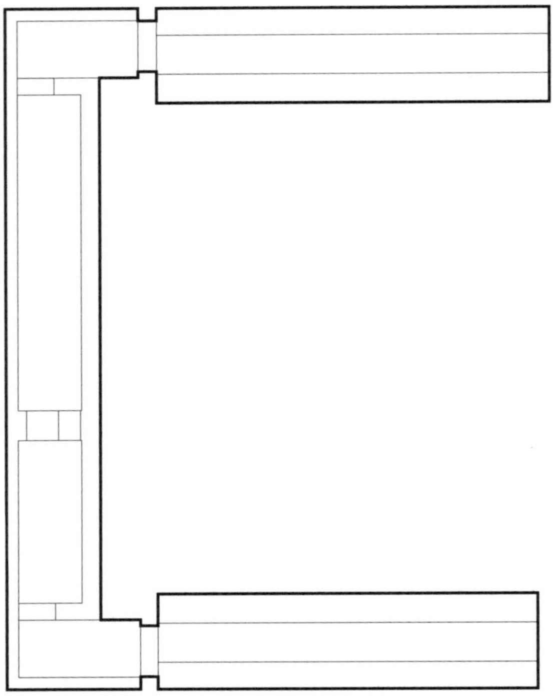

4 Iroko Housing

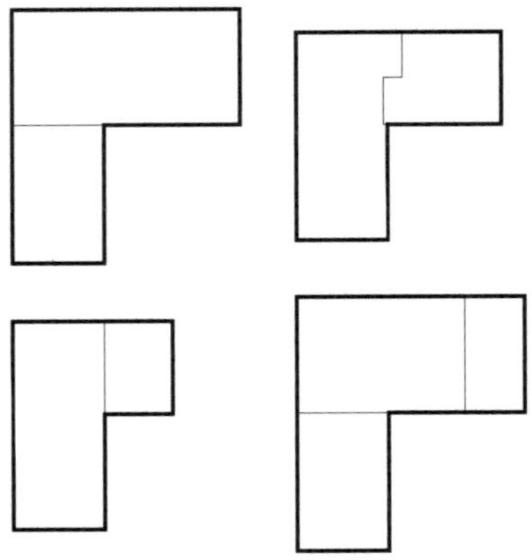

3 Wildgarten / Sonnenblumenhäuser

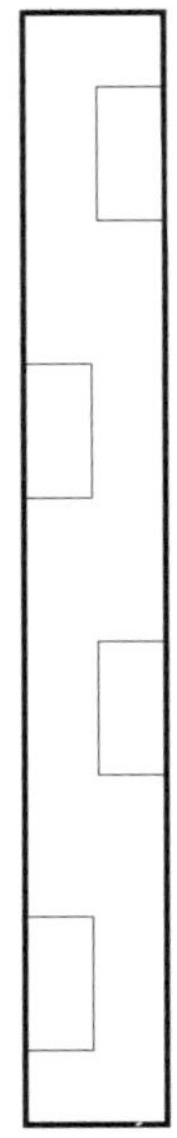

9 Social Housing in Granadero Baigoria

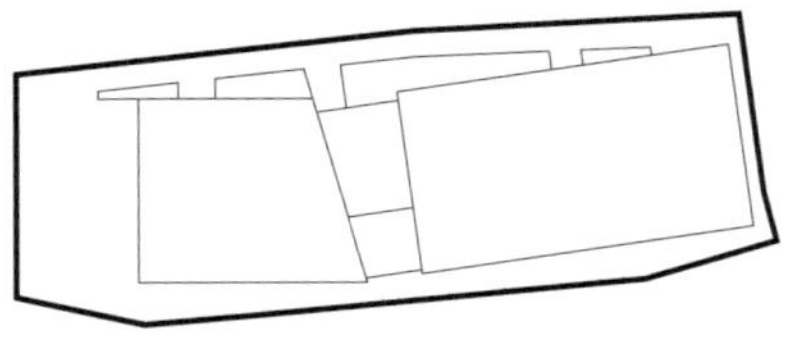

2 Buildings R and S in Pierre Loti Residential Area

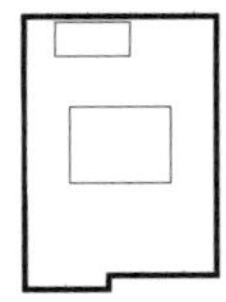

6 Wohnregal Apartments and Ateliers

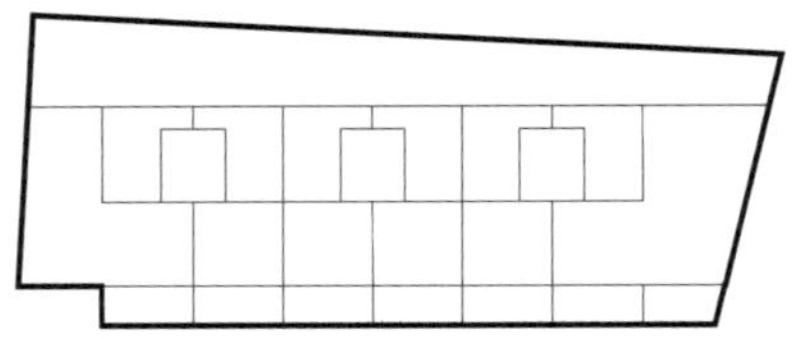

5 La Vecindad Plaza Mafalda

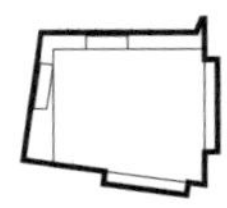

11 Yokohama Apartment

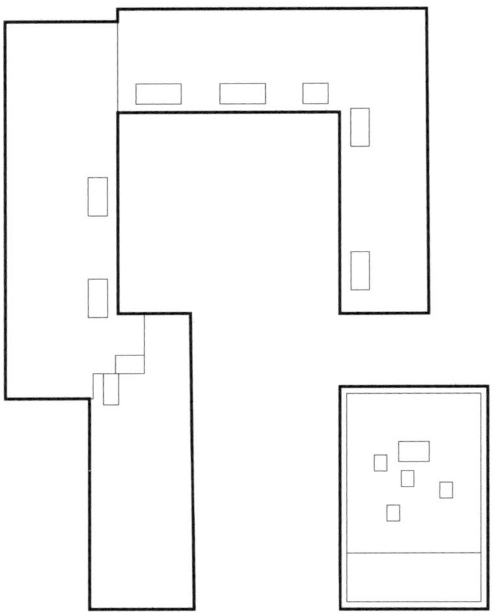

1 New Housing on Briesestraße

12 R50

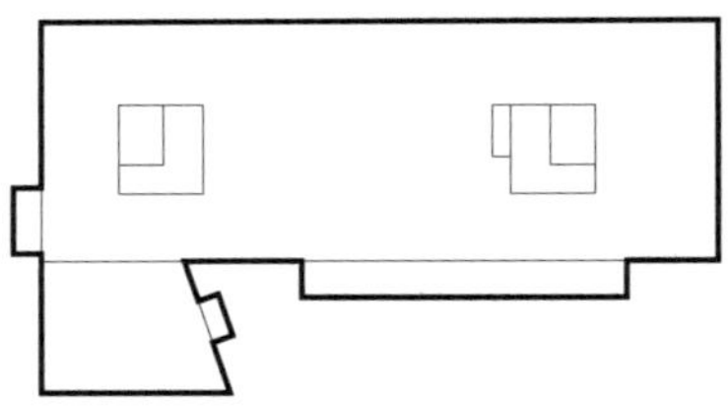

10 San Riemo

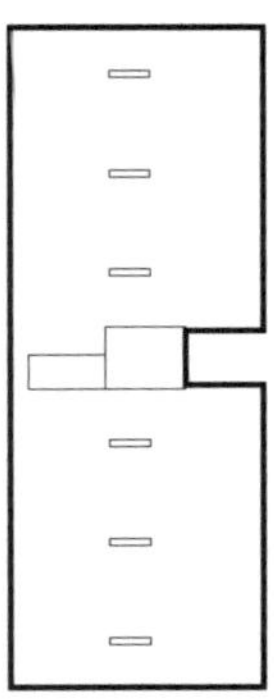

7 6×6 block

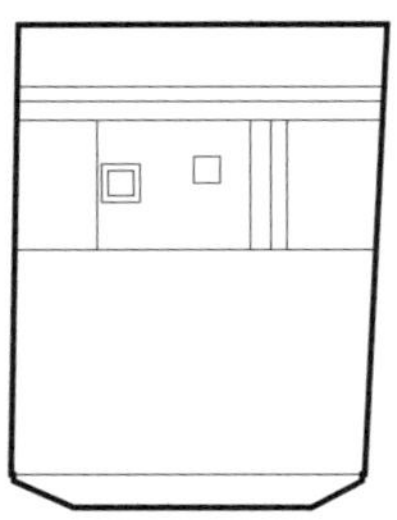

13 La Borda

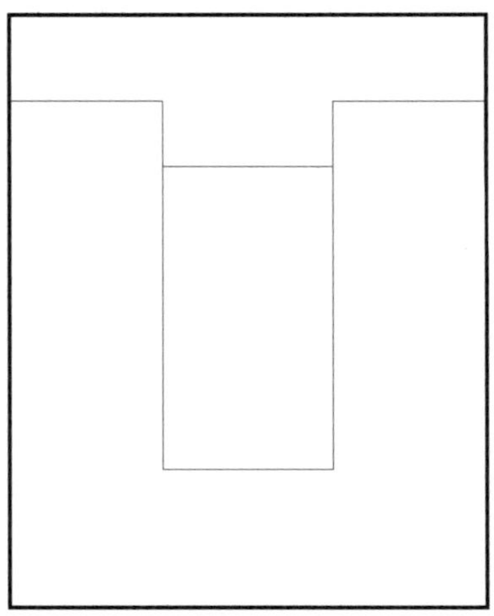

14 85 Social Dwellings in Cornellà

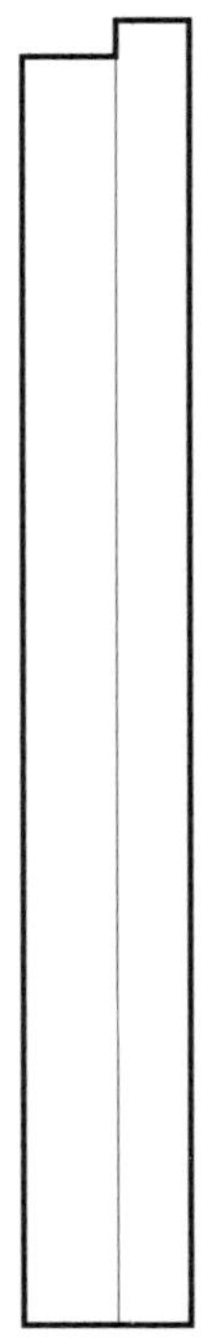

8 Residential building in Straßgang

Social Viability

The selected projects show how the relationship between the individual and communal in residential buildings is addressed with a view to social viability, which is a critical topic in multidisciplinary research on housing. They offer spatial solutions that balance the intimacy of individual dwellings with enabling or creating opportunities for interaction between residents. The outlined comparisons and established overlaps between projects suggest that access spaces dimensioned beyond minimal standards, including well-defined communal spaces such as courtyards and providing shared domestic spaces and amenities in an architectural project, help the social sustainability of multiunit residential buildings—but, depending on the context, different and sometimes opposite design decisions can help the same goal. The following chapters will give more information, including drawings and interviews with architects and residents, to show that the architectural complexity of each project requires a unique set of design decisions. These decisions are made according to the given spatial context determined by the building's size, orientation, and positioning and by the forms of tenure, ownership, and maintenance. While knowledge transfer from one design project to another has always been a part of architectural practice, acknowledging differences between individual needs and local cultural values is, too. Therefore, this book aimed not to begin formulating a universal design guide but to explore and present the potency of decisions made in architectural practice to inform future interdisciplinary research on housing. Their social implications are often discussed first, but the truth is that design decisions in architectural practice are made considering environmental implications and economic limitations simultaneously. Addressing such fundamental challenges and balancing between them in architectural practice will be introduced in the following two segments of the overview.

Figure 2
Footprints of the fourteen selected buildings drawn at the same scale

Determined ↔ Undetermined
The Economic Viability

The use of the antonyms *determined* and *undetermined* is borrowed from the slightly different title of Roger Riewe's recent lecture hosted by the Melbourne School of Design to start the discussion of shared decision-making between architects and inhabitants of multiunit residential buildings.[13] The lecture revisited some of the earlier work of Riegler Riewe Architects, including the multiunit residential building in Graz presented in this book. At the conceptual level, this affordable housing project differentiates between determined elements such as building structure and services and undetermined spaces. For the latter, inhabitants have been given a choice on how to use them and an opportunity to assert control. Although the reader will learn more from the chapter dedicated to this project, it is essential to clarify that by *undetermined*, Riegler Riewe do not imply empty but rather carefully planned and structured spaces to allow multiple uses and modifications by occupants. Such a design approach can be traced back to John Habraken's influential book *Supports: An Alternative to Mass Housing*, written in the 1960s with the proposition that residential buildings should be conceptualized and built as "supports" that allow inhabitants to take control of the infill or their "own immediate environment."[14] Today, the proposition is well understood by many architects and is finding practical application in myriad ways. To corroborate, several practitioners interviewed in this book have related their work or referred back to *Supports*, and most of the presented projects, in their own ways, address the balance between empowering residents and the architectural definition of the project. The distribution of design control and an understanding of housing as an activity whereby residents make contributions toward creating the built environment come from two of John Turner's books from the 1970s, *Freedom to Build: Dweller Control of the Housing Process* and *Housing by People: Towards Autonomy in Building Environments*, which are also referenced by serval architects in the discussions on their work.[15,16] The positivism about self-help or self-organized housing provision prevails through some of the following case studies, as it increasingly does in many other current research-related debates on housing. Still, the book

13. Roger Riewe, "determined / non-determined," guest lecture, Melbourne School of Design, March 14, 2023, https://msd.unimelb.edu.au/events/determined-non-determined.
14. John N. Habraken, *Supports: An Alternative to Mass Housing* (London: Architectural Press, 1972).
15. John F. C. Turner, *Housing by People: Towards Autonomy in Building Environments* (New York: Pantheon Books, 1976).
16. John F. C. Turner and Robert Fichter, *Freedom to Build: Dweller Control of the Housing Process* (New York: MacMillan, 1972).

explores a range of housing models. The discussion focuses on the value of architectural design and explores contemporary architectural practice in relation to seminal ideas originating more than half a century ago. It includes differentiation between determined and undetermined in an architectural project. It is observed as central or equivalent to spatial flexibility and adaptability, accepting the architectural difference between the two notions.[17]

An appreciation of the resident-centered approach is characteristic of all presented projects. In some, the emphasis is placed on spatial adaptability in the dwelling layout, enabling residents to use the space in multiple ways according to their individual and changing needs, with or without physical modification. In other projects, it is about incorporating input from the resident community during the design process. As the case studies show, the embedded spatial adaptability and collaborative or participatory design require that at least some parts or aspects of an architectural project are not determined by architects but are left undetermined to allow residents to assert control. The potential advantages observed in the selected projects were twofold. First, the indeterminacy suggests improved economic viability. If residential buildings are not flexible and cannot adapt to occupants' needs, they become redundant.[18] Second, as brought forward in the lecture by Cristina Gamboa Masdevall from Colin Word's preface to John Turner's book, "when residents make their own contribution to the design, construction, or management of their housing, both the process and environment stimulate individual and social well-being."[19,20]

The residents' contribution to the design process is most relevant for the projects developed by housing cooperatives La Borda, Kooperative Großstadt, and Iroko, as well as a self-organized building group (not a cooperative), R50. These four projects in particular have required developing an art of planning between determined and undetermined, adding complexity to architectural design. Conversations with architects involved with these projects reveal their efforts to work collaboratively with resident communities, requiring agency, additional hours, and commitments not foreseen in the traditional scope of work. The successes of these projects depended on architects' capability to work closely with the inhabitants and their skill to deliver innovative design solutions accommodating communal and individual needs on tight construction budgets. It may be important to emphasize that these projects are internationally acclaimed for their architectural outcomes, which is still relatively rare with self-organized housing undertakings.

The book recognizes the value added by architectural design and does not advocate developing and planning a multiunit residential project without adequate knowledge and professional support, which

17. Tatjana Schneider and Jeremy Till, *Flexible Housing* (London: Architectural Press, 2007).
18. Schneider and Till, *Flexible Housing.*
19. Christina Gamboa, "Infrastructures for Sustainable Living: Modes of Housing," guest lecture, Melbourne School of Design, August 26, 2020, https://edsc.unimelb.edu.au/studio-epsilon/lecture-repository/lacol.
20. Colin Ward, Preface to Turner, *Housing by People.*

can be the case with self-organized housing provision and participatory design processes. It is not uncommon for housing communities to try to drive projects with little professional input, resulting in inadequate architectural outcomes. Recent research on housing identifies the potential adverse effects of closed residential communities on the larger socio-spatial development. The exclusivity of some communities is associated with development costs, ownership rights, and other less apparent aspects.[21,22]

The book also explores the tools and mechanisms used to bring together architectural practices and self-organized housing provision. For example, an architectural competition was used to select architects by two housing cooperatives, an invited competition was used for Iroko, and an open architectural competition for the San Riemo building. The conversation with Iain Tuckett of Coin Street Community Builders, the social enterprise behind the Iroko housing cooperative, reveals how they selected and worked with architects. They have decided to move away from the model based on extensive consultations but to engage with architects through local representatives during and after the competition, as they found in their previous projects that some of the decision-making could improve if better informed by professional knowledge.

Architectural design perspective on the spatial relationship between determined and undetermined in selected multiunit residential buildings includes comparisons and a discussion on the following topics.

Figure 3
Structural grids of the fourteen selected buildings drawn at the same scale

Flexibility

Two of the selected projects incorporate negotiable boundaries between dwellings. While their load-bearing structures, building services, access spaces, and overall form are determined, they envisage and provide spatial mechanisms for changing boundaries between dwelling units so that they can expand or downsize. The dwellings of the building designed by Lacol are composed of modules called "basic dwelling configurations" and "satellite rooms." The satellite rooms can be attached or detached from basic dwelling configurations and thus exchanged between different households. Structural walls, made of mass timber, contain concealed door-size openings to facilitate an exchange. Similar spatial flexibility is incorporated into the architectural project in Munich by Summacumfemmer and Büro Juliane Greb, where the housing cooperative behind the project was keen to have rooms that can be associated and dissociated with several individual dwellings and used interchangeably between households based on their needs. As both projects are based on rental tenure, it makes it easier to foresee how such spatial changes could be regulated and

21. Gutzon Larsen, "Three Phases of Danish Co-housing."
22. Francesco Chiodelli and Valeria Baglione, "Living Together Privately: For a Cautious Reading of Co-housing," *Urban Research & Practice* 7, no. 1 (2014): 20–34.

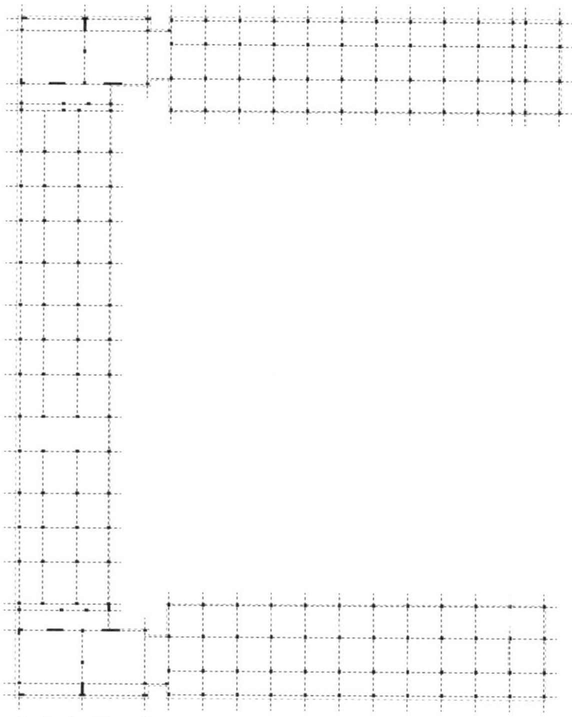

4 Iroko Housing

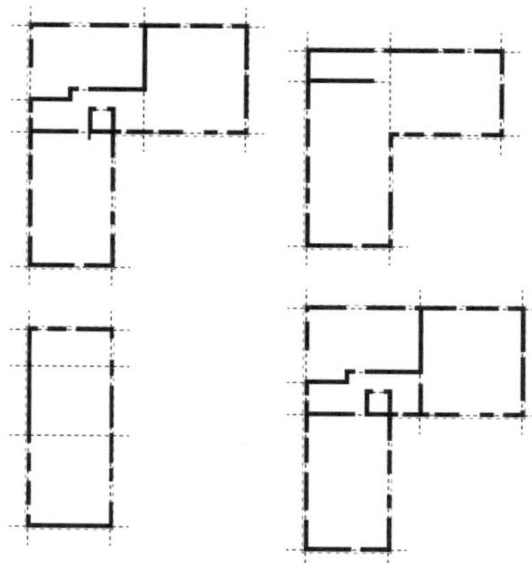

3 Wildgarten / Sonnenblumenhäuser

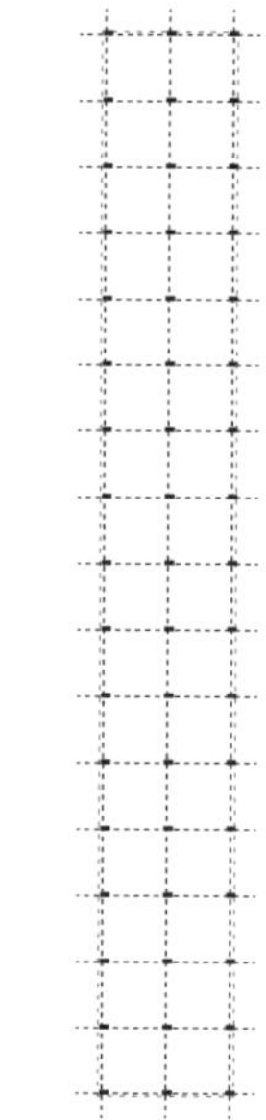

9 Social Housing in Granadero Baigoria

2 Buildings R and S in Pierre Loti Residential Area

6 Wohnregal Apartments and Ateliers

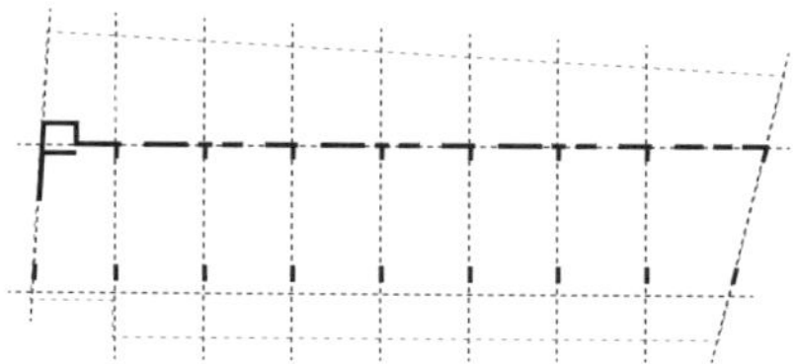

5 La Vecindad Plaza Mafalda

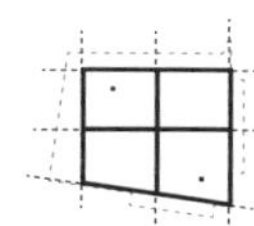

11 Yokohama Apartment

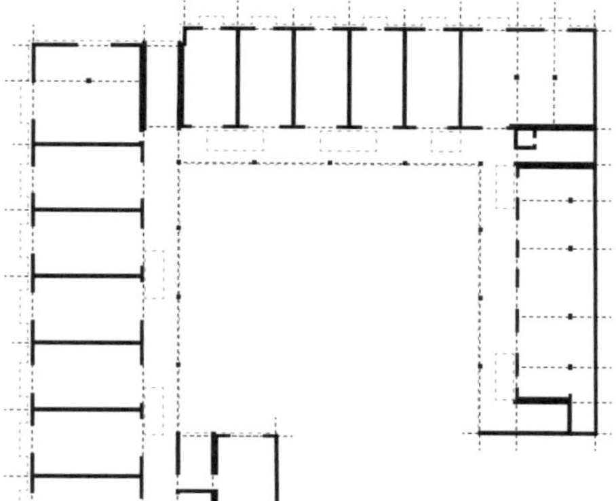
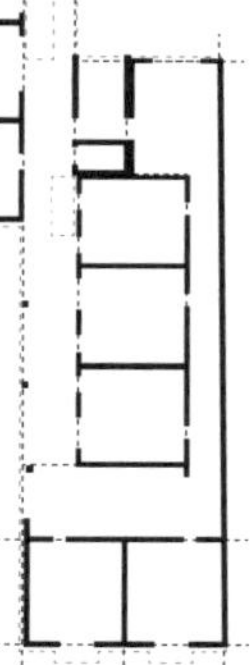

1 New Housing on Briesestraße

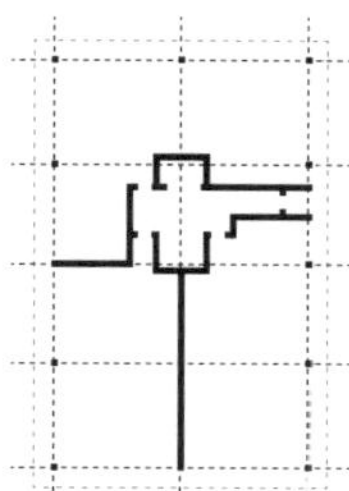

12 R50

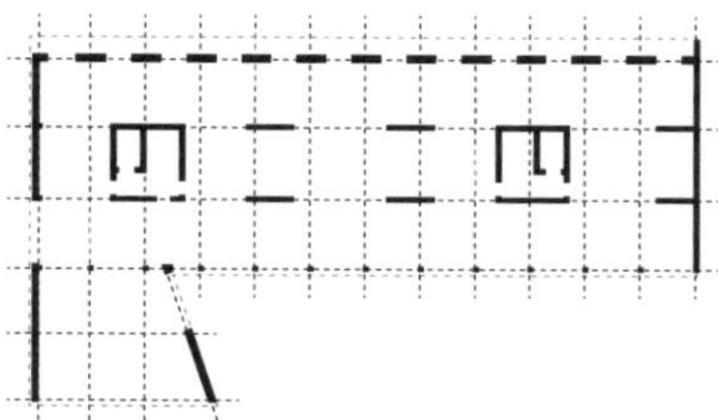

10 San Riemo

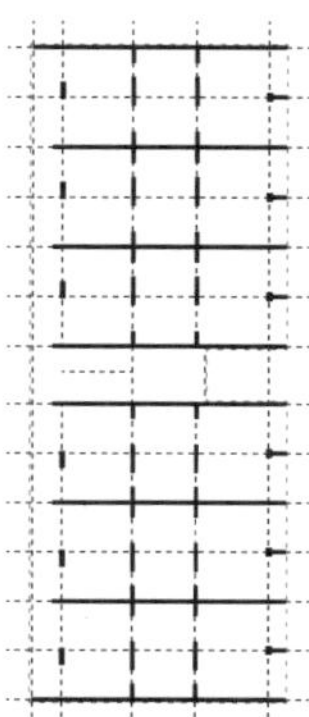

7 6×6 block

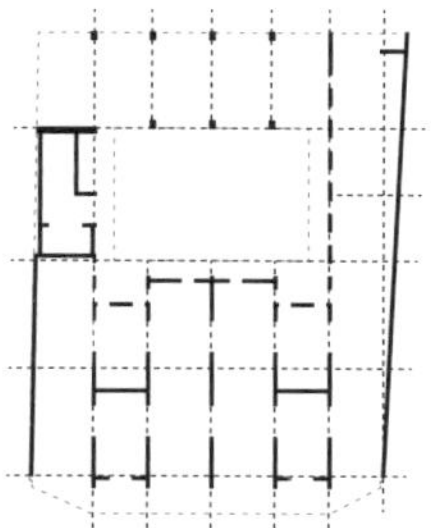

13 La Borda

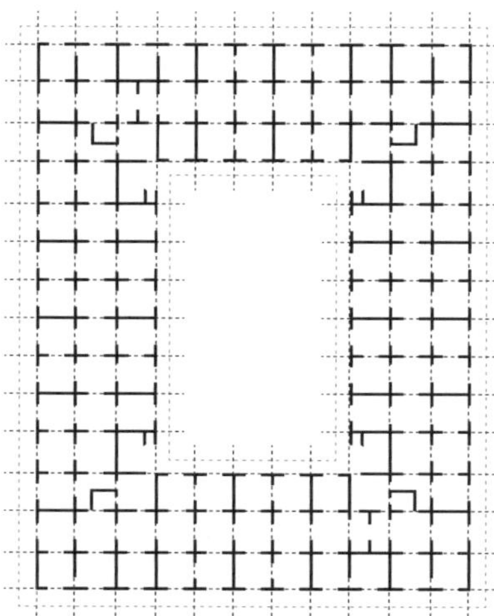

14 85 Social Dwellings in Cornellà

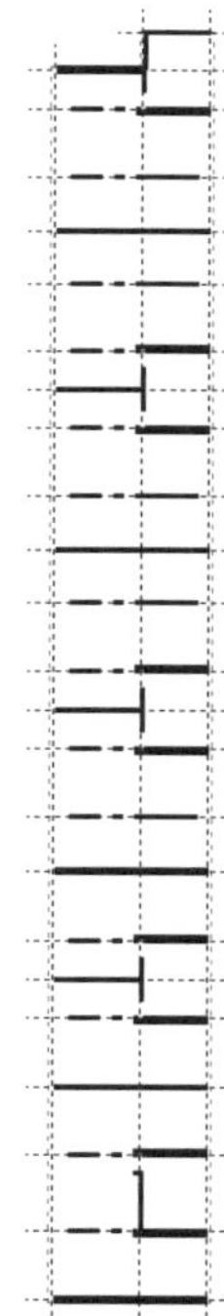

8 Residential building in Straßgang

negotiated between residents. In the first instance, the change of unit boundaries requires physical modification, while in the second, it is facilitated simply by opening or closing double doors. Spatial flexibility is also achieved in other ways. As mentioned earlier, some of the dwellings of the San Riemo building have access to shared living rooms, and most of the dwellings in the building in Berlin by EM2N can utilize access galleries as their outdoor areas. Such an expansion of private dwellings into shared spaces may be linked to the spatial relationship between determined and undetermined and observed as a form of spatial flexibility.

Adaptability

The use of individual rooms within dwellings is undetermined in architectural projects in Barcelona by Peris+Toral; in Munich by Summacumfemmer and Büro Juliane Greb; and in Girona by bosch. capdeferro. The building structure, dwelling boundaries, services, and access spaces are all determined. However, dwelling layouts are

Figure 4
6×6 Block building, Architects: bosch.capdeferro arquitectura

conceptualized as composites of identical rooms. The three projects provide alternatives to the conventional dwelling typologies based on a hierarchy of room sizing according to their use. Instead, rooms were made larger than prescribed by minimal building standards to allow multiple options in the first two named projects. In contrast, rooms in the project by bosch.capdeferro are as small as building regulations allow for rooms to be deemed habitable, but a pair of rooms can be connected with large sliding doors so that they can merge into one space. The conversations with residents from buildings in Girona and Barcelona provide insights into how the designed adaptability works in real life and capture their appreciation of the given freedom.

Connectivity

The discussion on the relationship between determined and undetermined with architects and residents of several projects has also gravitated toward sequencing spaces in the unit layout and the connectivity between them. In the dwelling layout by bosch.capdeferro in Girona, each room has three doorways. Such connectivity allows the same unit plan to meet diverse needs, accommodate different-sized households, and respond to diversified lifestyles. As outlined above, two small rooms can combine when the sliding doors are tucked in. The use of sliding doors in this project allows residents to convert their dwelling layout into an open plan configuration. Similarly, connectivity achieved in dwellings in Cornellà by Peris+Toral permits longitudinal views from one facade to the other, which makes them spacious and enables better daylighting and natural ventilation. The configuration of dwellings in Graz designed by Riegler Riewe employs similar principles. The three projects strategically use different door types, including sliding, folding, and pivoting single or double doors, to establish connectivity between spaces within dwellings. For example, folding doors employed in the building in Graz and in the R50 building also serve as subtle dividers between spaces even when they are open. In the San Riemo building, emphasis is placed on the use of double doors: when they are open, they combine two rooms rather than just open a passage from one room to another.

Architectural Definition and Residents' Contribution

Not all presented buildings were completed before the dwellings were handed over to residents. That, too, has to do with how much is determined by architects and what depends on residents' contribution, either as a way of asserting control over their dwelling space or a necessity born out of cost savings and, therefore, related to the economic viability of projects. At the conceptual level, it is captured in the

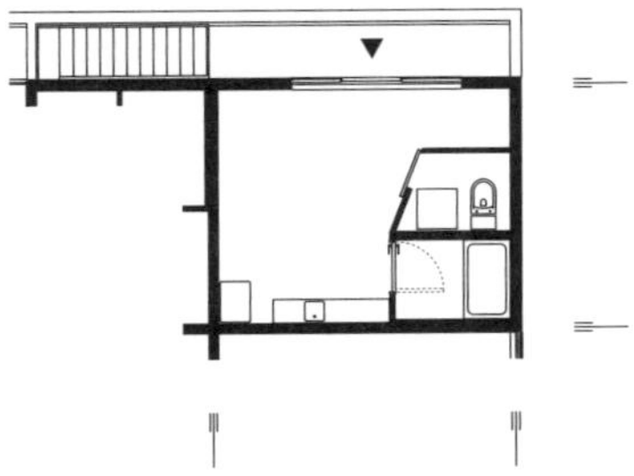

11 Yokohama Apartment

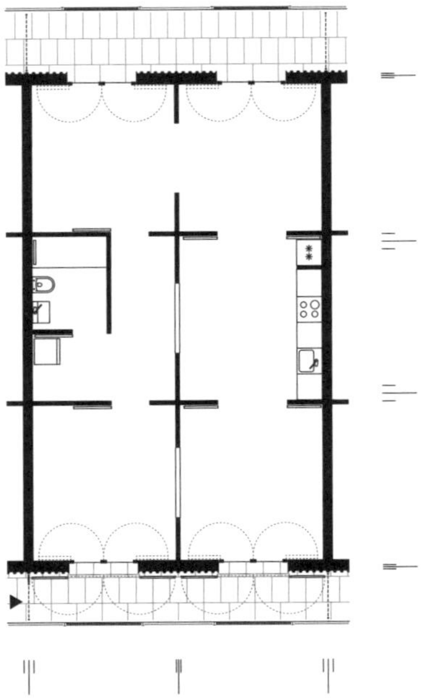

14 85 Social Dwellings in Cornellà

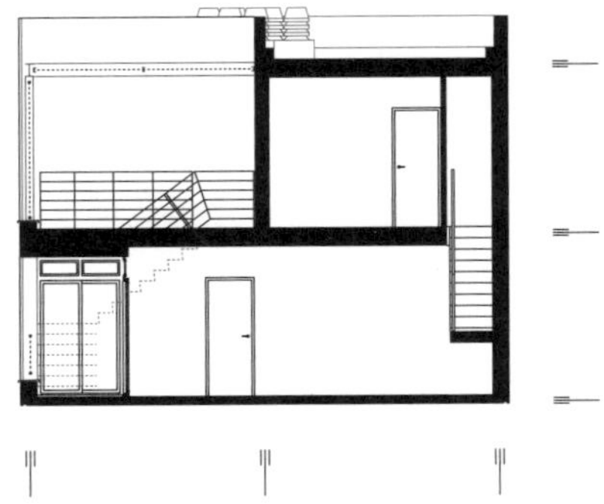

9 Social Housing in Granadero Baigoria

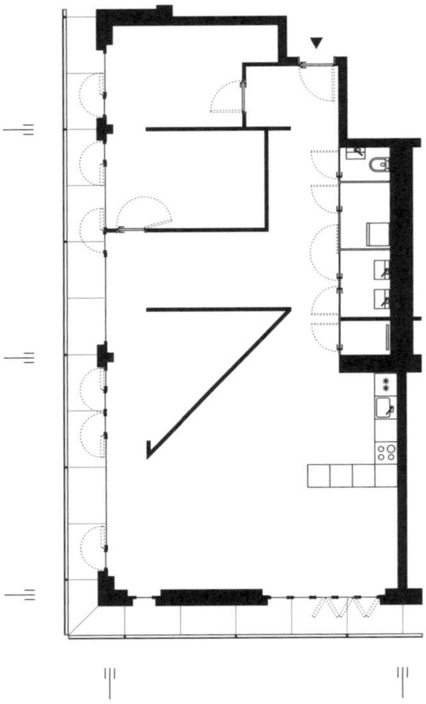

12 R50

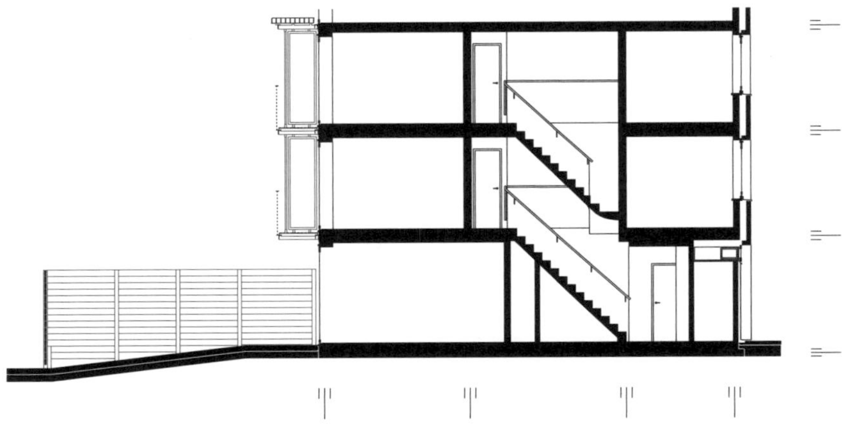

4 Iroko Housing

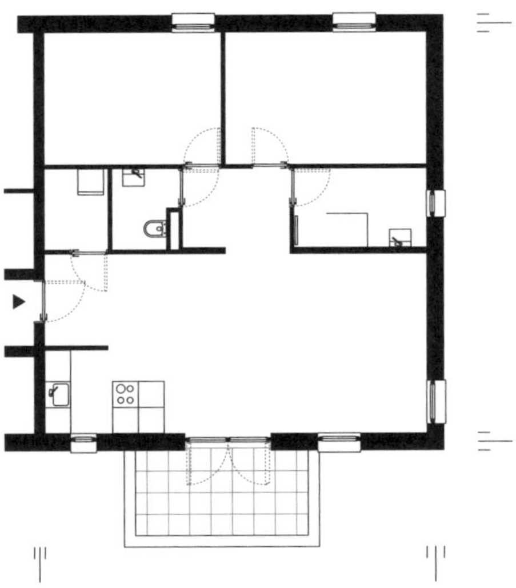

3 Wildgarten / Sonnenblumenhäuser

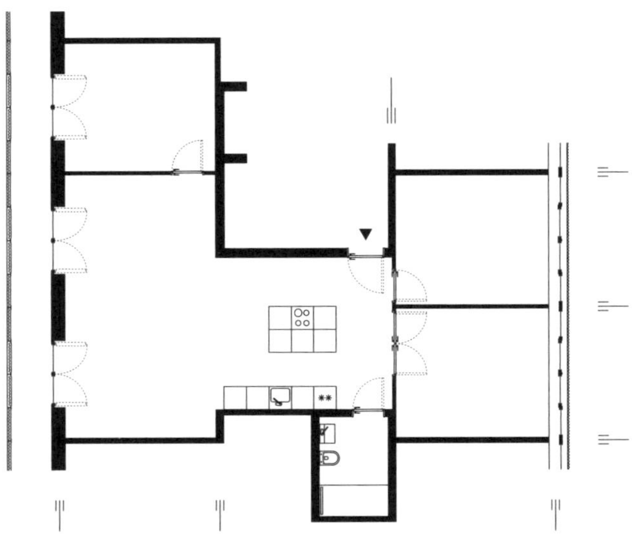

10 San Riemo

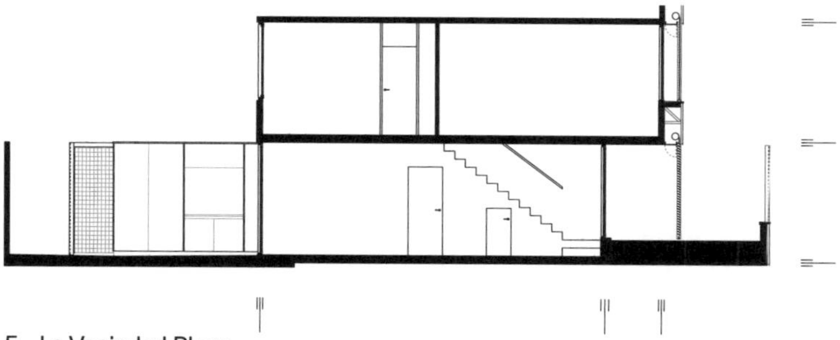

5 La Vecindad Plaza Mafalda

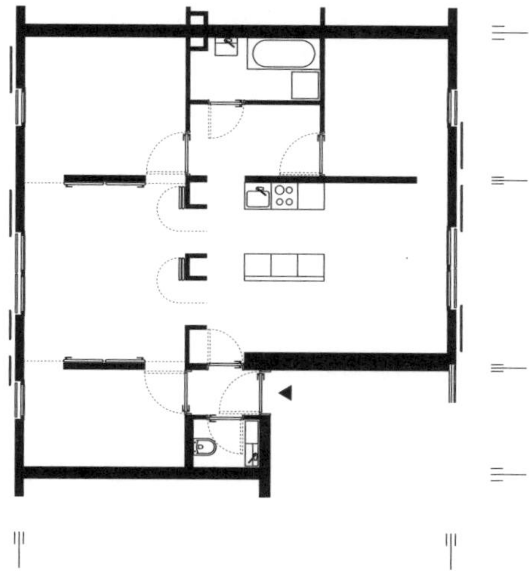

8 Residential building in Straßgang

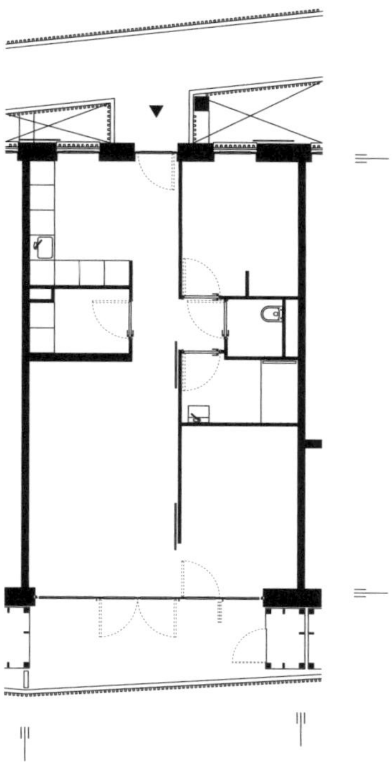

2 Buildings R and S in Pierre Loti Residential Area

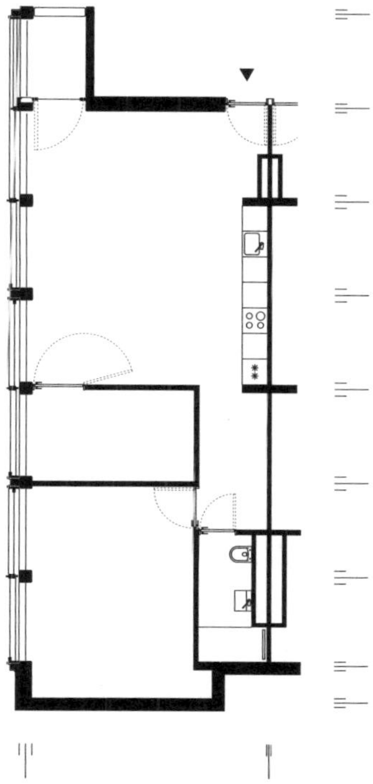

6 Wohnregal Apartments and Ateliers

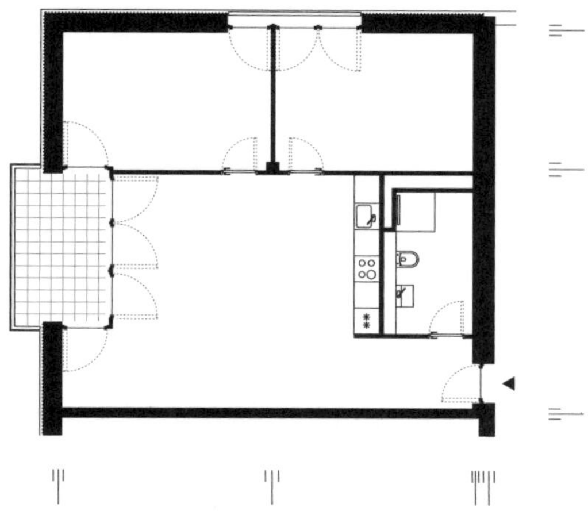

1 New Housing on Briesestraße

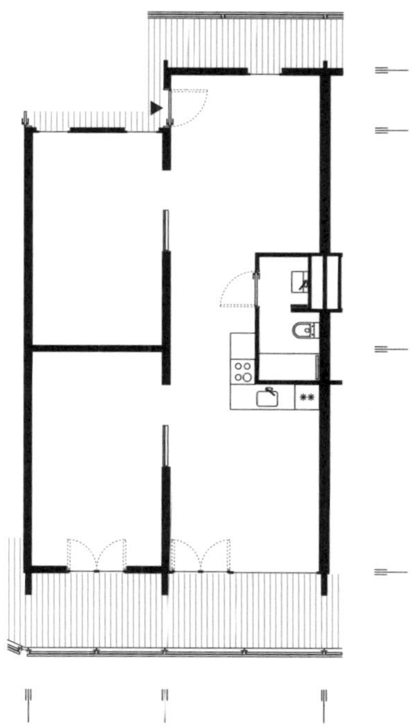

13 La Borda

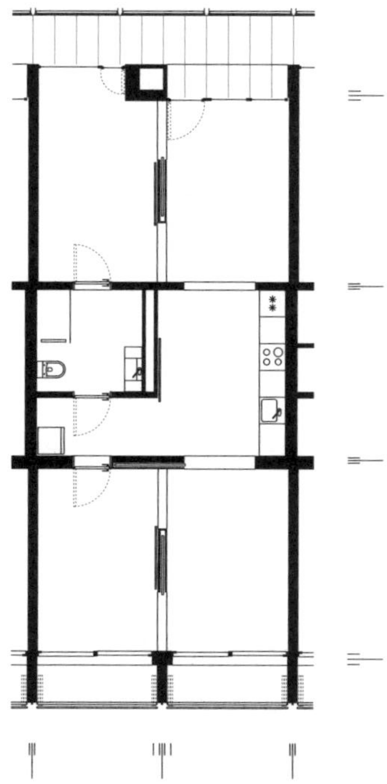

7 6×6 block

title of Anne Femmer's lecture "non-finito," which included the presentation of their design for the San Riemo building.[23] The conversation with Jesko Fezer about the collaborative design strategy for the R50 building in Berlin reveals that the group was able to postpone some decision-making but to progress with the design and construction when consensus was not reached or funding was not agreed upon. Construction work on the building for the La Borda housing cooperative was planned in two stages. The building was handed over to residents as the first phase was complete, and minimal regulatory requirements were met to allow people to move in. Residents have then continued working on the fittings and finishes of their dwellings. The communal areas were also incrementally completed. The conversation with Lacol Architects highlights the benefits but also challenges faced by residents and how that has informed their approach to other ongoing projects. A separate discussion with Marc Frohn about the building in Berlin designed by FAR frohn&rojas addresses construction methods. He explains how a strategic differentiation of construction works and building elements or layers according to their life spans in their project allowed more flexibility in conceptualizing the building, including planning unit layouts. The reliance on cost-effective building materials and finishes is explored in conversations with other architects and residents.

Economic Viability

The case studies provide insights into how the architectural significance of the determined and undetermined can be relevant to research efforts probing into the economic viability of housing. The presented comparisons and established overlaps between projects suggest that spatial flexibility, adaptability, connectivity in dwelling layouts, residents' involvement with aspects of the building construction, and careful planning of the construction works can be valuable in lowering the construction cost and helping residential buildings stay purposeful for longer.

23. Anne Femmer, "non-finito," guest lecture, Melbourne School of Design, August 17, 2022, https://edsc.unimelb.edu.au/studio-epsilon/lecture-repository/summacumfemmer.

Interior ↔ Exterior The Environmental Viability

The relationship between interior and exterior in architectural projects for multiunit residential buildings can be complex, and in this book, it is observed as significant to their environmental impact. It is important to clarify that the presented buildings are designed for different climates, allowing a varied continuum between indoor and outdoor domestic activities. It makes some comparisons difficult but also creates a good platform for discussing architectural design decision-making instead of design standards. The presented case studies show the relationship between the interior and exterior concerns various aspects, such as the provision of private outdoor areas, positioning and orientation of buildings, architectural treatment of the building envelope, and microclimate control. Related design decisions significantly impact residents' health and well-being, indoor environment quality and thermal comfort in dwellings, and overall energy consumption. A growing body of research in building physics is probing these and related topics. At the same time, there is, and should be, an increasing awareness of the embodied and operational carbon footprint in the building construction industry. However, the emphasis of this book's discussion is not on meeting the relevant building industry standards but on architectural practice and project-specific decision-making on the relationship between the building and the environment. It is partly done concerning carbon-neutral building and scientific knowledge originating outside the discipline of architecture, similar to how the relationship between individual and communal is addressed in the interdisciplinary research on housing. The growing body of research in leading peer-reviewed journals such as *Building and Environment*, *Architectural Science Review*, *Energy and Buildings*, *Journal of Building Physics*, and *Applied Thermal Engineering* addresses the environmental impact, thermal comfort, and the efficiency of energy consumption in residential buildings. Yet research undertaken in the building science domain does not often incorporate architectural design knowledge.[24] The related discussion presented in this book aims to highlight aspects of architectural practice that could benefit from closer links and integration with scientific methods relevant to the environmental viability of multiunit residential buildings.

24. Milica Vujovic, Djordje Stojanovic, Tina Salemi, and Michael Hensel, "Design and Science: Content Analysis of Published Peer-Reviewed Research over the Last Four Decades," *Frontiers of Architectural Research* 12, no. 3 (2023): 613–29, https://doi.org/10.1016/j.foar.2023.04.001.

Private Outdoor Areas

Access to backyards or gardens is commonly associated with an image of an individual house, a building typology characteristic of sub-urban areas. In contrast, the significance of private outdoor areas is often overlooked in planning multiunit residential buildings. When designing high-density residential structures, architects often face challenges in finding room for outdoor amenities and in balancing demands for privacy with the provision of outdoor access. In the discussion on the R50 building, Verena von Beckerath addresses the specific nature of private outdoor areas in multiunit residential buildings and their role as an extension of the dwelling interior rather than an autonomous feature. In the R50 building, a balcony-like steel grate floor forming the building's circumference, 100 meters long and less than a meter wide, is shared by three dwellings on each floor. In the building designed by EM2N, dwellings have a small private outdoor area facing the street and a right-to-use larger outdoor area that is part of the communal access gallery facing the courtyard. Significances of the continuum between communal and individual and the value of spatial adaptability allowing units to expand into communal areas in this project have already been identified. However, the structuring of the relationship between the interior and exterior is equally important, as it enables access to an outdoor environment directly from the individual units. Different design decisions are made to achieve similar objectives in other projects. For example, access from dwellings to the outdoor environment was one of the main drivers of the overall architectural definition of the project in Buenos Aires by adamo-faiden. The building comprises two rows of duplex units, placed one over the other, so the lower row units have access to back gardens, while the upper row dwellings have roof terraces.

Positioning and Orientation of Buildings

In the projects in Vienna by arenas basabe palacios and in Aytré by Guinée*Potin, the relationship between the buildings and the landscape is central to the design intent. In both projects, ground-floor units have private gardens next to the openly accessible landscape. The two named projects are good examples of the positioning and orientation of residential structures, essential for the intake of daylight and natural ventilation. In Vienna, the entire master plan for 1,000 dwellings is developed systemically following simple rules to ensure dwellings and outdoor communal areas have adequate southern exposure.

Indoor Environmental Quality, Thermal Comfort, and Microclimate Control

The building in Girona designed by bosch.capdeferro exploits southern exposure in its own way. It utilizes private winter gardens to preheat air, which is then distributed throughout the dwellings to reduce reliance on mechanical heating systems. The project is centered around microclimate control and creating breeze paths to improve thermal comfort and indoor air quality with minimal energy consumption. The courtyard of the building owned by housing cooperative La Borda performs similarly. In winter, it captures air that is heated by the sun. In summer, it opens to create a breeze and draw air from the north to help cool the building. An interview with one of the residents revealed that thermal comfort in the dwellings, along with the low energy bills, is one of the most loved qualities of that building.

In all fourteen projects, most dwellings are dually oriented to ensure natural cross ventilation and reduce reliance on energy-consuming environmental systems. The intent to achieve good indoor environmental quality but avoid costly technology for controlling air temperature and humidity comes across most clearly through the conversation with Ramon Bosch. He explains what architectural means and decisions have improved thermal comfort in the building and how creating different microclimates along the two main building facades benefits residents at other times of the year.

Building Envelopes

The architectural treatment of the building envelope is one of the topics discussed in relation to most projects. The associated design challenges are establishing an interface between the interior and exterior and creating an architectural expression of the building as its contribution to the surrounding environment. This is clearly articulated in the project by adamo-faiden, where the facade of a privately developed residential building creates a backdrop for a public square, and vegetation in the private gardens enlarges the city's green fund. This project, as well as the projects by bosch.capdeferro and Peris+Toral, exemplifies architectural strategies for making complex and layered facades, which help regulate indoor environmental conditions and protect the intimacy of dwellings. The three named projects incorporate inhabitable open-air space within the building envelope and use architectural means to create microclimates with air temperatures significantly lower than the surrounding environment in the summer. More information is available from the interview with Marcelo Faiden as part of the chapter on the project in Buenos Aires. The presented conversation addresses the knowledge transfer between their projects, a series of completed multiunit residential buildings incorporating gardens between the inner and outer layers of the facade as a seamless extension of dwellings, and a transition between inside and outside.

Rollable sunshades employed in projects in Girona and Barcelona and sliding screens of the building in Graz designed by Riegler Riewe provide protection from overheating. Still, they are also central to how the building is perceived from the exterior. These devices are operated by residents individually and manually. They are used in response to the same environmental conditions but according to diverse personal needs. As there is only a remote chance of these devices ever being aligned, their application contributes to the architectural expression by rendering the building's image dynamic and compound. It contrasts the uniformity imposed by the rationalized construction methods and the standardization often associated with multiunit residential buildings. The design challenge of overcoming the impersonal and monotonous image of multiunit residential buildings comes across most clearly in discussion with BBOA, who explain the fenestration strategy of their project in Granadero Baigorria. The project was part of a government-led initiative to provide affordable housing. The objective to lower the construction cost of seven buildings imposed many restrictions, including that all windows would be of the same dimensions. In an interview, Fernando Brunel and Tomás Balparda explain how they worked with the builders to make window frames not only the same but also out of a single aluminum bar to minimize material waste. However, they also explain a stream of design decisions concerning the individual dwelling layouts and grouping of units into clusters to offset the limitations imposed by the use of a single window dimension to achieve a specific architectural expression.

Not Fully Enclosed and Thermally Insulated Spaces

Thermal requirements can be different for shared spaces and dwellings. In several selected projects, communal spaces are not fully enclosed nor thermally insulated. Moreover, from the architectural point of view, they are neither entirely interior nor exterior. For example, the building in Yokohama includes a shared living room on the building's ground floor, equipped with a rarely used floor heating system. At the same time, with its large openings, this space doubles as an outdoor environment. The openness is deliberate in making this space more visible and accessible to the public, as the building is designed for an artist working and showcasing their work there while using it daily for domestic activities. Similarly, staircases turned into shared spaces and extensions of dwellings in the project in Granadero Baigorria designed by BBOA are treated as outdoor environments while they are inside the building volume. Not fully enclosing spaces and omitting

thermal insulation, windows, and doors in these and other projects was driven by cost savings. The rationale for designing communal spaces to a level of thermal comfort different from what is achieved in dwellings is that these spaces are used less frequently, for shorter periods, and for activities that require lower temperatures. The conversations with architects and residents of projects in Berlin, Munich, Vienna, and Barcelona provide more information on how such spaces are designed and used.

Environmental Impact of Building Materials

The decision-making on the selection of building materials, including considering environmental impact and embodied carbon footprint, was part of the discussion for most projects. Projects in Barcelona, Girona, and Yokohama have employed timber for the primary structure. Mass timber construction was considered but dropped in several other projects because of the associated cost. In addition, restrictions

Figure 5
Bonpland building,
Architects: adamo-faiden

imposed by the building regulations have been identified as one of the main hurdles for the broader use of timber and other regenerative materials in the construction of multiunit residential buildings. In the conversation about the project in Aytré, Hervé Potin also recognizes a shortage of building construction companies and workforce with knowledge and interest in working with regenerative building materials and vernacular construction techniques. In separate conversations with José Toral and Ramon Bosch, we explore the benefits and challenges of using wood and making structural walls and slabs of cross-laminated timber visible in the building interior. In addition to the choice of building materials in some of the chapters, the discussion focuses on the choice of construction methods in relation to their environmental impact. For example, the residential building in Berlin by FAR frohn&rojas employs prefabricated concrete construction and uses solutions tested and developed for industrial buildings.

Environmental Viability

The presented overview identifies overlaps and common threads between the selected projects in the provision of private outdoor areas, positioning and orientation of buildings, microclimate control, treatment of the building envelope, and the use of building materials and construction methods with an awareness of the associated carbon emissions. The design decisions concerning the listed aspects of selected projects are primarily driven by environmental implications, which are also addressed by the growing volume of research in building physics. The following chapters present design knowledge developed in architectural practice that can be useful to scientific and research-oriented undertakings in addition to architectural practice. The case studies aim to identify and explicate architectural design decisions impacting the environmental viability of multiunit residential buildings and to show how they correspond with other design objectives, such as social and economic.

The complexity of design decisions consistently referred to in this overview is in balancing different objectives: social, economic, and environmental. The following chapters will help better understand such a balancing act through greater detail while focusing on spatial antonyms: the individual and communal, the interior and exterior, and the determined and undetermined.

Projects

1

New Housing on Briesestraße, Berlin

EM2N

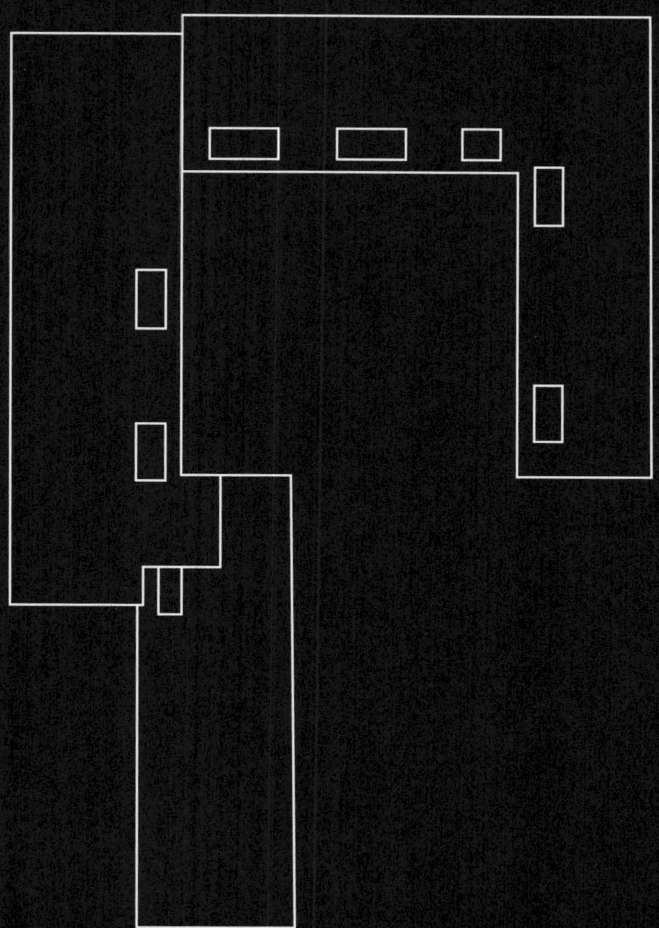

Infill Form

Figure 1
Site plan, drawing scale 1:2500

New Housing on Briesestraße, Berlin
EM2N

Year of completion: 2020
Number of units: 101

This project delivers affordable housing on an underutilized site in the inner city. It carefully structures outdoor spaces to improve the broader neighborhood, employs access galleries as extensions of individual dwellings, and facilitates interaction between residents.

Background

The project for New Housing on Briesestraße in Berlin was initiated through the ideas workshop New Forms of Urban Living, organized by the Berlin Senate Department of Urban Development and Environment in 2013, seeking new and experimental solutions for housing in the context of the city's eight nominated districts. The initiative opened the debate about inner-city densification through affordable and innovative housing development. The workshop resulted in the progressive competition brief for the site on Briesestraße, posing questions about future housing standards, changing demographics, community-building, and environmental impact. EM2N, founded by Mathias Müller and Daniel Niggli, working with MAN MADE LAND landscape architects, won the competition, held in 2016. It led to completing the building with 101 dwelling units for STADT UND LAND, one of Berlin's most prominent social and affordable housing providers, in 2020.

Infill Form

The building lot is at the center of a large city block populated with residential buildings of different scales and types.[1] The design proposal mediates between the existing structures to translate an infill planning strategy into an architectural form. In the public lecture hosted by the Melbourne School of Design on March 7, 2023, Verena Lindenmayer of EM2N presented their design proposal as a form composed of four building volumes positioned in response to the surrounding built context.[2] In this project, the spaces between the buildings are as important as the buildings themselves. The new and existing buildings work together, creating diverse outdoor spaces that link the new development with the city and ensure adequate daylighting, outlook prospects, and the privacy of individual dwellings.

Outdoor Spaces

To the west, one of the new building volumes is positioned at some distance from an existing residential structure to maintain a pedestrian link cutting transversally through the block. It also creates space for a landscaped area, continuing a green zone stretching through city blocks south of the site and tapping into a sizable public park. This landscaped pedestrian path is the first of three outdoor places defined by the building's form. The second, which can be observed as an extension of the first one, is created as one of the new building's volumes is pushed further in, so it stands back-to-back with an existing structure. This formal gesture makes room for a publicly accessible open area as an extension of the sidewalk. A convenience store facing this area contributes to its activation. Units on the ground floor, suitable for small businesses and live-work studios, are accessible from the street to help create active frontages. The ground-level treatment reinforces the building's relationship to the city and improves the neighborhood's amenities. The entrance to the underground garage is positioned at the eastern part of the site in Briesestraße to take advantage of the sloping terrain. The third outdoor space is an enclosed courtyard created by three new building volumes and an existing building's back wall. This courtyard, combining hard surfaces and landscaped areas, is available to residents only. There are two entrances, from north and south, from where one can take elevators and stairs to access galleries leading to dwellings.

Galleries

Three-meter-wide open-air access galleries are one of the defining features of this project. They have a dual purpose in providing access from the courtyard to individual units and space for private dwellings to expand into. The latter is particularly valuable, as most units in the building are studios or one-bedroom units. Utilizing access galleries as an outdoor extension of dwellings benefits residents' well-being and health.

Most dwellings have their living areas facing the gallery. Floor-to-ceiling glazing creates a direct link and a visual connection between private living rooms and communal space. Cutouts in the floors of the galleries are strategically positioned next to the building's facade to protect the intimacy of dwellings and improve daylight intake.

The boundary between communal access routes and private dwelling extensions is marked on the floor of galleries as part of the architectural project to ensure that fire escape routes are not compromised. At the same time, the floor marks prompt residents on how the space can be used or appropriated. The boundary between individual and communal is subtle, and architectural means are only suggestive. Residents were left to decide how to use this additional space and negotiate thresholds. Photos capturing personal items, toys, potted flowers, chairs, tables, and other personal items on access galleries as evidence of domesticity were made by Andrew Alberts six months after residents moved in.

The oversized access galleries create space for interaction between residents. The project rests on the basis that people want to live collectively and desire contact with their next-door neighbors. As galleries overlook the courtyard, poised as a social center of the new development, they also support the relationship between individual dwellings and the entire housing community. Such a spatial configuration, incorporating galleries overlooking the courtyard, was important during socially challenging times imposed by the recent pandemic. As part of the Window Flicks initiative, when local venues were closed, the courtyard of the New Housing on Briesestraße was among Berlin's residential spaces occasionally turned into open-air cinemas.[3] The galleries were an auditorium, and the back wall of an adjacent building was a projection screen, allowing residents to share the feeling of watching a movie together while sitting in front of their dwellings.

1. The building lot is at the center of a large city block between Briesestraße and Kienitzer Straße in the Rollberg neighborhood of the Neukölln district in Berlin.
2. Verena Lindenmayer, "Urban Social Housing," guest lecture, Melbourne School of Design, March 7, 2023, https://msd.unimelb.edu.au/events/urban-social-housing-lecture.
3. Window Flicks was a cultural project and a campaign that aimed to support cinemas in Berlin during the lockdown imposed by the COVID-19 pandemic and create a community experience by projecting movies onto building walls of residential courtyards to be viewed from dwellings.

Lindenmayer explained that open-air access galleries, commonly used in southern Europe where the climate is more temperate, are also known to be historically used in Germany, giving an example of residential buildings in Dessau designed by Hannes Meyer and the Bauhaus Dessau Architectural Department.[4,5] This access type is often favored in multiunit residential buildings for economic reasons and is employed as a cost-saving measure. However, Lindenmayer emphasized that EM2N's approach was also driven by spatial qualities related to the transition between indoor and outdoor environments associated with structures such as pergolas, arcades, and arbors. She underlined EM2N's interest in the social value of access spaces in multiunit residential buildings.[6]

Units

The development has a range of unit types and sizes, assembled into four building volumes. The smallest in size, studios, are in the building's part facing north. Two-room units are positioned along the western facade, while three-room units occupy the building's corners. Units for group living, each operating as a cluster of five autonomous dwellings with a shared kitchen and living room, are on all levels above the ground floor, in the building volume overlooking the extension of the sidewalk. More units for group living are in the building's part on the eastern edge of the lot. These are designed as duplex units to offset limitations imposed by their single orientation. All dwellings, apart from those for group living, have dual orientation, either north-south or west-east, to secure daylight and natural ventilation. Living areas face the gallery, and sleeping rooms are placed toward the street with mature trees and less noise. Eighteen barrier-free dwellings are distributed throughout the building.

Affordability

The choice of open-air access galleries and staircases was driven by an intention to lower the construction cost, but that is not the only design decision contributing to housing affordability. Before the architectural completion was launched, it was first considered if the existing car garage that occupied a part of the lot allocated for development should be demolished to create room for the housing or if the existing structure could be retained and reused to reduce the cost and environmental impact of the new development.[7] This idea was quickly discarded because the existing structure was unsuitable for efficient space usage, and floor-to-ceiling height was below the minimum required for multiunit housing standards.

Including only a few parking spaces in this development, made possible with the recent relaxation of car parking requirements in Berlin, has contributed to lower construction costs. However, the main savings were made through design decisions. The building structure is made of concrete, deemed the most viable option. Efforts were made to use only the minimum of building material. Load-bearing walls are placed between units, reducing most structural spans to as little as 4 meters, allowing for thinner concrete slabs. There are four staircases and only two elevator shafts in the building. Selecting durable and affordable finishing materials is also part of the same strategy. Linoleum flooring is used in the unit interior. Concrete is exposed in the exterior, on the floor and underside of slabs forming galleries. The building has a plaster facade facing the courtyard and an industrial aluminum-clad one facing the streets

4. Lindenmayer. "Urban Social Housing."
5. Laubenganghaus, in Dessau-Törten Settlement, designed by Hannes Meyer and the Bauhaus Dessau Architectural Department in 1929.
6. Lindenmayer. "Urban Social Housing."
7. Lindenmayer. "Urban Social Housing."

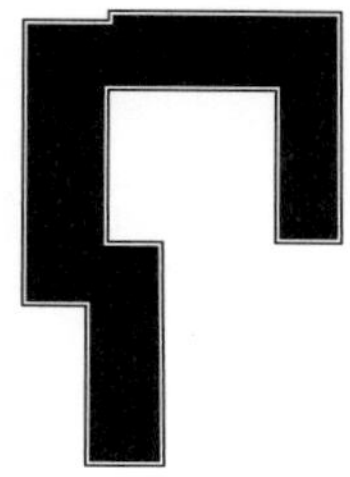

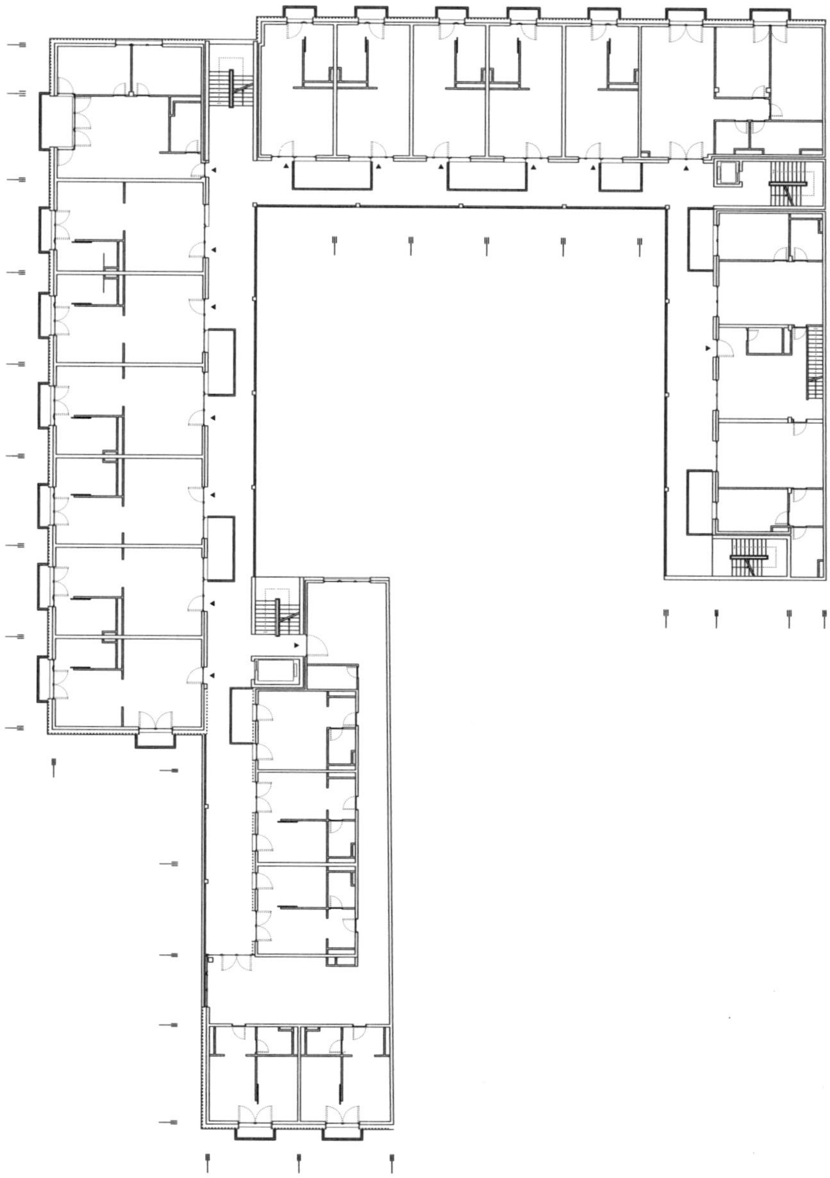

Figure 2
Typical floor plan,
drawing scale 1:500

In conversation

The following section, an edited interview with Verena Lindenmayer, former associate at EM2N and project development lead recorded on April 6, 2023, provides further information from the architects' perspective.

DS What design decisions have contributed to reducing the construction cost?

VL To give you the context first, I would like to emphasize that all units are for rental tenure, some are subsidized, and some are rented according to the market price. The requirement for subsidized units in Berlin at the time was 30 percent; it has recently increased to 50 percent. Many affordable providers are struggling as construction costs have increased. At the same time, the demand for affordable housing is enormous. We made many design decisions to reduce the construction cost, affecting space planning, choice of building materials, and construction methods. A strategy of utilizing minimal structural spans illustrates how the three aspects work together in reducing the amount of concrete needed for construction. Building service installations are bundled together. Standardized bathrooms of adjacent units are placed back-to-back for this reason. However, we don't see cost saving as an obstacle but as a design challenge and a need to be inventive. Our approach employs open-air access galleries to reduce the cost of development and to establish an important communal space. It is not just access but a place where people meet and spend time.

DS What design decisions do you find most impactful on the relationship between individual and communal?

VL We made a critical decision concerning the dwelling unit layout to have living rooms face access galleries, understanding that privacy is compromised. We have reinforced the link between the private living room and a communal access gallery with floor-to-ceiling windows. We did this contrary to what you will find in many buildings from the 1960s, when open-air galleries were frequent in low-cost housing. Instead of making access to minimal dimensions, we made it a generous size to become an extension of individual dwellings and a place where people can meet.

DS How is the role of outdoor spaces relevant to the overall building form?

VL Besides responding to the surroundings, the building form is crafted for gallery access type turned into a shared space. It is also driven by the distribution of dwellings, their orientation, and the need for outdoor areas around the building. As the project developed, we had to fine-tune the building form to balance these aspects. We had a slightly different idea for the competition stage from what was built. We first proposed that the courtyard be open, with a pedestrian thoroughfare connecting two passages that became secured entrances as the project developed. We proposed a communal roof terrace, which was impossible because of budget constraints. In our competition entry, there was no pedestrian link where we now have it along the western edge of the site. Initially, we thought there could be a landscaped area only between our building and the existing one and that units on the ground floor would benefit from more privacy. However, as the design developed, we decided to close the courtyard off to make it for residents only to create a safe environment for children and meet other planning requirements. The outdoor area on the southern side is open to the public, and this space has a different character. The convenience store, located on the ground floor, is run by the residents but is open to the public, too. You can buy coffee and basic things there. We have maintained our initial aims to provide communal areas for residents, such as galleries and the courtyard, and building an actual part of the surrounding Rollberg neighborhood. The outdoor area on the southern side and access to units from the street are important in this regard. There are more communal spaces inside the building, integrated into the dwellings for group living, sometimes called clustered apartments, composed of autonomous units with a shared living room and a kitchen, currently attractive to the young and aging population and single parents.

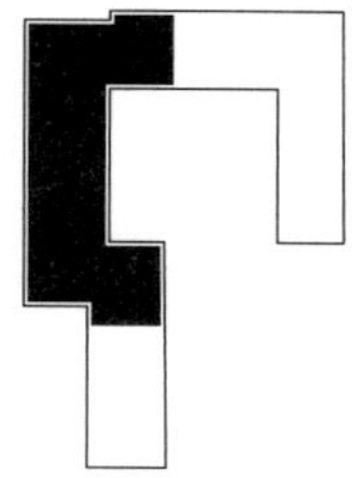

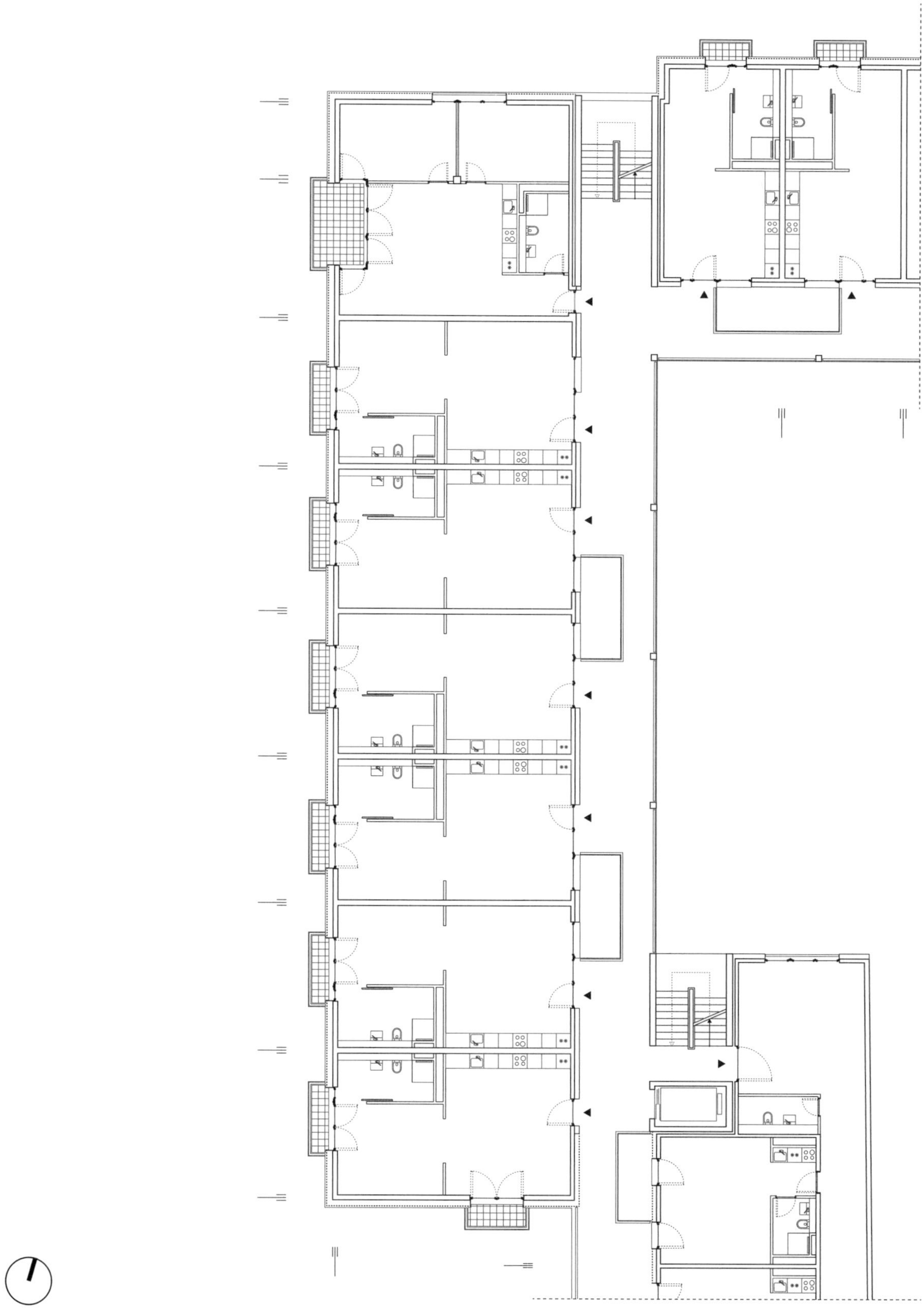

Figure 3
Typical floor plan, segment, drawing scale 1:250

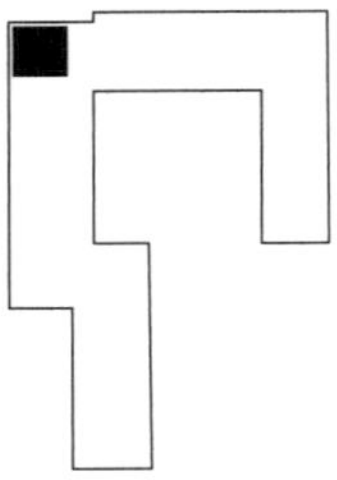

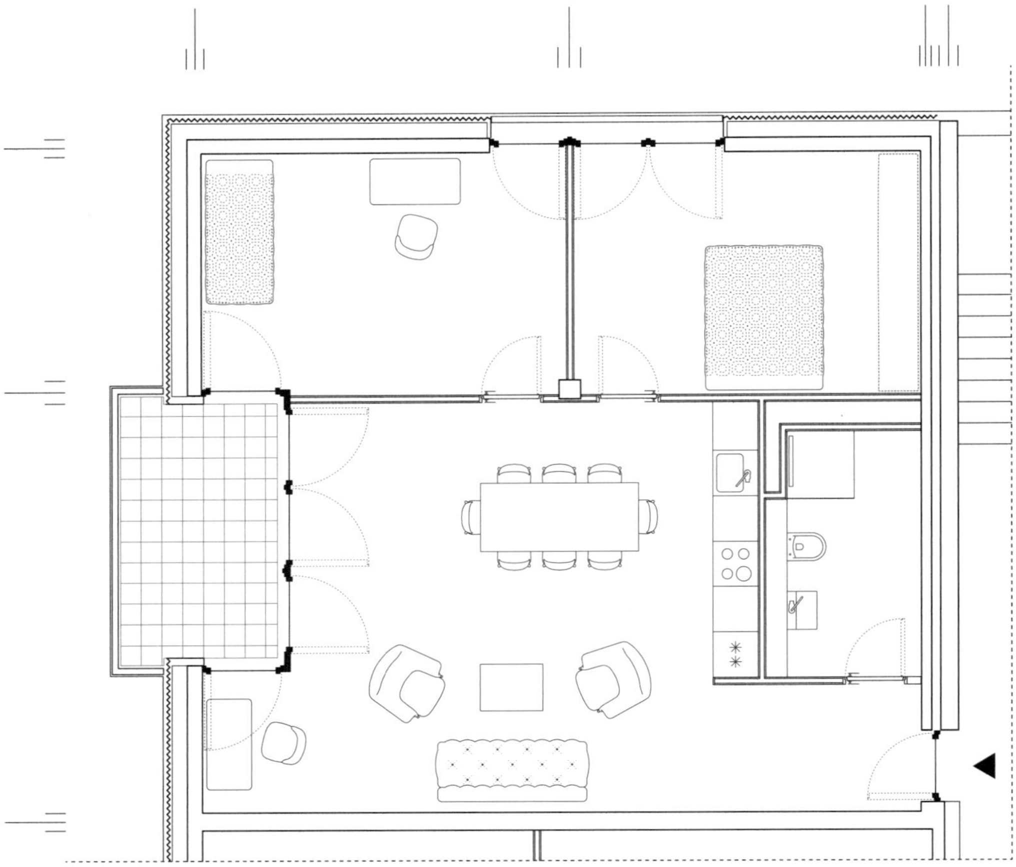

Figure 4
Sample unit layout, drawing scale 1:100

DS How spontaneous is the use of access galleries, and what did you have to do as designers to make the concept work in real life?

VL We insisted on enabling the appropriation of access galleries by residents. It was not easy to do so because of the firefighting regulations, which are very strict in Germany. We had to ensure escape routes were not compromised and put much effort into convincing everyone that the zoning approach we established using different floor finish colors would work. Without residents taking over that space, we would have vast empty spaces. If residents did not actively use galleries, they could become a no-man's-land, prone to derelict behavior, not unknown in large housing estates. When people moved in, there was some anxiety about what would happen. However, they started bringing chairs and pots outside after a few weeks. I think people are generally happy with the setup whereby other residents are passing by their living rooms. There were some complaints about group visits and tours. On an everyday basis, it works fine. STADT UND LAND, the housing provider who owns and manages the building, has undertaken steps to inform and prepare people applying for tenancy contracts about the specific form of housing the building offers. So, people knew what to expect, and yet there was a significant number of applications. You could say it is down to the demand for affordable housing, but now that the building is used, we can see that people want to live in a community.

"If residents did not actively use galleries, they could become a no-man's-land, prone to derelict behavior, not unknown in large housing estates. When people moved in, there was some anxiety about what would happen. However, they started bringing chairs and pots outside after a few weeks."

DS What design decisions did you take to accommodate diverse and changing housing needs?

VL Initially, we assumed that structural columns rather than walls would give more flexibility for the unit layout and a possibility to change over the building life span, estimated to be fifty years according to current standards. However, our client, STADT UND LAND, an affordable housing provider with tremendous experience and an extensive portfolio, saw it more feasible to relocate residents between units when their needs change than to plan to adapt the unit structure or size. They do well in practice to help people replace one larger with two smaller units if needed. In this development, as many as eighty units are small, either studios or one-bedroom units, in response to the demand. It has allowed us to place structural walls at a short distance from each other, resulting in a bookshelf-like structure. There are only a few partitions within dwellings. Units are handed over to residents as generic spaces, with only basic finishes specified by the provider, with electrical and all other installations, but without kitchens. It allows, or necessitates, residents to assert control over their dwelling space. Photos by Andrew Alberts available from our website show a variety of domestic interiors created by residents.

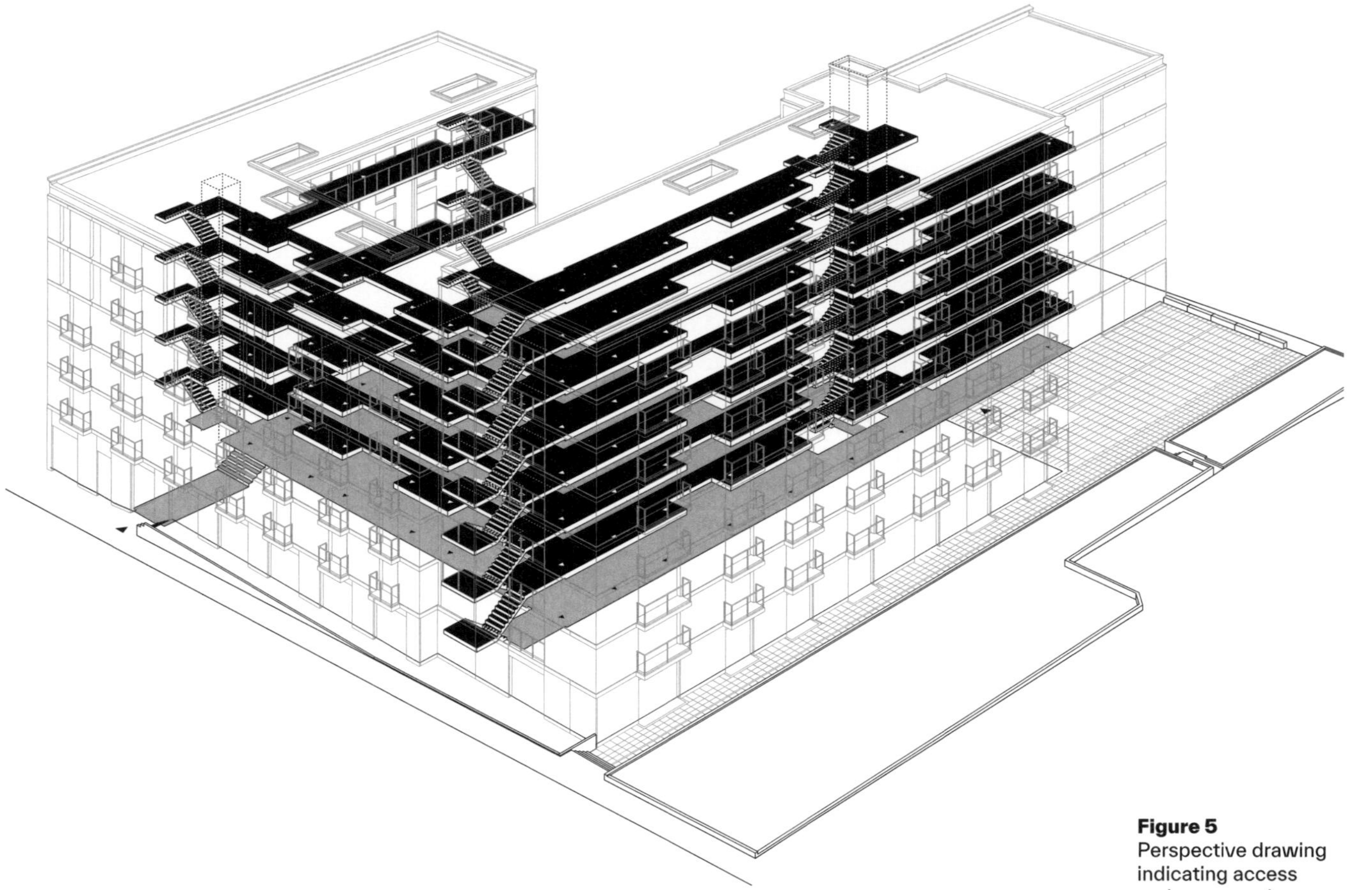

Figure 5
Perspective drawing indicating access and communal spaces in the building.

In conversation

The following section is an edited interview recorded with one of the residents on April 23, 2023. They live on the fifth floor with their partner and daughter.

DS What are the main communal spaces in and around the building, and how are they used?

DB A small outdoor area next to the Kienitzer Straße is an important communal and public space. It is used mainly by residents but is an open public space. We have a convenience store called *Späti* in our building facing it. These shops are typical for Berlin and can be found in most blocks in the inner city. I would say that they have a social value in the first place. They usually sell tobacco, snacks, drinks, and basic items and are open late into the night and on the weekends. They are often run by the people who live nearby and are spots where locals meet. A group of residents has started running the Späti in our building. I was part of it. But it was not sustainable; we all had too much going on. We therefore reached out to a group that manages cultural activities as we thought it would be important to have such a store to support social momentum among the residents. Now, that group rents the space from the housing provider who owns and manages the building. Several residents remain involved in running it. It works very well as a gathering spot. It can be rented for events, such as kids' birthday parties. Cultural events sometimes occur in the outdoor area next to the Kienitzer Straße. Last week, there was a concert by a group helping people with long-term illnesses. Three residential units with floor-to-ceiling windows face that public space as the shop does. It adds to the character of that space. At the same time, these units have less privacy. For some people, it works. I know someone who lives in one of them and always keeps their door open. For others, it doesn't. I know that someone has moved out.

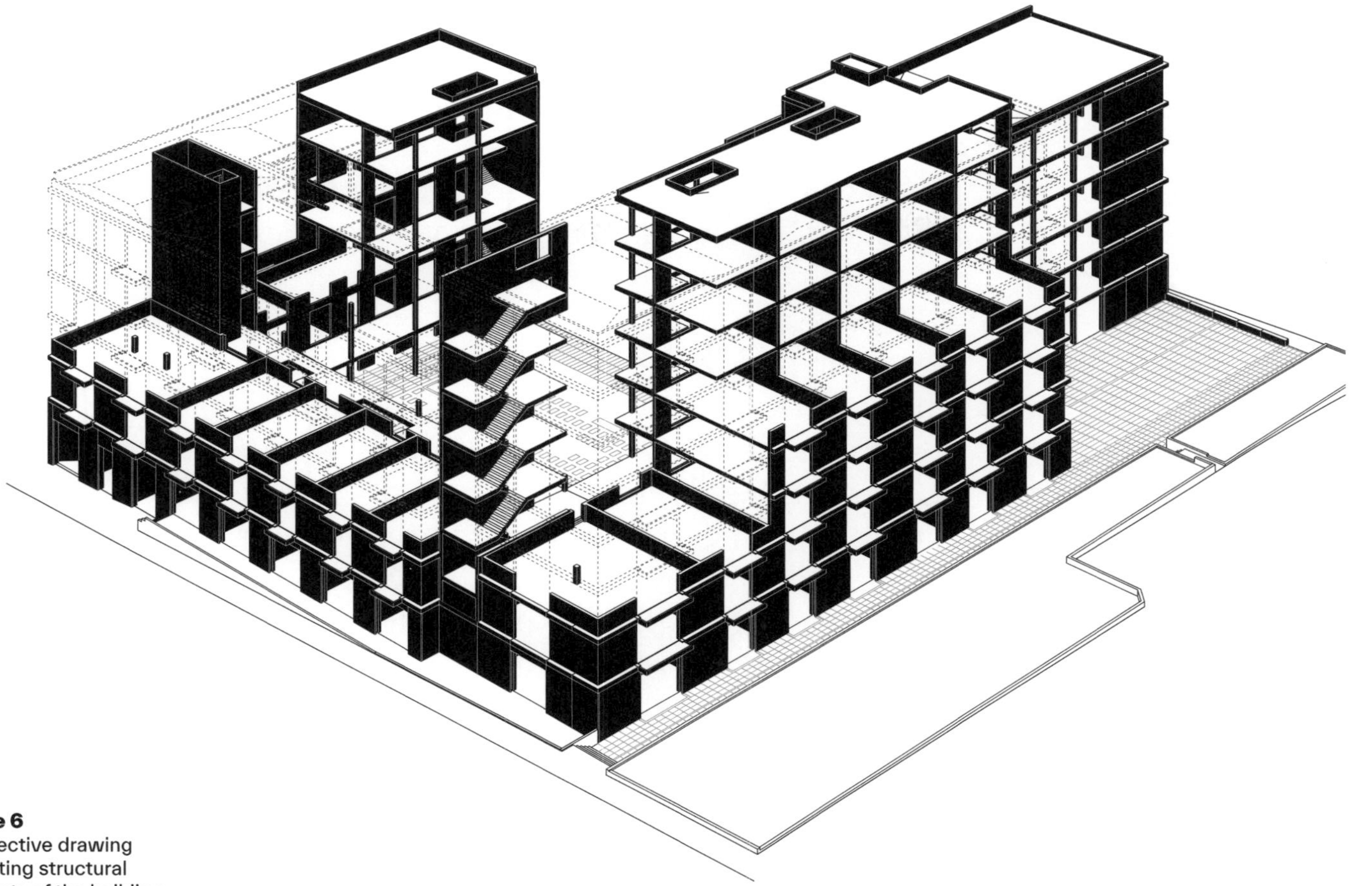

Figure 6
Perspective drawing indicating structural elements of the building.

DS I expected that you would start with the courtyard. Is it the main communal space?

DB The courtyard is accessible by residents only. It is partially landscaped. Five trees that are growing there are 4 meters tall now. There is also a sand pit. Children mainly use the courtyard. Many playgrounds are around the building, so children have a big choice. I think older kids like to explore the area, and mainly younger children play in the courtyard. Most units overlook the courtyard via access galleries, so parents can keep an eye on them while they are playing. We can hear when parents call children in for dinner. It feels like having your garden. The space is enclosed by the building on three sides and a fire barrier wall, which amplifies the sound coming from the courtyard, but it has not been much of an issue until now. Once a year, in summer, we have large gatherings in the courtyard with food and everything. These are called summer fests. In the first two years, these events were self-initiated by residents, and last year, it was organized by STADT UND LAND, the housing provider who owns and manages the building.

DS What about the units on the ground floor? Do they benefit from direct access to the courtyard?

DB The courtyard zone, just next to the building, is used by the ground-floor units. There are no fences or anything like that, but the space is appropriated by people who live there. It contributes to keeping that space active. Some units on the ground floor face the public space on one side and the courtyard on the other. Privacy is an issue for some of the residents there. These units are used as ateliers, and many people use them as a workspace.

DS I trust that most of the interaction between residents unfolds on outdoor access galleries encircling the courtyard. How are they used?

DB Walkways or access galleries are halfway between communal and individual. That was the idea behind the project. It was explained to us by STADT UND LAND when we expressed interest in the rental agreement. And it works in practice. It generates random encounters between people. Many residents will have their dinner or glass of wine there in the summer. Some are more casual and may come out in their pajamas, while others may dress up more formally to have dinner there. In winter, galleries are used sparingly. Some areas are decorated for Christmas. But as soon as it gets warmer, galleries go back to life. Yesterday was the first warm day of the year, and it was very nice to see plenty of activity. We can also see children often playing there. Rails are of great help to those learning to walk. A few years older kids find it amusing to run through the galleries.

DS Most units have living rooms facing open-air access galleries with floor-to-ceiling glass doors. Do you feel the intimacy of one's home is compromised with such an arrangement between individual and communal space?

DB People deal with it differently. I suppose it depends on their preferences. Some residents have mounted folios onto the glass to make it translucent rather than transparent. Most have curtains of different kinds. Some are not fussed with it, and you can see their entire living room as you pass by. Mostly, it is plants that I mentioned before, which are used to provide a bit of a barrier. Some plants are turning into hedge walls for that reason. We have a plant next to the glass door in the interior. But our unit is atypical, as it is on the corner of the building. We do not have a dedicated space in the galleries that we can use. We are often tempted to have breakfast at the access gallery in front of our dwelling when it is sunny. But we have a large private outdoor area facing the street. Most units have both, and you can choose between a private outdoor space facing the street and a less private area facing the courtyard.

DS Are there any shared amenities in the building?

DB There is bicycle parking in the courtyard, but other than that, I don't think we have any shared facilities, such as a communal laundry. I understand the social value of having one. But I think everyone prefers to have their washing machine in their units. All units are equipped with adequate installations. But I think we could use a communal dryer.

DS Do you notice any physical or architectural means that help regulate the relationship between individual and communal use of access galleries?

DB There are marks on the floor to help regulate where residents can place their things. I think there is an informal gardening rivalry in the building, resulting in some spectacular plants growing everywhere. Planting pots and perhaps some furniture or toys are occasionally placed on the other side of the marking line, for which we get prompt notices from the building manager.

Figure 7
Perspective drawing of the building envelope.

“I think there is an informal gardening rivalry in the building, resulting in some spectacular plants growing everywhere. Planting pots and perhaps some furniture or toys are occasionally placed on the other side of the marking line, for which we get prompt notices from the building manager.”

DS Besides the physical barriers, or their deliberate omission, that you have just described, are there any other regulations or ways of regulating the noise impact?

DB We love regulations in Germany, so there are some guidelines for quiet hours at certain times during the day and night. The noise made by people socializing in the galleries or the sound coming from the courtyard is not an issue. More of a concern is if someone tries to put a painting on the wall in their dwelling. There is a high chance they will have to drill into the concrete, which vibrates throughout the entire building. The first three months were challenging when we moved in and did touch-ups in our units. We have a WhatsApp group for residents, with almost 100 members, where complaints about noise from building work are reported regularly. The same communication is used for neighborly staff, for example, if you need to borrow something, such as a drill, if you are out of flour when shops are closed, or if you need someone to take your delivery if you are not home.

DS Can you describe your unit's layout and how it fits your needs?

DB We are happy with the unit layout. We have three rooms. My partner and I use one of the rooms as an office. Now that our child is growing up, that room will be used differently, and our home office will shrink to a desk space, probably somewhere in the living room. We are not thinking about changing the layout. However, one of our neighbors with an identical unit is considering splitting the living room into two spaces to create a home office. I also know that in several units for group living, residents have obtained approval from the building owner to reduce their living rooms to create another bedroom, reducing the share of rent met by each habitant. The building owner does provide kitchens on request, but we have built our own. Finishes in the apartment are neutral, white plastered walls and a gray linoleum floor, which we liked, but I know that some residents have covered it with a laminated floor instead.

DS How do you find daylighting and natural ventilation in your unit, and is your dwelling comfortable?

DB Our unit has plenty of daylight on the fifth floor. As our apartment is on the corner of the block and some distance from the adjacent block, we have views down the street and over treetops. Our loggia facing the street is spacious. Big pivoting and tilting glass doors separate the interior from the exterior. When we use these doors in summer, we reshuffle furniture in the living room to move it out of the pivoting path and turn our sofa toward the loggia. Like all other units in the building, our unit has dual orientation, enabling natural ventilation. Windows can be tilted inward for ventilation without creating too much draft. Our bathroom has a ventilation shaft. Most units have bathrooms oriented toward the street. The bathrooms' dimensions are very generous. I think this has to do with barrier-free access regulations. But it is funny to see tiny units with very large bathrooms. I know that some people keep wardrobes in their bathrooms for that reason.

2

Buildings R and S in Pierre Loti Residential Area, Aytré

Guinée*Potin
with Alterlab Architects

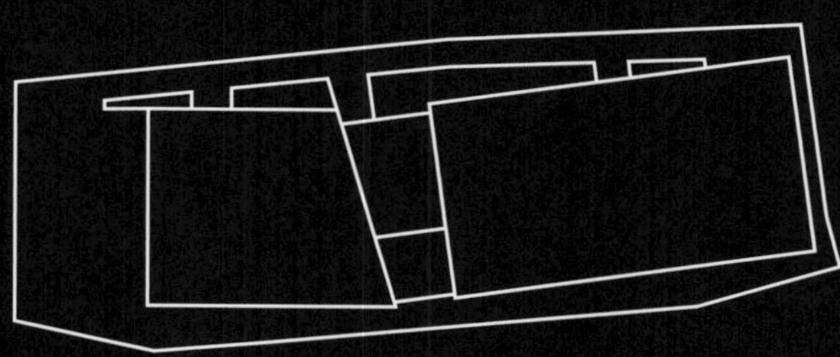

Amalgam

Figure 1
Site plan, drawing scale 1:2500

Buildings R and S in Pierre Loti Residential Area, Aytré

Guinée*Potin with Alterlab Architects

Year of completion: 2017
Number of units: 64

Recent multiunit residential projects by Guinée*Potin are often on sites forming edges between urban and rural environments. Their work is innovative and usually centered on the relationship between the built form and the surrounding landscape. They have tested and applied vernacular construction methods and regenerative building materials across various residential projects.

This project is part of the larger redevelopment plan for the Pierre Loti neighborhood located in the municipality of Aytré near La Rochelle, a port town on the Bay of Biscay in southwest France. The site is just across the road from the spontaneously built low-rise fabric, near the sizable wetlands with rich biodiversity, and only one kilometer from the large Atlantic Ocean beach. The Pierre Loti residential area was built by the state between 1957 and 1968 in response to a high housing demand.[1] As with other similar developments from this period in France and other countries, the response to the housing provision pressure often was to build as many units as possible while only a minimum of communal facilities was provided, and little emphasis was placed on the spaces between buildings. The neighborhood was created from scratch. It provided approximately 400 social housing units in mid-rise, freestanding buildings optimistically named after remote archipelagos, such as the Galapagos, Fiji, and the Balearic Islands. The analogy between isolated and remote buildings and islands lending themselves to the building names was not intentional but must have become apparent over time. After four decades, the deteriorating buildings and the lack of amenities contributed to the worsening of housing conditions and the poor image of the neighborhood. In response, the local government engaged with Habitat 17, one of the leading affordable housing providers in the region, to undertake an ambitious renewal project. The planning process included public consultations with the residents of the area. It was followed by the formulation of a master plan aiming to maintain the density, renew the housing stock, create more landscaped areas, and help fashion a new identity for the entire residential area.[2] First, the Canary Island building was removed to make room for the new residential developments on the site's southeast corner. Once the new facilities were ready, with approximately 170 homes and residents relocated, two more buildings were demolished, including the 200-meter-long one named Antilles, and replaced with landscaped areas.

Once the new master plan was drafted, architectural competitions were held for smaller segments. Guinée*Potin Architects won the competition for the site with two buildings, Réunion (Building R) and Seychelles (Building S), and developed the project in collaboration with Alterlab Architects.

Siting

The site for the Buildings R and S is on the fringe of the Pierre Loti residential area. The project for the two buildings negotiates between the retained social housing buildings, an existing low-rise, and other concurrently built residential structures. The two buildings are separated by a street which runs longitudinally across the residential area. They create an ensemble, but they also differ. These differences are generated in response to their immediate surroundings. Building R is closer to a busy road connecting Aytré to La Rochelle and is more visible from a distance. It has an elongated rectangular footprint, and its height varies between three and five floors. Its roof comprises five gable roofs, and its overall form resembles a composite of a multiunit residential building with one- and two-story detached homes placed on top of it. Building S has almost a cubical form, a flat roof, and a height of four floors. Building R has outdoor gallery access and thirty-one units, while building S has indoor corridor access and thirty-three units.

Envelope

What unifies the two new buildings is the architectural treatment of their facades, central to understanding the entire urban renewal project and efforts taken to change the identity of residential areas previously associated with large, monotonous buildings and the ill-defined spaces between them. The facades of the two buildings are complex and layered. The dominant building material is larch, applied differently for the railing, cladding of the walls separating the interior and exterior, and shutters protecting glazed surfaces. The railing comprises battens held by a galvanized steel structure, forming horizontal bands that dominate the project's overall appearance. The facade cladding is shiplap with vertical joints. Folding and sliding shutters are made from slightly narrower slats. The three ways of applying the same building material produce a patchwork of vertical lines, which, along with the weathering texture of the larch, help articulate the building envelope. The architectural treatment of the facades is completed with highly visible and vividly colored polycarbonate storage boxes, distinctly shaped as garden sheds or beach huts. These are placed in private outdoor areas to separate individual dwelling units, in addition to providing storage space. Gable roofs, extensive private outdoor areas, a wood-clad facade, and the incorporated storage sheds help create a distinct appearance for the two multiunit residential buildings, halfway between rural and urban.

Vernacular Architecture

During their lecture hosted by the Melbourne School of Design on March 9, 2022, Anne-Flore Guinée and Hervé Potin explained how their early career travels to Africa had invoked a long-term interest in vernacular architecture, which continued to thread through their practice.[3] They presented three different multiunit residential projects in a build-up to the discussion of their work in Aytré to illustrate the point. Some common denominators between these projects are their siting at an edge between urban and rural and the connection between residential buildings and the surrounding landscape. They also involve innovative use of vernacular construction methods and regenerative building materials such as timber and

1. The influx of people relocating from Algeria after the country finally gained its independence in 1962, is estimated at close to 1 million, which added pressure on the housing system in France.
2. Phytolab, "Quartier Pierre Loti," accessed March 22, 2022, https://www.phytolab.fr/project/quartier-pierre-loti/.
3. Anne-Flore Guinée and Hervé Potin, "Sustainable and Affordable Collective Social Housing," guest lecture, Melbourne School of Design, March 9, 2021, https://msd.unimelb.edu.au/events/msd-at-home-with-anne-flore-guinee-and-herve-potin.

straw. The first presented was the project for 16 dwelling units in Chantepie, near Rennes, where they started to develop construction methods later employed at Aytré, using concrete for the primary skeleton structure, with secondary structure and cladding done in timber.[4] It was followed by the presentation of work with a self-organized housing group on the reuse of existing structures and the conversion of an agricultural farm into dwellings for 12 households at La Montagne, near Nantes.[5] The third project presented was for 105 subsidized and affordable housing units in six residential buildings at the urban edge close to large agricultural greenhouses in Rezé, also near Nantes.[6] Because of its size, the last referenced work is the closest match to the formal and organizational principles of the project in Aytré. However, all projects are relevant to this discussion, as they harbor a rural character and qualities while maintaining the efficiency of multiunit residential buildings in urban environments. This is achieved by carefully structuring the relationship between dwellings and private and communal outdoor areas and links between the buildings and the surrounding landscape as much as it is by the choice of building materials and techniques resulting in built forms widely associated with country, individual homes, and barns.

Amalgam

The achieved architectural expression of this project epitomizes the opposite of the housing estate built in the 1960s, which was dominated by repetitive fenestration and the absence of private outdoor areas. It is an amalgam of urban multiunit residential buildings associated with qualities of pastoral life, such as access to the outdoor environment, landscape, and gardening. To the south, ground-floor units of Buildings R and S have gardens facing publicly accessible landscaped areas designed as orchards and productive gardens. These units can be accessed from the landscaped area via private gardens and bridge-like platforms laid over a depression in the terrain, which, along with fences and plants, are employed to protect their privacy. To the north, both buildings have open-air parking lots. Communal bicycle storage is next to Building R, while part of the ground floor in Building S is utilized for car parking. A small convenience store is on the corner of Building R, closest to the street that runs longitudinally through the residential area.

The building structure is a concrete skeleton system, with beams and slabs cantilevering from the main building volume to form private outdoor areas and access galleries. These cantilevers protect the facade wall from the weather and contribute to thermal comfort and microclimate in the dwellings.

Units

A vertical core with stairs and elevators is in the center of both buildings. Open-air galleries on the north side provide access to the dwellings of Building R. Up to six units are on the same floor, three on each side of the core. The distribution of units and their layouts repeat across the floors. Level four has one, and level five has two units fewer as the building form changes on the upper floors. Building R is split into two parts as open-air access galleries cut through the middle of the building from the north to the south facade on all floors. It creates a gap in the built form populated with communal platforms. Two units are entered from the platform, while other dwellings are entered from the north via bridges, creating distance between access spaces and private rooms. Dwellings vary from one- to three-bed configurations. All units are dually oriented to secure access to daylight and natural ventilation. Day and night zones are made explicit in the unit layout. All units have access to large, south-facing private outdoor areas. Access to dwellings in Building S is via an indoor corridor, while the dual orientation of most units is achieved as they occupy building corners.

4. Guinée*Potin, "105 Housing Units, Rezé," accessed August 8, 2023, http://www.guineepotin.fr/index.php?/pages-projets/reze---la-jaguere/.
5. Guinée*Potin, "16 Intermediate Dwellings, Chantepie," accessed August 8, 2023, http://www.guineepotin.fr/index.php?/pages-projets/chantepie/.
6. Guinée*Potin, "12 Participatory Housing and Collective Premises in La Montagne," accessed August 8, 2023, http://www.guineepotin.fr/index.php?/projets/la-montagne---12-logements-collectifs/.

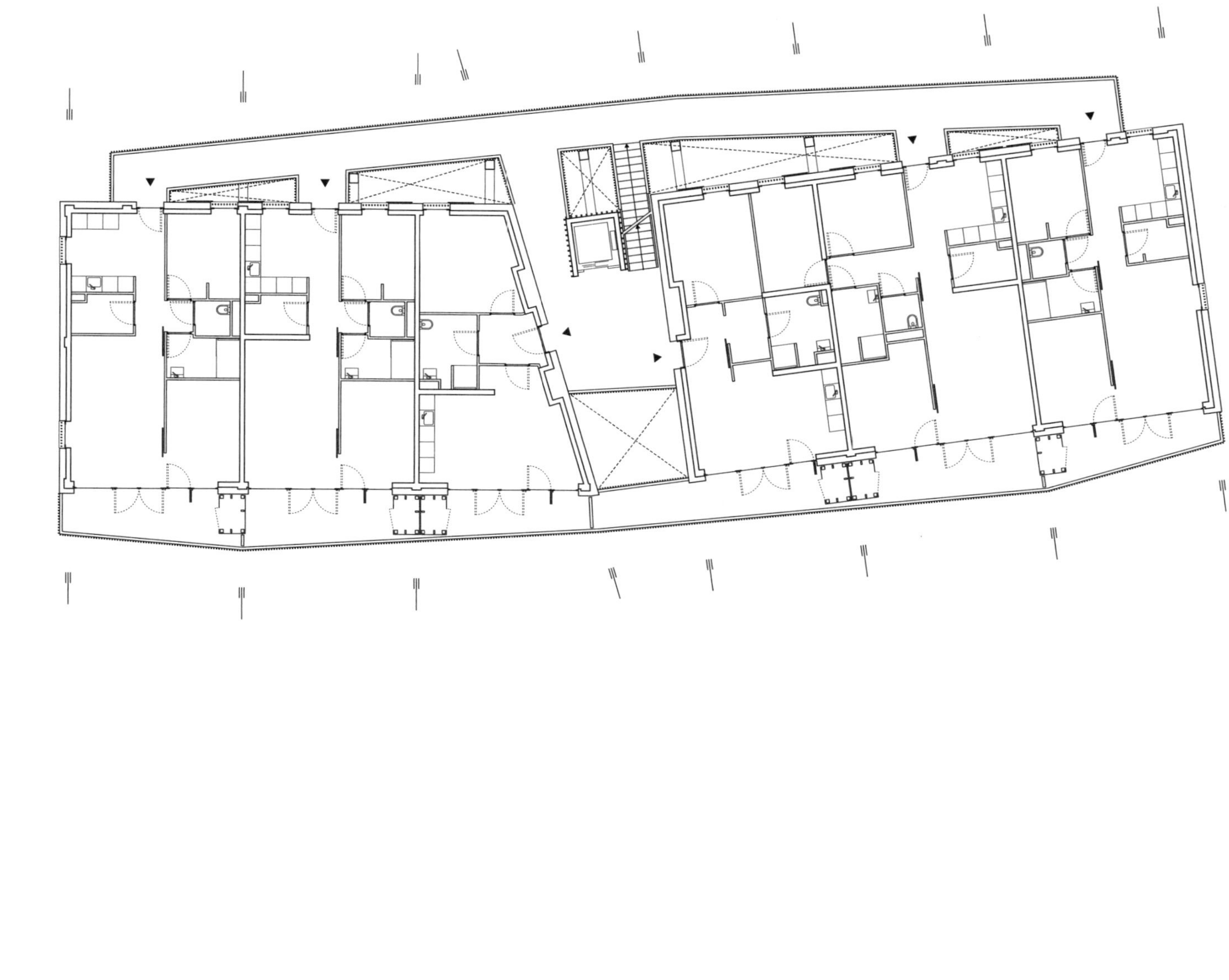

Figure 2
Typical floor plan,
drawing scale 1:250

In conversation

The following segment, an edited interview with Hervé Potin recorded on June 30, 2023, provides further information about the project from the architects' perspective.

DS The project for the renewal of the residential area involved the demolition of some buildings and relocating residents as part of the social housing program. Did you have an opportunity to interact with the resident community, and have you had a chance to incorporate their feedback into the design proposal?

HP We had two public presentations to the local community of residents, composed of people who live in this neighborhood. Some were living in buildings demolished as part of the renewal project. Some of them were relocated to new buildings, including the ones we designed. In parallel with the project for Buildings R and S, other schemes for three sites in the same residential areas unfolded. We were all part of the same consultation process. At that time, we did not know who would move into the buildings we were designing. The renewal project, as well as the initial development, was subsidized by the government, and people are allocated or given rental tenure through the procedure determined by the local government and Habitat 17, the housing provider behind the project. Some of the buildings had to be demolished. They were not too bad regarding unit layout and spatial standards; however, most were in poor condition. There was hardly any thermal insulation. There is always a dilemma if a building should be retrofitted instead. One of the main issues was that the existing buildings had no relationship to the landscape.

DS Can you talk more about the relationship between dwellings and landscape?

HP Dwellings have a dual, north-south orientation. It maximizes the views from the dwelling and improves natural ventilation and intake of daylight. At the same time, we created distance between access galleries and the windows of dwellings. We have small bridges you must cross to get to the unit to protect the intimacy of homes. Looking at the typical floor plan of Building R, you can see that we have divided it into two blocks to insert a platform between them on each floor. We could have had another small unit there, but we thought it was important to maintain views to the north and south and to make this space generous. Residents of the two adjacent units use it as an extension of their dwellings. When I last visited the building, I saw that they kept bicycles and had tables and chairs there.

DS Did the master plan or the competition brief articulate how the missing relationship between the buildings and the landscape should be achieved, and were there any requirements for communal spaces in the new buildings?

HP The competition brief did not include any provisions for communal areas. However, we took the initiative in that regard. We worked closely with the landscape architects. Our project is about the relationship between the dwelling and the landscape or the outdoor environment. We have done it by focusing on the sequencing of spaces one goes through on the way home. It concerns the transition from public to private and the relationship with the outdoor environment. It includes passing the fence, going through an entry, walking along an elevated walkway while observing the landscape, and entering the dwelling directly from an outdoor environment. In this project, one's landscape experience starts at the ground level and continues in the communal access areas and the dwellings.

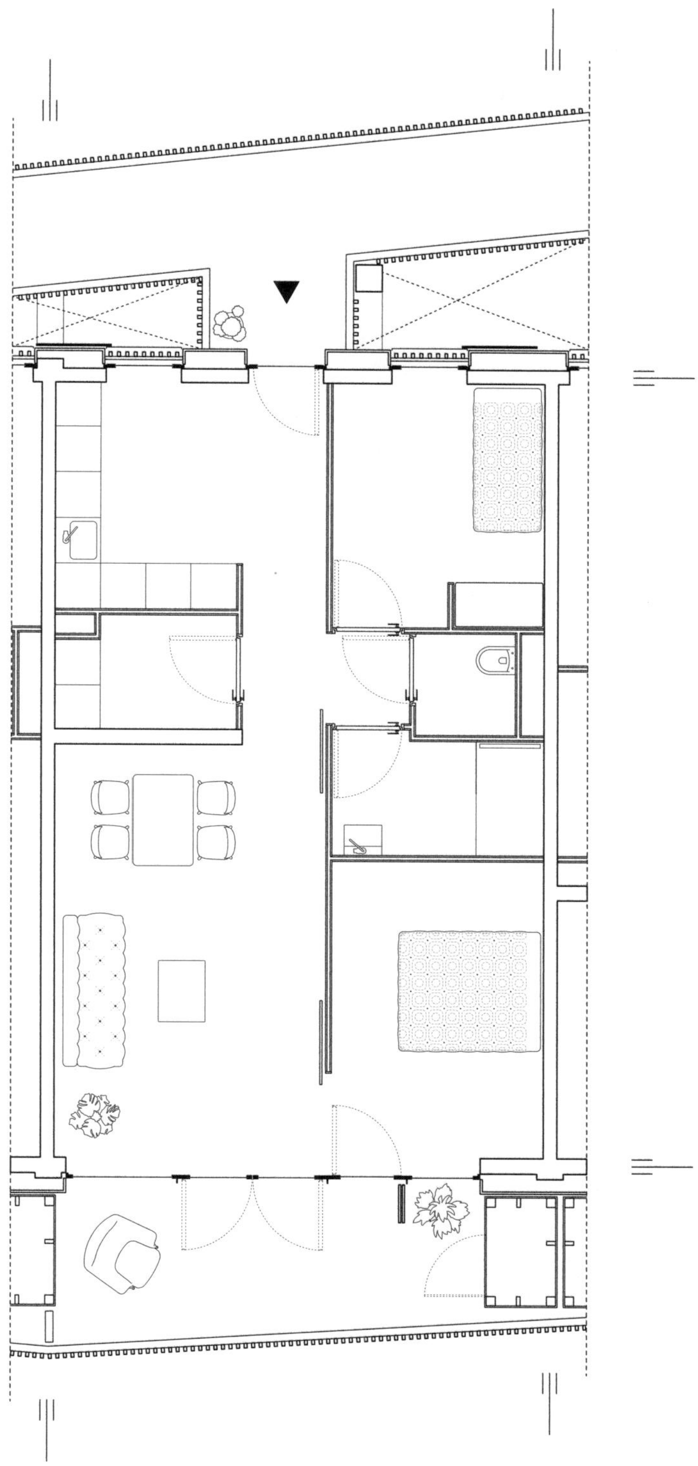

Figure 3
Sample unit layout, drawing scale 1:100

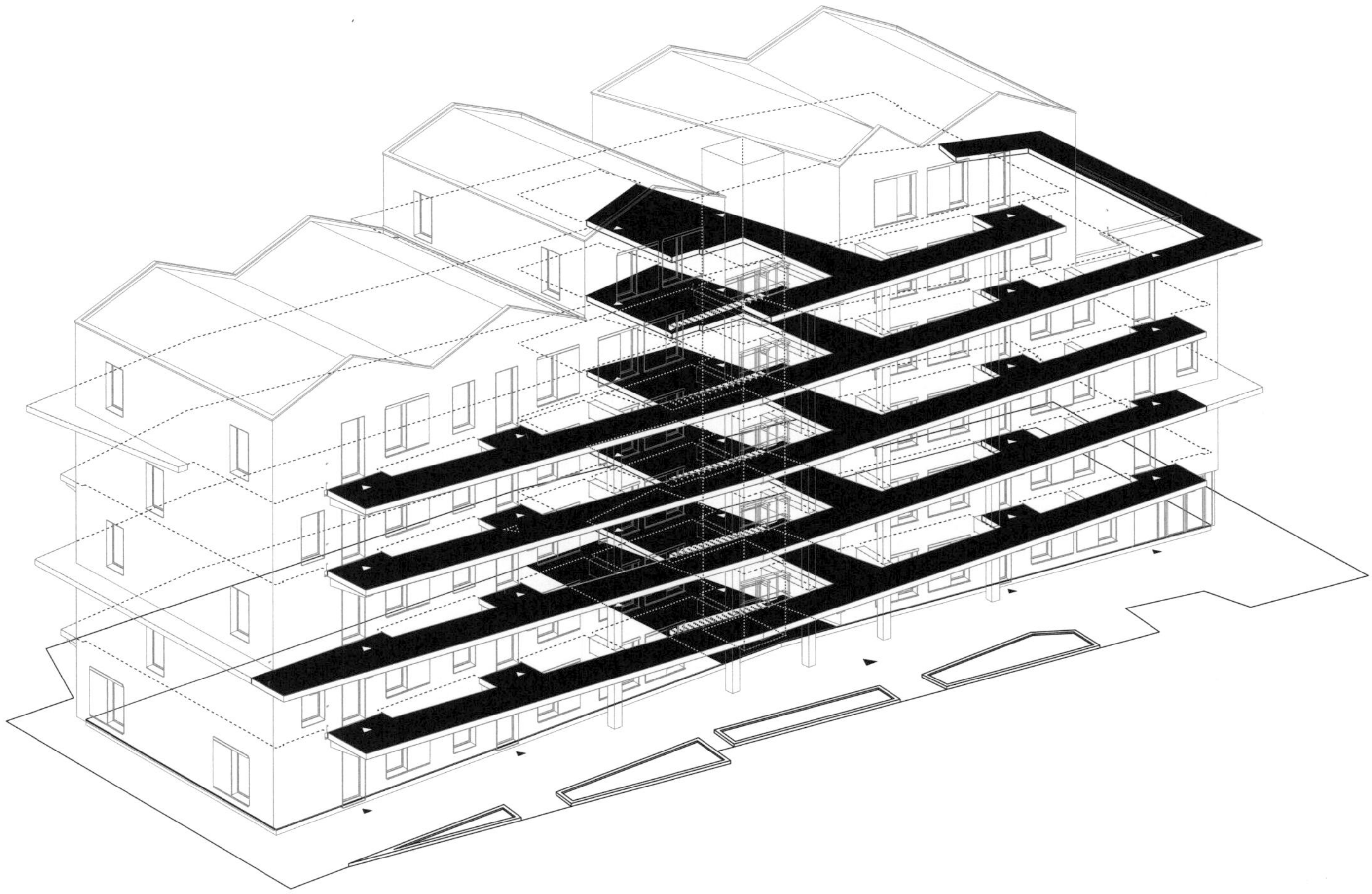

Figure 4
Perspective drawing indicating access and communal spaces in the building.

DS What is the relationship with the landscape for the units on the ground floor?

HP The inclusion of private gardens for units on the ground was part of the brief. Those units are planned and designed for larger households. Some are duplex units meant to be closer to an individual house typology. The aim was to provide a greater diversity of dwelling types. In practice, it works well. These gardens are used by residents; it is excellent for children to play and grow edible vegetables. They also provide more privacy to units as the public landscaped area, which includes a children's playground, is just in front of them. This area is part of the master plan, not designed by us.

DS Buildings R and S are part of the same project but very different. What was the reason for employing different access types for the two buildings?

HP The brief suggested two different access types for the two buildings. I understand it was a response to the repetitive and homogenous character of the residential area built in the 1960s. It was also driven by differences in the shape of the two lots. We made their footprint slightly irregular. One building is elongated, and the other is more compact and nearly square in footprint. We added slight inflections to those geometric figures, which make buildings appear different when viewed from the surroundings. We wanted to move away from the homogenous and impersonal nature of the old development.

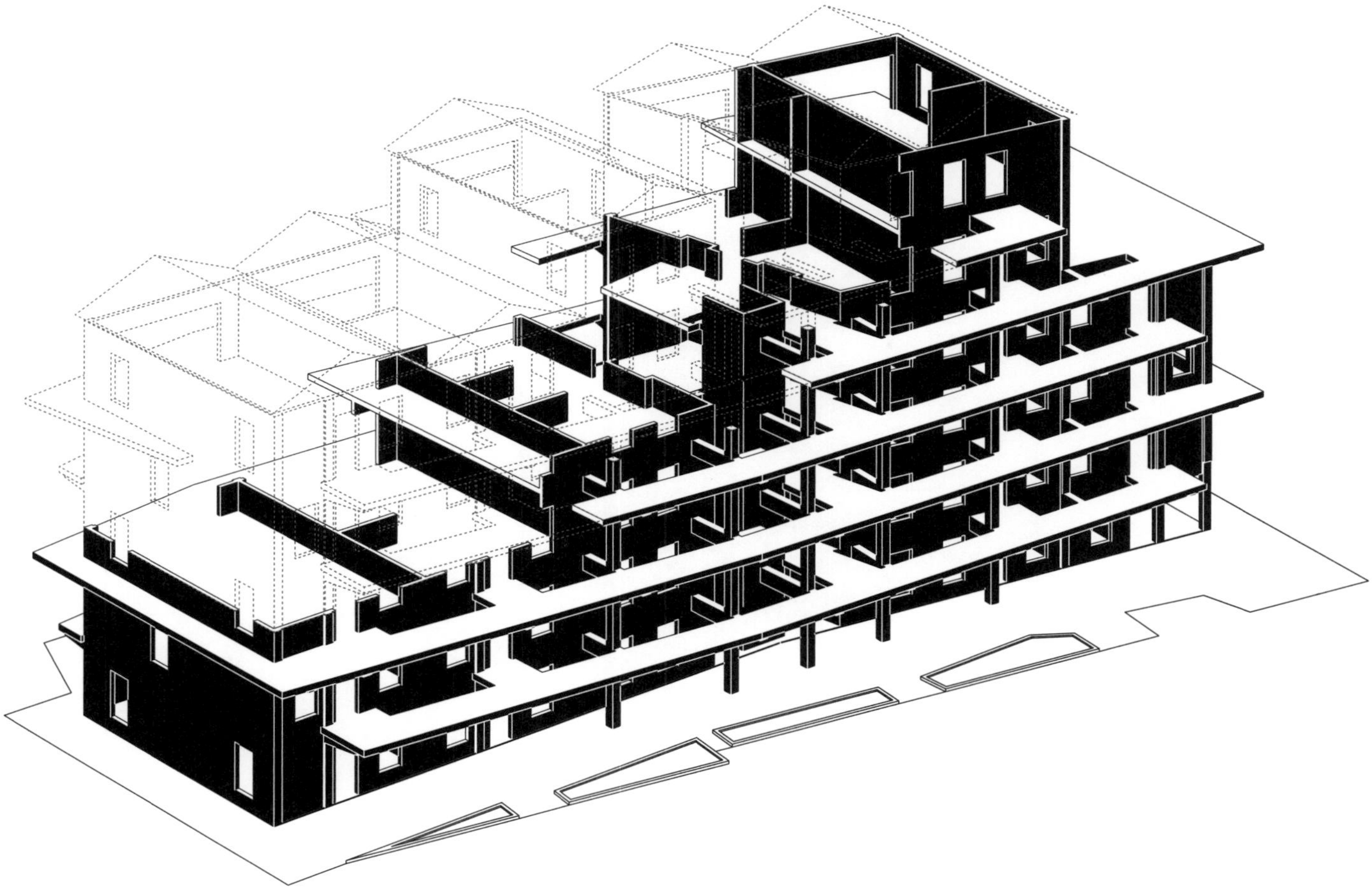

Figure 5
Perspective drawing indicating structural elements of the building.

DS We opened the conversation about the relationship between inside and outside with a question about the relationship between the landscape and the building. Can you speak more about private outdoor areas in this project in the context of this relationship?

HP We have achieved that units have around 15 square meters of private outdoor areas. The brief did not explicitly demand such size, but we wanted to make them as big as possible. The climate of Nantes has hot summers, and outdoor areas can be used for a large part of the year. The site is not far from the beach, which adds to the expectation of an outdoor environment as part of the dwelling. Finally, it is very different from how it was done in the buildings we were trying to replace, which did not include any private outdoor environment. It was essential to change the images of the residential area as much as to provide an amenity. Historically, the importance of outdoor spaces attached to dwellings was often overlooked in social housing projects. We wanted to create large outdoor areas where people can spend time and keep their plants. We have deliberately made all openings facing private outdoor areas extensive. They are composed of three panels, which connect one or two rooms to the terrace, depending on the unit type. It almost lets you remove a part of the wall to have a better relationship between inside and outside when you want to. We have also added storage boxes. As dwellings are not very big, we thought it would be helpful for all the stuff people usually keep on their terraces in multiunit residential buildings. We have used storage boxes to cheer up the building facade by making them look like garden sheds and adding a bit of color.

Figure 6
Perspective drawing of the building envelope.

“Our project is about the relationship between the dwelling and the landscape or the outdoor environment. We have done it by focusing on the sequencing of spaces one goes through on the way home. It concerns the transition from public to private and the relationship with the outdoor environment. It includes passing the fence, going through an entry, walking along an elevated walkway while observing the landscape, and entering the dwelling directly from an outdoor environment.”

DS The storage boxes are a great add-on to the building facade. Wood for cladding is another critical decision impacting the architectural expression.

HP In this project, we used larch, *mélèze* in French, a very durable wood, and it is not demanding in terms of maintenance. It is probably superior to most wood cladding options and rarely used in social housing projects. We would have liked to use timber for the primary structure, too. However, we had to use concrete because of the cost associated with timber construction. The underside of the concrete slab and beams are visible from the exterior. We had to include thermal breaks in both the beams and slabs, which has added some cost. The concrete beams and slabs cantilever to create the communal access galleries and private outdoor areas. They are also crucial in protecting the facade walls from the weather and for providing shade. On the top floors, where we don't have such protection, we have retractable shading devices made of canvas.

DS I am also interested in your choice of building materials for other projects.

HP We have developed a good understanding of regenerative building materials and vernacular construction techniques through our practice. In 2014 we completed a project, the Center for Discovery, Scientific Culture and Research on the Environment and Biodiversity, in La Roche-sur-Yon, using straw thatch for its roof and walls. We have used tree trunks as columns supporting the roof structure of its more recently completed addition. I mentioned that we used concrete for the primary structure in this project, but we have also used cross-laminated timber or solid wood in other projects. Some of our buildings have mixed structures composed of concrete slabs and timber columns. We use timber cladding frequently and straw-based products for insulation. Buildings R and S have mineral wool insulation, which was not our preference. We are currently working on a project for seventy-one low-carbon housing units in Rennes, where we could apply solid wood for the primary structure, straw-based thermal insulation, and clay for the exterior finish.[7] The challenges with regenerative building materials are compliance with the building regulations, cost, finding the skilled workforce to apply them, and working out architectural detailing.

DS How does your project contribute to environmental sustainability?

HP We are very interested in the environmental impact of the buildings we design. As with this project, we try to avoid technology in achieving objectives, including environmental benefits. We can accomplish a lot by ensuring dwellings are dually oriented and living rooms face south. Positioning and dimensioning the buildings to make the most of the given physical context is essential to protecting dwellings from overheating and utilizing natural ventilation. In this project, rainwater irrigates the landscape, and solar panels are used for water heating.

7. Guinée*Potin, "71 Low Carbon Housing Units, Rennes," accessed August 8, 2023, http://www.guineepotin.fr/index.php?/projets/71-logements-bas-carbone-courrouze/.

3 Wildgarten / Sonnenblumenhäuser, Vienna

arenas basabe palacios arquitectos
with M & S Architekten / Buschina & Partner

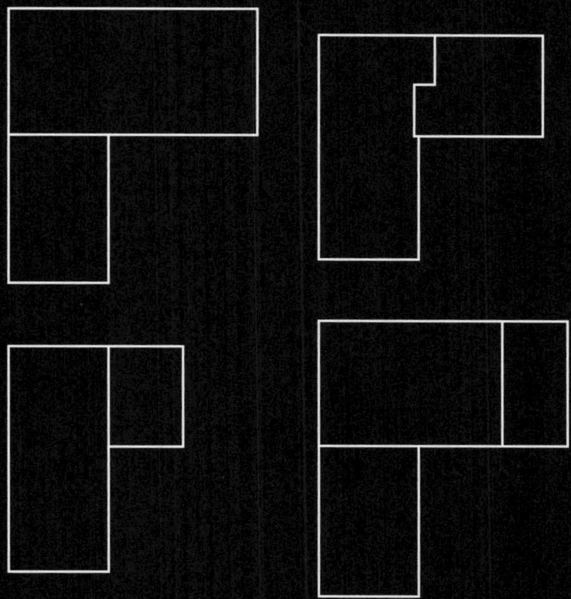

Homogenous Heterogeneous

Wildgarten / Sonnenblumenhäuser, Vienna

arenas basabe palacios arquitectos
with M & S Architekten / Buschina & Partner

Year of completion: 2022
Number of units: 82

This project was initiated in 2009 through Europan, a platform for architectural competitions and implementation of projects.[1] The entry, titled "Garten>Hof" by arenas basabe palacios arquitectos was the winner for Europan 10, Austria.[2,3] Subsequently, it was developed into the Emil-Behring-Weg, Meidling master plan adopted by the Vienna City Council in 2015. The master plan incorporated the proposition for a new residential neighborhood, Wildgarten, with approximately 1,000 dwellings. It was produced collaboratively between arenas basabe palacios, their local partner architects M&S Architekten, and multiple design consultants.[4] Citizens, institutions, and Austrian Real Estate, the landowner, were involved in the process. The master plan was endorsed by the United Nations Department of Economic and Social Affairs for

1. Europan Europe, "What is Europan," accessed March 30, 2023, https://www.europan-europe.eu/en/#what-is-europan.
2. Europan, "Garten>HOF," in *Inventing Urbanity: Regeneration, Revitalization, Colonization*, ed. Didier Rebois (Montreuil: Europan, 2010), 154–55.
3. arenas basabe palacios arquitectos, "Gartenhof," accessed March 30, 2023, https://arenasbasabepalacios.com/en/2009/06/26/gartenhof/.
4. arenas basabe palacios arquitectos, "Wildgarten," accessed March 30, 2023, https://arenasbasabepalacios.com/en/2015/09/25/wildgarten/.

Figure 1
Site plan, drawing scale 1:2500

its collaborative design process contributing to Sustainable Development Goal 11: Making cities and human settlements inclusive, safe, and sustainable.[5] A new residential neighborhood has been gradually and segmentally built by multiple developers, affordable housing providers, and self-organized cooperatives working with various architects. Sonnenblumenhäuser, a development comprised of eleven multiunit residential buildings designed by arenas basabe palacios in collaboration with Buschina & Partner, was completed in 2022.[6]

Site

The project site on Vienna's periphery was used for livestock farming during World War Two and as a veterinary center subsequently. In the late 1980s, it was earmarked for residential development as part of the urban densification strategy by the City of Vienna. The surroundings include a fragmented fabric of single-family homes with productive gardens to the south and west, one of Vienna's major cemeteries to the north, and a train line and industrial buildings being repurposed as part of the same strategy to the east.

Homogenous Framework

The competition entry was a systemic design proposal.[3] It was based on a flexible framework stipulating development across a matrix of building lots according to a set of rules. Each lot is square, with a side length of 21 meters, and incorporates a communal garden. One cannot build inside the garden, a smaller square with a side length of 12 meters, but only in the 9-meter-wide zone around it and only in a way that does not block the garden's exposure to the southern sun. The formula created a grid of L-shaped buildable parcels with an area of 360 square meters attached to 144-square-meter green areas and separated by open access spaces, including streets, pedestrian paths, and landscaped areas. Such a rules-based approach has provided a homogenous framework. At the same time, it enabled stakeholders to negotiate building types and sizes while securing a relationship between the buildings and the landscape. The framework remained essential throughout the master planning and subsequent development of architectural projects. The outcome is best observed in the site plan drawing.

Heterogeneous Fabric

During the initial stages of the project development, starting with the competition phase and transitioning to the master plan, little emphasis was placed on the building design. The focus was on the positioning of buildings and their orientation and volume, thus creating a system to enact a dialogue between stakeholders in the development process. A gradation of five possible building volumes was established, ranging from XS size, corresponding to individual homes, to XL size, occupying several lots and suitable for large multiunit buildings, usually delivered by institutional developers. Building scales S, M, and L were nominated for housing cooperatives and private developers. With such a definition, the master plan utilized placeholders instead of architecturally defined buildings that were swapped or altered according to consideration of economic, social, and environmental aspects throughout the design process. It enabled input on diverse factors critical to forming a new residential neighborhood. The main advantage of the proposed system was enabling negotiation between different participants in the process and providing flexibility within the overarching framework. This allowed demand and investment capacities to inform the density of the development. It enabled the coexistence of high- and low-density propositions and resulted in a heterogeneous built fabric suitable for diverse housing typologies. Using a set of rules helped structure the project as an open process instead of fixing the proposal early on a single vision. It also helped to establish a strategy for gradual implementation. The approach postulated the entire site as a communal landscape into which housing and supporting amenities were introduced incrementally.

Common Land

During a public lecture hosted by the Melbourne School of Design on August 3, 2021, Luis Basabe presented the architects' intent to address the 10-hectare site as common land.[7] He suggested that space does not have to be public or private only and expressed his interest in exploring spatial forms and organizations beyond a simplistic duality between the two. The master plan is conceptualized on open-access principles, yet it includes carefully structured outdoor spaces. It creates a tight relationship between dwelling and landscape, harnessing the advantages of a site on the outskirts of the urban area. To better explain architectural means to achieve open yet structured outdoor spaces, Basabe referred to the allotment gardens designed by Carl Theodor Sorensen, where such spatial condition was created by tall oval hedges.[8,9] Similar means, vegetation and landscape treatment, are used to establish soft thresholds between spaces in Wildgarten, allowing continuity and openness of the landscape.

In the Wildgarten master plan, structuring spaces between buildings helped control the overall built density and provide amenities for the new residential neighborhood. The space

5. United Nations Department of Economic and Social Affairs Sustainable Development, "Wildgarten Quartier: An Innovative Ecological and Democratic Neighborhood in Vienna, Austria," accessed March 7, 2023, https://sdgs.un.org/partnerships/wildgarten-quartier-innovative-ecological-and-democratic-neighborhood-vienna-austria.
6. arenas basabe palacios arquitectos, "Sonnenblumenhäuser," accessed March 30, 2023, https://arenasbasabepalacios.com/blog/2022/07/10/die-sonneblumenhauser/.
7. Luis Basabe, "Multiplayer City: Flexible Urban Supports for Complex Social Processes," guest lecture, Melbourne School of Design, August 3, 2021, https://edsc.unimelb.edu.au/studio-epsilon/lecture-repository/arenas-basabe-palacios.
8. Allotment Gardens, Naerum, Copenhagen, were designed by Carl Theodor Sorensen in 1948.
9. Basabe, "Multiplayer City."

between buildings includes pedestrian access routes and recreational and play areas.

The spaces between buildings also incorporate an uncultivated landscape network. Basabe explained the intention to support biological diversity in the new neighborhood, referring to the notion of the "third landscape" and the work of landscape architect Gilles Clément.[10,11] In the Wildgarten, the space between buildings includes tall grass and shrubs to provide refuge for native wildlife species. The same also provides residents with direct contact with nature.

Other landscaped areas between buildings are designed as city parks with mowed grass for active use. As there are no hard boundaries, these areas are offered to residents for joint use and as an extension of their gardens. To explain, Basabe showed a summertime photo of residents jointly using a lawn between their buildings. The image captured a moment of spontaneous interaction between people in that space. Four garden hoses held by people in the photo supply water from the surrounding buildings, allowing a viewer a glimpse into the projected dynamics between the individual and communal and illustrating the architects' intent behind the common land concept.[12]

Clusters

The Sonnenblumenhäuser development is a segment of the Wildgarten neighborhood. Its size, rather than the master plan's, is suitable for comparison with other projects in this book. This development comprises eighty-two dwellings across eleven buildings. Along with the associated landscaped areas, it occupies a rectangular site with sides measuring approximately 150 and 70 meters. The physical scope of the project is indicated in the provided site plan and a roof plan at the scale of 1:500.

The new street grid, part of the master plan, defines two clusters of buildings: a compact one, with four buildings; and an elongated one, with seven more. The typical floor plan drawing at the scale of 1:250 of the cluster of four buildings is provided to show unit layouts and the relationship between dwellings and outdoor areas. Inside the two clusters, the space between the buildings is the communal outdoor spaces and part of the larger network, incorporating uncultivated landscapes and maintained park-like areas. Square gardens are attached to each building according to the principles established in the competition entry. Ten buildings of the Sonnenblumenhäuser development have an L-shaped footprint, defining the square gardens' north and east edges. The square gardens' remaining edges are left open to allow southern exposure. The exception is the large building positioned at the northern tip of the elongated cluster. It has seven floors, a footprint occupying the entire lot, and it contains the highest number of dwelling units. It forms frontage to a public space together with buildings that are part of the other developmental segments.

The remaining buildings of the Sonnenblumenhäuser development are of different heights, ranging from one to four floors. Exterior walls are built with a monolithic clay block system commonly used in residential building construction in Austria, while two different finishes are applied to the facade. Yellow ceramic tiles are applied only to elevations facing southeast, while all other elevations are covered in plain white stucco. The choice of different building materials is part of the architectural expression. However, it is also driven by cost-effectiveness. More costly and durable materials are applied on elevations exposed to the sun.

The dimensioning of buildings, their positioning, and using a single vertical core per building enable efficient dwelling unit layouts with dual orientation, good daylighting, and natural ventilation. The private outdoor spaces include roof terraces, balconies with massive solid parapets, or gardens at the ground level. Unit variants range from one- to four-bed dwellings. All variants have a clear division between day and night activity zones. The day zone, incorporating an access lobby, kitchen, and dining and living rooms, is oriented south toward the garden. The typical floor plan varies from 8 to 10 meters in width and contains up to three units. Load-bearing elements are predominantly perimeter walls and the central access core, allowing a large and open plan configuration of the day zones.

Backdrop

The presented design approach recognizes a multitude of decisions leading to the housing provision and creation of the built environment. Basabe clarified this stance by referring to Sam Davis's book *The Form of Housing*, which discusses how housing provision has evolved to become much more complex over time and now involves multiple stakeholders, unlike in the primitive phase when resident, developer, builder, and designer were the same person or group of persons.[13] He also referred to John F. C. Turner's diagram differentiating between heteronomous and autonomous housing systems to clarify further how these processes and stakeholders interact with architecture.[14] In his view, an example of the former is a centralized form of housing whereby the provider—the public sector, usually the State or other large-scale institution—undertakes the planning, building, and managing of housing. At the same time, the latter is a self-organized form whereby residents are engaged and work with different stakeholders to create housing.

10. Gilles Clément, "In Practice: Gilles Clément on the Planetary Garden," *The Architectural Review*, no. 1478 (February 16, 2021), https://www.architectural-review.com/essays/in-practice/in-practice-gilles-clement-on-the-planetary-garden.
11. Basabe, "Multiplayer City."
12. Basabe, "Multiplayer City."
13. Sam Davies, *The Form of Housing* (New York: Van Nostrand Reinhold, 1977).
14. John F. C. Turner, *Housing by People* (New York: Pantheon Books, 1976).

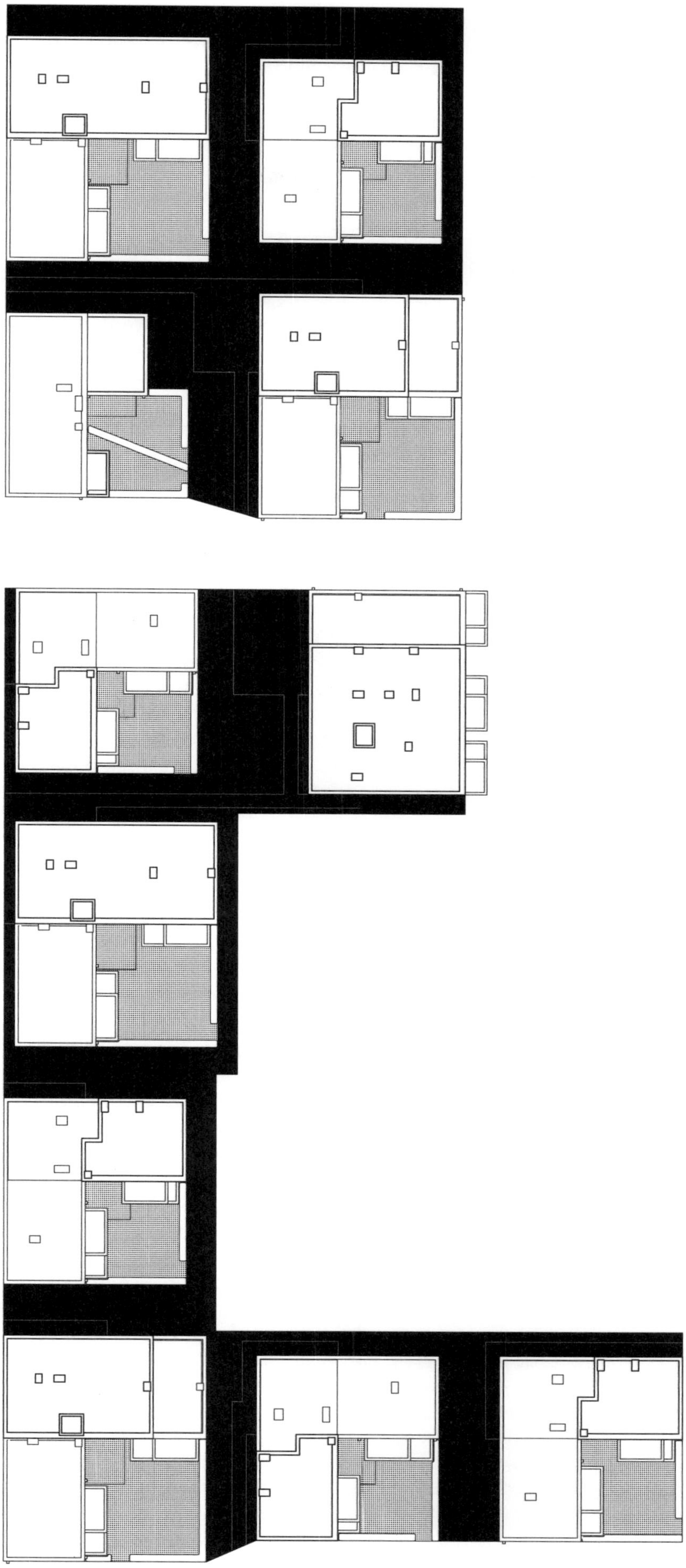

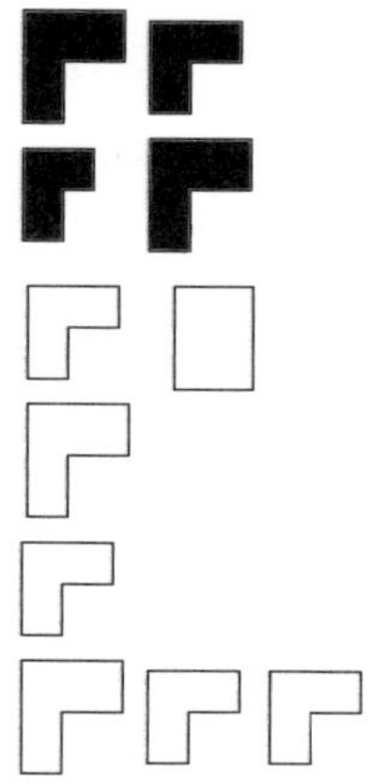

Figure 2
Roof plan, drawing not to scale

In an interview for this book, Basabe recalled John Habraken's influence and how it interacts with the understanding of housing as a complex system with multiple actors.[15] He said: "We try to organize space with clear supports but keep our intervention as low as possible. And I don't mean on the ground level. It just happens it is often some form of demarcation or landscape gesture. It is instead a minimal intervention making sure that the spaces we design are livable and that their appropriation by the people is possible. Here, I can refer to [Henri] Lefebvre, harnessing the power of 'differential' space and unlocking the potential of things that could happen. We understand the city as a process. We are interested in spatial flexibility as an integral part of that process."[16] The concept of "supports" has been employed by arenas basabe palacios across multiple projects to develop an approach that differentiates between what is and what is not controlled in the design process. In the Wildgarten master plan, the same concept is scaled up and applied to a design strategy and a framework centered on creating outdoor spaces in a residential development of diverse typologies and densities.

In conversation

The following section, an edited interview with Luis Basabe recorded on January 25, 2023, provides further information about the project from the architects' perspective.

DS **You said before that Wildgarten is not simply about the duality between the public and private and that the relationship between the two in the project is more complex than just being opposites. Can you tell us more about how you see this relationship in the context of your project?**

LB We address the topic of the suburban environment by questioning the duality between public and private. I will first describe the local context in Spain, Austria, and other European countries. We have a street as an infrastructural space, not an actual place. Then we have gates that take you into enclaves, into the fenced-off property owned and maintained individually or collectively. In this project, we aimed to break this duality, but not by introducing a semipublic space, which is a vague concept in our view, or should I say, it is something that we never fully understood. The project was about developing public-private partnerships as much as finding ways to use space. In the Wildgarten master plan, we tried to establish an approach based on common land, a default condition across Europe five centuries ago. The concept has been lost as modern society developed, and today, we can find common land only within the enclaves of space that I described. Present-day city structure is associated with the duality of individual and communal. The urban fabric of Vienna is dominated by a closed block structure that does not work with the common land approach. It is preferred because it does not create in-between conditions, so the space is either public or private.

Given the site's context, we saw an opportunity to create such an in-between condition based on the concept of *Allmende*, or common land.[17] The idea has been part of many other projects, such as Tempelhofer Field in Berlin, whereby land that belongs to the community or a municipality is publicly accessible.[18] In that project, just as in Wildgarten, it is not so much a matter of ownership but rather membership. There is a right of use, and there are specific rules. That requires management, or software as we call it. We have created a soccer field, but also the team that plays on it. There are multiple stakeholders in the project and different housing forms that make intensive use of that open space.

15. John N. Habraken, *Supports: An Alternative to Mass Housing* (London: Architectural Press, 1972).
16. Henri Lefebvre, *The Production of Space* (Cambridge, MA: Blackwell, 1991).
17. *Allmende* means "common land," "commons," "shared resources."
18. Tempelhofer Field is a recreational area in Berlin occupying the site of the former Tempelhof Airport.

Figure 3
Typical floor plan, drawing scale 1:250

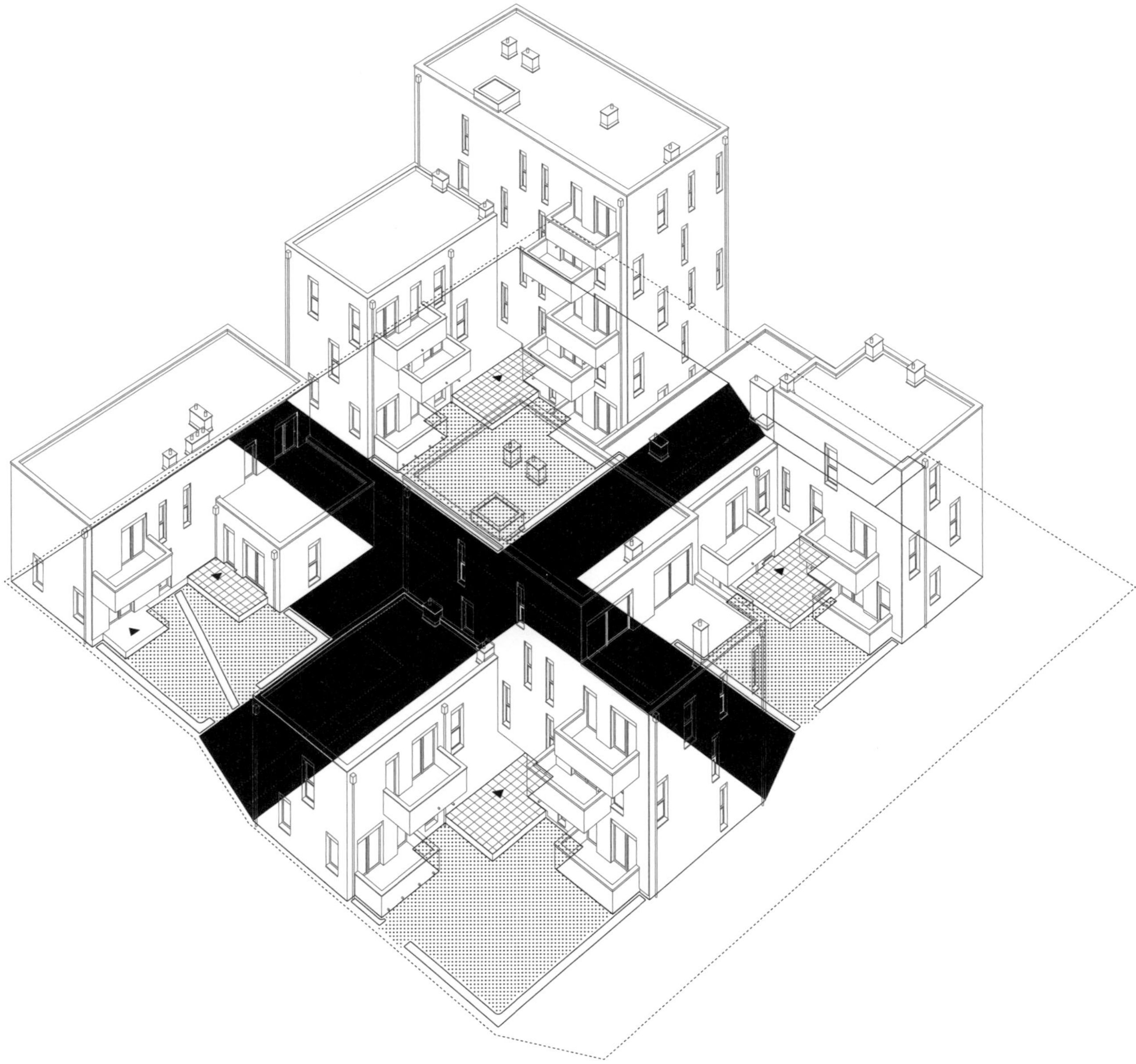

Figure 4
Perspective drawing indicating access and communal spaces.

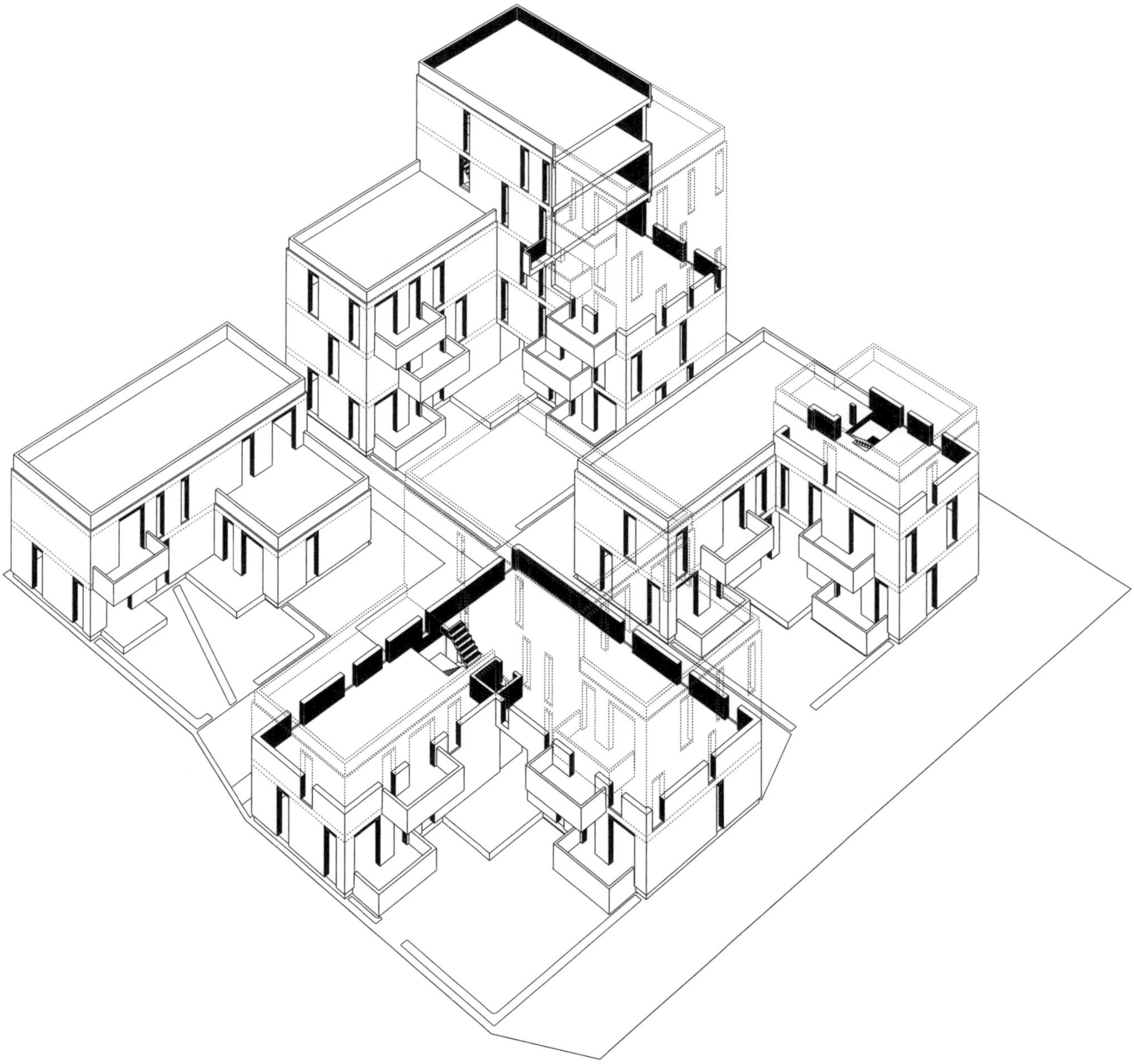

Figure 5
Perspective drawing indicating structural elements of the building.

Figure 6
Perspective drawing of the building envelopes.

DS What architectural means do you use to structure or facilitate such a dynamic relationship between the public and private?

LB We started the project by looking into the symbols of European suburbs, such as gardens with fences or intensively maintained hedges, and by understanding them as objects that sit in the common land. That became the underlying structure of the project. Therefore, it is not about a simple divide between public and private but their relationship. They are not always the opposite ends, as their relationship is fluid and changing. In the Wildgarten master plan, we have a network of streets required by planners providing access, complying with firefighting regulations, etc., that is, of course, public, and we have common land. Inside the common land, we have private gardens, as objects that are not strictly private but shared between groups of residents, as they are associated with individual buildings ranging in size between three and ten units. In the master plan, we have larger buildings, labeled "X" and "XL," that do not have their own gardens and rely on a more direct relationship with the commons.

DS Could you explain a little more how the space between buildings is structured in this project?

LB Our main contribution to this project is creating a framework for different architects selected by housing providers and developers to deliver diverse projects. Of course, we wanted continuity between them, as outdoor areas are central to this project. And again, if you zoom in and look at Sonnenblumenhäuser, it is not about designing eleven buildings and some open areas but creating a condition whereby spaces are both inside and outside, and one is never entirely outside or inside.

In a master plan, the distinction between the interior and exterior may not be as straightforward as in a single building. At Wildgarten, you are constantly surrounded by buildings, and you don't perceive single structures but always the ensemble. Sometimes it can be hard to differentiate where one stops and the other one starts. In that sense, you are always inside. When you are somewhere between the buildings, you don't necessarily have the impression that you are in the park. Thomas Proksch, the landscape planner on the project, insisted on the importance of small outdoor spaces that are the size of a room or that are not vast open spaces. The size is essential to have different qualities, that is, be sunny or shady, with trimmed grass or wild shrubs. Part of the same strategy is establishing six easily identifiable public squares next to taller buildings with commercial or social amenities. There is continuity, but there is diversity, too. It breaks the simplistic duality again.

DS Is the relationship between inside and outside equally dynamic in the project?

LB I am impressed with the domestic spatial thresholds we learned about in India. There is never a wall that divides the space but rather an intermediate space. For example, between inside and outside, there is *otla*, a kind of veranda that provides a transition between inside and outside.

Rather than the fence, the space provides a threshold between the two properties in the Wildgarten master plan. There are no fences, only vegetation in the form of 80-centimeter-wide strips, providing habitat for small wildlife species. Residents have engaged with the idea, and some have added birdhouses there. So, it is not walls we have used as an architectural means to divide space but another space that we have created. We have employed the same thinking about the layout of individual dwelling units. We have separated individual sleeping rooms from the communal living room by inserting a tiny space in between. Similarly, the garden provides another threshold that separates a group of dwellings from the commons.

DS Your Europan competition entry was based on a flexible framework stipulating development across a matrix of building lots according to several simple rules. The master plan, too, was developed around rules defining spaces between buildings as much as the positioning and orientation of buildings.

LB All buildings in the Wildgarten master plan are like little arrows facing north. Consequently, all gardens are open to the south. It creates a compact tissue with great proximity between buildings. Sometimes, we have 5 meters between buildings and even fewer if you consider the cantilevering balconies. This condition can be compared to the old town of Venice. But at the same time, we have secured plenty of sunlight coming through the gardens and good natural ventilation through the dual orientation of units. That way, we made the most of the southern exposure, which is an asset in the Austrian climate, and we have decided to signify that with the choice of the finishing material and the use of a bright yellow color.

DS Changing the topic now, what design decisions were important for the project cost?

LB The eleven buildings we have designed were developed for the market, not affordable or social housing. It was important to be aware of the construction cost, and we worked closely on this with our local partners utilizing local and efficient construction methods. Our approach to landscape, leaving a part of it intact to provide natural habitats for wildlife, requiring no maintenance, also helped reduce the development cost.

"In a master plan, the distinction between the interior and exterior may not be as straightforward as in a single building. At Wildgarten, you are constantly surrounded by buildings, and you don't perceive single structures but always the ensemble. Sometimes it can be hard to differentiate where one stops and the other one starts."

DS Your undersigning of spatial adaptability may not necessarily be tied to the changes in the unit layout, either by retrofitting or employing devices such as movable partitions. To conclude the conversation, can you underline what spatial flexibility results from your systemic approach empowering multiple stakeholders during the design process?

LB We introduced a pattern that accommodates diverse developments. It includes developments like the one we have designed, but also large public housing buildings that are part of the same program that delivered the Karl-Marx-Hof.[19] It also includes buildings for four self-organized housing groups, a high percentage of the overall development, even for Vienna standards. We combine subsidized rental, private rental, and owner-occupied tenancies in one project. There are small buildings, almost the size of an individual home, with only three units. For example, a mother and two sons own one of the smallest buildings with three units. You could almost say this is a single household, and their garden is equivalent to a farmhouse garden. At the same time, we have very large buildings of 10,000 square meters for public housing. We are interested in the flexibility that provides plurality and diversity, which we hold as essential values. It is not just about employing different typologies but enabling multiple stakeholders as producers of the city's built environment.

19. The Karl-Marx-Hof Gemeindebau (social housing) in Vienna, designed by Karl Ehn and Otto Wagner, was built from 1927 to 1930 for 5,000 residents.

arenas basabe palacios arquitectos
with M & S Architekten / Buschina & Partner

In conversation

The following section is an edited transcript of conversations with Katharina Kirsch-Soriano da Silva and Leonhard Schilling from Caritas, an organization supporting neighborhood initiatives and civil society engagement. They have been engaged with the project since 2015, working closely with housing associations and residents of the Wildgarten neighborhood on day-to-day matters and initiatives. They have communicated with the residents from the area during the planning process and have followed the implementation of housing projects delivered by different developers.

DS The master plan is based on the common land concept and open-access principles. What are the main challenges to implementing the idea, and how does it work in practice?

KK The *Allmende* or common land concept creates possibilities for people to meet and interact, including residents from different buildings. It helps relationships form and grow. But we must be aware that there are groups with varying interests regarding common spaces, and the negotiation processes between these interests can, in my experience, be resolved through communication and community work and not so much through planning. The open-access concept is not necessarily understood by everyone immediately and may not be easily implemented in everyday life. That's why communication matters. At Wildgarten, we have different housing forms or tenancies. We have private ownership, private rental, several forms of subsidized rental, some of which are public housing Gemeindebau, and four housing cooperatives. They all have their specifics, but I think there is a difference in how people perceive outdoor areas related to the form of housing. It is a little bit different if dwellings are owned or rented. Rental tenants are aware of rules for common spaces as they are often part of the tenancy agreement, but some homeowners are not fully onboard with the idea of free access. As there are multiple developers in Wildgarten, we have no insight into all the details of contractual agreements regulating legal allowances concerning the servitude of access in outdoor areas surrounding residential buildings. As far as we know, some ownership contracts include servitude of passage through communal areas of the development along a specific path but do not specify if this is for everyone or just other residents of the same development. We have learned from Wildgarten how important precision is in legal documents so that we can make the best use of innovative ideas such as the open-access concept.

LS The use of outdoor areas in Wildgarten is an exciting topic. The master plan creates openness, porosity, and fluency, and people can go where they want. Still, when you implement the plan, there are many little nuisances that you must resolve on an entirely different level. Yesterday I had a conversation with several disgruntled homeowners from smaller buildings. They felt the intimacy of their homes was impacted by people circulating freely between the buildings. They are unhappy because people from other, larger buildings are using the open green areas or children's playgrounds next to their buildings. Children make noise when they play, and there is an issue with dog owners, particularly those not keeping their dogs on leashes. So you can understand that their privacy is compromised. At the same time, I don't think the answer is to close or privatize those problematic areas. We don't have this issue in most of the neighborhood, as trees, hedges, and bushes have matured and have established boundaries and buffers that protect privacy. The privacy issue is reported in the newest part of the development, where residents moved in last summer. So it is not only the implementation of an architectural project but also the needed time for people to get used to it and learn to live with each other. Our role is to help bring residents together to find solutions. As I said before, fine details are important to the larger picture of the master plan. Wildgarten is a complex project. Its implementation is a long process requiring communication.

DS The master plan emphasizes a link between housing and nature. How did residents take to it in real life?

KK The concept is attractive to young families. In my experience, this is often the case with new residential districts in Vienna. At Wildgarten, we have a mixed but predominantly young population and plenty of children to whom access to open spaces and landscaped areas incorporated into the neighborhood is important.

LS Residents have engaged with the more-than-human-habitat concept. Some of the participative processes we facilitate are with small groups keen on topics such as enlarging habitats for lizards, providing water sources for hedgehogs, or calling attention to light pollution.

DS How are the open spaces and landscaped areas maintained?

LS Our role is to disseminate information from the planning level and how things are thought of to the level of realization and how things are carried out. We help by passing on the information we have from landscape architects and planners regarding landscape maintenance. Several gardening firms are maintaining different parts of the neighborhood, commissioned by different developers and housing associations. They all have their own techniques and approaches. It requires a bit of coordination. It is vital to know when and how to do it. Landscaped areas are mowed only twice a year. The ecological concept of Wildgarten is that grass and shrubs should grow tall to provide a habitat for insects and small animals and help create an ecosystem within the residential development. It also helps people navigate open-access areas. When grass is tall, there is a high likelihood of people staying on the paved path, but when the grass is low, they may wander off—particularly children—and get closer to private dwellings.

arenas basabe palacios arquitectos
with M&S Architekten / Buschina & Partner

DS Where are the cars?

LS Another enormous quality of Wildgarten is a car-free environment. There is a good bus service, and people use bicycles to get to the nearest train station. A new train station is planned closer to the development, but it will probably take a few more years. Cars are kept at the perimeter of the residential district. There is ample underground and on-street parking along the road on the district's eastern and southern edges, which is only a short walk to most buildings. It means children can play safely and move freely as their parents allow. I feel residents appreciate this aspect.

"[...] there is a difference in how people perceive outdoor areas related to the form of housing. It is a little bit different if dwellings are owned or rented. Rental tenants are aware of rules for common spaces as they are often part of the tenancy agreement, but some homeowners are not fully onboard with the idea of free access."

DS What helps community cohesion at Wildgarten in addition to the open-access landscape?

KK The neighborhood center is the primary indoor communal space, a space for social life and interaction in the neighborhood, and the outdoor space around it with benches, green space, and gardening areas is also important. Furthermore, there are smaller outdoor places distributed throughout the master plan.

LS I work at the neighborhood center twice weekly to meet with residents to help them with self-organized initiatives. There is space they can use to work on joint initiatives such as the development of ecosystems that we spoke about earlier or to work with youth and children. There is an informal café where people can meet to get to know each other. Rooms can be booked for various purposes, such as birthday parties or yoga classes. Next to the center is a large open area with mature trees predating the new neighborhood. This space is for recreation, but we also use it for cultural programs such as summer picnics or open-air cinema that attract people from the neighborhood and beyond.

4 Iroko Housing, London

Haworth Tompkins

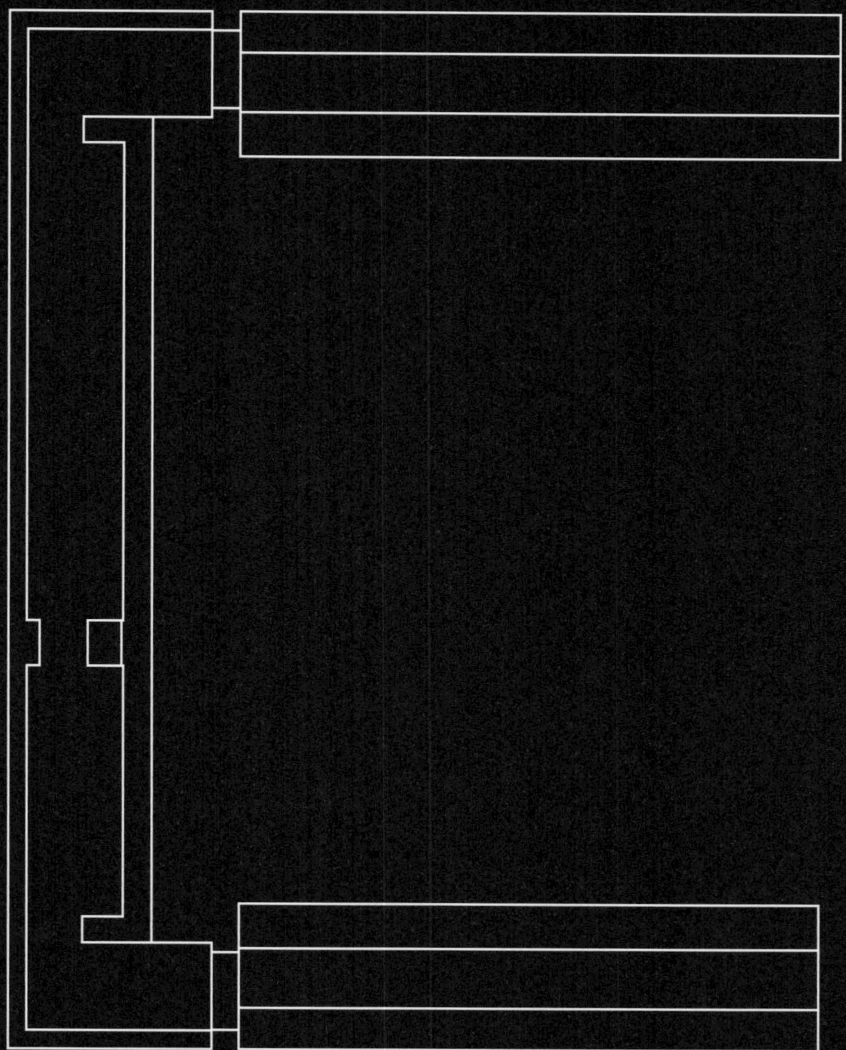

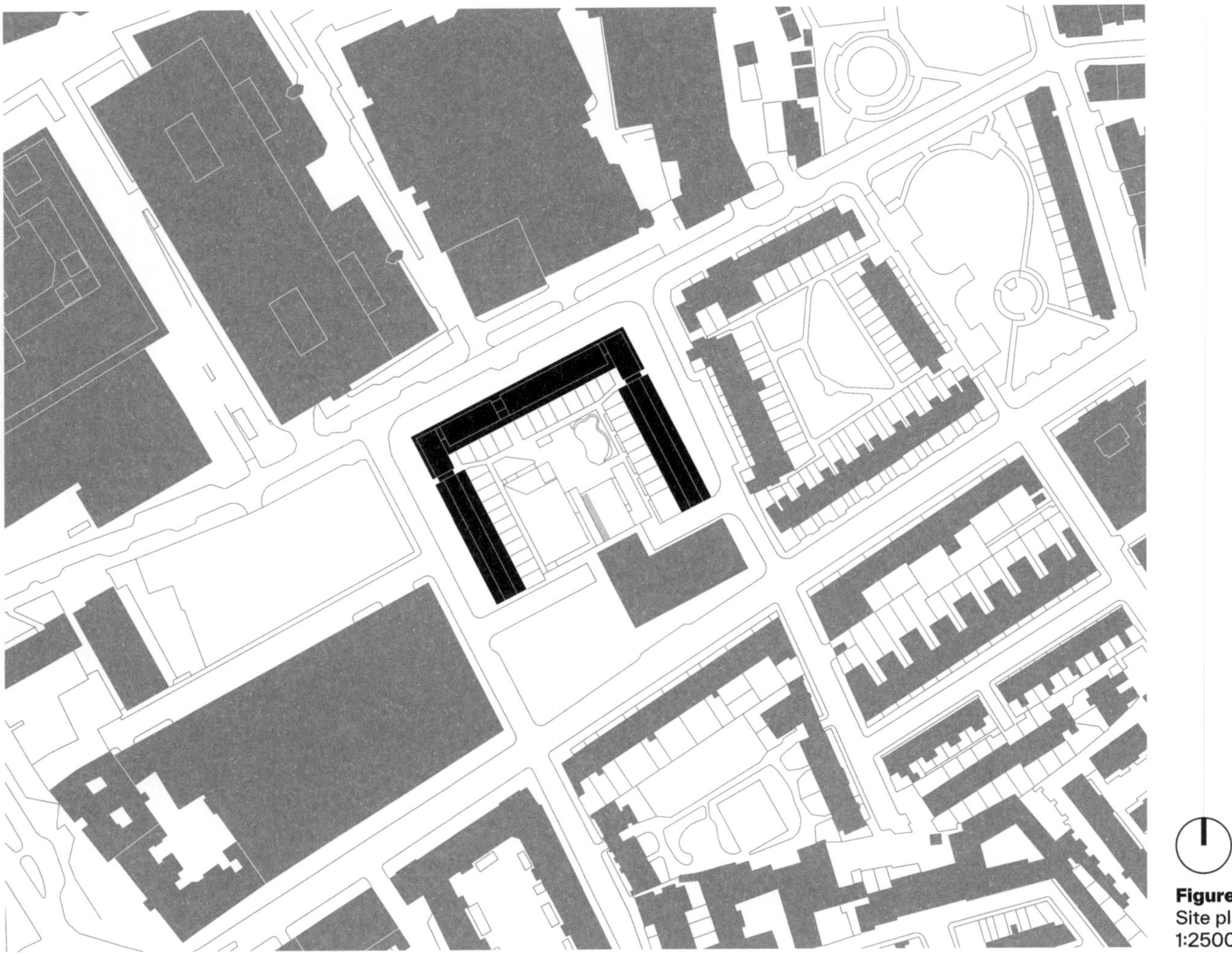

Figure 1
Site plan, drawing scale 1:2500

Iroko Housing, London
Haworth Tompkins

Year of completion: 2004
Number of units: 59

Renewed interest and the growing body of research on self-organized housing models suggest another and closer look at the success of Iroko Housing, completed in 2004. The outcomes of this project are valuable for understanding potentials arising from the collaboration between architectural practice and social enterprise. Iroko Housing is part of a large and still ongoing regeneration project in Central London driven by local residents that started more than four decades ago following a set of unique and interconnected actions and circumstances, including: (1) a prolonged grassroots campaign expressing concerns about the deteriorating population and the amenity of the neighborhood; (2) the formation of a social enterprise with a mission to address these concerns; (3) planning authorities' support for the local groups; (4) the local government's willingness to sell its land to a not-for-profit organization; and (5) an occurrence of unfavorable economic momentum for commercial development.

There Is Another Way

The completed parts of the regeneration project for the South Bank area near the Waterloo Bridge on the River Thames, besides Iroko Housing, include three more residential developments set up as housing cooperatives; a public park, Bernie Spain Gardens; the riverside walk; underground car parking; and the adaptive reuse of a historical building, Oxo Tower Wharf, which now houses restaurants, exhibition venues, and retail. The development is led by Coin Street Community Builders (CSCB), a not-for-profit organization established to deliver public service objectives, including affordable housing. The organization was formed in the early 1980s off the back of public protests involving local communities who wanted to stay in the area and demanded support from the government to create a livable neighborhood with homes and amenities. Local groups opposed a commercial scheme prioritizing office space and a hotel. They started a campaign under the motto "There Is Another Way" and formulated an alternative strategy for regeneration.[1] The two schemes were under consideration, but after long deliberation and a coinciding economic recession in the UK, planning authorities backed the local initiative. The planners mandated affordable housing as part of the development, reducing the available land's commercial potential. Finally, in 1984, Greater London Council lent some of the purchase amount and sold 13 acres of its land in the South Bank area to CSCB.[2]

The Architecture of Engagement

In 1997, with the benefit of experience from the completion of other residential developments in the South Bank area, CSCB organized an invited competition and selected Haworth Tompkins to deliver an architectural project for Iroko Housing. It was one of the pivotal moments for this architectural practice, which has continued working with social housing providers to date. Their design scheme for affordable homes and inclusive communities involving Peabody Trust and other developers, with almost 600 units, was completed last year at Fish Island on the Hertford Union Canal in east London.[3]

Graham Haworth reflected on the importance of the community's positive involvement in this project's planning process. He pointed out that the overall regeneration objectives for the South Bank area, and consequently the brief for Iroko Housing, were established according to the local groups' needs rather than driven by the property market and that the involvement of indigenous communities has added the benefit of local knowledge and cultural values to the project.[4] The architectural intent for Iroko Housing started to take shape during the competition phase based on the input provided by local community groups. Residents of adjacent housing developments were involved and have provided input on the relationship between the building and the street, the creation of the communal courtyard for residents, and the selection of housing typologies suitable for large families. These inputs were central to the architectural definition and the overall built form.

Hollow Square

The architectural intent for Iroko Housing is structured around the provision of the central courtyard, accessible to all residents, and a perimeter defined by the built form. This is read in the floor plan and referred to as a "hollow square" by the architects, who have shaped such a diagram according to the existing street pattern.[5] The project encompasses the entire city block with sides measuring approximately 100 by 100 meters. The site is separated from a busy public walkway along the River Thames only by a narrow zone of civic and commercial buildings.

Three edges of the block are defined with rows of townhouses merged into a single structure. Part of the fourth edge, built a few years later, is the community center, providing services to the entire neighborhood, including a childcare facility and function room with a roof terrace for hire. The community center, too, was designed by Haworth Tompkins, and today, CSCB uses part of the building for its offices. The remaining buildable area along the fourth edge of the block is yet to be utilized. Current plans are for another residential building that would close the block as the original design intent envisaged.

The central courtyard is designed to provide amenities and help create a sense of community among residents. It includes play areas for children, and it is partially landscaped. A deep soil area for trees and several large planters are part of it. The vegetation, introduced twenty years ago, makes this inner part of the block appear very green today. This central space can be accessed directly from all townhouses forming the three edges of the block and from the main lobby serving units on the upper floors. It is viewed from dwellings and communal access spaces. The building facade facing the courtyard has floor-to-ceiling openings and is clad in timber, while the brick facade with smaller windows faces the street. The fenestration and use of building materials reflect the difference in the character of the inner communal courtyard and the building's outer perimeter, forming the public domain.

1. Coin Street, "Our Story," accessed March 5, 2023, https://www.coinstreet.org/about-us/our-story.
2. Andrew Bibby, "Coin Street: Case Study," accessed May 25, 2023, http://www.andrewbibby.com/socialenterprise/coin-street.html.
3. Haworth Tompkins, "Neptune Wharf at Fish Island Village, 2022," accessed May 25, 2023, https://www.haworthtompkins.com/work/neptune-wharf-at-fish-island-village.
4. Graham Haworth, "Coin Street Housing: The Architecture of Engagement," in *Sustainable Urban Design: An Environmental Approach*, ed. Adam Ritchie and Randall Thomas (New York: Taylor & Francis, 2008), 116–37.
5. Haworth Tompkins, "Iroko Housing, 2004," accessed May 25, 2023, https://www.haworthtompkins.com/work/iroko-housing.

Underneath the entire block, a basement of a former industrial building is converted into a large publicly accessible car park. A florist shop and a convenience store occupy two corners on the ground floor. Access to these shops and the underground car park is separated from the residential part of the building.

Cross-Subsidy

It is important to clarify that the overall regeneration project led by CSCB includes facilities that generate revenue utilized as cross-subsidy for maintaining public spaces and providing affordable housing.[6] The already mentioned underground car park is leased to one of the leading parking providers in central London. Several spaces across the area, including the florist and convenience store on the ground floor of the building, are rented to retailers, businesses, and restaurants. Some income is generated from advertising billboards. It is a deliberate economic strategy implemented by CSCB to support the running and maintenance of public facilities that tackle social problems, generate change, and improve the community. The role of CSCB was to devise an overall development strategy for the area based on a range of smaller ideas and projects through an incremental implementation of mutually supporting programs, including the improvement of housing conditions. They run infrastructure, organize events, train local communities, and forge links with institutions and local businesses.

Approximately two-thirds of the funding for the Iroko development came from the borrowings made by CSCB and the Coin Street Housing Cooperative formed by it.[7] The remaining one-third came from government subsidies. The contributions coming from CSCB have enabled better housing quality, reflected in the provision of spacious dwellings and private outdoor areas. The cross-subsidy secured and instrumentalized through social enterprise has contributed to utilizing a terraced house (townhouse) typology and keeping development density in check as preferred by residents.

During his lecture hosted by the Melbourne School of Design on August 24, 2021, Graham Haworth referred to the Victorian terrace at Stanley Crescent Garden in Kensington, on the other side of central London, as a precedent for what both the local community and architects wanted to achieve in this project.[7] Their aim was to create spacious dwellings suitable for large households, with access to a large communal garden, something rarely associated with affordable and subsidized housing. Today, the cost of freehold for a six-bed terrace house, with period features and access to the communal garden at Stanley Crescent Garden, sells for millions of pounds sterling. Although the Iroko units are not for sale, as they belong to the housing cooperative, and the difference in real estate market appreciation for the two neighborhoods remains, the current market value of the precedent illustrates what this project has achieved in providing homes for vulnerable and needy groups, including key workers and immigrant families.

Iroko Housing is set up as a cooperative. The building is owned by the housing cooperative, while tenants, as members of the cooperative, have security, pay a fairer rent, and actively participate in the management and maintenance of the building. CSCB runs a training program to help tenants understand and manage their responsibilities.[8]

Units

The project comprises 59 units, including 32 townhouses, 16 duplex units, and 11 flats, all combined into a single structure. Townhouses have three floors. Together, their volumes constitute the base of the overall built form. There are two variants of this dwelling type. Rows of narrower townhouses, measuring 4.2 meters in width, form the eastern and western edges of the site. A row of wider variants, with a 5.2-meter distance between party walls, populates a row of townhouses along the northern side of the site.

The layout is similar in the two variants. The entrance is from the street via a small recess, providing an interface with the public domain and storage for utilities, including electricity and gas meters and bins. The entrance lobby, kitchen, and living room are on the ground floor. Private gardens are at the back and have direct access to the communal courtyard. On level one, a pair of rooms face opposite facades. They can be used as additional living spaces or bedrooms. Three more bedrooms are on level three. All rooms facing the inner side of the block have a narrow balcony accessed through double glass doors. The narrower townhouse variants have an additional room on level four and access to a private roof terrace. Duplex units are placed on top of townhouses along the northern edge and accessed via a communal access gallery on the inner side of the block. Their kitchens and living rooms are on the lower level, while two bedrooms are on the upper level. Stairs are positioned along the access gallery to protect the dwelling's privacy. The access gallery is 2.4 meters wide and serves as a front yard where residents interact and can keep their plants and outdoor furniture. Eight smaller apartments in the two corners of the building, just above retail units, on levels one and two, add diversity to the mix of dwellings. These one- and two-bedroom units are predominantly oriented toward the street and are accessed by the stairs. Three more atypical units can be found in the part of the building closest to the community center.

6. Coin Street, "Our Story."
7. Graham Haworth, "Iroko Housing," guest lecture, Melbourne School of Design, August 24, 2021, https://edsc.unimelb.edu.au/studio-epsilon/lecture-repository/haworth-tompkins.
8. Coin Street, "Iroko Housing Co-op," accessed May 25, 2023, https://www.coinstreet.org/about-us/our-developments/iroko-housing-co-op.

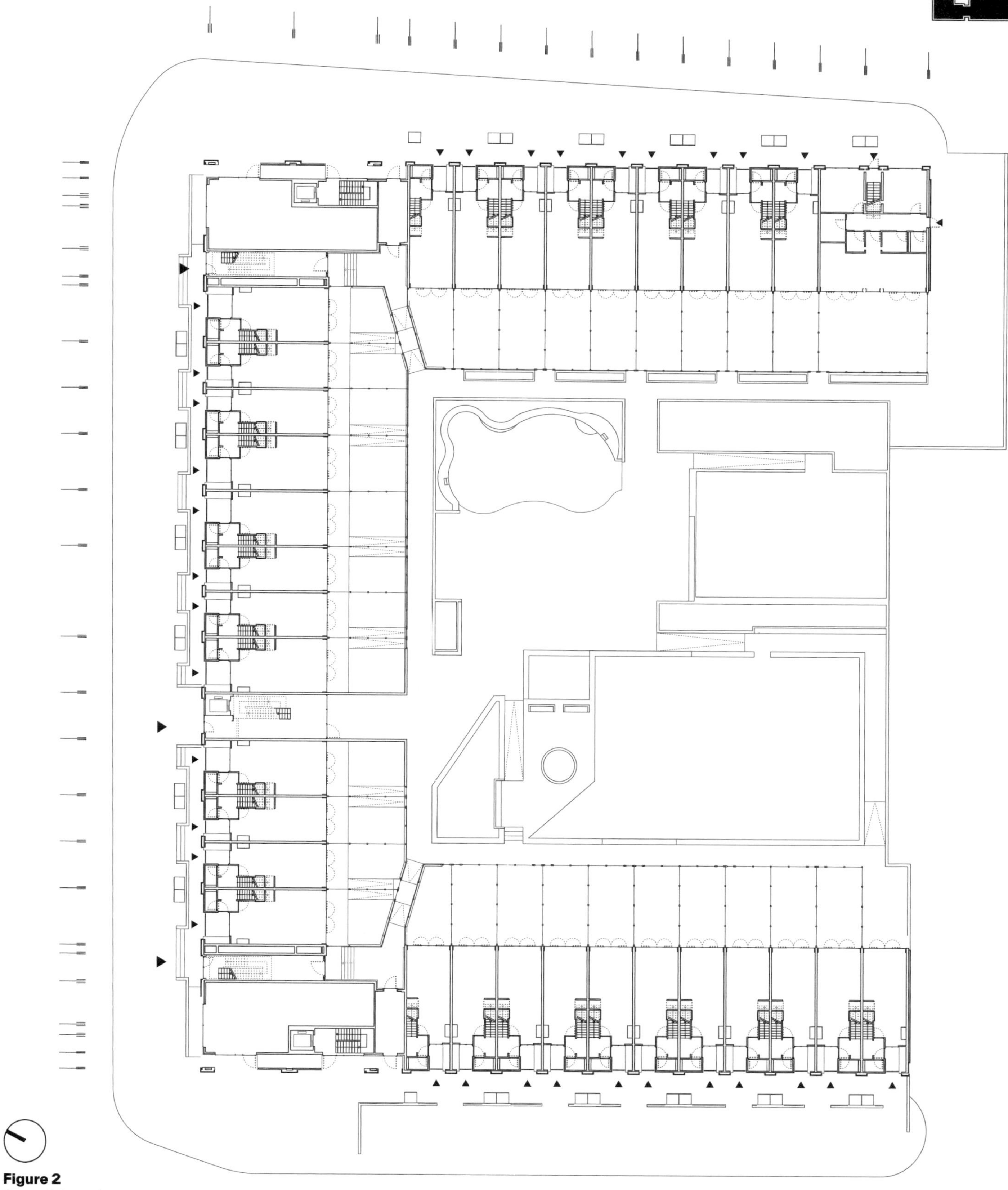

Figure 2
Ground floor plan,
drawing scale 1:500

In conversation

The following segment, an edited interview with Graham Haworth recorded on June 27, 2023, provides further information about the project from the architect's perspective.

DS What are the main reasons for employing a "hollow square" diagram in this project?

GH It had something to do with the scale and location of the site. We explored various configurations before we settled for the hollow square option. That form gave us a balance between the intimacy of dwellings and the presence of the building in the inner city. We worked with two architectural expressions, a hard urban edge on the outside and a soft or organic inside where we have planting and landscape. The hollow square configuration also allowed us to reconcile two scales, one of the dwellings and the other of the city.

DS What was the involvement of local representatives and their role in the design process?

GH Residents from the adjacent buildings that formed part of CSCB were powerful voices in judging the competition. They were right in there from the beginning. And then, after the competition, they stayed involved in the interim reviews right up to planning. CSCB developed a project brief, and their input was instrumental in settling for the townhouse typology. By then, they had already completed three other housing projects, and we benefited from their experience. Mulberry Housing, a low-key project, is immediately east of our site. On Broadwall Street, closer to Oxo Tower Wharf, is a row of elegant townhouses designed by Lifschutz Davidson Architects.[9] CSCB had tenant representatives from those two housing cooperatives involved in the design process for Iroko Housing. As I said, they were part of the interview panel and workgroup we regularly met. We had a series of workshops with them throughout the competition stage and after during the project development.

DS The two main communal spaces are the central courtyard and the gallery, providing access to the duplex units located on the upper levels. Could you tell us more about their roles and relationship to the built form?

GH Communal courtyards are often associated with apartment buildings. Usually, units are accessed via galleries, which are part of the courtyard on the inner side of the block. However, our architectural proposition employed townhouse typology, where you go from the street through a dwelling to access a communal garden. We used townhouses to establish the block's perimeter. In the north wing toward the National Theatre, we placed a row of duplex units that we call "maisonettes" on top of the townhouses. We have created a communal access gallery reached by an elevator and stairs in the middle of that wing. Only a limited number of residents use the access gallery. It has helped create a smaller community within the community, which has positively appropriated this space. All townhouses and maisonettes are looking into the courtyard, adding passive surveillance, and the idea was that the central space would help create a sense of community. The brief included the sunken ball game area, children's play area with climbing frames, and seating areas. We initially had ideas that everybody could wander through and use that space. We thought workers from adjacent office buildings would come and have lunch there, but the client group representatives were dead against it for lots of different reasons, and in the end, we settled on a closed private courtyard.

9. Lifschutz Davidson Sandilands, "Broadwall Housing," accessed May 25, 2023, https://lds-uk.com/projects/residential/broadwall-housing/.

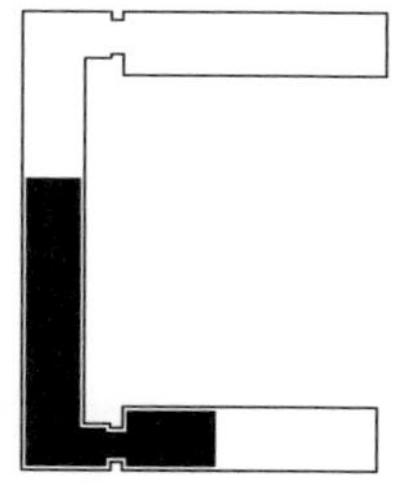

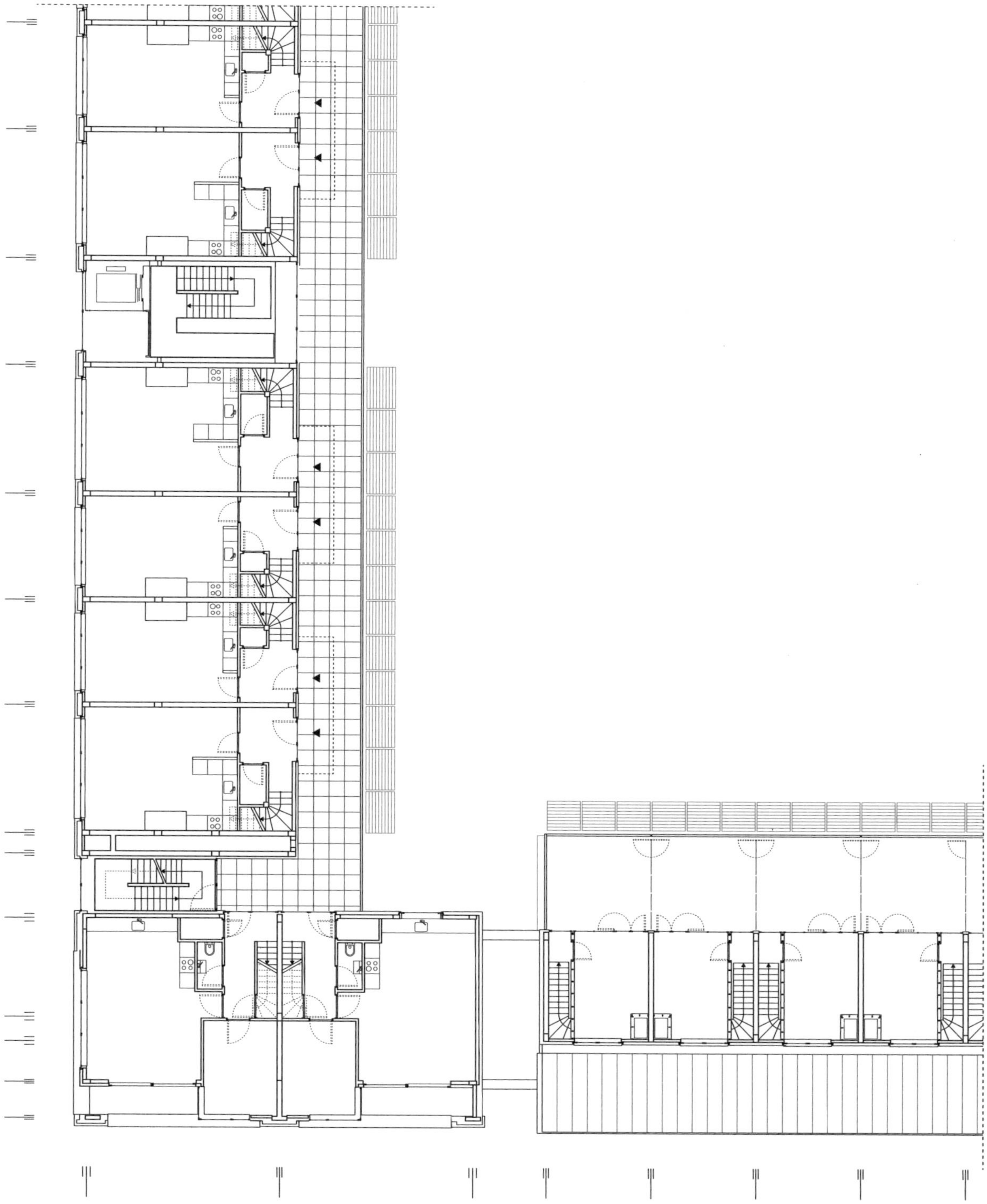

Figure 3
Segment of the first floor plan, drawing scale 1:250

DS What input did local representatives provide during the design process, and how did it affect the architectural project?

GH To illustrate, we had proposed that the community building would be placed along Upper Ground Street, closer to the National Theatre, thinking the two facilities could relate in some way. Their feedback was to place it on the opposite end of the site, along the busier Stanford Street, to shield dwellings from the noise. I already mentioned our debate about the courtyard. They supported the idea of the communal courtyard, but we had much discussion on the character of that space. How does the privacy gradient work if it should be public, permeable, or private? We received good input about dwelling units, too. For example, the recessed entries were debated during the competition stage. They asked practical questions, such as where can we put our fruits and vegetables? Where do we put our trainers? Where do we put our bicycles? In response to those inquiries, we created a secured lobby facing the street in each unit. We also discussed the relationship between private gardens and the communal courtyard, and the outcome was the fences that you can see today. Interestingly, I took a group of Dutch architects to see the building approximately five years after its completion, and they could not fathom the idea of fences and private gardens. They would have preferred a low wall and openness between the private dwellings and the communal courtyard. A little private garden is a British thing, so it was important to close that space off as representatives of the resident community requested. They wanted privacy, a safe environment for young children, and room for productive gardens.

DS Did you have much interaction with residents after they moved in?

GH I think the only place where the involvement or residents tailed off is post-occupancy evaluation. It wasn't easy to stay involved and continue monitoring once the building was handed over. It is always good to know whether the things you have designed are working. The building industry has moved on, and post-occupancy evaluation procedures are much more structured in more recent projects. We would have preferred more feedback for Iroko Housing. We received a call from them after the Grenfell Tower tragedy. The housing cooperative was concerned, and we had to reconnect to clarify that the timber cladding on the inner facades was not an issue. The building is not a high-rise, and it has a concrete structure. Overall, I think that the building is aging well. The maintenance thus far has been minimal. Hardwood on the courtyard facade proved resilient and required only cleaning for some dirt staining, as the wall acts as a splashback to outdoor walkways.

"We have created a communal access gallery reached by an elevator and stairs in the middle of that wing. Only a limited number of residents use the access gallery. It has helped create a smaller community within the community, which has positively appropriated this space. All townhouses and maisonettes are looking into the courtyard, adding passive surveillance, and the idea was that the central space would help create a sense of community."

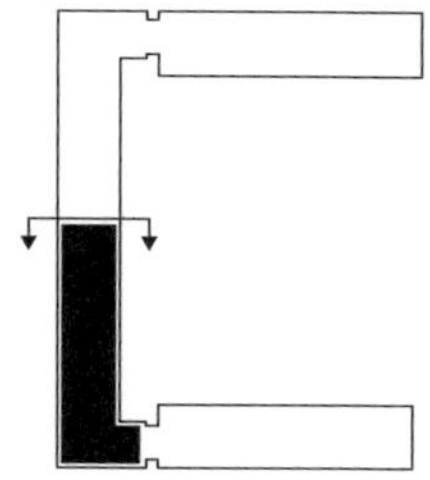

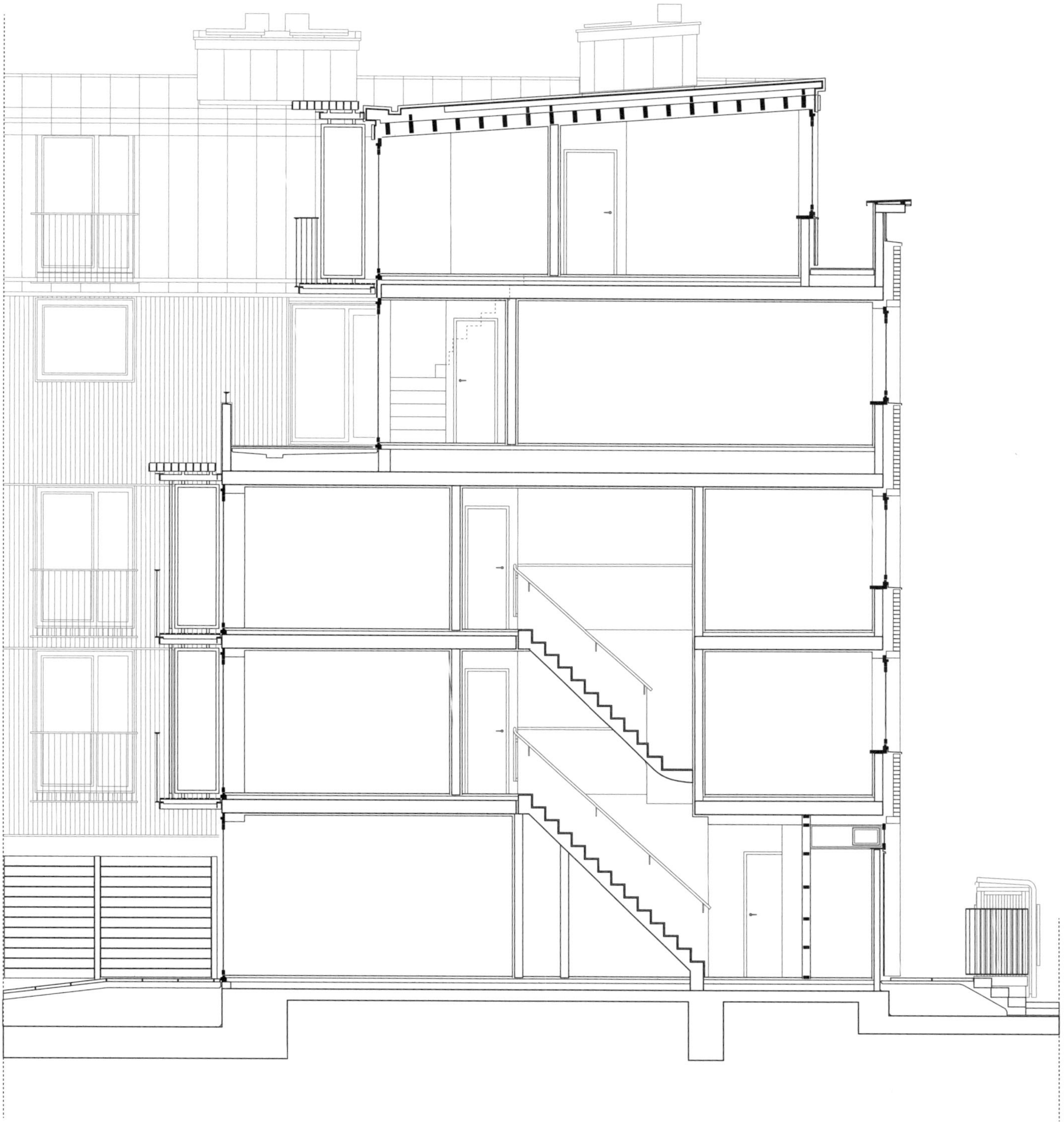

Figure 4
Cross section,
drawing scale 1:100

DS This project was designed and built just before environmental awareness and requirements started to pick up in the construction industry. What were the main provisions in this regard?

GH It is true that environmental objectives have become much more onerous in the meantime, but environmental implications were always high on our agenda. We are interested in the performance of our buildings and often take steps to understand the environmental impact of their operation. Iroko Housing units are equipped with individual heat recovery plants. Initially, those plants were not appropriately used, and CSCB has provided some training. Residents did not have the benefit of soft landings, which are much more prevalent today. The building has solar panels and relies on natural ventilation as all units are dually oriented.

DS Some of the Iroko dwellings have up to five bedrooms, as they were designed for families according to the input from the Council and local groups involved in the design process. Was there a projection that households would grow or shrink?

GH The development was planned for 360 occupants. At first, 260 people were living there. When Lambeth London Borough Council and CSCB offered homes to people on the housing registrar, they made the allowance for population growth. It was expected that families would grow and that there would be more children. However, five years into the building's use, the number of residents remained roughly the same. I suppose that some children become young adults, that there must have been some family separations, and that, after all, there were not as many children as projected because we know that the number of children decreased from 114 to 65 according to the same census.

DS Could you apply the knowledge developed in this project to other residential buildings you have designed?

GH Quite a lot of it. I would say establishing a scale of the community in the first place. The way we have clustered units around the access gallery to form a smaller community and the way we have helped create a larger community around the communal courtyard is something we have applied in a much larger project in East London. The knowledge transfer also includes utilizing duplex and triplex units and gallery access to provide natural light to units. It is helpful in meeting housing design standards that have become more stringent regarding the orientation of dwellings. Also, the attention to the landscape is relevant. And most important, identifying key stakeholders and consulting communities during the planning process.

DS This project provides homes for vulnerable and needy groups, including key workers and immigrant families, yet the units are of the highest spatial standards. I understand this is in part made possible through cross-subsidies provided by CSCB. Was there a pressure to design and build higher density at the time?

GH At that time, Iroko Housing was considered a good-density project. Its density is measured at 79 units per hectare. Today, our practice is looking into schemes with as many as 500 units per hectare. But even according to older standards, the project was against the market. The funding stream from the government was important, but even more, the autonomy of the housing group, who were able to set their own space standards because of their own funding channels. I think the chances of something like that happening again are remote. Today, we would probably be looking to add several more floors to a project of a similar kind to maintain viability.

DS Did the project address the spatial adaptability of dwellings?

GH In this project, spatial adaptability is inherent to the size of units. They are a bit like Victorian terraced houses, which are known for their flexibility in the vertical sense rather than horizontal. Depending on the household size, occupants can decide whether to have rooms on level one as a secondary living space or as bedrooms. The additional room with access to the private roof terrace, found in the narrower variant of townhouses, is suitable for working from home. At the time we designed the building, not much emphasis was given to working from home, and we didn't necessarily plan for it, but I think it comes in very handy today.

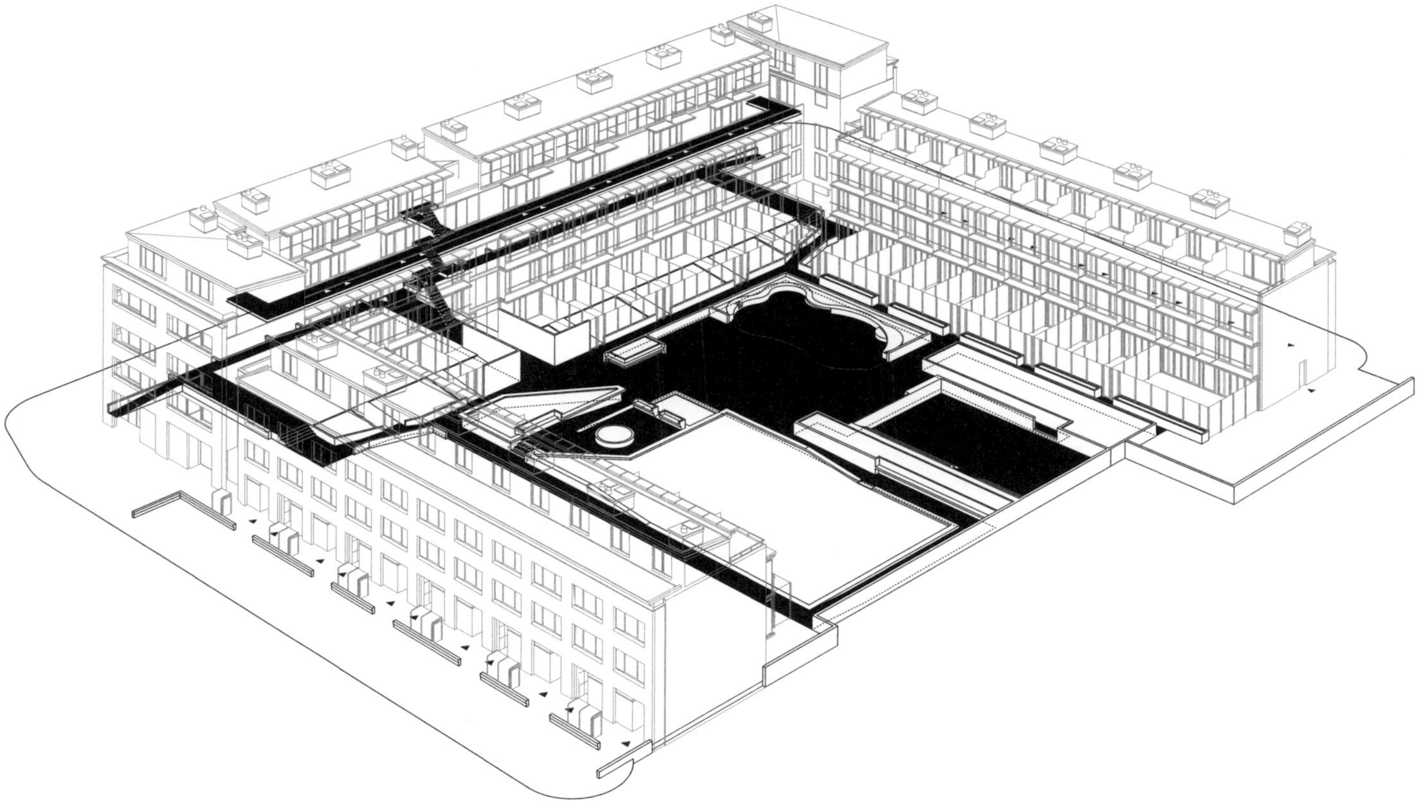

Figure 5
Perspective drawing
indicating access
and communal spaces.

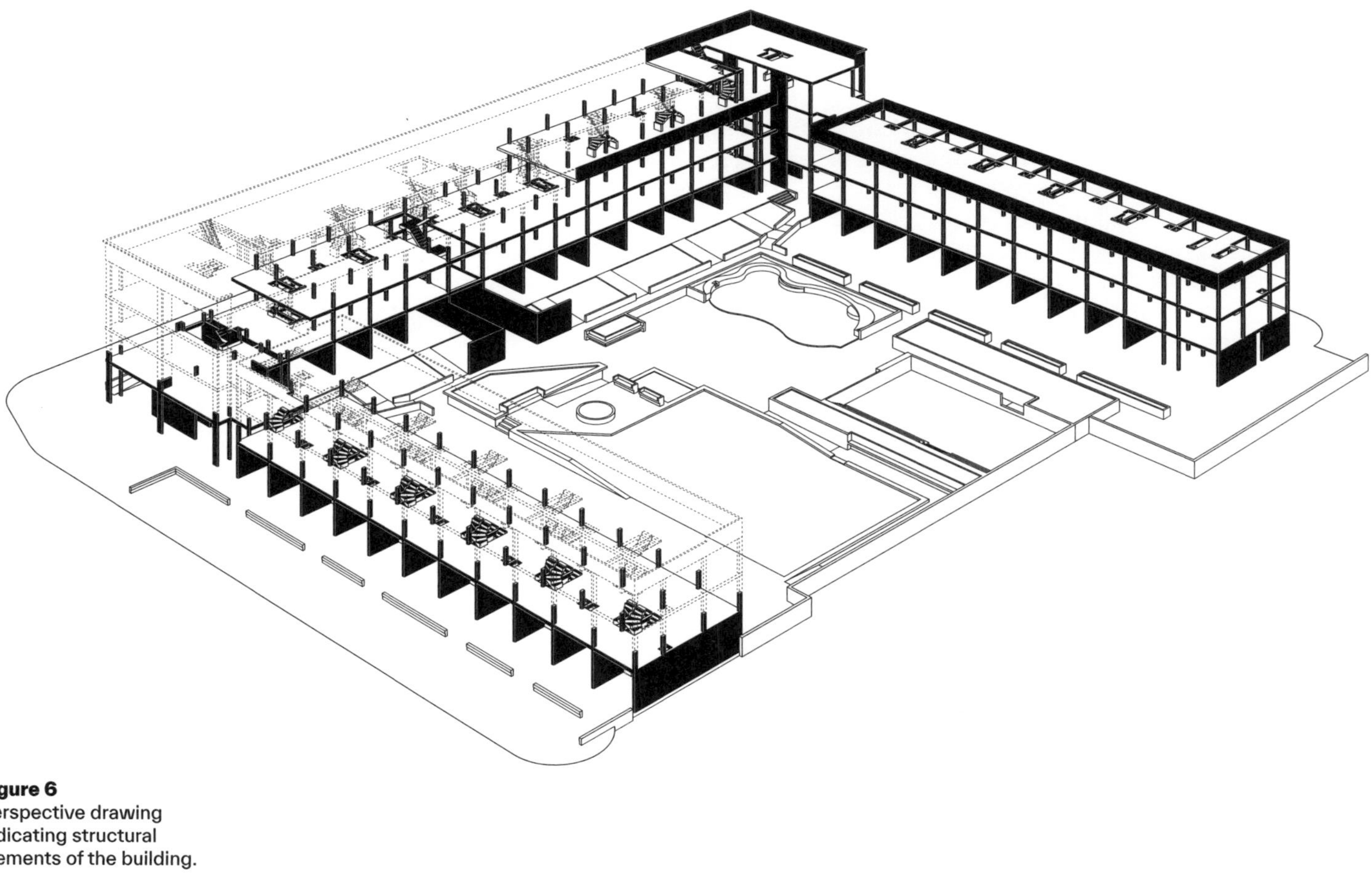

Figure 6
Perspective drawing
indicating structural
elements of the building.

In conversation

The following section is an edited interview recorded on August 9, 2023, with a local resident and Group Director at Coin Street Community Builders (CSCB), Iain Tuckett.

DS We have tried speaking to architects and residents for each project in this book. We have an architects' perspective on Iroko Housing. We would like to know more about the links between the architectural project and social enterprise.

IT Iroko was our fourth housing cooperative, part of the regeneration project for the South Bank area. Our board, which runs the CSCB organization and oversees projects, includes local residents, some of whom are members of housing cooperatives. We always wanted to involve people, and anyone local could come. Our organization is set as a trust, and we have a group for housing, a group for commercial, and another one for outdoor spaces. In short, the Iroko housing development was led by local residents and the CSCB organization.

DS Is an invited architectural design competition an adequate mechanism for involving local representatives in the design process?

IT We relied on consultations when developing our first housing cooperative, which served as a next-door example we mentioned previously. In that project, the housing group met regularly with architects, which was a bit of a disaster. What happened was that architects would present to this group of people with little housing knowledge other than the experience we all have living somewhere. We think we know about housing, but most don't have the experience of developing housing. The architect would present three options. The bit silly option, the one that was like, okay. And one that they wanted, and you know it. It's very easy. I'm not saying to manipulate but to bring people along with you. I remember when we were choosing the brick, and there were exactly even numbers as to which brick color and type to use. And so, the person who abstained was sent out on a taxi to look at some housing done with that brick. Still, that person couldn't decide. Finally, the taxi driver took the decision. Therefore, you know, that process hadn't really worked. This is why we introduced architectural competitions overseen by local residents, including myself. It does not exclude consultations—especially when you go for planning, when local communities must be brought along.

DS What mechanisms did you use to work with architects in the development process?

IT It's probably important to understand that we held an architectural design competition. We have done this quite often, so we got it down to a nice art. The first thing is the rough brief. We wanted family housing, and we also wanted to build a neighborhood center that was to come later. The Council was very keen to accommodate large households. We settled for five-bedroom units suitable for families of eight and a mix of smaller units and flats. We engaged a quantity surveyor very early on to give us a rough cost based on the brief. We knew having them on your side was essential, and we let architects appoint other consultants. We interviewed eight architects. They presented design approaches. And based on that, we selected four. Those four all came together. We spent a day looking at the site and responding to their questions. We had an example next door, a housing scheme built in 1988. In that scheme, you go through your back door, you get into your private garden, you go through it, and you get into a communal garden. Such a housing concept can be found across London. But dwellings like that are pretty large and occupied by wealthy people. We did not see why social housing shouldn't be just as good. Each architect worked with the construction quantity surveyor company we had appointed because we didn't want schemes that were way out of the set budget. Halfway through, each of the teams presented where they were at, and we gave feedback. One scheme did not work for us, but the other three were very good. We were surprised by how many units all teams managed to get on. We selected Haworth Tompkins. Following our feedback, they placed the neighborhood center against the busier road and positioned housing on the other three sides of the block. I think it's an excellent scheme. It weathers well, too.

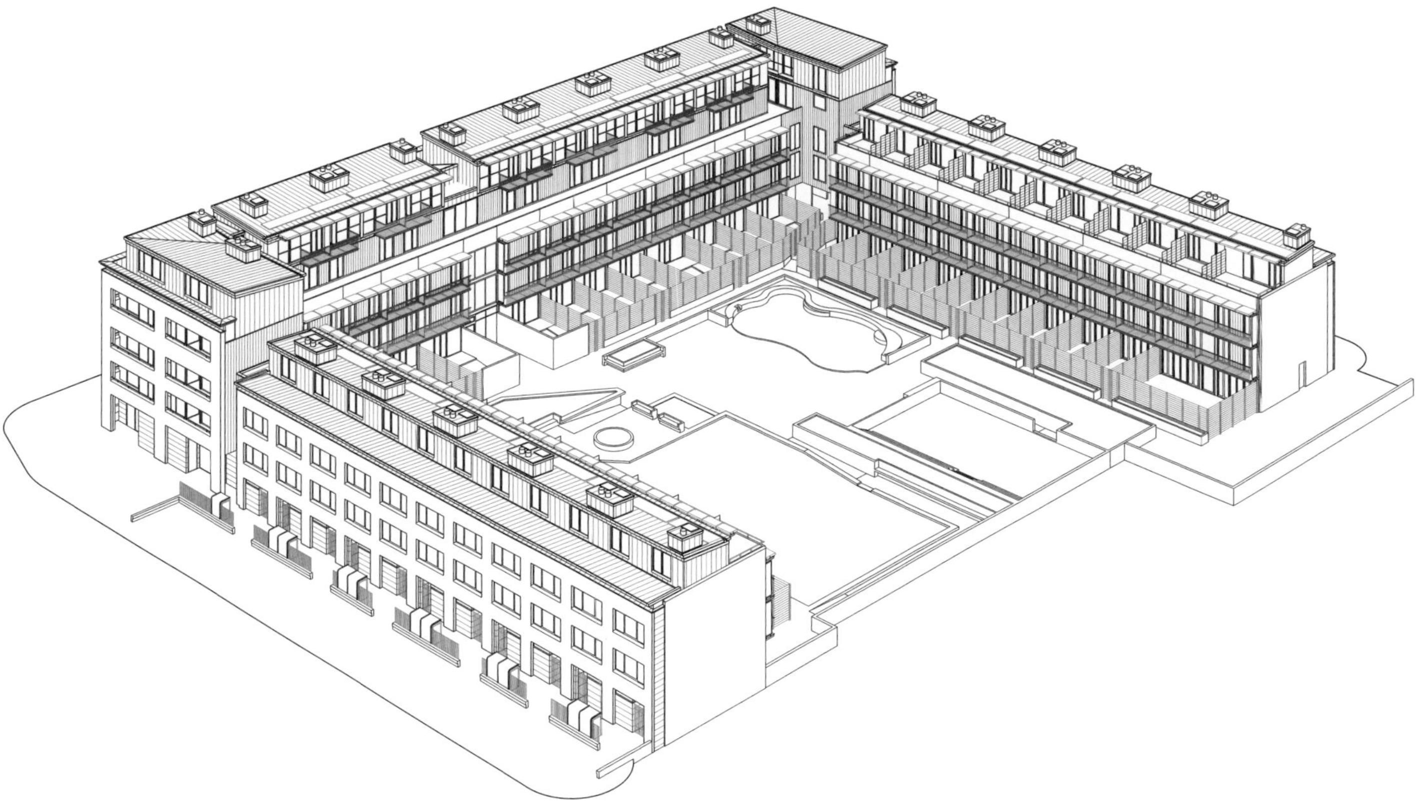

Figure 7
Perspective drawing of the building envelope.

"I remember when we were choosing the brick, and there were exactly even numbers as to which brick color and type to use. And so, the person who abstained was sent out on a taxi to look at some housing done with that brick. Still, that person couldn't decide. Finally, the taxi driver took the decision. Therefore, you know, that process hadn't really worked."

DS You mentioned the Council wanted large units, and CSCB, too, wanted and succeeded in achieving specific spatial standards, which are rare in subsidized housing today.

IT We wanted construction to pay for itself. That was not possible with Iroko. We built into the brief spatial requirements exceeding government standards, which are now abolished as they do. We set environmental standards to include solar water heating and heat exchange systems. We applied for a housing grant from the government, but it had a ceiling, and anything else you had to borrow. We also knew that if we borrowed as much as it took, the rents over the many years you calculate would have been too high. So, we decided to cross-subsidize it using CSCB commercial income.

DS Can you tell me more about how cross-subsidies work?

IT The public car park underneath the building effectively covers the cost of groundwork and foundations for the Iroko building. We did not have the money in our back pocket, but CSCB had the ability to borrow because of the commercial activity it undertakes. That borrowing has been recently paid off. It was great as it was. It enabled the provision of private gardens on the ground level, roof terraces, and additional rooms on the east and west wings, from where you could look out your windows and see Tate Modern.

DS I understand that the organization's commercial activity and capacity to engage with the public domain, rather than maintaining a narrow focus on housing affordability, was essential to improving housing conditions.

IT We have set up a registered housing association called Coin Street Secondary (CSS) housing cooperative, which has long-term leases from CSCB for the land for housing developments and receives public grants. It allows CSCB to focus on the public realm, the commercial side, and that sort of stuff, and CSS to focus on housing. Iroko is one of its primary housing cooperatives. CSCB provides the cross-subsidies we mentioned. CSS is responsible for the loan and cyclical maintenance, including external bits of the building and lifts. Maintenance of dwellings and communal areas is the responsibility of Iroko as a primary housing cooperative. They also look after allocations and management themselves. Each of the four cooperatives is slightly different.

DS Is the development scale critical for the ability to cross-subsidize housing and, the other way around, for housing to subsidize public amenities?

IT In fact, on the adjacent site, just south of the National Theatre, we are doing a major scheme that involves quite a lot of private housing to fund the public swimming and indoor leisure center, which was needed because we brought a lot of people into this area. Traditionally, local authorities used to provide communal facilities. Doesn't happen. They don't even manage to get developers of really big schemes to contribute substantially to public amenities. In this area on the South Bank, we work with Lambeth Council. We do our stretch for the riverside and Bernie Spain Gardens. We were involved in setting up the Jubilee Gardens trust.

DS Why is it rare to see grassroots initiatives turned into projects for neighborhood regeneration and housing development, such as this one led by CSCB?

IT The grants have been reduced since we started doing housing cooperatives. The government essentially made housing associations build private housing for sale to subsidize social housing. They've done the same to local authorities; they don't get the old rate support from the government and have to rely on other means. A target for new developments in London is that half of it should be open-market housing. And there is reliance on a shared ownership model. Housing has become extraordinarily expensive in this area.

DS To conclude, what are your views on the potential of self-organized, local community groups in housing provision?

IT We use the term *community anchors*, and that's a term that's been used for quite a time for organizations that are based in the neighborhood and support other groups and have links with local authorities and regional government. We have invested enormous amounts of time in getting the government to adopt a social enterprise strategy. We showed that we can go a long way if communities can bid for land and if there's government money around to help. I believe in redesigning the State from the neighborhood upward and that governments can help bring different people together to try and find a way through problem areas.

5 La Vecindad Plaza Mafalda, Buenos Aires

adamo-faiden

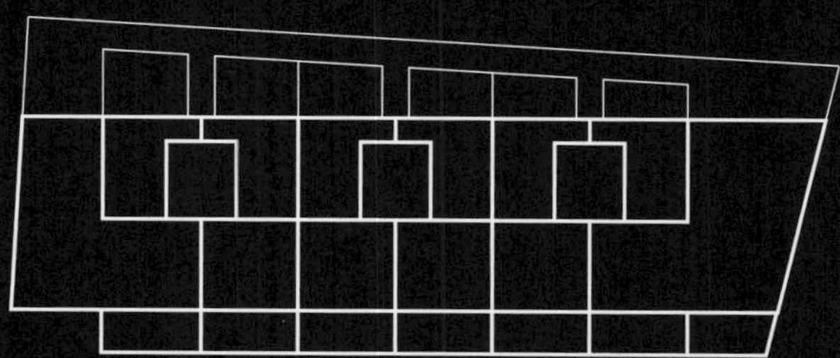

The Building and the City

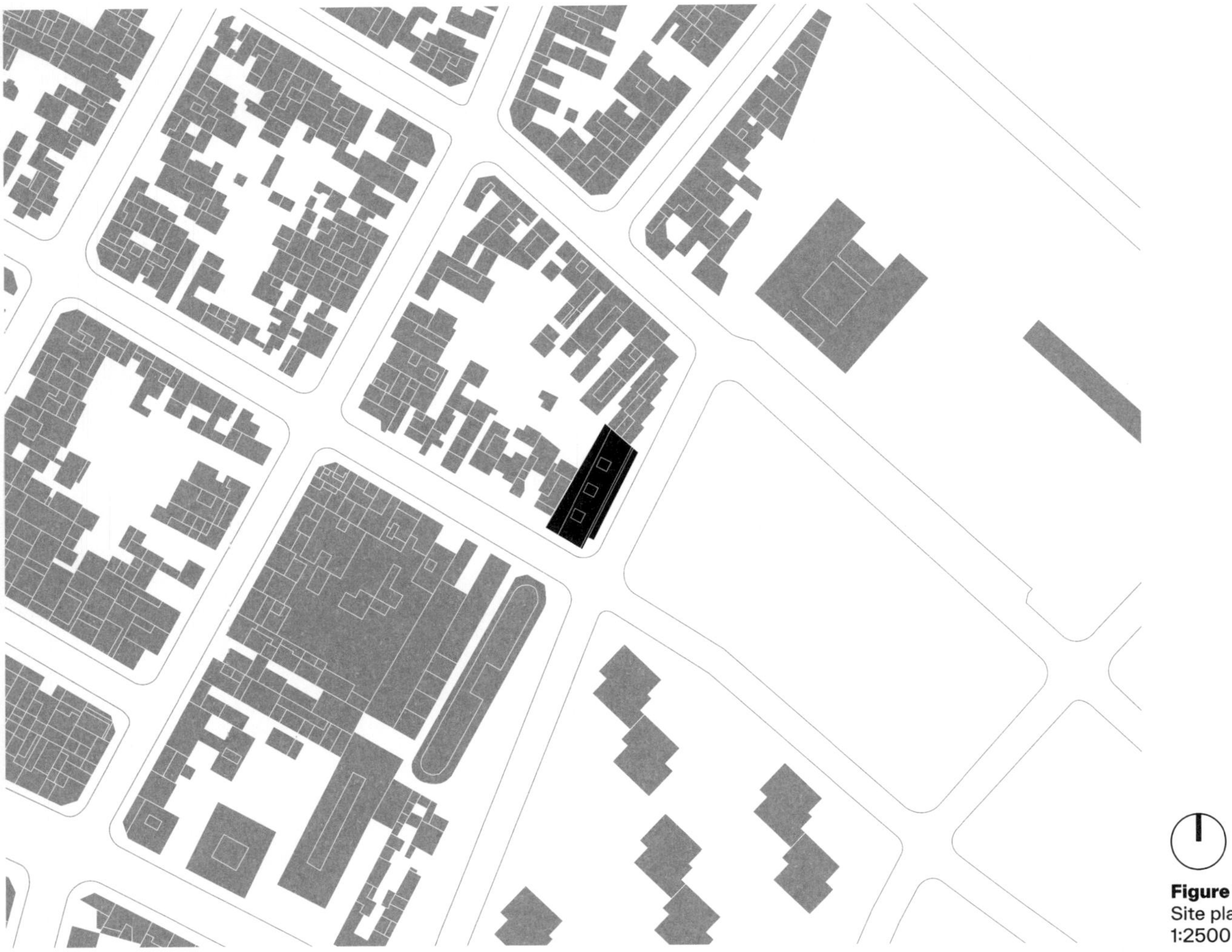

Figure 1
Site plan, drawing scale 1:2500

La Vecindad Plaza Mafalda, Buenos Aires
adamo-faiden

Year of completion: 2018
Number of units: 12

The building provides a backdrop to the public park and occupies the corner of two streets in the Colegiales district of Buenos Aires. The relationship between the building and the city is central to its architectural intent and will be discussed from multiple aspects. The architectural project prioritizes access to the private outdoor environment. It contains two rows of townhouses, placed one on top of the other and merged into one structure to improve the usage of available space and make the most of the view over the open green area across the street.

Section

During a public lecture hosted by the Melbourne School of Design on September 8, 2021, Marcelo Faiden suggested that their design intent can be best understood through

1. Marcelo Faiden, "I Love Living in the City," guest lecture, Melbourne School of Design, September 8, 2021, https://edsc.unimelb.edu.au/studio-epsilon/lecture-repository/adamo-faiden.

the building section.[1] This drawing shows two units belonging to two rows of townhouses merged into one structure. It also shows the relationship between dwellings and the private outdoor environment. All units have two levels, one for the living area with a kitchen and the other for bedrooms. However, dwelling layouts are such that the use of levels is inverted between the two rows. Duplexes of the lower row have their living rooms on the ground floor and their bedrooms on level one. The upper units have their bedrooms on level three and living areas on level four. Dwellings of the lower row benefit from the private patios at the back, while the upper-row units have private landscaped areas on the building's roof.

The sectional drawing also shows how the building sits on the pedestal formed by the car parking garage, half sunken into the terrain. The residential part of the building is pulled away from the street to make room for a strip of private gardens on the garage's roof, standing approximately 2 meters above the street level. This way, units of the lower row have small private landscaped areas at the front protecting them from the street. Back patios, which are larger, paved, and equipped with built-in amenities, are used as an extension to the living rooms. Today, a few years after the building's completion, diverse vegetation added by residents grows in front gardens and makes an integral part of the building facade.

The upper row of units benefits from a setback on level four, where building volume is pulled further away from the street. The formal gesture creates room for planters, which are incorporated into the building envelope. Like the front gardens, these planters help protect privacy, contribute to architectural expression, and improve the amenity of the upper units' living rooms. The private landscaped areas on the building's roof are primary outdoor spaces for the upper row of units.

Units

This building has a concrete skeleton structure, with vertical load-bearing plates concealed in party walls. These walls are perpendicular to the building facade, allowing for large fenestration, daylighting, and views toward the park. All units have two bedrooms, except the first and last in the row, which have one and two additional bedrooms. All living rooms occupy an 8-meter-deep space, stretching from one building facade to the other for better daylighting and cross ventilation. The entrance to all units is via their living areas. Access to lower units is from the back alley or via private stairs connected to the underground car parking. Upper units are entered via the gallery on level three, reached by elevator or communal stairs from the entrance lobby on the ground floor or underground parking level. The only communal spaces are the building's entrance lobby, back alley, and third-floor gallery.

The seamless floor finish of terrazzo tiles is applied in the entrance lobby, stairs, outdoor patios, and living rooms. The connection between the inside and outside environment is reinforced using the same floor finish in living rooms and patios and the floor-to-ceiling glazing between the two spaces. Kitchens are separated from the living area by a built-in element combining a kitchen bench and overhead storage. Bedrooms have timber flooring.

Envelope

The building envelope is complex and composed of layers and interstitial space. The building facade facing the street is designed as a backdrop for the existing park and trees. On the ground floor and the roof of the building, this facade incorporates a full-story height steel mesh. Almost the entire building's frontage is glass, protected with rollable aluminum shutters. It enables residents to control the intake of daylight and protect their privacy, and it is essential to the architectural expression of the building. These shutters are an integral part of the building facade. Pulley mechanisms are concealed in cavities in the concrete structure clad with finely corrugated aluminum panels. The building's appearance is dominated by the patchwork of horizontal and vertical lines, materialized through a careful choice of building materials and textures. The finishing layer of the back facade is concrete with the texture of vertical lines.

The architecture studio, adamo-faiden, has been developing a unique architectural knowledge and command of building materials in designing residential building envelopes with multiple layers. Generally, their designs include the outer layer, usually perforated steel mesh, which provides sun protection, and the inner layer, floor-to-ceiling glazing, as the thermal barrier. They often incorporate soil and plants in the intermediate space between the two layers to regulate temperature and increase humidity. Their earlier projects on extensions to single-family homes, such as extensions for Nuñez and Piñeiro Houses, and smaller multiunit residential buildings, such as Lago and Martos Houses, could be observed as prototypes.[2–5] Their more recent project for the seven-story building on Bonpland Street in Buenos Aires, which will be addressed in the conversation with the architects in the following segment, also incorporates soil containers and plants to filter light and create microclimates between the interior and exterior spaces.[6]

2. adamo-faiden, "Ampliacion casa Nunez," accessed April 25, 2023, https://adamo-faiden.com/index.php/projects/data/af-casa-nunez.
3. adamo-faiden, "Casa Pinerio," accessed April 25, 2023, https://adamo-faiden.com/index.php/projects/data/af-casa-pineiro.
4. adamo-faiden. "Casa Lago," accessed April 25, 2023, https://adamo-faiden.com/index.php/projects/data/af-casas-lago.
5. adamo-faiden, "Casa Martos," accessed April 25, 2023, https://adamo-faiden.com/index.php/projects/data/af-casa-martos.
6. adamo-faiden, "Edificio Bonpland 2169," accessed April 25, 2023, https://adamo-faiden.com/index.php/projects/data/af-bonpland-2169.

In conversation

The following text, an edited transcript of an interview with Marcelo Faiden, recorded on April 11, 2023, provides further information about the project from the architect's perspective.

DS My first question is about the relationship between individual and communal aspects of the project. How do you see the relationship between the two?

MF As an architect, I can think of the two extremes. One would be zero shared spaces. There would be no corridors, no access space, just individual units. The opposite is if everything is shared. Perhaps you could go as far as not having individual units. Both are possible, but most often, it is something in between. There are many in-between scenarios, and as architects, we try to find the right balance for each project. In this project, the intent is closer to the first extreme. There are no shared facilities, and access spaces are minimal. We wanted to use all the space available for dwellings and make them as spacious as possible. The idea behind the development was to create conditions where people can live in proximity to each other, while ensuring the privacy of individual dwellings and residents' comfort is achieved. The intent was to combine multiple dwellings in a single building while keeping the qualities of a single-family, detached house. We have used spatial devices, which we have tested and developed in other projects, to create patios with outdoor kitchens and gardens with plants that people own and care for. It is important to emphasize that the project is an infill development. In the first place, it is about making houses in the city.

DS It is important to emphasize that this building does not create a closed community but one that wants to be part of the city. But I also want to ask what is the building giving back to the city?

MF The architectural expression of this building incorporates vegetation. Maybe we could say that part of the giving back is the building's facade, which creates a backdrop to the public space and adds to the green fund of the city. Front gardens, which we created on the garage's roof, just above the street level, form a significant green area. They are extensions of dwellings, as they are an extension of the park. Plants from these elevated gardens merge with canopies of trees growing on the sidewalk in front of the building. They enlarge the city's vegetation fund and perhaps create a natural habitat for species of birds and insects. These are all different kinds of communities, as I mentioned earlier.

DS I understand there are no communal amenities in the building, but could one go as far as to say that the development is not driven by the intention to create a community?

MF There is a question of what the community is and what makes one part of the community. Most of our housing projects are in the inner city and part of vibrant neighborhoods with plenty of street life. The same is true for this project. A large public square in front of the building is a communal space important to this building's residents and residents of other buildings. It is the best possible example of the relationship between the building and the city and how the city is the community of residents from different buildings.

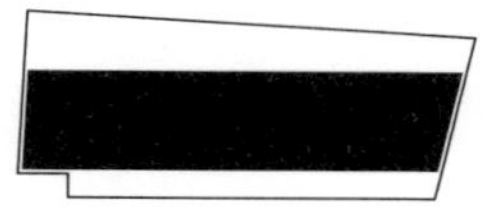

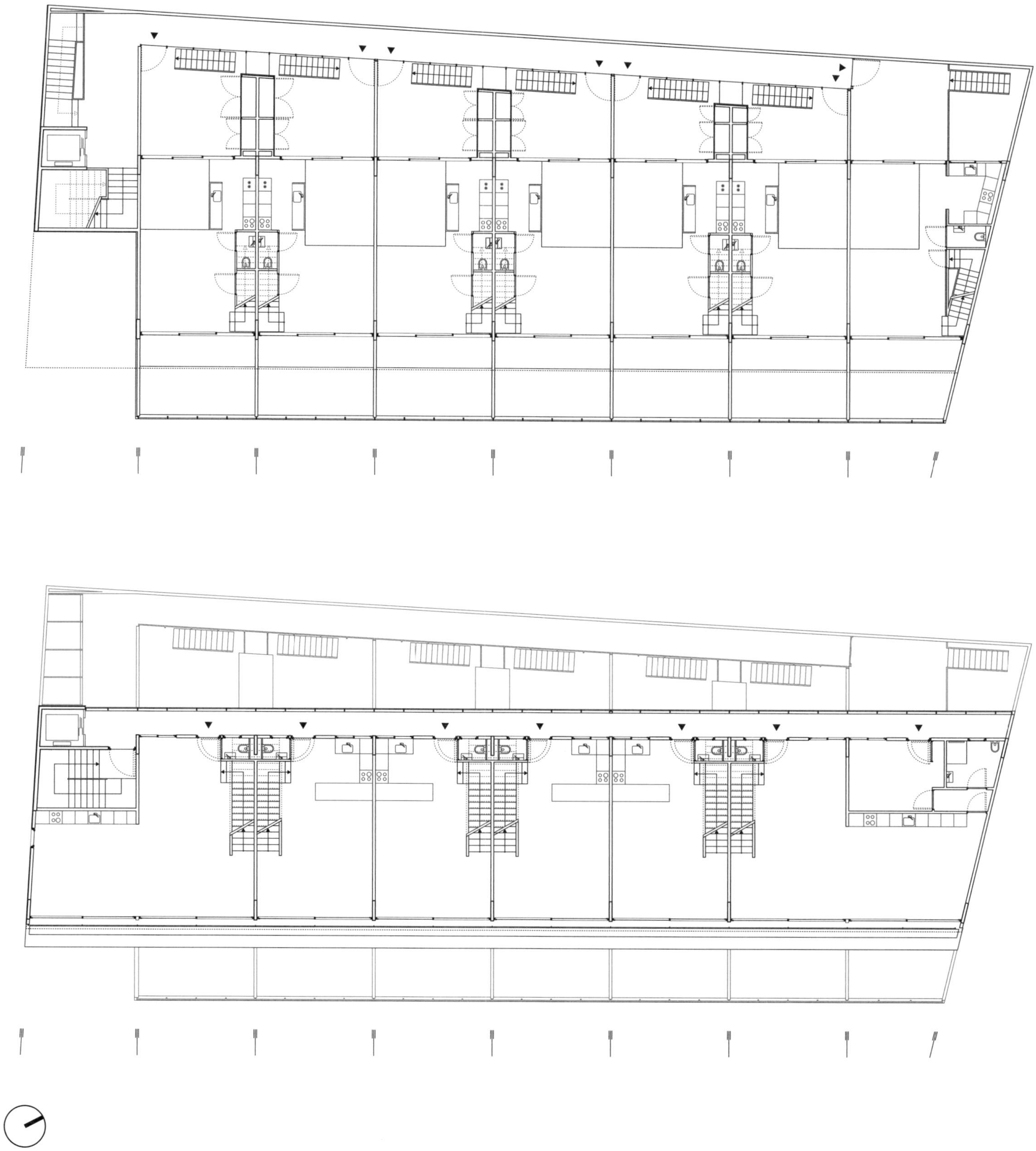

Figure 2
Levels 1 and 3 floor plans, drawing scale 1:250

DS On some residential projects you designed, you were not just architects but have been involved in their initiation. Was it the same with this project?

MF This project was a direct commission. We were approached by a visionary developer who wanted to work with us. It was a good experience for both parties. It was nice to work with a developer for a change. I say this because most of our preceding multiunit residential projects, such as the Arribeños and Conesa Buildings, were developed through *fideicomiso*, which is a form of a property trust, where we, the architects, have had a role in initiating the project, finding available land, attracting investors, and working with residents.[7,8] As we generated projects, we did not have to make compromises that architects sometimes make. The most important part of the process is that architects start working before developers. It changes the nature of the conversation and the outcomes.

"Maybe we could say that part of the giving back is the building's facade, which creates a backdrop to the public space and adds to the green fund of the city."

DS It reinforces what you said about the relationship between the building and the city. Is such a self-initiated approach to housing provision that you have just described rooted in the cultural and economic context of Buenos Aires and Argentina?

MF In Argentina, as in many other countries, there is a lack of systemic supply of affordable housing. Instead, housing provision is often an individual undertaking. However, in Argentina, it is widespread to invest savings into property rather than depositing money in banks. Inflation is so high that it can render savings void. Our currency has probably dropped in value between the start and end of our meeting. Not long ago, in 2001, we had an institutional crisis and the collapse of the banking system. People lost their savings. Consequently, their trust in financial institutions has vanished. It is why our middle class is keen to invest their savings into property development, frequently unfolding at a small scale. It often includes individual home extensions, development through lot subdivision, and self-organized trusts. This is where we found opportunities to apply architectural design, and it is the context in which we have grounded the beginning of our architectural practice. In addition to practice resulting in built projects, we initiated an experimental project exploring using air rights at the systemic level to increase the housing provision in Buenos Aires.[9] We have indeed grown since and now work on some larger projects.

DS You make initiating and delivering multiunit residential projects sound easy. How do you do it?

MF It is not easy. Many stakeholders in the project, such as engineers and lawyers, are engaged in the process. You must know the city, how it changes, and how those changes affect land and property values. You must predict what will happen in three years or by the time your project is complete. You need to know in advance how much your building will cost, so you need a good understanding of building construction. It is not straightforward. You must gauge and work out different options. You add value with good design. And then you start asking people, friends, and family first if they are interested in investing and want to live there. You try to balance individual interests and identify communal benefits.

7. adamo-faiden, "Edificio Aribenos 3182," accessed April 25, 2023, https://adamo-faiden.com/index.php/projects/data/af-edificio-arribenos-3182.
8. adamo-faiden, "Edificio Conesa 4560," accessed April 25, 2023, https://adamo-faiden.com/index.php/projects/data/af-edificio-conesa-4560.
9. adamo-faiden, "Casa Murere," accessed April 25, 2023, https://adamo-faiden.com/index.php/projects/data/af-casa-murere.

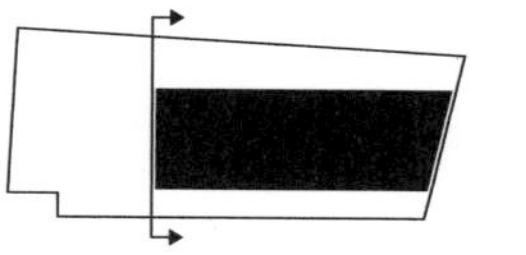

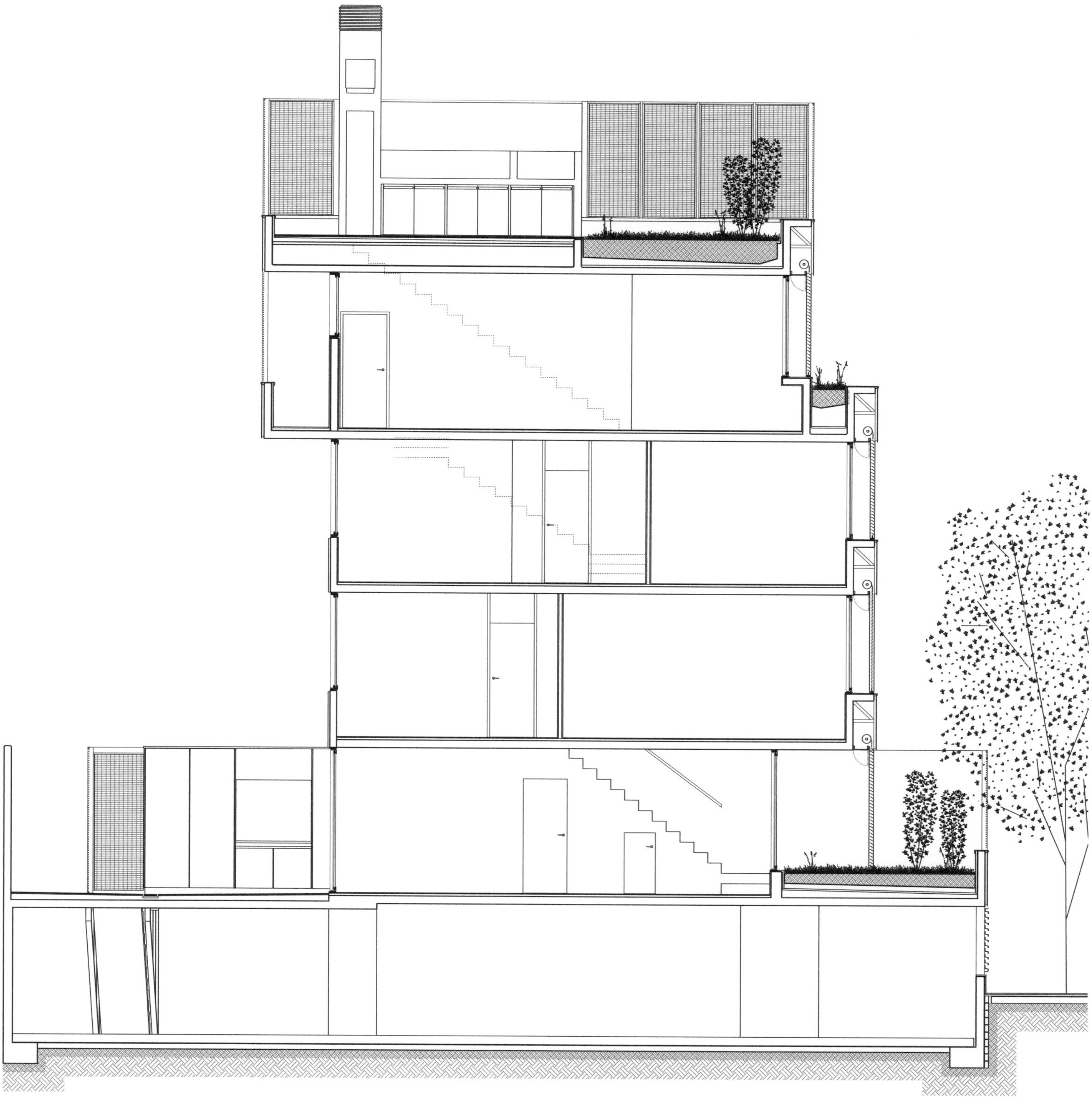

Figure 3
Cross section, drawing
scale 1:100

DS Did your work on *fideicomiso* projects result in a universal solution, a prototype, that can be used as a baseline on different sites?

MF One of the contributors to the practice we have developed was the availability of buildable land in the inner city at a relatively low cost, although this is also changing fast. These opportunities would present themselves as leftovers and imperfect lots. Therefore, in addition to finding buildable parcels, it was equally critical to propose what to build. We have designed a sequence of projects utilizing narrow and deep lots, often comprised of lofts and one-bedroom units—as we knew, those are in demand in certain parts of the city. It's not just the size of the unit that is relevant, but the way of living and the very relationship between people and buildings. As architects, we have been developing spatial devices specific to such contexts related to spatial organization, using cost-effective and durable building materials, creating microclimates, and structuring the building envelope as a habitable space. An architectural project is a form of knowledge and much more than a building.

DS I want to ask specifically about the building you designed and completed in 2019 on Bonpland Street, not far from Plaza Mafalda. Does it encapsulate the knowledge you have developed through the sequence of projects?

MF Building on Bonpland Street is one of the projects procured through *fideicomiso* that exemplifies some of the key principles we have been developing over the years. The building is on a narrow lot between two other buildings, typical for Buenos Aires. Its floor plan is organized into five zones. There is an access core in the middle and a loft or open space on each side. That is three zones. I will explain the remaining two later. Let me clarify the dwellings first. Units are designed without partitions. There was an understanding that we were not designing homes for nuclear families. Our intention was to create space with possibilities and to step back and let residents take control of it. During the development process, investors were keen on different uses. Some were after dwelling space, some wanted an office space, and some had an idea to run a small hotel there. Our response was always yes, it can be all of that. The building was completed shortly before the pandemic, and many of these plans instantly changed. The openness and universality of our approach came in very handy. Today, these units are occupied differently by residents as homes, ateliers, offices, or both. There is a very nice bookshop on level four selling art books. It proved that all of those uses fit. I am always fascinated to see what happens after residents assert control and how they appropriate the open space we have designed. I always appreciate any opportunity to learn about their furniture choices as they make a significant difference in a space without partitions.

DS One of the topics we try to address in conversations on most projects in this book is the relationship between the interior and exterior. The building envelope is particularly elaborate and almost always a critical feature of your work. How does it work in this project?

MF I can answer by speaking about the two remaining zones, out of five, in the floor plan of the building on Bonpland Street, which we refer to as "perimeter gardens." These gardens are contained within the building envelope, which operates as a ventilated facade with an inner and outer layer. Vegetation growing from soil flush with the floor level, between the two facade layers, filters the light, and changes the microclimate by lowering air temperature and increasing air humidity. The inner facade layer is floor-to-ceiling glazing that forms the thermal barrier. The outer layer is a porous metal mesh that protects it from the sun. The interstitial space between them, where the gardens are, is 2 meters wide.

DS The building on the Plaza Mafalda and the building on Bonpland Street have different physical contexts. The two projects are not the same. Still, could you draw parallels between them?

MF They are different, but we could say there is a similarity in the architectural structuring of the envelope's layers, which was done to shield intimacy and improve safety, in addition to creating a microclimate and a garden extension of dwelling space. In the building on the Plaza Mafalda, units on the ground floor have an aluminum shutter between the inner glazing and outer metal mesh for protection, designed as an integral part of the building facade.

DS Did you consider spatial adaptability in your design?

MF We try to put structure out of the way and make dwellings more flexible. It leaves more options for residents. We have also planned for the potential extension of units on the ground floor into the parking level. Several residents have already done it according to the specifications that we have provided. The garage level has access to daylight, making its parts suitable for gradual conversion into guest rooms or ateliers. It is a form of spatial adaptability embedded in the project.

DS What design decisions have impacted the construction cost of the building on Plaza Mafalda?

MF We employ locally available materials commonly used in the construction industry. However, we use the minimum of building materials to achieve design goals. Using less building material means less embodied carbon, which is important for the environmental impact of the building, as it is for the cost. Sometimes, we increase the cost of the concrete structure by insisting it is limited to specific dimensions to conceal it within walls. Sometimes, we increase the budget by insisting on high-performance glazing. Investment in building structures is important in the long run, and glazing is important for efficient energy use.

In conversation

The following section is an edited interview with a resident who is the developer behind the project, recorded on May 9, 2023. They live in one of the townhouses of the upper row with their family of four.

DS What was the rationale for undertaking the development?

SD As a developer, I found a lot suitable for small or medium-scale residential development, only 200 meters from where I lived. I knew the neighborhood was very well suited for what we were trying to do. Also, as a developer, I have created the brand La Vecindad to offer an alternative to the residential property market dominated by apartments.[10] You may know that most people in the inner part of Buenos Aires live in apartments. There are individual houses, too, but they are few. We realized there is a demand for different housing solutions, halfway between flats and houses. We wanted to try small and medium-scale developments that are typologically closer to townhouses and imply a form of communal living. Hence the brand name. *Vecindad* is a Hispanic concept representing a neighborhood and a residential community. It is historically tied to communal living in buildings with shared patios.

DS Was there a need to build more units to increase the profit?

SD The development was not about building more units or lowering the cost of construction to make revenue but making ownership of an individual house with a garden in the inner city more plausible. To a large extent, planning regulations define the number of units, building height, and more. We went through many scenarios to find the best way to use the lot and make this specific form of housing less costly. By specific, I mean living in the inner city and having access to a garden. I was also keen to add value with good design. We were looking for architects capable of delivering medium-scale residential projects at the highest level.

DS How do you see the building as a resident?

SD My family and I wanted to move from an apartment to a house. As our family grew, we needed more room, but most of all, we wanted to have better access to private outdoor space and a garden, and that was more important to us than some advantages that apartment buildings offer, such as better views, access to some amenities, and security. Overall, a house costs more than an apartment, but per square meter, an apartment costs more than a house. We weighed between the price and what we got in each scenario and decided living in a house was a better option for us.

DS It seems that the scale of the development was critical to the project.

SD In Argentina, the coexistence of individual and communal ownership in the same development is enabled by *Propiedad Horizontal* regulations. Fifty or more years ago, these regulations were commonly used to facilitate residential developments comprised of only two or three units on a lot. The experience of living in such developments was closer to living in a house than an apartment. It looked like a possible solution to what my family was looking for. It contrasted with today's mainstream development, dominated by large multiunit residential buildings and apartment living.

10. Campania de Inversion y Desarrollo, "Vivendas La Vecidad y Atico," accessed April 28, 2023, https://cid.com.ar/la-vecindad/.

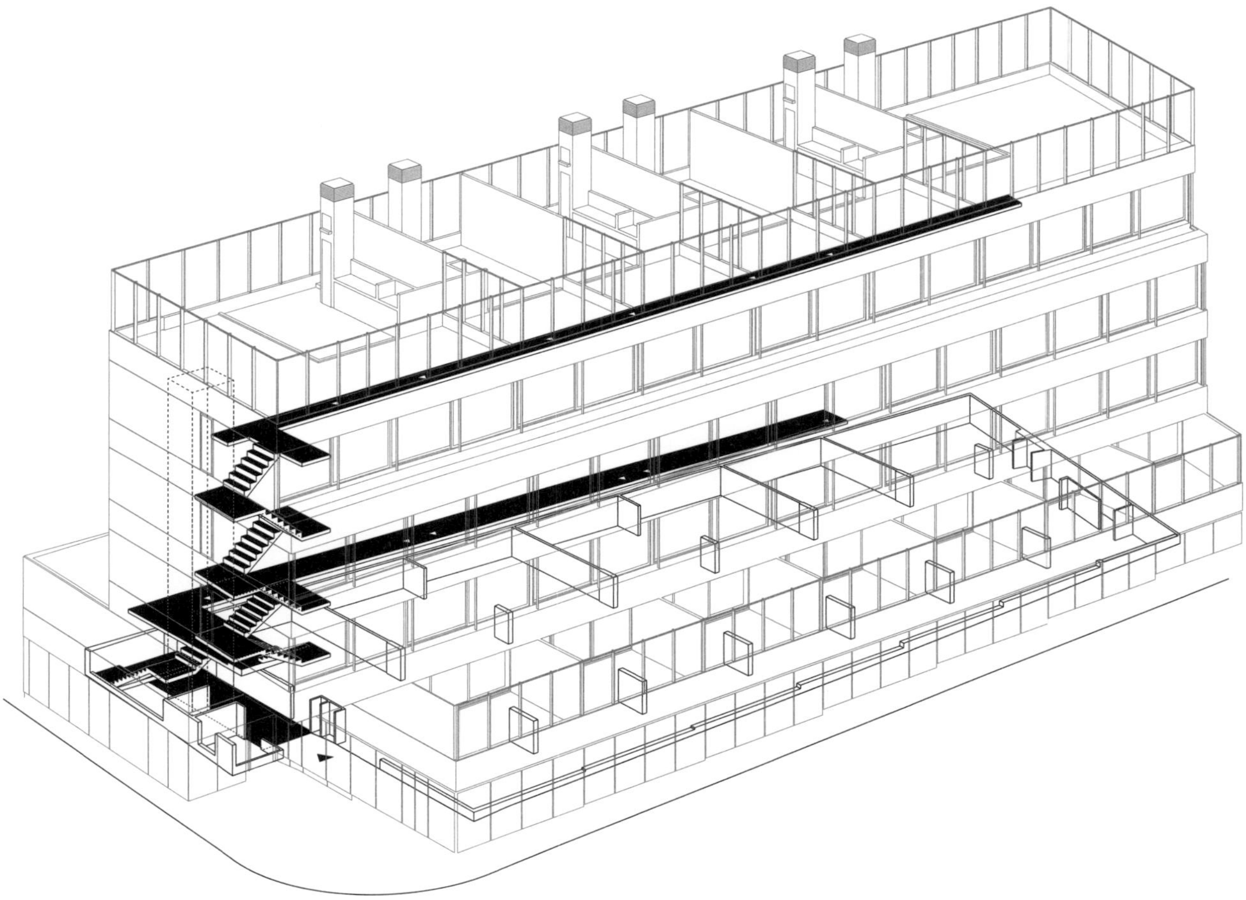

Figure 4
Perspective drawing indicating access and communal spaces in the building.

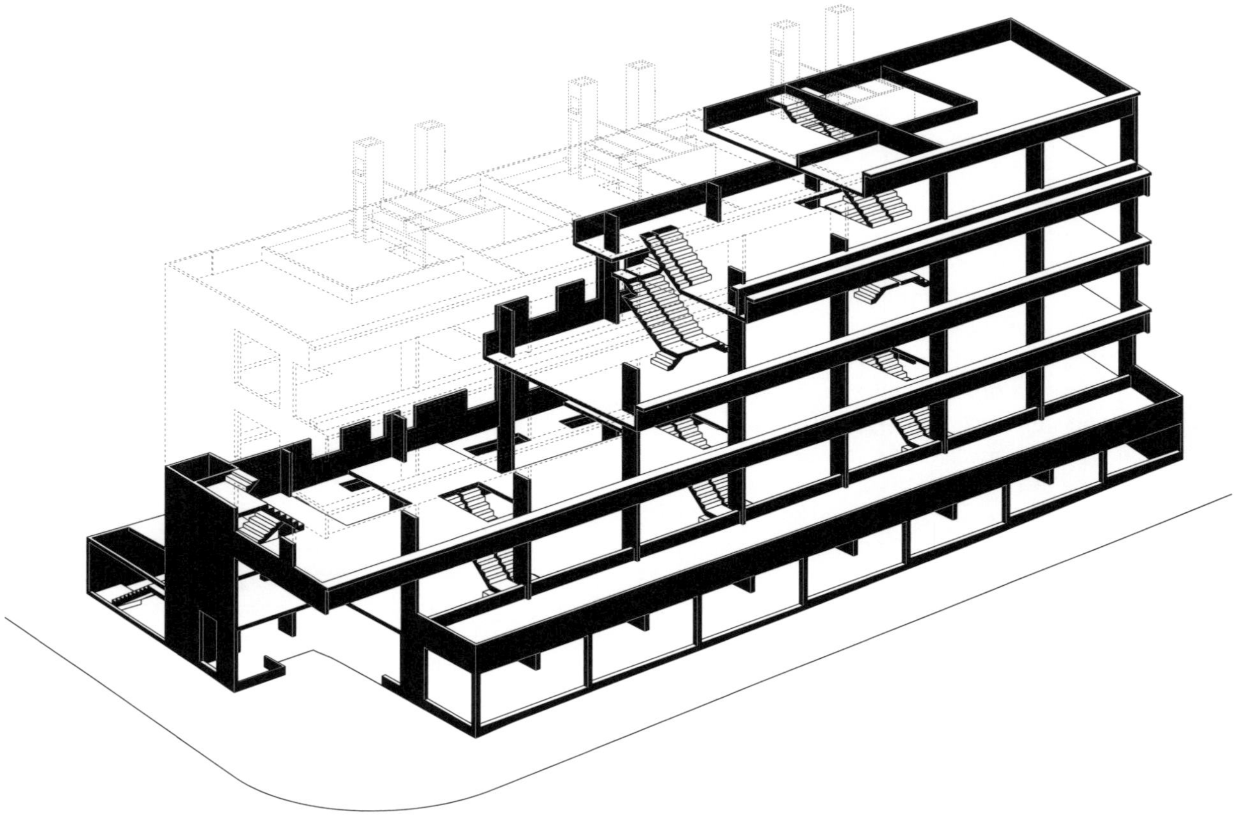

Figure 5
Perspective drawing indicating structural elements of the building.

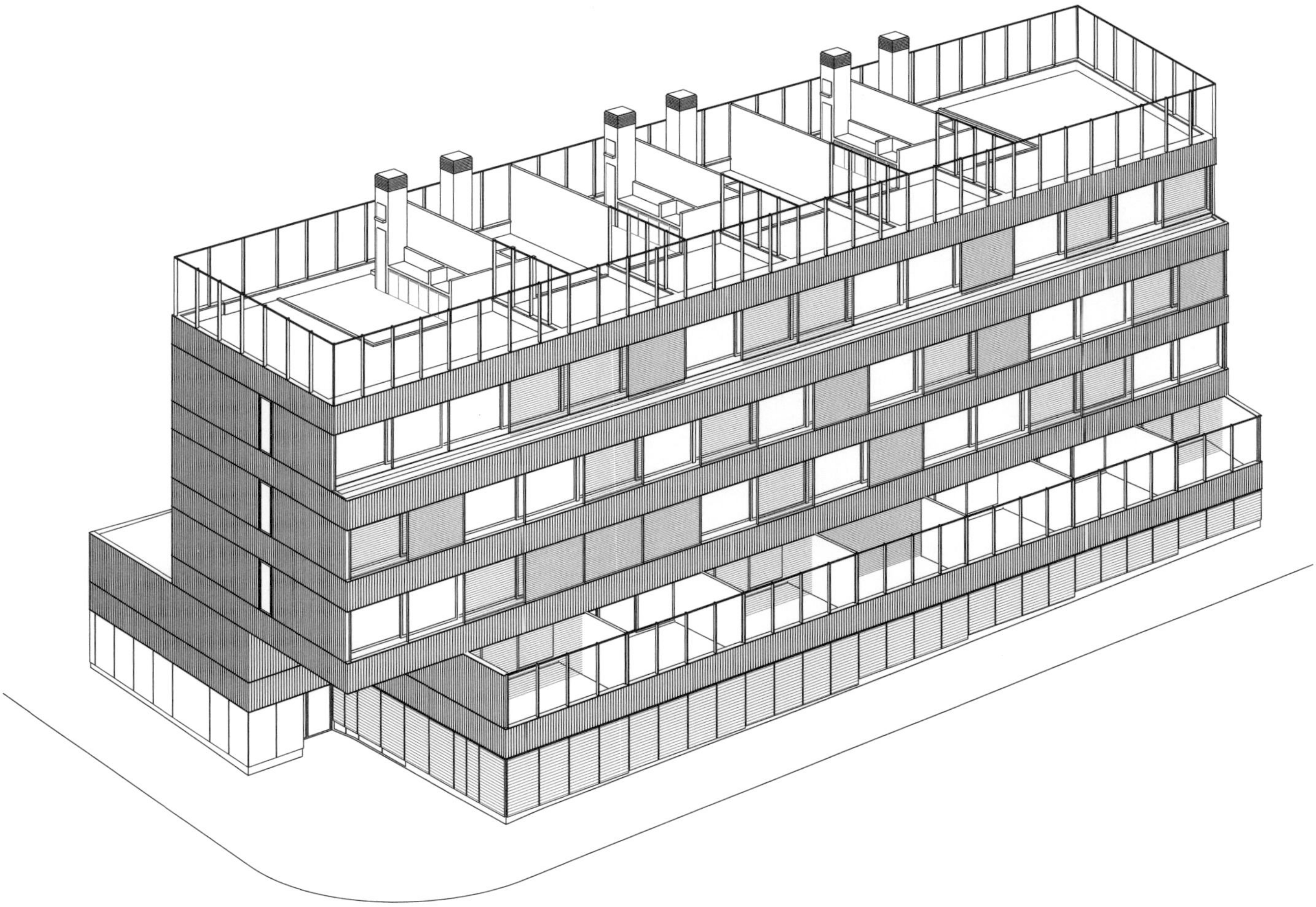

Figure 6
Perspective drawing of the building envelope.

DS How would you describe the residential community created with the development and how people who live in the building interact?

SD Unit layout and size are informed by market demand and are specifically made for the needs of young families. I mentioned earlier that we were targeting a specific market segment by developing a niche product. There are plenty of children in the building. Similar daily routines between different families have helped social cohesion between residents. Generally, people who live there know each other. We have a WhatsApp group for practical reasons.

DS Why did you decide to minimize communally owned spaces in the building?

SD One may expect to find shared facilities in the building, such as a communal kitchen or garden. However, that was never part of our plan. The communal amenities available to residents are those near the building. The biggest one is the public square just across the street, and other amenities are nearby. One of the essential reasons for omitting shared facilities is the maintenance cost. As a developer and resident, I am interested in how buildings are managed and how they age. If we had amenities, those would increase the cost of development and maintenance, an essential aspect of any development.

All units but one in this development are privately owned. That one unit is for rental, and it is communally owned. The income it generates is part of the maintenance cost plan. It reduces the surcharge associated with multiunit residential developments.

DS You mentioned that access to private outdoor space was one of the draws for your family to move from an apartment to a building comprised of twelve townhouses.

SD Yes, access to private outdoor areas was one of the key reasons we wanted to live in a building like this one. The building occupies approximately two-thirds of the lot, while the rest is outdoor space, and we have a green roof.

DS Can you describe the use of private outdoor areas and comment on the relationship between indoor and outdoor spaces in the building?

SD We live in one of the units of the upper row, and our garden is on the roof of the building, so we must take a flight of stairs from our living room to the garden. This garden incorporates a patio with a basic outdoor kitchen. We, developers and architects, have decided not to have built-in shading for roof gardens, thinking that the uncovered outdoor space would provide an experience closer to the garden or backyard. A significant part of the roof is a green roof covered in grass. Children play football there. It is ideal for gatherings. We have added a retractable shading device, and some neighbors have done similar, but it would be good to have at least a little bit of the permanent cover.

DS Is the relationship between indoor and outdoor spaces different for units with a living room on the ground floor?

SD Units in the lower row have access to the garden and the patio at the same level as their living rooms and a visual link to it, which is better in my view. They use outdoor space all year around, while we mainly use roof gardens in summer, less in the winter. Their outdoor kitchens are well connected to indoor kitchens.

"All units but one in this development are privately owned. That one unit is for rental, and it is communally owned. The income it generates is part of the maintenance cost plan. It reduces the surcharge associated with multiunit residential developments."

DS Is there enough daylight, and do you feel comfortable in your home?

SD On level three, where our living room is, we have built-in planters in front of our windows, and the view is over treetops. It is very nice. We have a continuous strip of windows stretching from wall to wall in each room. We also have automated blinds or shutters, which are important as the building is exposed to the sun from the east, where the park is, in the mornings. These blinds are an important feature of the architectural concept. There is plenty of daylight inside the unit throughout the day, and it is naturally ventilated because it has a dual aspect.

6 Wohnregal, Berlin

FAR frohn&rojas

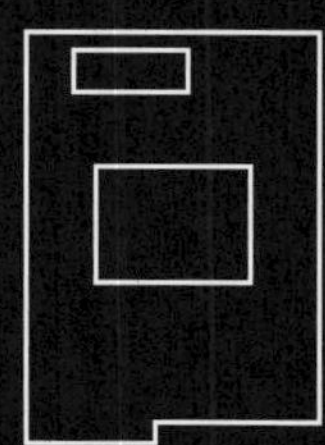

Repurposing

Figure 1
Site plan, drawing scale 1:2500

Wohnregal, Berlin
FAR frohn&rojas

Year of completion: 2019
Number of units: 11

The environmental impact of the building industry, including the choice of construction methods and materials, is more scrutinized than ever. An increase in the use of plant-based materials, such as timber and straw that can be restored, and materials that can be extracted with less harm to the environment, such as clay, are being increasingly explored.[1,2] Contemporary efforts to replace dominant construction methods include cross-pollination between vernacular building techniques and digital fabrication.[3] Current research efforts try to minimize waste, neutralize carbon emissions, and maximize reuse in building construction. Yet researchers and the construction industry still need to learn how to achieve these goals while meeting the demand. Today construction continues to depend on concrete and other building materials that do not fit

1. S. Bourbia, H. Kazeoui, and Rafik Belarbi, "A Review on Recent Research on Bio-Based Building Materials and Their Applications," *Materials for Renewable and Sustainable Energy* 12, no. 5 (2023): 117–139, https://doi.org/10.1007/s40243-023-00234-7.
2. Shubbar Ali Abdulhussein, Monower Sadique, Patryk Kot, and William Atherton, "Future of Clay-Based Construction Materials – A Review," *Construction and Building Materials* 210 (2019): 172–87, https://doi.org/10.1016/j.conbuildmat.2019.03.206.

the bill. Some of the projects presented in this book demonstrate the use of timber for the primary construction, as well as the hurdles they have run into, including the prohibitive cost and compliance with building regulations, namely fire rating. It shows that concrete is still difficult to replace in constructing multiunit residential buildings as the material for the primary structure.

Repurposing

This project explores the innovative, cleaner, and more efficient use of concrete through precast construction. The design approach revisited an established building construction method traditionally used for industrial facilities to find its application in a residential building for rental tenure in inner Berlin. Intriguingly, the project incorporated other building solutions and products against their original purpose. The following segments will discuss the repurposing of building solutions employed for this building's primary structure, facade, and other elements.

TT-type Slabs

This building has a precast concrete structure, including TT-type slabs, columns, and beams. TT-type slabs are widely used in industrial buildings and warehouses and are not commonly used in residential buildings. As their names suggest, they comprise two vertical down-stand beams and a horizontal flange. When precast elements are in place next to each other in construction, their flanges often serve as the formwork for an additional layer of concrete cast on-site. Therefore, the construction with TT-type slabs is often not precast exclusively, but it is significantly faster and requires less formwork. A range of related slab solutions are used in the construction industry, such as composite slabs, but few can combine such a large span capacity with most of the manufacturing done off-site.

The strategy behind this project was to engage with locally based manufacturers in a carefully planned construction process, using affordable building materials, minimizing waste, and reducing the time needed for on-site assembly.[4] The precast elements for this project were produced by manufacturers and facilities experienced in prefabricated panel construction, which have been widely used in Germany and other countries in answering high housing demands in the past. Such building systems were utilized for high-volume building, successfully lowering the cost and increasing the speed of construction.[5] On the downside, they resulted in a repetitive dwelling layout. This project, however, employs a precast skeleton frame rather than a precast panel system. It explores the potential of the TT-type slabs for their large spans and ability to carry high loads, for which they are primarily used in industrial buildings. In this residential project, they are employed to provide greater flexibility in unit layout planning in conjunction with streamlining the construction process.

TT-type slabs are usually manufactured over 20 meters long and 2.4 or 2.5 meters wide. In this project, they were employed to span the distance from one facade to another. They were produced in the factory setting and transported to the site, along with other elements of the building's primary structure. This allowed for a quick assembly of the primary structure, followed by other on-site works. In this project, the TT-type slabs are supported by precast beams and columns positioned at the perimeter of the building, allowing for the interior of the building to be free of structural elements.

During his lecture at the Melbourne School of Design on November 11, 2021, Marc Frohn presented the project's twofold aim to reduce construction costs by standardizing building elements and to avoid spatial uniformity by enabling the diversity and customization of dwelling units.[5] He suggested that the building can be understood as a composite of warehouses stacked one over the other.

Wohnregal

The project's name, Wohnregal, translates as "residential shelf," and is borrowed from an earlier residential building realized almost forty years ago also in Berlin.[6] The two projects have a similar number of units, and both incorporate precast concrete elements but formally remain very different. They are instead linked by housing affordability pursued through innovative building construction and their interest in enabling spatial flexibility and customization of dwellings. The earlier Wohnregal, an experimental and subsidized housing project, was also conceived as a series of stacked units, although not as warehouses, but as individual houses. Precast panels were employed as the primary structure, while wood was used for the secondary structure in partitions and fittings. The idea was to enable residents to take things into their own hands and build their own house between precast panels. The project by FAR frohn&rojas does not attempt to engage residents in the same way. Yet it makes a related distinction between the primary structure and other building elements to enable diverse and emerging dwelling demands.

Units

During his lecture at the Melbourne School of Design, Marc Frohn clarified that the project addresses the demand for affordable

3. James Stevens and Ralph Nelson, *Digital Vernacular Architectural Principles, Tools, and Processes* (New York: Routledge, 2015).
4. FAR frohn&rojas, "Wohnregal," accessed May 8, 2023, https://www.f-a-r.net/.
5. Marc Frohn, "Wohnregal," research symposium, the Housing Assembly: Creating Socially Valuable Housing, Architecture vs Housing: Four Case Studies, Melbourne School of Design, November 5, 2021, https://edsc.unimelb.edu.au/studio-epsilon/lecture-repository/far-frohn-and-rojas.
6. Wohnregal was an experimental and subsidized housing project designed by Peter Sturzbecher, Kjell Nylund, and Christof Puttfarken for the Internationale Bauaustellung (IBA) Berlin, 1987.

housing and requirements for diverse unit layouts for changing lifestyles and household structures.[7] This development provides rental live-and-work ateliers rather than residential-only units. The building is in the Moabit area, in inner Berlin, now a multicultural residential neighborhood which has been attractive to artists and younger people. Its peripheral location changed to more central with the removal of the Berlin Wall. The area has a heterogeneous structure characterized by open blocks and mature trees. The building is at the corner of one such open block. It receives daylight from three sides while attached to an existing structure on the south.

The building has a ground level and five floors. It measures 17 by 12 meters in footprint. A single unit occupies the ground floor, while the upper floors contain two units each. These units are accessed via a vertical core containing an elevator and stairs. Six TT-type components are placed in the east–west direction and aligned with the rows of columns along the building's facades. Their length is approximately 12 meters, and their width is 2.2 meters. Units on the first two floors are of similar sizes and have a single aspect. Their layouts are slightly different. The three upper floors contain one larger unit with dual aspects with up to three bedrooms and a smaller studio.

Curtain Wall

The building's east and west facades are fully glazed. Following the same logic of repurposing an industrial solution for the building's structure, the building facade is a curtain wall formed by fixed and sliding glass panels ordinarily used as doors in solid walls of residential buildings. The operable floor-to-ceiling panels are 2.2 meters wide. When open, they remove significant areas of the building envelope to transform the indoor living environment into an outdoor one.

The concrete structure, behind glass panels, is thermally protected by the building envelope. Yet columns, beams, and TT slabs are visible from the street. The railing, a repurposed floor grid attached to concrete walls in the interior, adds to the articulation of the building facade. The north facade, with the entrance to the building, is dominated by an open stairwell and a stainless-steel mesh stretched across all floors. The building's corners are occupied by small private outdoor spaces facing north.

Building Systems

The Wohnregal project explores the streamlined use of concrete to achieve architectural, economic, and environmental objectives. It utilizes precast construction and offers itself to the discussion at the intersection between architectural design and building systems. The main advantages of prefabricated building systems result from higher precision and more efficient workflows in a controlled environment. Currently, FAR frohn&rojas are exploring the knowledge and building construction methods developed in this project on a significantly larger development with 124 residential units.[8] These efforts rely on the use of precast concrete for primary construction. The emerging alternatives, providing a lower embodied and operational carbon footprint, include modular building systems, such as WikiHouse Skylark, utilizing blocks digitally manufactured from plywood panels.[9] These blocks are reusable and can be assembled and disassembled. They are digitally fabricated, highly precise, and available in different sizes and series, providing more choices and flexibility. However, the system remains suitable for small buildings only with up to two or three levels and, therefore, not necessarily applicable for sites where only taller structures can justify the use of available land.

7. Frohn, "Wohnregal."
8. FAR frohn&rojas, "Lion-Feuchtwanger-Strasse 61," accessed May 8, 2023, https://www.f-a-r.net/.
9. WikiHouse, "WikiHouse Skylark," accessed May 5, 2023, https://www.wikihouse.cc/product.

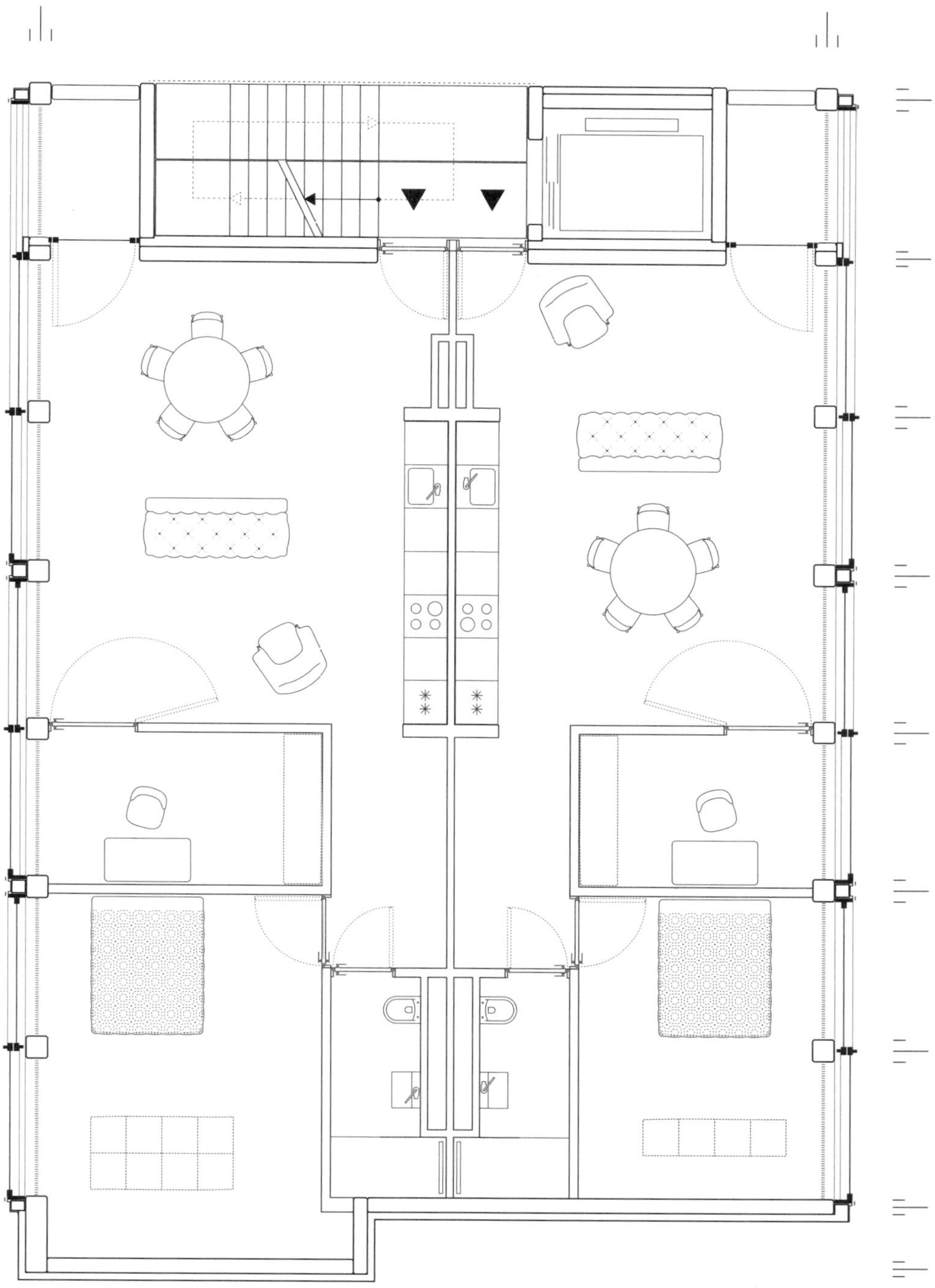

Figure 2
Level 2 floor plan, drawing scale 1:100

In conversation

The following section, an edited interview with Marc Frohn, recorded on April 14, 2023, provides further information about the project from the architect's perspective.

DS One of the most intriguing aspects of this project, for me, is the repurposing of building methods and products to achieve goals specific to residential buildings, namely reducing the cost of construction to improve housing affordability and responding to changing lifestyles.

MF We started the project by looking at another realm, not residential buildings. We looked at industrial buildings because they allow high-level flexibility. These facilities are designed and built not to restrict movement and workflows but to be used in many ways. When you design a warehouse, you may not know and plan what goes on there, but you want to create room for different processes and activities to unfold. We tried to separate how dwellings are planned from the main structure. There is no structural support within the building. We do have a vertical access core and shafts for services. However, structural columns are pushed out to the facade of the building. It created the possibility to plan each unit differently. I am not saying that we wanted to change units every week, month, or year, but to create options in designing their layouts, which is not achieved in residential buildings often enough.

DS This project adds a line of inquiry to this book, which combines architectural design and building construction. The flexibility you mentioned also has to do with the construction and maintenance of the residential building, just as it does with the unit layouts.

MF We have explored the distinction between the primary structure and the other construction works. On one side, you have a precast concrete structure; on the other, you have drywalls, facade walls, services, fittings, and everything else. There is a hierarchy, and there are different life cycles to them. The concrete could easily last eighty years; other things must be replaced in twenty or thirty years. The spatial changes that we foresee are part of those cycles.

DS I understand your interest in precast construction partially relates to a local building tradition.

MF Cost saving is a promise that has been associated with prefabrication for decades, if not a century. We deliberately intended to work with locally based manufacturers and utilize knowledge developed in the past. We continued a particular tradition, but we also did things differently. *Plattenbau*, or panel construction, has been used extensively in Germany in the past, but it implied repetition. Although the unit layouts were optimized, they had to be identical because of the construction method. As the precast wall was structural, they had to be aligned, which meant the unit layout had to be the same. In my view, that is very different from what prefabrication allows today. We employed TT-type slabs in this project, which have been used for decades, too. We just saw it as advantageous for what we were proposing. The system has already been tested, developed, and optimized to perfection. The reliability and availability are good reasons for using it. We just had to find a way to make it work in a residential building.

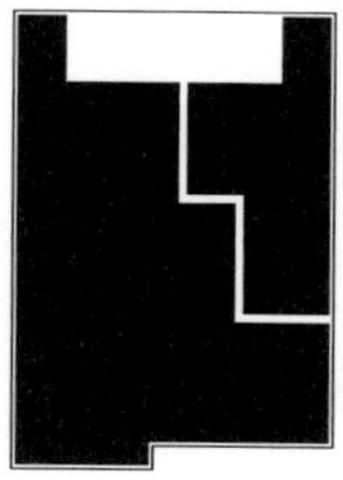

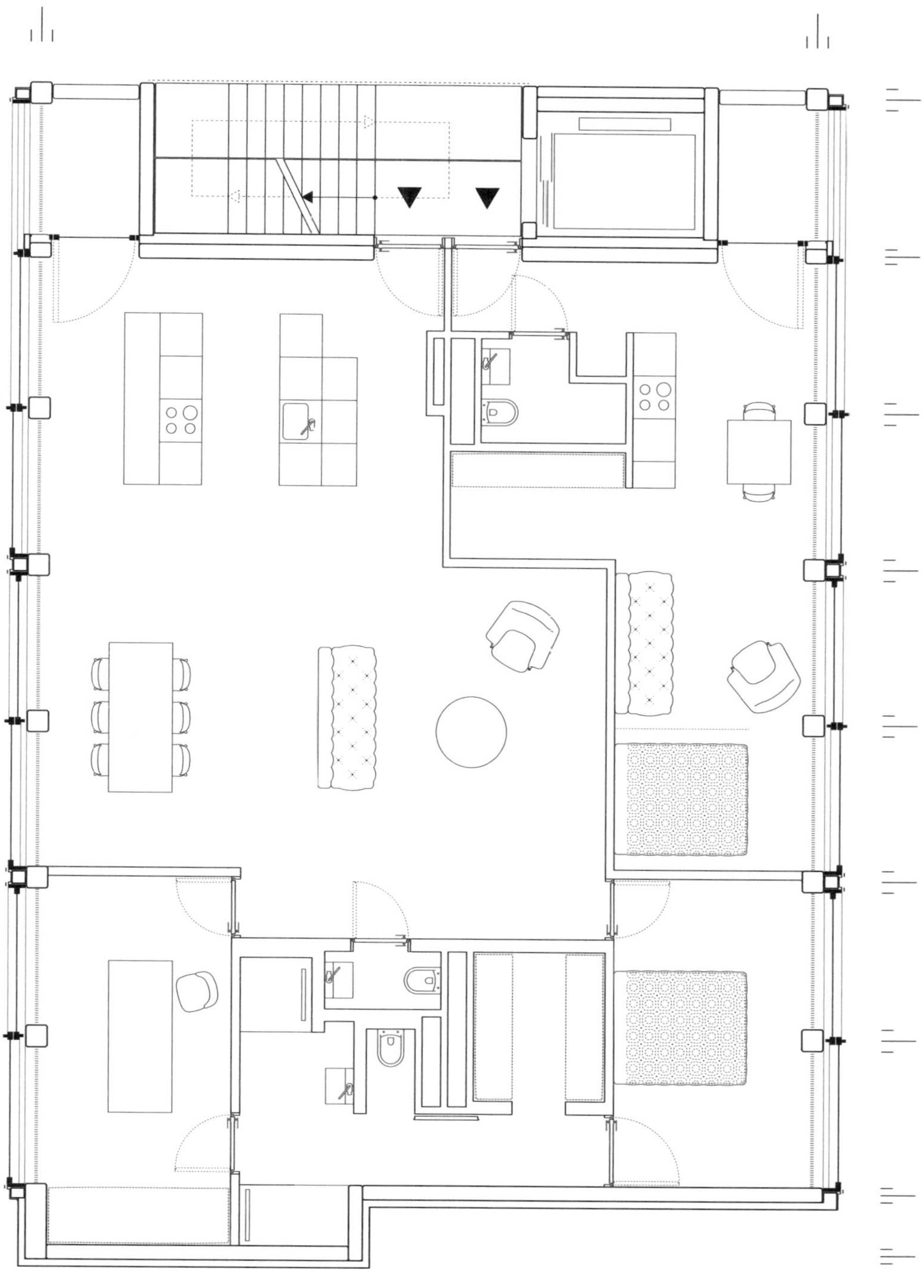

Figure 3
Level 5 floor plan, drawing scale 1:100

DS TT-type slabs eliminate the need for formwork but still require in situ concrete.

MF For what it is worth, I would like to clarify that construction with TT does not always necessitate the in situ layer of concrete. In this project, a layer of in situ concrete is cast over TT elements to bind them together. Before the concrete was cast, connections between them were loose. Tape was placed between them to hold the concrete while it was still liquid. That layer of concrete adds mass that stabilizes the structure of the building. On top of it, we have sound insulation, screed, and a thin layer of mineral industrial flooring. Adding in situ concrete allows for sound insulation to be done correctly. The legal framework around acoustical requirements is rigorous.

DS What were the main challenges you have faced in working with the precast construction?

MF This project is about a building system as much as the building itself. As a system, it is much more than the sum of its physical parts. It includes a network of stakeholders, knowledge developed, infrastructure, and logistics. Technically, you can do anything with precast concrete but must balance it with the cost. In this project, there was a necessity to lower the construction cost. When we started, some bits were counterintuitive to us. What appeared easily done was costly and difficult to achieve, while things we thought impossible were quickly done. You get a better sense of the pieces once you see how they are made. For example, the standard axial distance between down-stands at the factory we were working with is 1.2 meters, but the multiple did not work with our site. You must recalibrate the casting table to change the axial distance. That comes with a cost. Instead, we got what we wanted by inserting a form board on each side. So, it was about getting involved with the manufacturing process to develop an understanding of how elements are made and assembled and how the logistics of the process work. We had to visit factories located on the outskirts of Berlin frequently. We are a relatively young practice, and initially, we didn't necessarily have the respect of the local manufacturers we wished for. These manufacturers have all been in the business long enough. They have previously delivered large projects with the *Plattenbau* system we mentioned. However, we have teamed up with an engineer, IB Paasche, who had substantial experience in the field and had worked with the same factories before. It helped us sway their views and test things that perhaps would not be tested and ordinarily used in the construction of a residential building.

DS **Was there a possibility to integrate channels for electrical and other installations into precast elements?**

MF Horizontal installations, such as electricity and heating, are laid on the concrete cast on-site, along with sound insulation. Vertical installations attached to concrete elements are visible, but most are in drywalls. Tubing for installations is not integrated into TT-type slabs for this project. It is something we would like to explore in the future.

DS **The environmental question is inevitable if we are speaking of concrete.**

MF The carbon implications of building with concrete are real. If we must use concrete, the question becomes how to minimize its environmental impact. Precast elements and prefabrication in construction reduce the quantity of material to achieve specific goals. Less waste is generated in factory conditions during the manufacturing of pieces. Regarding embodied carbon, prefabricated construction is advantageous as individual elements can be reused or replaced. The digital twin models, now increasingly used in building construction, let you identify individual elements and plan around their life spans. With prefabricated construction, we can access individual elements and groups of elements and selectively repair or replace them. It increases the longevity of built structures. We also work with timber. I believe the selection of building materials always depends on a larger context.

“Cost saving is a promise that has been associated with prefabrication for decades, if not a century. We deliberately intended to work with locally based manufacturers and utilize knowledge developed in the past.”

DS The building envelope is as intriguing as the precast structure of this project.

MF We have the facade made of floor-to-ceiling sliding panels. The intent was to enable the building to open in spring and summer. The climate sort allows for that, and large tree canopies in front of the building make that prospect even more attractive. One can be in their living room and feel the breeze as if they are outside.

DS Does it mean the living room floor can be flooded if it rains and you forget to close the windows?

MF You should avoid that, but if you forget to close the windows when it rains, you may need to wipe the floor surface. It is a hard industrial floor, but it should not happen often. The aluminum profiling includes a standard drain or a shallow gutter.

DS You have repurposed an industrial product for the building's structure and have done the same with the facade.

MF We used sliding windows to create a curtain wall from those typically used in multilayered walls. They were made to our order, and wind loads were calculated, but an existing window production line was used. The facade is a curtain wall composed of aluminum frames and glass panels, protecting the concrete structure so that costly thermal breaks are unnecessary. The panels are triple-glazed and meet all regulatory requirements. It achieves the architectural expression we wanted. The concrete construction is legible from the outside.

DS The fin-tubed radiators and railings are just behind the glass and part of the building facade, in a way. Are these two elements also repurposed industrial products?

MF The railing is made of fiber-reinforced polymer. We have used a standardized product initially designed for catwalks in industrial buildings. We thought it could do a good job of protecting people from falling out of the building. It is a simple solution and quite beautiful architecturally. Such railings let daylight through but provide a visual barrier to some extent. The fin-tubed radiators are more commonly used in residential buildings. We used them as they fit well with the curtain wall and railings.

DS Can the knowledge gained from this project be applied to address the broader issue of housing affordability?

MF One of the drivers behind this project was to get involved with the housing provision by rethinking the construction process. We have done that to a certain extent by innovatively employing a well-developed precast concrete construction method and repurposing the existing building solutions. The best way to test what we were doing was by building, but to do that, we had to develop an entire system. As an architect, I wanted to improve rental tenure conditions by designing for cost-efficient construction of units suited to contemporary needs. The whole development is for rental. The rental revenue was a necessity for the viability of the project. Traditionally, in Berlin, rental tenure was and still is very common. We have self-build groups and housing cooperatives, all great models, but rental tenure is still a dominant housing segment in Berlin. The contemporary housing needs include the growing demand for work from home. We completed the building just before the pandemic, and the demand for live and work units increased. But even before that, it was clear that working from home was becoming more prevalent.

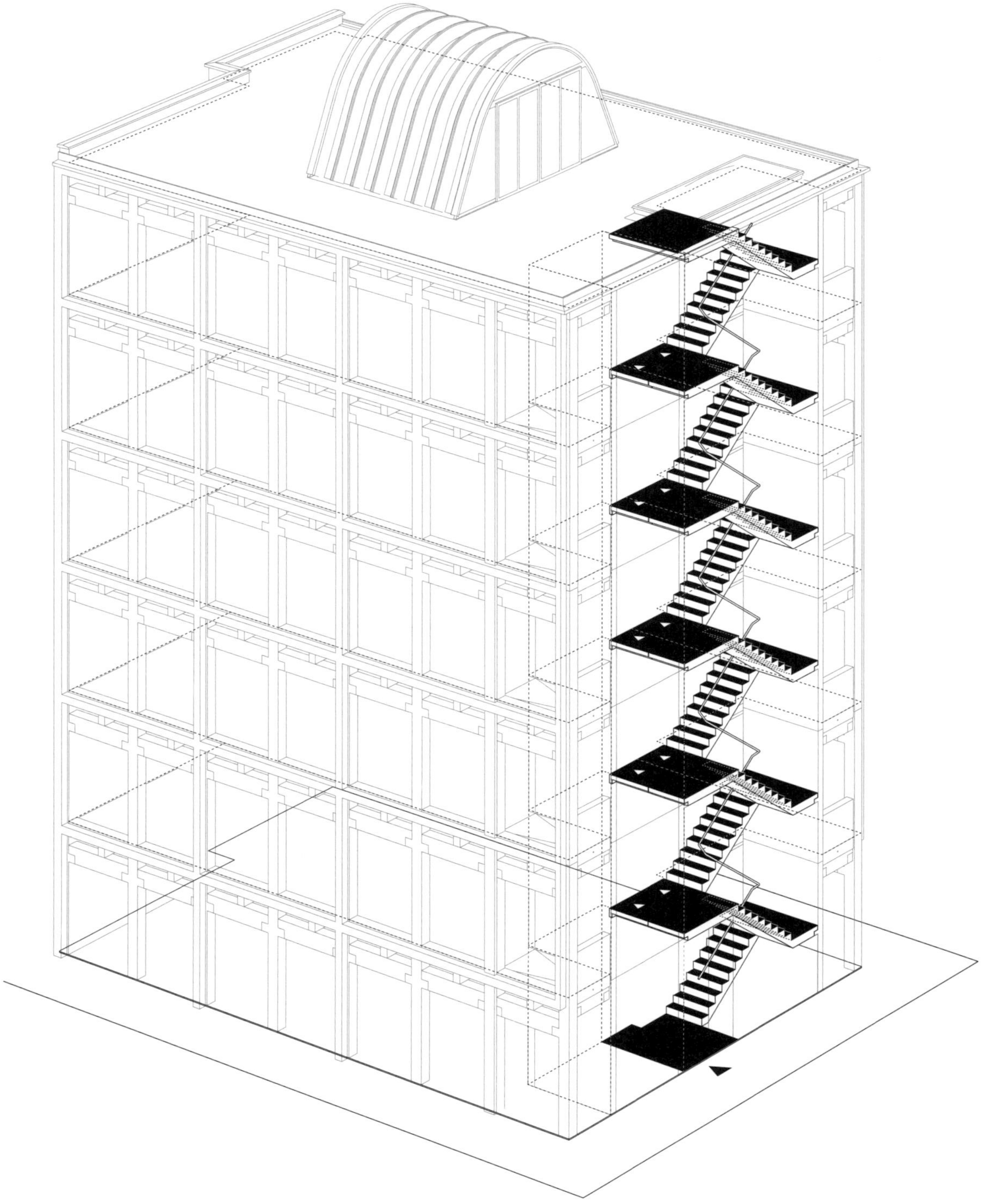

Figure 4
Perspective drawing indicating access and communal spaces in the building.

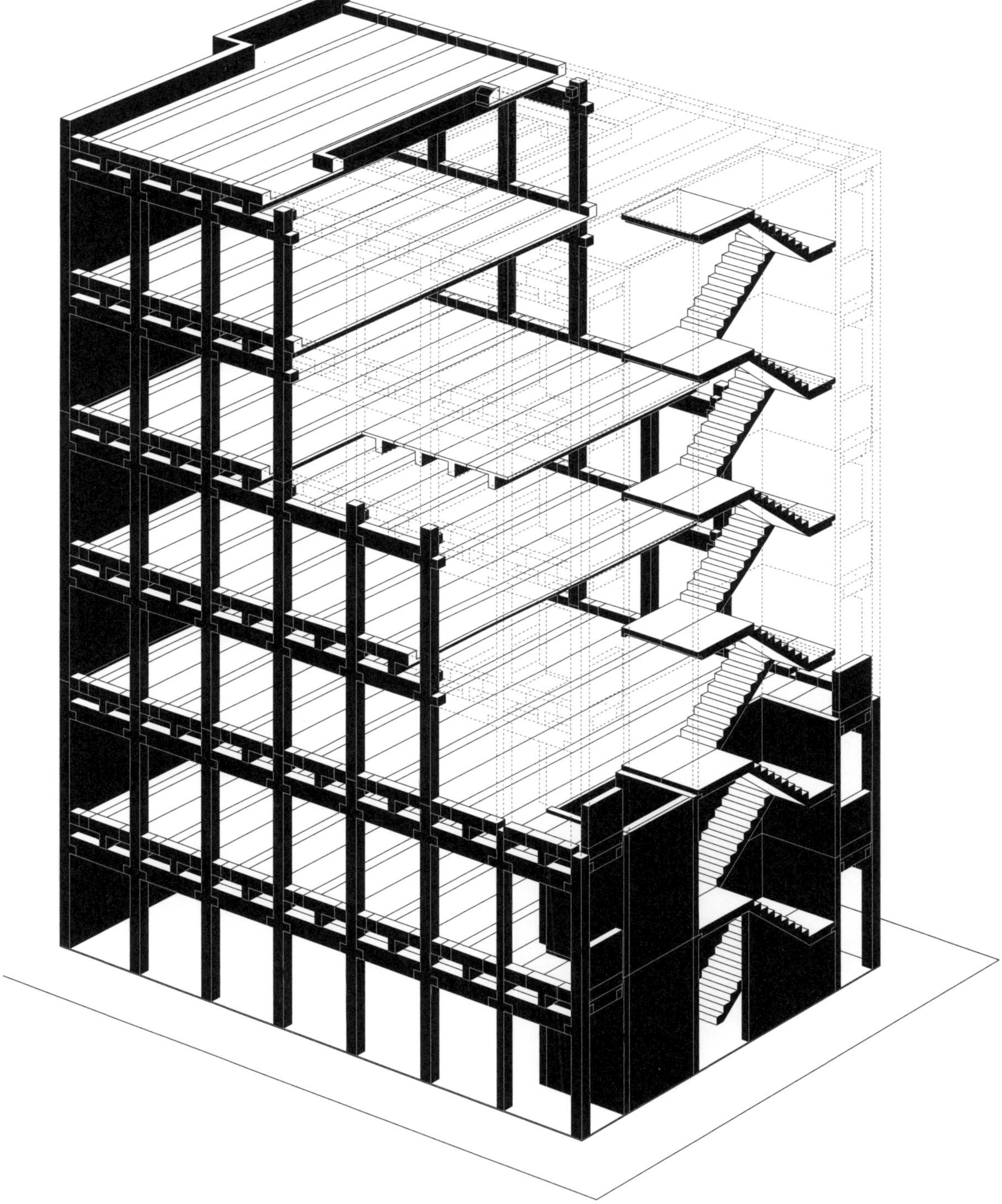

Figure 5
Perspective drawing indicating structural elements of the building.

In conversation

The following section is an edited interview with one of the residents, recorded on May 12, 2023. They live on the second floor.

DS The building has no communal areas besides an open-air stairwell providing access to units. Rather than asking about the relationship between the individual and communal, for this and a few other projects in this book, it may be more relevant to ask about the relationship between the building and the neighborhood first.

PP Our neighborhood is not affected by gentrification as some other areas of Berlin, where almost the entire population has changed. The Moabit area is still very much indigenous. It is a residential and safe neighborhood, although surrounded by industrial buildings. The main street has many grocery shops, convenience stores, and fast-food restaurants. There are plenty of small public parks. But no amenities, such as recreational facilities and cultural buildings, are close to the building. The area does not attract people from other parts of the city. I think many have never been here. However, it does attract younger people working in creative industries, like me. I lived in this neighborhood before moving into this building. When I first saw this building, with its glass facade, as there are not many around, I thought it might be something for the well-off people, and I was unsure if the structure fits the context.

I remember reading a novel by Anke Stelling that touches on glass facades of new residential buildings, housing, and gentrification and gives a bit of context on these topics specific to Berlin. I don't know if you care to know that rents in Berlin have now caught up with other German cities. Before, the cost of housing was lower, and everyone was renting. However, I was looking for a place to rent when units in this building were advertised, and I now live here on the second floor with my partner.

DS How would you describe the resident community of the building?

PP Some people have moved out, and new tenants have moved in, but only a few. I think the smaller units have changed residents. Most residents are mainly middle-aged. I like to joke that you wouldn't be able to live here if you were older than fifty because the windows are so hard to open. They require a strong pull. There are no children either. Most residents work from home, but I think this is now the default. I believe that residents in this building work from home just as much as any other building. I go to my office once or twice a week, and so does my partner, and the rest of the week, we work from home.

DS Did you have a chance to meet other residents of the building?

PP I have lived here for three years now. Occasionally, I've been invited to social gatherings in other dwellings. It was the usual drinks and people getting to know each other. I want to say we know each other, but not really. We meet in the stairwell, by the elevator, and by the entrance to the building, and we exchange greetings. We take parcels from couriers for each other, which is a form of contact between us. It is handy if you are not at home at the time of delivery or if the courier is in a rush and leaves everything with whomever they find first. I became friends with one of the residents. We meet outside the routines I described.

Figure 6
Perspective drawing of
the building envelope.

DS You mentioned floor-to-ceiling windows twice. Firstly, for their part in characterizing the building's appearance and secondly as being challenging to operate. Can you tell me a bit more about how you use them?

PP The sliding windows are big and heavy. The column does not let you get a good grip. So opening windows requires a bit of effort. It may sound like I am making it too big of a deal now. It is good exercise. We love the idea that you can open large windows, and it was one of the things that attracted us to get this unit. We face the street, and the large trees make it even more attractive. However, we don't do that very often. Perhaps because of the street noise. Unfortunately, my partner is allergic to pollen. In spring, you get the urge to open sliding windows, but the air is most saturated with allergens at that time of the year. We are also conscious that we don't want to forget to close our windows when it rains.

DS Are you comfortable living in a dwelling with such a large, glazed surface?

PP Yes, I love the dwelling and street relationship. Having big windows makes you feel you are outdoors. The best bit is that you don't have to open them to feel that way. I enjoyed seeing the street and what was happening there. As I often work from home, I see the same people passing by. I know other residents would be keen to put curtains up in our units.

"I lived in this neighborhood before moving into this building. When I first saw this building, with its glass facade, as there are not many around, I thought it might be something for the well-off people, and I was unsure if the structure fits the context."

DS How do you use the small private outdoor area on the north facade?

PP We don't spend much time there, but we find it an essential amenity of the unit. That door leading to that space tilts and turns. We keep the tilt open most of the time. It is important for cross-ventilation.

DS How do you find soundproofing in the building?

PP We don't hear our neighbors. We are separated from the unit on the same floor, not only by the wall but also by back-to-back and built-in kitchens and wardrobes. However, inside the dwelling, there are no acoustic barriers between rooms. It becomes a bit difficult when two of us work from home and have meetings simultaneously. I think the dwelling should have better separation between rooms. On the one hand, I like the large living room, but on the other, I wonder if some of that should have been used for a corridor to create more distance between spaces.

DS Is there enough daylight and adequate ventilation in your unit?

PP The indoor air quality is excellent, the rooms are a good size, and the living room in particular. The breeze between the door on the north facade and sliding windows on the east facade provides good natural ventilation. Thermal comfort is excellent. We are never too cold in winter nor too hot in summer.

DS How do you find building materials in your dwelling?

PP I like the concrete ceiling and the distinct character it gives to the space. The industrial floor is easy to maintain and comfortable. Floor heating would be good to have. I appreciate the built-in storage and the kitchen.

7

6×6 Block, Girona

bosch.capdeferro arquitectura

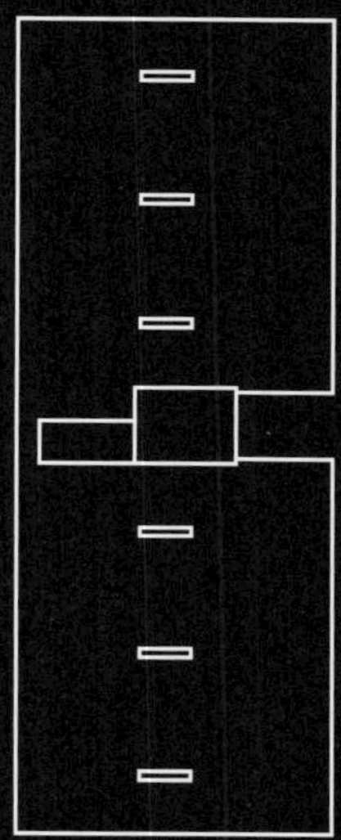

Adaptability

Figure 1
Site plan, drawing scale 1:2500

6 × 6 Block, Girona
bosch.capdeferro arquitectura

Year of completion: 2020
Number of units: 35

This building is located outside the historical center of Girona, in an area characterized by the regular street grid populated with civic and multiunit residential buildings. It is next to a small park with basic amenities and a children's playground. The project has a clear environmental focus and combines a high level of spatial adaptability with efficient use of space by employing a generic unit configuration.

Envelope

This building is designed to respond to seasonal weather changes. It has two main facades with distinct roles and architectural expressions. The north facade contains open-air access galleries, and the south facade is where dwellings have private winter gardens. Both facades have two architectural layers, the inner and outer.

The outer layer of the south facade is composed of bespoke and standardized elements attached to the building's load-bearing structure. It is developed between architects and local manufacturers through full-scale testing, and it includes foldable glass panels, low parapet walls with aluminum cladding, railings, and sunshade supports. The inner layer is a thermal barrier, mainly composed of sliding glass doors. Between these two layers are 100-centimeter-wide private outdoor areas. When the glass panels of the outer layer are shut, the sun warms the trapped air. In winter, the air temperature between the two facade layers can increase by ten degrees Celsius. From there, the ventilation system distributes the preheated and filtrated air into the dwelling interior.

In summer, when glass panels of the south facade's outer layer are folded, winter gardens transform into shaded terraces. Rollable timber blinds are attached to the inner wall to protect large glass surfaces from sun exposure and reduce heat gain. The blinds are long enough to create canopies over private outdoor areas. They are traditionally used in this region and are part of the local culture. As they become visible from the street, they contribute to the architectural expression of the south facade.

The outer layer of the north facade is formed by railings and slender bracing elements positioned at 3 meters throughout the entire facade. The inner layer is an insulated wall clad with spruce wood panels. The same finish is applied to the tilted underside of the slabs. Between the two layers are 110-centimeter-wide access galleries serving three units on each side of the vertical core. Entrance zones to dwellings are given more room, as the facade wall is pushed back to create a 185-centimeter-deep area where residents can put potted plants, small tables, and chairs. This additional space is meant to be appropriated by residents to help negotiate the interface between the private and communal, as dwellings overlook access areas while relying on the intake of air and daylight via large windows and glass doors. Purposively, the communal access galleries are designed to serve as an outdoor extension of dwellings. In summer, the microclimate on the north side benefits from the shadow created by the building, and the ventilation system changes intake direction to introduce cooler air from that side.

A Generic Unit

Floor plans are consistent across all six levels. All dwelling units have the same generic configuration and a dual orientation with 6-meter frontages on the north and south facades. There are six units per floor, apart from the ground level. There are six rooms per unit, including kitchens and bathrooms. A pair of identical rooms is by each facade, while kitchens and bathrooms are slightly smaller and placed in the central zone of the building. Confidence in a generic unit layout and coincidental or deliberate reliance on the value of six across the project, captured by its name, has contributed to the apparent repetition in the building floor plans. However, this setup has created a highly adaptable space.

The generic unit has a floor area of approximately 70 square meters but can be used in many ways. This is achieved by carefully dimensioning rooms, establishing links between them, and maximizing access to daylight and natural ventilation. Rooms have a minimum of three doors. The limited width of individual rooms is offset by the possibility of connecting them into a single space with large sliding doors. It allows using two rooms as one space or the entire unit as an open plan configuration when needed.

Adaptability

The architect's website features a sequence of six drawings showing how the generic unit can be used in different ways.[1] The same unit, with the unchanged configuration of walls, is presented as a one-, two-, and three-bedroom layout in the first three drawings. The increase in the number of bedrooms is at the expense of the home office first and the dining area second. The dining room is moved into the central zone and combined with the kitchen in the three-bed layout. These three options respond to the needs of growing nuclear families and show how the generic unit can accommodate diverse households and lifestyles. The fourth drawing shows a two-bed layout prepared for dinner with 32 people around a long table starching throughout the entire dwelling, from one building's facade to the other. The fourth and fifth drawings show how the same space can be used as a workplace for an organization with seven members and a nursery for young children.

Reuse

The capacity to introduce other uses, such as a workplace or communal amenity, instead of dwelling in any one unit of the building without undertaking construction works is one of the main qualities of the project. Beyond accommodating different and changing lifestyles, the generic unit configuration allows for introducing nonresidential uses as presented in architectural drawings described in the previous paragraph. Other drawings produced by architects show a pop-up café, a communal kitchen, and a gym, all efficiently fitted into the same generic unit. These drawings demonstrate how

1. Bosch Capdeferro Arquitectura, "6×6 Block," accessed September 3, 2023, https://www.boschcapdeferro.com/en/work/6x6-block.html.

a residential-only building can transition into a multipurpose one. This is relevant to a broader question of reusing built structures and how housing interacts with other essential programs in today's urban environments.

Building Materials

The choice of building materials and construction methods have contributed to reducing carbon embodied in the construction of the building. Above the ground level, the primary building material is locally sourced cross-laminated timber. It is used for load-bearing beams and columns, walls, and floor slabs, all produced off-site. Concrete is cast over timber slabs, adding thermal mass, fire resistance, and stiffness to the building structure with its weight and offering a durable and easily maintained floor finish throughout the interior. Sliding doors are integrated into partition walls to enable occupants to combine individual rooms or create an open plan configuration. When open, these wide doorways help cross ventilation, allow the intake of natural light deeply in the interior, and create views across the entire dwelling, measuring 12 meters from one facade to the other. Natural cross ventilation is supported with ceiling fans and, along with the previously described natural heating and cooling of the dwelling interior, improves indoor air quality and thermal comfort using only minimal energy. The ceiling height is lower in the central zone of the dwelling where kitchens and bathrooms are to accommodate the exhaust heat recovery unit.

Air and Atmosphere

During a public lecture hosted by the Melbourne School of Design on November 5, 2021, Ramon Bosch discussed links between several artworks and their architectural project for this residential building introducing some of the critical decisions during the design process.[2] First, he evoked J. M. W. Turner's painting and the painter's understanding of physical processes in the atmosphere as the gaseous layer that envelops the planet.[3] He suggested a parallel to thinking of air as a design medium in an architectural project. It corresponds to how the design of the 6×6 Block enables the built form to respond to climatic conditions and weather changes. Air movement, indeed, is one of the central topics of the project. It is linked to the building's overall form, unit layout, and structuring of the building envelope. Second, he referenced a painting by Ramón Casas to speak about the phenomenological understanding of the atmosphere and human perception of physical phenomena such as light, shadow, heat, and humidity before explaining how these phenomena were central to their architectural take on the dwelling interior.[4]

Decantation

Other references made by Ramon Bosch include representational techniques practiced by Pablo Picasso and Alberto Giacometti.[5,6] Picasso's decantation technique, whereby the artist uses only minimal graphic means, a few lines, to capture complex forms of objects, served him to explain the role of cross-laminated timber walls and slabs in the project. Indeed, the photo taken during the construction, showing only cross-laminated timber components, is one of the most striking images of the project. It is not difficult to see how these party walls define the form of the building as they provide structural stability and harbor the basis for the project's spatial organization and adaptability.

Sedimentation

On the other hand, Giacometti's technique of sedimentation, whereby the artist draws multiple lines one over another to graphically define a form of an object, served Ramon Bosch to discuss further the relationship between the built form and its use.[7,8] He showed a drawing of a generic dwelling unit layout, with superimposed graphic layers corresponding to multiple furniture configurations predicted by architects. Here one can see the analogy between numerous line traces defining a form in the artistic technique of sedimentation and superimposed traces of different furniture configurations defining the position of walls and dimensions of rooms as architects' intention to design for different ways of living.

2. Ramon Bosch, "6×6 Block," research symposium, the Housing Assembly: Creating Socially Valuable Housing, Architecture vs Housing: Four Case Studies, Melbourne School of Design, 5 November 2021, https://edsc.unimelb.edu.au/studio-epsilon/lecture-repository/bosch-capdeferro.
3. J. M. W. Turner, *Waves Breaking Against the Wind*, 1840, oil on canvas. Tate, London.
4. Ramón Casas, *Interior al aire libre*, 1892, oil on canvas. Carmen Thyssen-Bornemisza collection, Barcelona.
5. Bosch, "6×6 Block."
6. Pablo Picasso, *The Bull* series, 1945, lithograph. Museum of Modern Art, New York.
7. Bosch, "6×6 Block."
8. Alberto Giacometti, *Head of a Man*, 1961, drawing. Private collection.

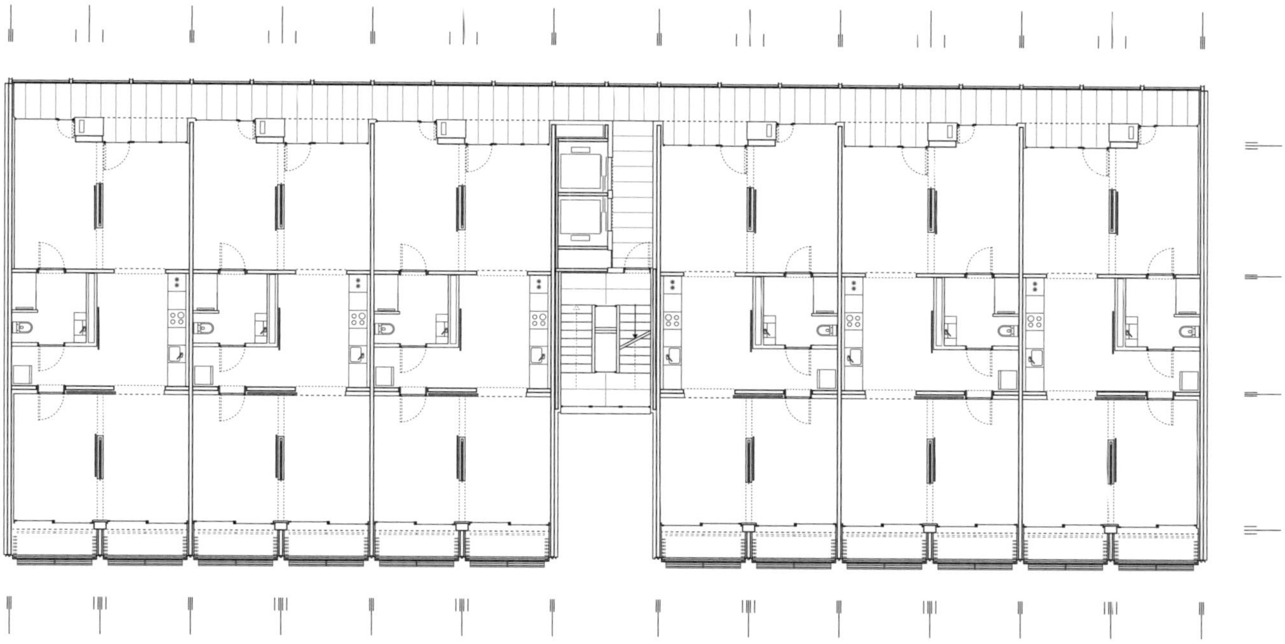

Figure 2
Typical floor plan, drawing scale 1:250

In conversation

The following section, an edited interview with Ramon Bosch recorded on June 16, 2023, provides further information about the project from the architect's perspective.

DS How does this building support a sense of community between residents?

RB As architects, we tried creating opportunities for people to interact, but a lot depends on residents. Approximately 100 people live in the building, and we wanted to help establish a community. I know that residents often get together on Wednesdays when the weather is nice, and we have joined them once or twice. These meetings are self-initiated. I understand they discuss practical things, but I believe these meetings are mainly social events.

DS You have enabled private dwellings to extend into the communal access galleries. Were you concerned about compromising the intimacy of homes when combining open galley access and dual orientation of dwellings?

RB We know that the intimacy of one's home, essential in our culture, could be disrupted if neighbors pass by the windows. However, in this building, there are only three units on each side of the vertical core, so we are not looking at high-volume traffic. It was essential that units are dually oriented, and we did not want to compromise that in the first place. But we discussed it during the design development. At one point, we wanted to include built-in shutters that residents could operate to protect privacy but decided it was unnecessary and even aggressive.

DS What design decisions have created opportunities for people to interact?

RB Access galleries provide opportunities for neighbors to meet. People use them to get to their units, but they also serve as extensions of private dwellings. We have created that bit of additional space, just by the entrance of each unit, to establish an interface between the communal and individual. That space is part of the gallery, but at the same time, it belongs to private dwellings. In summer, people bring out their chairs and spend time there. They open large glass doors to connect their dwellings with the communal access area. These doors are single-panel, floor-to-ceiling, and 1.8 meters wide.

DS Some of your drawings show that a generic unit you have designed for this project can be more than a dwelling. You show a possibility to include communal facilities for residents of the building, but also commercial spaces that would be accessible to the public.

RB The relationship between the building and the city is as important as the relationship between the individual and communal. Zoning regulations in most cities are based on segregation and monofunctional planning. Today, most master plans still differentiate between the blue and red zones, where one is housing and the other is commercial. However, the reality is different and more complex. If you see a doctor, lawyer, or architect, you will likely find their workplace a repurposed dwelling space. In response, we have designed spaces suitable for other uses, not only housing. We have established room dimensions and links between them to meet dwelling requirements and have shown in our drawing how they can be converted into workplaces. Moreover, we have explored how units can be converted from private dwellings into communal spaces, such as a shared kitchen, gym, or nursery, serving the entire community, not just a single household. In that way, the project mediates between private, communal, and public.

6

DS The building is designed to respond to weather changes. The south facade provides a preheated air supply in winter, while cooler air is introduced from the north in the summer. The north facade also allows access to the outdoor environment, which is helpful during the summer. For me, this is the best possible example of the relationship between the interior and exterior of a residential building.

RB The envelope of this building is designed as a habitable space and an interface with the outdoor environment. Air movement and intake of daylight, as much as air temperature and humidity, are part of our thinking about the unit layout. At least for a moment, we consider dwellings as outdoor rather than indoor environments during the design process. I like to describe the building as a composite of the load-bearing structure and openings or windows and doors. For us, the building is a provider of physical and climatic support. Looking at the facade, you will see nothing apart from operable openings and structure. The project makes the most of Girona's temperate climate, where the microclimate can be successfully controlled without much technology. We can open windows and roll down the shades when the weather changes, and we can follow our instincts to expose ourselves to the sun in winter and hide from it in the summer.

DS The photo of the primary timber structure, taken during the construction, is one of the most striking images of the project for me. I am not suggesting that everything else required for the building to operate is less relevant. However, given the growing expectations from timber-based materials in the future of housing provision worldwide, I am curious to learn more about it.

RB It is fascinating how architects are concerned with hiding timber but not concrete, brick, or other materials. Is it the texture of wood that we like, or environmental consciousness that is reflected by the material? Structural timber panels arrived at the site ready for assembly. It took only six weeks to complete the assembly on-site. At that point, you could see the entire building. You could count units, and you could see each room. It felt like only doors and windows were missing, but it was far from completing the building. Party walls, made of cross-laminated panels, provide bracing and rigidity to the building. Slab panels, also made from cross-laminated timber, run from one facade to another. They are 3 meters wide, 16 meters long, and only 15 centimeters thick. It is the biggest panel size produced in the Basque country. We have two such panels for each unit. We insisted on utilizing locally sourced building materials for environmental reasons and aimed to use only the minimum. Floor slabs have spans of approximately 4 meters running perpendicular to the facade, and they are supported by beams and walls. The aim was to reduce the amount of timber by having smaller spans.

"At least for a moment, we consider dwellings as outdoor rather than indoor environments during the design process. I like to describe the building as a composite of the load-bearing structure and openings or windows and doors. For us, the building is a provider of physical and climatic support."

DS What challenges did you face when opting for a timber structure?

RB This project was the first time we used structural timber at the scale of a multiunit residential building, and we were dealing with building regulations still centered on other building materials. We had to consider how to meet acoustic and fire protection requirements carefully. Floor slab panels had to be separated between the units to provide better soundproofing. We could not leave timber walls exposed as much as we wanted to. We used recycled cellulose panels that are porous and allow timber to absorb and release humidity while achieving fire rating standards and providing sound insulation. Cellulose panels are attached to timber walls with pliant perforated profiles, allowing them to vibrate and absorb the sound.

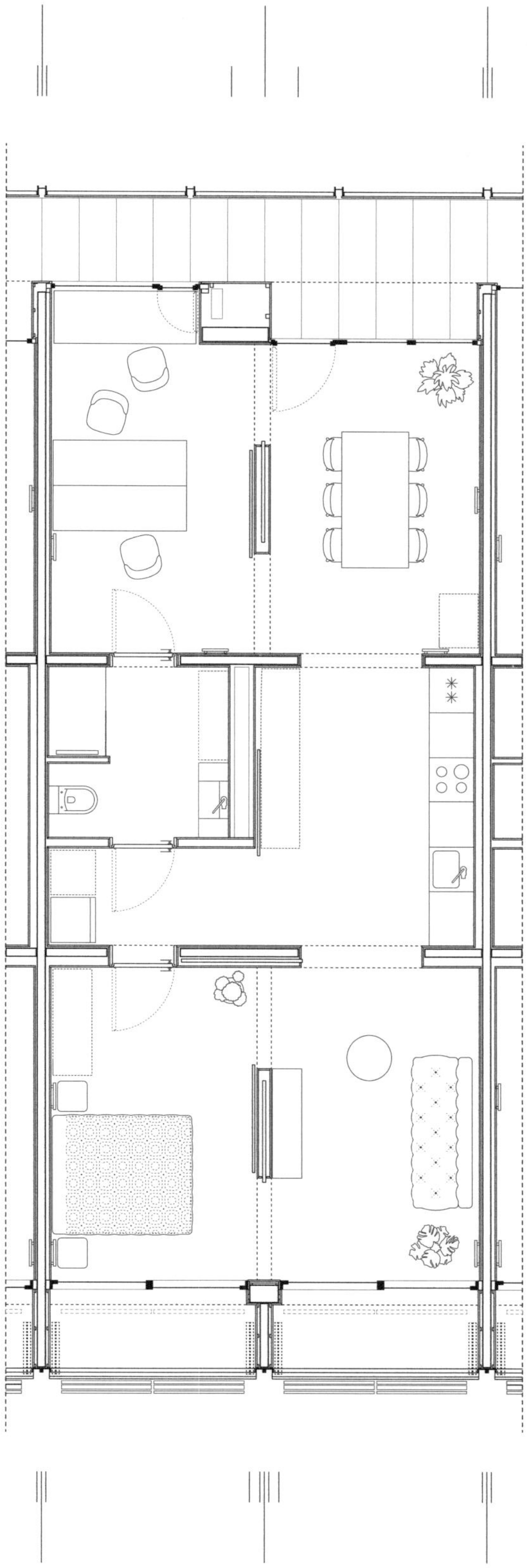

Figure 3
Sample unit layout, drawing scale 1:100

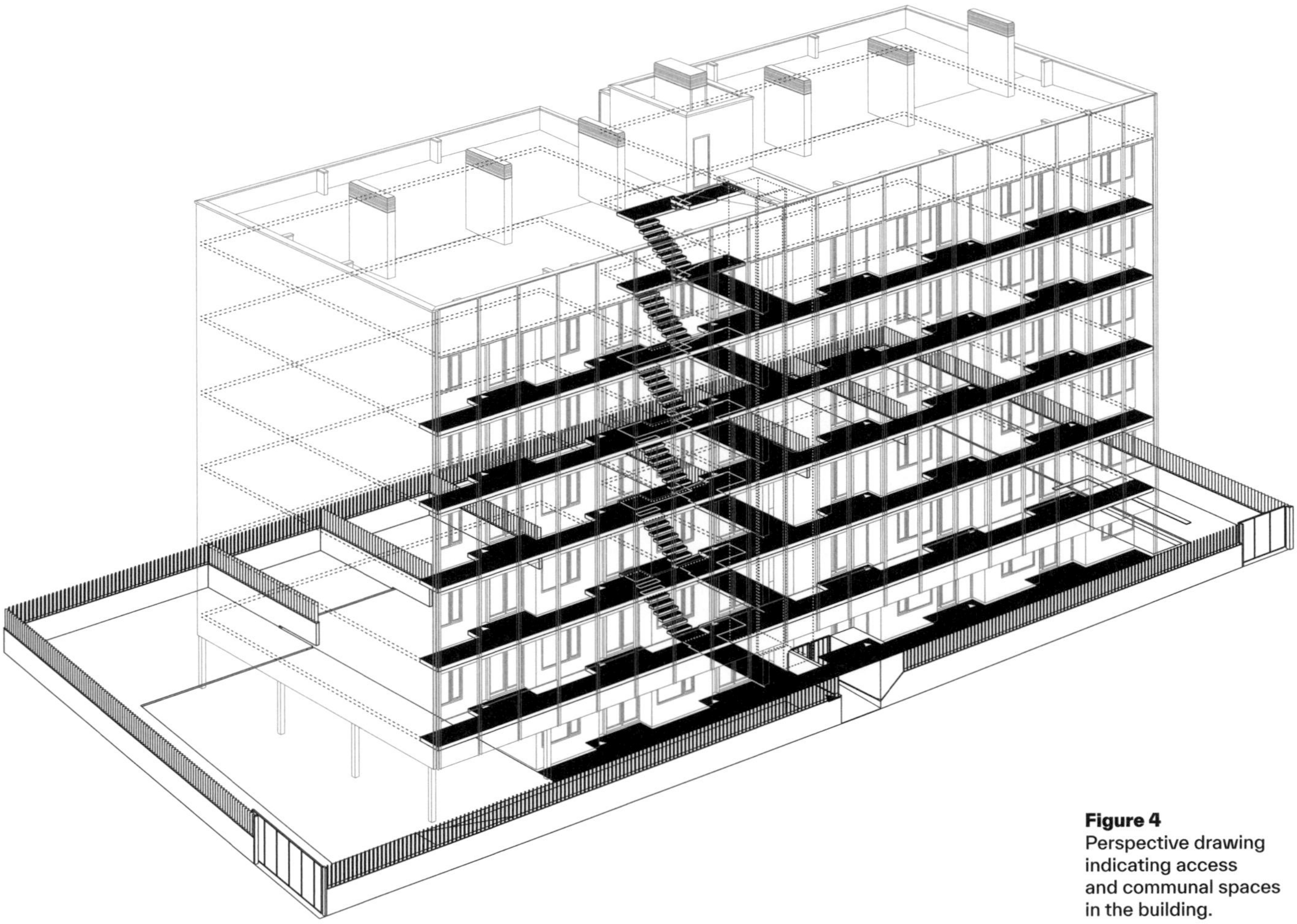

Figure 4
Perspective drawing indicating access and communal spaces in the building.

DS Concrete is introduced as a floor finish in this project. What is its role?

RB Even if it appears contradictory for a project utilizing a dry construction system, we decided to introduce a 7-centimeter-thick layer of concrete cast over the timber slab to add weight and thermal mass to the building. It adds fire protection and acoustic insulation that timber does not have. Its weight stiffens the building's structure. Its mass is also essential for thermodynamics. Traditionally, in our part of the world, thermal comfort in buildings has relied on thermal mass. In winter, the concrete floor of this building is heated by the sun during the daytime via the sun-catching south facade. The heat is gradually released throughout the evening.

We are currently experimenting with clay on a much smaller scale and finding it less resistant and more challenging to work with. Separately, we are working on another multiunit residential project in Barcelona, where we can apply some of the lessons learned from the 6×6 Block. For example, we have found a way to expose the underside of the timber slabs. We are looking for ways to avoid adding layers of material to the timber construction, reducing the construction cost and time.

DS What design decisions were most impactful in lowering the construction cost of this project?

RB A simple answer would be modularity, but the building industry has evolved beyond that. It is not only about repetition and standardization but also about finding the easiest way to achieve goals and solutions specific to each project. This project was about making one standardized unit to be built cost-effectively but used flexibly to accommodate diverse housing needs. To achieve this goal, we came up with a design to be manufactured by local enterprises, which is probably the main contributor to the lower construction cost. All the companies involved in the construction of the buildings are based within a 60-kilometer radius. It allowed us to visit workshops and factories and work closely with manufacturers. As I mentioned, the trees are cut, and panels are produced just a bit further away, in the Basque country.

DS Dwellings units are highly adaptable. As your drawings show, units can accommodate families of different sizes and structures. Their layout allows change in how the space is used without undertaking construction or retrofitting. Can you clarify if there is a link between spatial adaptability and housing affordability in this project?

RB The minimum width of a single room in multiunit residential buildings is 280 centimeters, by the standards in Catalonia. Units in this project have two pairs of well-connected rooms of those dimensions. If you go by minimal standards, it is two rooms, but residents can also decide to use the two rooms as one larger space. Each room has at least three doors to allow more connectivity. Moreover, all electrical installations are done so rooms can be used differently. The supply lines are not inside the walls but in conduits attached to the walls. By making units adaptable, we have managed to use the space more efficiently, achieve a high number of units, and make the best use of the building's frontage.

DS You have recently won a competition to design a building with 50 social housing units in Girona. Will you be applying the same design principles in that project?

RB You could say that the 6×6 Block is a generic building. We are building on that knowledge in our current projects. I am unsure if the social housing project in Girona will go ahead, even though we have won the competition and the building construction company has been appointed. It would have been an excellent opportunity to continue what we started with the 6×6 Block, to evolve this project in both the plan and section, and to include more communal facilities. However, we are using a similar timber construction method for a social housing project in Barcelona that I mentioned, which is nearing completion.

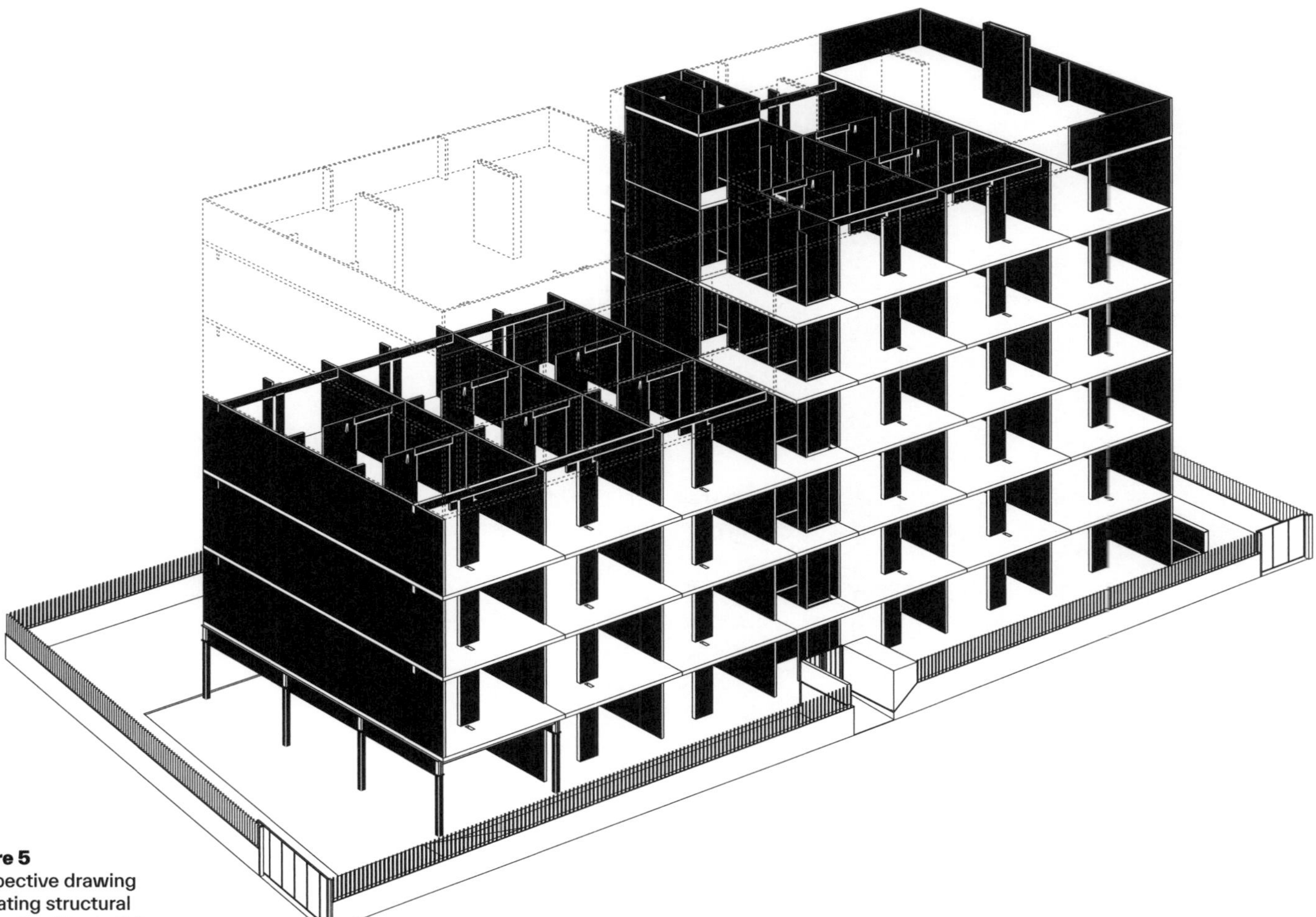

Figure 5
Perspective drawing indicating structural elements of the building.

In conversation

The following section, an edited interview with one of the residents, was recorded on July 23, 2023. They live on the ground floor with their family.

DS How would you describe the building and its built context?

MS This building differs from other buildings in the same area. It is not typical, and people are aware of it in a positive way. When I give someone, such as taxi drivers or the parents of my children's friends, the address and call it a timber building, they often tell me they know the building. Our area is not exactly an affluent residential neighborhood. It is located on the southern fringe of Girona, close to Salt, one of the most vulnerable municipalities in Catalonia, with large housing estates built fifty or sixty years ago, some as social housing. In my view, this building adds architectural quality, which has improved the neighborhood's amenity by changing its perception. It has attracted people with diverse purchasing power to move there. I understand that most residents in our building have relocated from regional Catalonia, and many are young couples. But the group is diverse, and residents are of all generations.

DS What do you think of the design decision to use glass panels to separate private dwellings from access galleries?

MS I don't feel the intimacy is compromised as people pass in front of each other's dwellings, even though we have floor-to-ceiling windows facing access galleries. Some residents use curtains, and we do the same in the evenings. During the daytime, I prefer to have the view out. For example, I can see kids playing in front of our entrance door from my kitchen.

DS Is there a sense of community among residents, and do you feel the building design has contributed to it?

MS Compared to other multiunit buildings where I lived, this one creates more possibilities for encounters between residents. We meet spontaneously when entering or exiting our units. I feel the sense of community has been made very quickly among inhabitants. Perhaps the building design, with an environmental focus, has created a common ground. I was one of the first to purchase the unit. I got to know other residents as they were moving into their dwellings. We created a WhatsApp group first, and then someone initiated the "Beers & Neighbors" gathering, which now takes place every Wednesday evening in the outdoor area on the ground floor by the east end of the building. There is a tree and a large table where people gather. Not everyone joins these meetings, but they are very popular with residents. More recently, residents have formed another group interested in establishing a communal productive garden. I have to say I've never been to these meetings because of my work schedule, but my mother, who lives in a unit next to ours, regularly attends these meetings. My mother is retired, and she has more time. It is great to see her extending her social network and establishing friendships with other residents.

Figure 6
Perspective drawing of the building envelope.

DS Like all other units in the building, your unit has two outdoor spaces. One is in front of your unit on the north side, and the other is at the back on the south. How do you use them?

MS Our dwelling is on the ground floor, and compared to residents living on other floors, we have additional space in front of our entrance, between the walkway and fence separating the building from the street. We keep large pots with bay leaf plants there, giving us more protection from the street, which is relatively quiet anyway. There is a pedestrian path and a wide green area in front of the building, not the street. We also have a back garden, which is one of the main reasons I chose this unit. If I have guests or my children's friends over, we use the front garden, which is almost 3 meters wide. During the summer, in the mornings, when there is shade on that side of the building, I can sometimes hear a couple from level one having breakfast on their terrace. Many residents keep coffee tables and chairs on the access gallery, but the upper levels have less intimacy than we do on the ground level, as they can be seen from the park. The south facade is more private for all units, as is our back garden on that side. I like having my coffee or dinner there, and my children spend a lot of time playing outdoors. One of them is into gymnastics, so we have some equipment there. I do the gardening, and we have a composter. Access to private outdoor space is one of the main reasons we moved from Barcelona to Girona, and we are delighted with it.

DS How would you describe thermal comfort, daylight, and ventilation in your dwelling?

MS The back garden gets hot in the summer but is always fine indoors. Rollable shading devices are handy, although they are a bit hard to operate. I require help from my children. The breeze we can create by opening doors on the two facades is beneficial. The average temperature in our apartment is 25 degrees Celsius, and our electricity bill is extremely low. We have plenty of daylight because of those large windows, even though our unit is on the ground floor. Bright colors of walls also help. This is even more pronounced in winter, as we get more direct exposure to the sun from the south. We have a winter garden which warms up and is very comfortable without additional heating throughout the year. I appreciate having the southern winter garden facing the backyard. The sun heats the air with a greenhouse effect. Even if it is freezing outside in winter, I can comfortably sit in a chair and read and write there. We have had no defects since we moved in. Everything in the building is thought through, including the construction methods and the architectural details.

DS You mentioned earlier that your mother lives next door to you. Learning more about the building from the intergenerational perspective would be valuable.

MS The units are small, but the space is just enough because of the layout. The autonomy of each unit is as important as the proximity between them. It allows us to operate as independent households while jointly using the outdoor area in front of the entrances of our units. It's very convenient from a parenting perspective because I can always count on my mother's presence when the kids arrive from school. My other neighbor next door is my mum's age, and I can count on her when my work schedule demands. At the same time, I think they benefit from interaction with children. I am sure there is also a female understanding between us because they always know the right time to appear and detect the moments when we need our privacy.

"When they were smaller, my children shared one room, and we used the space closest to the entrance as a dining area and the room at the back as a living space. But we have changed that to the configuration I have described first. And it is great that the use of the dwelling space could be changed easily so they can have their own rooms."

DS How do you find the layout of your dwelling?

MS Our living room is objectively a bit narrow. Perhaps it is a counterbalance of having multiple bedrooms. My bedroom, which is at the back and separated from the living room by the kitchen, provides an opportunity to enlarge the living space when needed. The children's rooms are one at the back and one at the front. When they were smaller, my children shared one room, and we used the space closest to the entrance as a dining area and the room at the back as a living space. But we have changed that to the configuration I have described first. And it is great that the use of the dwelling space could be changed easily so they can have their own rooms. I think it is essential for children to have their intimacy. They can keep their stuff in their rooms, which, from my point of view, helps keep the dwelling neat. We have only one bathroom, and I prefer it that way. The second bathroom would consume the space. Sliding doors are not entirely soundproof, which is an issue, but I still like that we can connect rooms during the day and separate them in the evening. The soundproofing between units is excellent. It is tricky to place all the furniture in our rooms, as there are multiple doorways, but again, I would not want to close any of them. Although our unit is not very big, it feels spacious because rooms can be connected when the sliding doors open and because of the longitudinal views throughout the interior.

8 Residential Building in Straßgang, Graz

Riegler Riewe Architects

Determined and Undetermined

Figure 1
Site plan, drawing scale 1:2500

Residential Building in Straßgang, Graz

Riegler Riewe Architects

Year of completion: 1994
Number of units: 24

This project was extensively published in architecture periodicals and well-known books providing various overviews of multiunit residential buildings, such as the *Floor Plan Manual*, *Flexible Housing*, and *Housing: New Alternatives, New Systems*.[1-3] It is one of the early works of Riegler Riewe Architects, who have since delivered multiple internationally significant and complex architectural projects. It predates most projects in this book by almost three decades. While housing needs and lifestyles have changed and the design standards and construction methods for multiunit residential buildings have evolved over the last thirty years, this project can be compared to more recent designs by the spatial adaptability embedded in the unit layout, treatment of the building envelope, and attention to affordability as its key driver.

This building is in the southwest metropolitan zone of Graz and part of a large but spontaneously planned residential area between the highway to the west, the railway to the east, and the two streets from which several dead-end roads lead to groups of multiunit

1. Oliver Heckmann and Frederikke Schneider, *Floor Plan Manual Housing* (Basel: Birkhäuser, 2018).
2. Tatjana Schneider and Jeremy Till, *Flexible Housing* (London: Architectural Press, 2007).
3. Manuel Gausa, ed., *Housing: New Alternatives, New Systems* (Barcelona: ACTAR and Birkhäuser, 1998).

buildings. Riegler Riewe Architects, when still an emerging practice, were commissioned for this project by the housing cooperative Eisenbahnersiedlungsgesellschaft based on their competition proposal for another building in which they engaged with cost-efficient housing provision. The building is 80 meters long, only 10 meters wide, and has ground and two floors. It shares an underground car park and outdoor area with another concurrently completed residential structure of similar dimensions, sitting 40 meters away.

Determined and Undetermined

During his lecture at the Melbourne School of Design on March 14, 2023, Roger Riewe presented an architectural approach that mediates between determined and non-determined, applied to various projects, not only housing.[4] The relationship between the two is a reoccurring topic in the practice of Riegler Riewe Architects. In slightly altered forms, it has lent itself to the title of their monograph, *Definite Indefinite*, and a series of lectures, such as "Conditioned Openness" at the Architectural Association.[5,6] In this project, the unit layout includes determined and undetermined elements. Determined elements are wet cores and kitchens placed in the central zone of the building. The undetermined is space on both sides of the central zone, occupying areas by the building facades. The undetermined space is not left void but carefully designed and prepared for residents to assert control. This is achieved by positioning architectural elements such as load-bearing walls, partitions, and different door types so that that space can be used flexibly and rooms can be connected in multiple ways. Other less visible enablers of spatial adaptability in this project include electrical wiring and floor heating. Electrical sockets are positioned to support different room layouts, not a single predetermined one. The omission of wall-mounted piping and heaters adds more freedom in how furniture can be placed and how the space can be utilized. During his lecture, Roger Riewe explained that their insistence on minimizing the determinacy in this project was to enable diverse and changing lifestyles and how it contrasted with the intention of the local municipality, which was keen on the unit layout for nuclear families.

Units

Dwelling units are of three sizes, measuring 46, 75, and 96 square meters. There are six units of the smallest size, fifteen of the medium size, and three of the largest size in the building. Ground, level one, and level two floor plans are identical. A pair of units on each floor is served by the same staircase, apart from units at both buildings' ends, where a staircase serves a single unit per floor. Access spaces are minimal, and elevators are not included.

Half-rooms

There are two variants for units of small and medium sizes. Small units can be either two-room or two-and-a-half-room configurations, and medium-sized dwellings are four- or four-and-a-half rooms.[7] The difference between dwelling variants of the same size is in the kitchen position, which enables variable use of the half-room area measuring 7.4 square meters. By building standards, space of that size does not constitute a habitable room. Still, as it will be discussed, its availability and usage have a significant impact on the overall spatial organization of a dwelling.

One way of using half-rooms is proposed by the architects, and the other by the municipality.[8] In the dwelling variants proposed by architects, kitchens were placed between rooms in the central zone of the building. Such centrally positioned kitchens give more choices. In smaller units, residents can choose to have a living room on either side of the building. In larger units, it allows more flexibility in how rooms adjacent to the living room can be used. The half-room can be utilized as an extension of the living area but also as a kid's room, a guest room, or a study, which is why variants incorporating a centrally positioned kitchen are referred to as a two-and-a-half or four-and-a-half configuration. However, as the local municipality preferred a more conventional solution, where the half-room area by the facade is utilized as a kitchen, the outcome was a compromise. The project includes an equal split between the number of dwellings with kitchens in the central zone and dwellings with kitchens by the facade. The presented segment of the typical floor, drawn at a 1:250 scale, plan shows both options. The typical floor plan, drawn at a 1:500 scale, shows the distribution of units, including the three largest, created by the union of the two dwellings of small size, positioned at the south end of the building. They have six rooms and kitchens in the central zone, which creates a choice between a large living room or a smaller living room and an additional bedroom.

It may be helpful to draw a quick parallel with another well-known but unbuilt project for residential buildings in Ceuta by ACTAR architects produced around the same time the building in Straßgang was completed.[9] That project introduced the ABC Design System using prefabricated elements for the storage, bathroom, and kitchen of a dwelling. The role of these three elements, which would be positioned in the unit according to residents' preferences in Ceuta, is similar to the role of determined elements in Straßgang. The resemblance between the two

4. Roger Riewe, "Determined / non-determined," guest lecture, Melbourne School of Design, September 8, 2021, https://msd.unimelb.edu.au/events/determined-non-determined.
5. Florian Riegler and Roger Riewe, *Definite Indefinite* (New York: Springer. 2001).
6. Roger Riewe, "Conditioned Openness," guest lecture, AA School of Architecture, London, November 29, 1995, https://www.youtube.com/watch?v=P6lUQETfxpl.
7. RieglerRiewe, "Wohnbebauung Graz-Strassgang," accessed May 29, 2023, https://rieglerriewe.co.at/de/projekte/stadt-und-wohnen/114-wohnbebauung-graz-strassgang.
8. Riewe, "Determined / non-determined."
9. Actar Arquitectura, "ABC Housing in Ceuta," in Manuel Gausa, ed., *Housing: New Alternatives, New Systems.*

projects is not only in elements' purposes but in their potential to enable spatial adaptability or support non-determined space, as Riegler Riewe Architects have put it.

Doors

This project utilizes four different door types in the unit layout: sliding, folding, and two sizes of pivoting doors. These specific door types are employed strategically to create links between rooms and are essential to accommodating change and different ways of using the generic layout. For instance, sliding doors positioned perpendicular to the building facade enable half-rooms to operate as extensions of larger rooms. Floor-to-ceiling folding doors, set in the central zone and parallel to the facade, have a different role. They allow residents to divide space into rooms or use it as an open plan configuration. Even when open, they serve as dividers between different activity zones within an open plan layout. Pivoting doors are placed at the entrance to the unit and in bedrooms to establish clear boundaries between the private dwelling and communal access and clear thresholds between individual rooms and spaces used by the entire household. All rooms have at least two doors, increasing the connectivity between spaces within the dwelling. All units are entered via a small lobby. From there, one can access the half room or proceed to other rooms using the other door.

Envelope

The differentiation between structural elements and the nonstructural facade is another important characteristic of this architectural project. The load-bearing elements in this building are concrete walls and vertical cores. Structural walls are perpendicular to the facade, positioned 3 and 4 meters apart, and serve as partitions between rooms and units. There are five vertical cores in the building and no corridors or access galleries. As a result, the building is a composite of five smaller buildings, each composed of identical units and minimal access space. However, this is not obvious on the building's facade, which transpires as a monolith form. The nonstructural facade is made of prefabricated concrete elements. All windows are floor-to-ceiling, with either double or single panels pivoting 180 degrees inward. These large openings enhance the relationship between the interior and exterior and help offset the omission of conventional private outdoor spaces. Sliding sunscreens, installed in front of the windows, can move to either side.

In most photos of the building exterior, screen panels are not aligned, as they are operated independently by residents. They add a dynamic layer to the facade otherwise defined by a repetitive pattern of openings. Besides supporting privacy and providing sun protection, they are essential for the architectural expression of the building. Like sliding and folding doors in the dwelling interior, sunscreens are designed and standardized by architects for this project. Galvanized steel rails, attached to concrete panels, are also part of the architectural expression. The sliding screens in the east facade are made of perforated steel mesh, while the west facade's panels are made of nylon fabric.

Affordability

One of the critical requirements in the project's brief was to reduce the construction cost by approximately one-fifth of the budget used for multiunit residential buildings at the time. During his lecture, Roger Riewe explained that such a requirement was a novelty, and not many architects were attracted by such a brief.[10] In a short interview related to the Austrian exhibition at the Venice Architecture Biennale in 2008, "Residential Building as Motivation," Florian Riegler and Roger Riewe discussed architects' role in improving housing affordability and suggested that the challenge could be met only with innovation across multiple aspects. They suggested that minimally dimensioned dwellings are not an answer to improving affordability, as there are many more facets to that question.[11] Changing tendencies and housing demands, which contribute to the increasing diversity of collective living forms and include vulnerable and elderly residents, are some of the topics they brought forward. That conversation is relevant to understanding how this project's architectural design ideas and innovation in unit layout and utilization of building materials have contributed to housing affordability along with introducing the spatial flexibility needed to accommodate such changing forms of housing.

In addition to the previously discussed unit layout and the embedded spatial adaptability, the way the units are accessed in this project is also an important contributor to the lower construction cost and better space utilization. Access to units directly from the vertical core, such as in this project, is less common in today's low-rise multiunit residential buildings. Access galleries and corridors are often preferred. However, the ratio between access and dwelling floor area may be more efficient when horizontal access spaces, such as corridors and galleries, are omitted. Building fewer galleries may offset the cost of multiple staircases and therefore help to lower development costs. Another advantage of core over gallery access to dually oriented units is that communal areas compromise neither of the dwelling's prospects.

10. Riewe, "Determined / non-determined."
11. Florian Riegler and Roger Riewe, "Residential Building as Motivation," interview with Werner Sewing, Raum Film, accessed March 5, 2023, https://a-clip.de/riegler_riewe/.

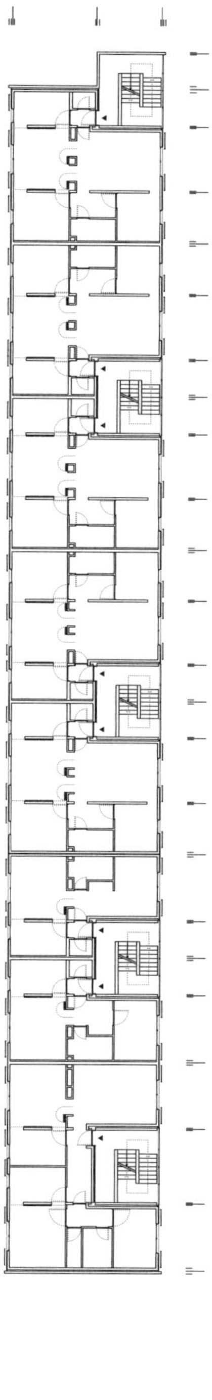

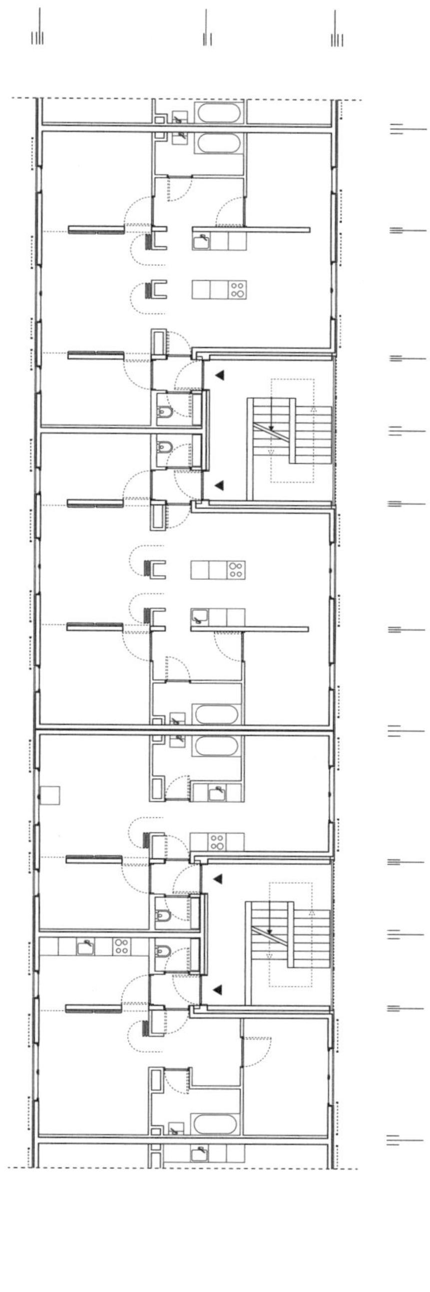

Figure 2
Typical floor plan, drawing scale 1:500

Figure 3
Segment of the typical floor plan, drawing scale 1:250

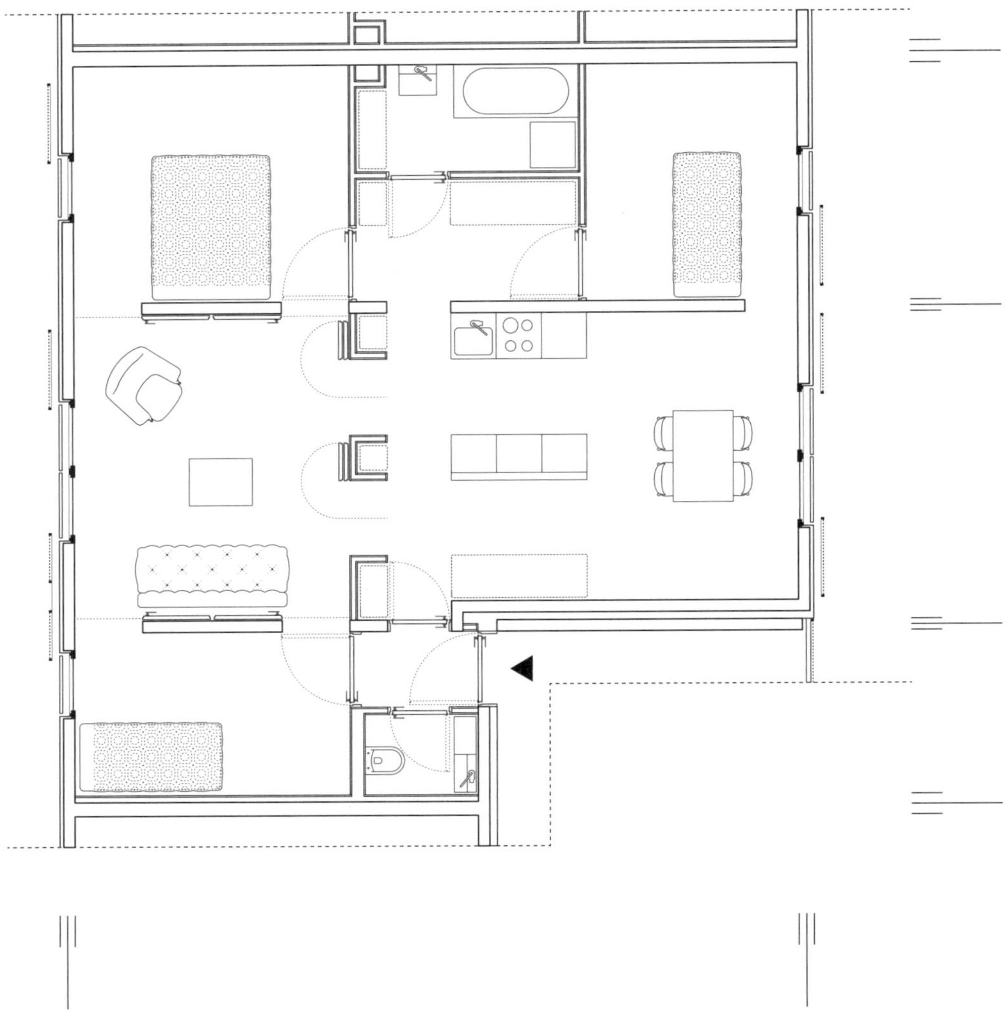

Figure 4
Sample unit layout, drawing scale 1:100

In conversation

The following section, an edited interview with Roger Riewe, recorded on April 18, 2023, provides further information about the project from the architect's perspective.

DS The project had a limited budget, which you managed with design decisions. Units are modest in size, access spaces are minimal, and the building has no shared facilities. How did you address the relationship between individual and communal in the project?

RR We wanted to create a condition where outdoor space around the building is used collectively. Children were the first to embrace the idea by playing behind the building, where we designed a hard-surface plateau and a landscaped area as part of the space shared with an adjacent residential building. With the project's physical context and budget constraints, we didn't see the value of introducing private gardens, as they would always be observed from the windows of dwellings on floors one and two. The same applies to those units on upper levels; they, too, do not have a private outdoor environment. Instead, we have communal outdoor space in this project.

DS Ground-floor units' windows face the communal outdoor areas behind the building and a street in front. Still, you make them floor-to-ceiling windows, consistent with the openings on the upper floors. Was there a privacy concern?

RR I believe you could say so. We had reports of curious architects visiting the building and inspecting the sliding shutters while residents had their morning coffee. Apart from that, it is true that units on the ground floor are more exposed. However, we avoided using fences of any kind in the project. We wanted people to interact in the space formed by the two new buildings. The landscaped area at the back was meant to be a buffer. In the front, where we have the street or vehicular access to the adjacent development, we have used permeable pavers and vegetation to establish a 2-meter-wide zone separating the building from the pathway, which is the primary access to the building.

DS Can you tell if the character and use of the outdoor areas have changed over time?

RR Funny enough, shrubs that were planted there in a certain grid according to our landscape plan were moved around and closer to the building by residents. Over time, some Christmas trees have been added, and shrubs have grown tall. It is all very green now. Residents from ground-floor units appropriated a narrow hard surface strip adjacent to the building from the very start. Without owning that space, they started by putting their chairs and sun umbrellas there. Now, they are treating large parts of the landscaped area as their backyards.

DS The project aims to accommodate spatial adaptability with an innovative unit layout. Can you explain what the residents' role during the design process was?

RR Rooms are loosely defined in the unit layout. Some rooms have three doors. That creates openness and the possibility to use the space in different ways. We wanted residents to decide how to live and not insist on predetermined housing typologies. During the design process, we had meetings with people allocated to live there. But these meetings sometimes went differently than we expected. Some residents asked for doors removed; luckily, we did not have to do that. The layout we proposed was flexible enough to meet the diverse needs, including nuclear families, as demanded by the municipality.

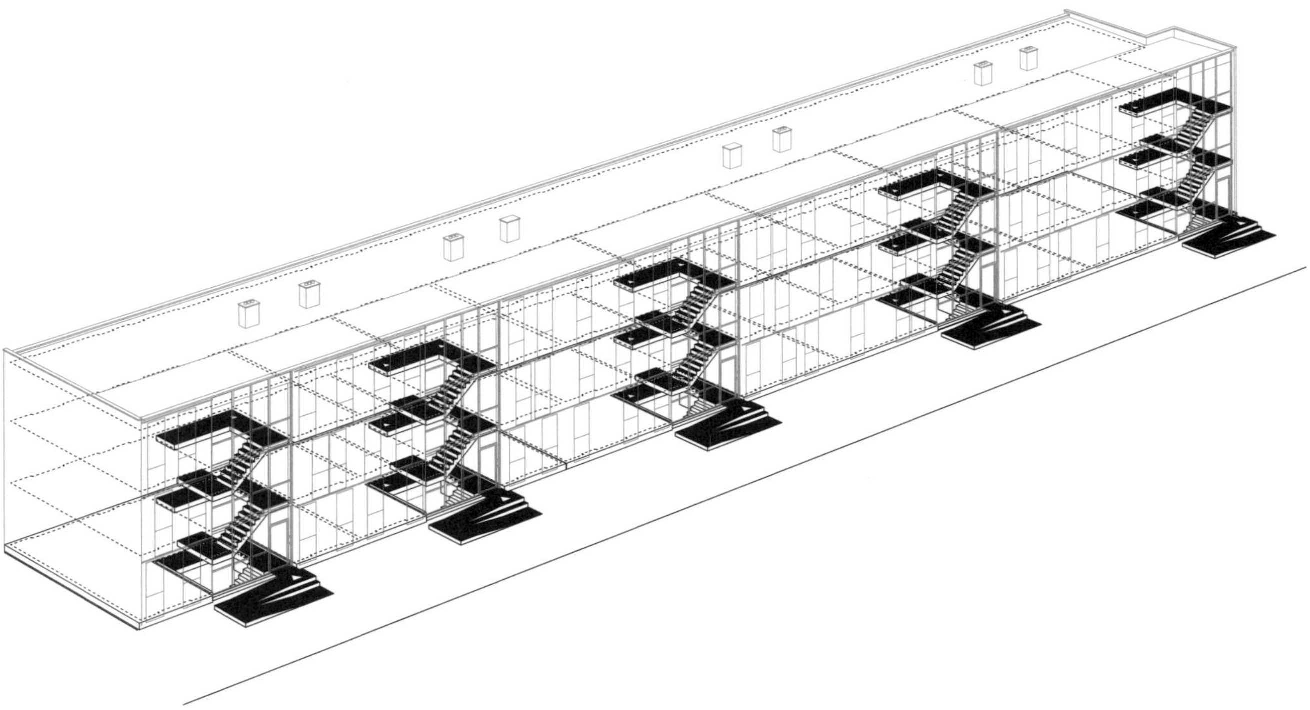

Figure 5
Perspective drawing indicating access and communal spaces in the building.

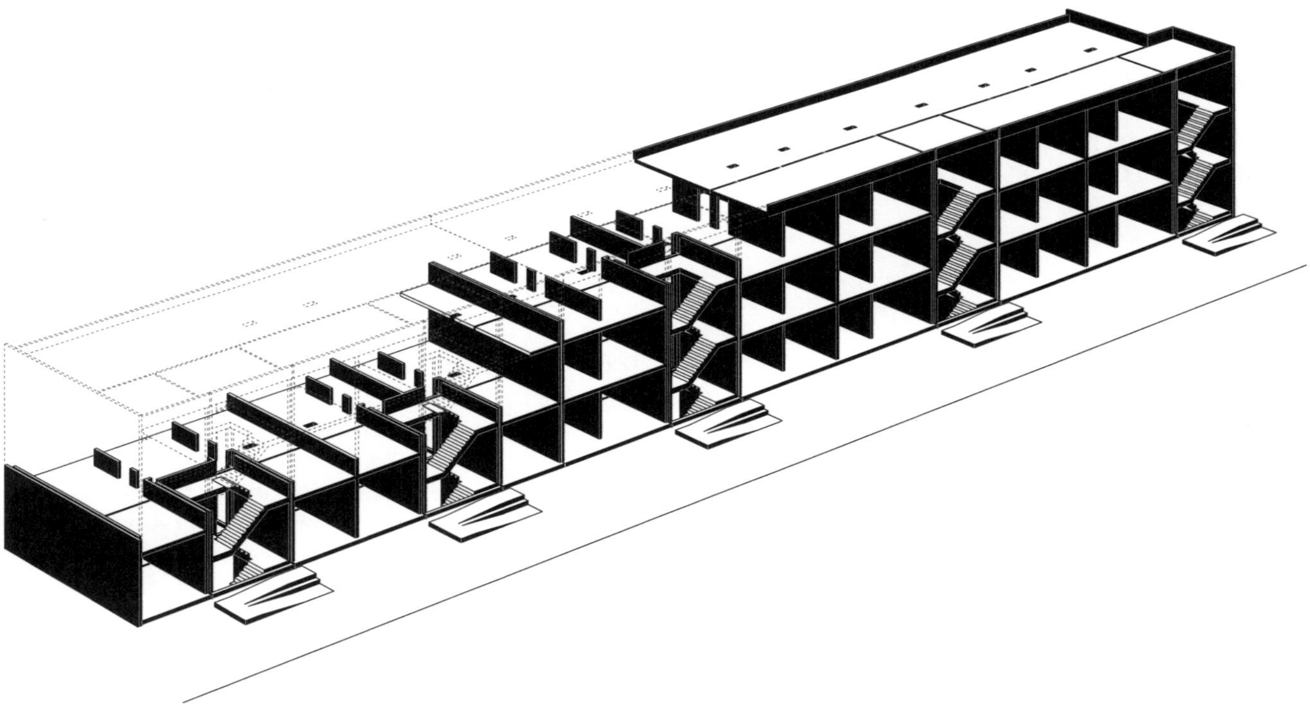

Figure 6
Perspective drawing indicating structural elements of the building.

DS Were you interested in what happens after residents move in?

RR Yes, very much so. Our second book, *Definite Indefinite*, showed photos of dwelling interiors after a few years had passed since the residents moved in.[12] It was almost like a survey. We wanted to show how the space is inhabited, and we wanted to do it with photos capturing domesticity. I remember meeting with book editors Nikolaus Kuhnert of *ARCH+* and Ernst Hubeli of the Swiss architectural magazine *werk, bauen + wohnen* and discussing presenting an architectural project with photos portraying everyday life. It was not very usual then, but I believe it is much more common today. The photos were taken by Bas Princen, now a widely acclaimed photographer of architecture and urban landscapes. He was a contributor to GAM, *Graz Architecture Magazine*, published by the Faculty of Architecture of Graz University of Technology, where I was the editor. We met at Berlage Institute, where I was teaching.

DS How do you understand the relationship between the resident community and the architectural project?

RR Ideally, they are one. For example, one of Graz's most desirable residential projects, Terrassenhaussiedlung, designed by Werkgruppe Graz, was developed as social housing.[13] But at the time, there were concerns that the project was unfit because of its size, choice of building materials, access spaces, and how open spaces are structured. Ultimately, it was deemed unviable for social housing, and the developer ended up putting it on the market. People who eventually moved in showed appreciation for what architecture had to offer. They wanted to live there and formed tight communities. That contributed to the project's longevity and made sense of an architectural project.

DS It appears that you may not be an advocate for participative design processes, and yet enabling residents to take control over domestic spaces appears essential to you.

RR We wanted to avoid creating dwellings based on individual preferences, which could prohibit flexibility and, therefore, would be restrictive to other occupants in the future. One of the projects that significantly influenced me while I was still studying was La MéMé student housing by Belgian architect Lucien Kroll.[14] The architectural project was developed after extensive consultations with students, enabling them to make decisions about the building layout and facade. Individual preferences have resulted in many unusual dwellings, including very tall or narrow spaces. The idea was that units would be reconfigured when new tenants arrived. The project included a large span structure, movable partitions, standardized and replaceable parts of the building facade, and arrangement of building services that would enable the change. But it never happened. These very specific units remain the same to date, and what happens is that new tenants apply for dwellings based on their characteristics.

12. Riegler and Riewe, *Definite Indefinite*.
13. The Werkgruppe Graz (Eugen Gross, Friedrich Gross-Rannsbach, Werner Hollomey, and Hermann Pichler) designed the terraced housing estate in Graz-Sankt Peter built between 1972 and 1978.
14. La MéMé student housing at the Catholic University of Louvain, by Belgian architect Lucien Kroll, was built between 1970 and 1972.

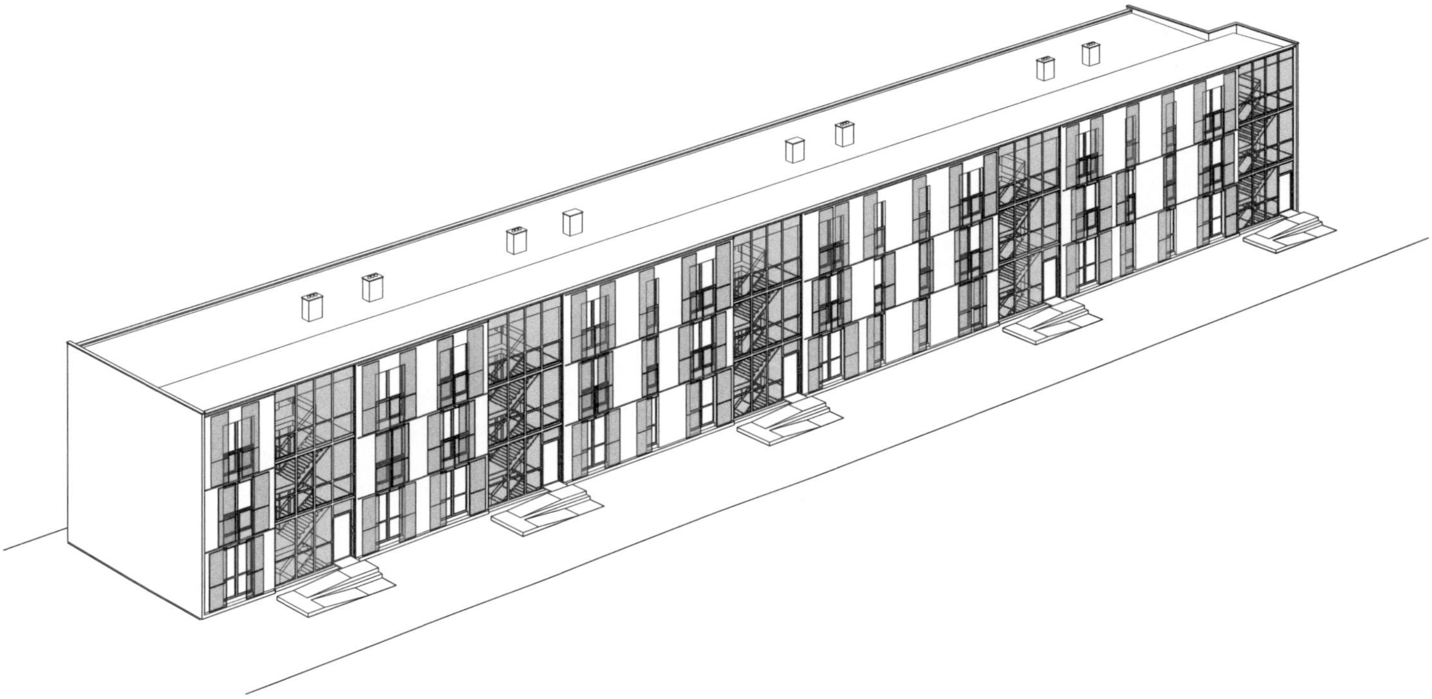

Figure 7
Perspective drawing of the building envelope.

DS This project is for subsidized housing. It usually implies tight construction budgets. Can you clarify what design decisions contributed to the lower-cost construction?

RR The earlier project we did for an architectural competition, which we did not win, served as the basis for the project in Straßgang. We had already developed ideas on how to lower construction costs through that competition entry. It included core access typology, omitting elevators, making partitions structural, and making the most of standardization. We used as little building material as possible. To minimize the use of concrete, we introduced only small spans. To do that, we made all partitions structural. The savings are substantial. With spans of 6 meters, the slab thickness is 24 centimeters. But if the spans are 4 meters, the slab is 19 centimeters thick. Across the 80-meter-long building, it is a significant savings. The unit layout repeats, allowing the reuse of formwork throughout the building. The facade is made of precast concrete sandwich panels. The wall thickness is only 22.5 centimeters. It saved space, although that would not be possible today, as standards have changed. We standardized everything we could in the building. There are only two or three panel sizes for the entire building. There are only two window types. All sunscreens are the same dimensions. At the same time, we managed to balance all that repetition with design decisions. If you look at the building's facade, it is not that repetitive.

"Rooms are loosely defined in the unit layout. Some rooms have three doors. That creates openness and the possibility to use the space in different ways. We wanted residents to decide how to live and not insist on predetermined housing typologies."

DS During your lecture at the Melbourne School of Design, you mentioned that the building was initially intended for rental tenure, but some residents are now owner-occupiers. Could you please explain how this came about and how it contributes to making housing more affordable?

RR The project was developed by a housing cooperative with support from the local municipality. Tenants were not owners and were paying rent, but that rent was deducted from the property value. After ten years, tenants were offered to buy the units where they lived, which some have done. It is done through a form of hire purchase agreement. In the process, tenants have saved some money as the cost of added value tax is less for rent than for the purchase.

9

Social Housing in Granadero Baigorria, Rosario

BBOA – Balparda Brunel Oficina de Arquitectura

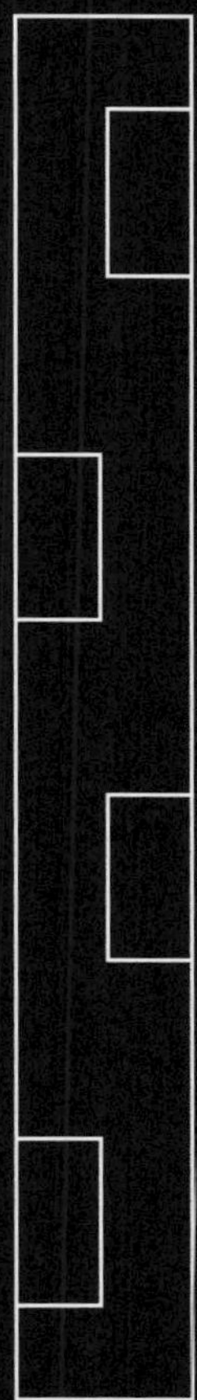

Between Buildings

Figure 1
Site plan, drawing scale 1:2500

Social Housing in Granadero Baigorria, Rosario

BBOA – Balparda Brunel Oficina de Arquitectura

Year of completion: 2015
Number of units: 147

The design outcomes, including the fenestration of the buildings' facades, the structuring of a sizable residential development into smaller spatial segments, and the architectural treatment of access spaces are achieved against the stringent budget, restrictive planning standards, and a conservative design brief.

Background

This project is in Granadero Baigorria, a small town near Rosario in Argentina. It was a part of the large-scale program started by the government to improve the supply of affordable housing across the country.[1] The program aimed to utilize land owned by various state agencies and engage with the construction industry in building new dwellings and the financial sector in securing favorable long-term loans to help

1. The Programa de Crédito Argentino del Bicentenario (PRO.CRE.AR) was started in 2012 and discontinued in 2018.

first-time home buyers. The government identified close to 100 sites, provided preliminary design, and invited companies working in the building construction industry to submit expressions of interest to deliver projects with fixed budgets. A procurement route was established for building construction companies to lead projects and employ architects to develop the design based on the preliminary scheme. One such preliminary scheme on the land acquired from the National Railway System was the basis of the agreement with the banks and building contractors and, thus, binding for further design development in this project.

Design Brief

During their lecture hosted by the Melbourne School of Design, Fernando Brunel and Tomás Balparda presented challenges faced by their newly formed practice Balparda Brunel Oficina de Arquitectura, commissioned to work on this project within the outlined setup.[2] They found themselves working with cost-saving restrictions imposed by the construction budget and limitations of the government's schematic design proposal, determining the positioning of buildings, their volumes, access typology, and the number of units and their layout. Their main concerns regarding the proposed scheme were the relationship between the new buildings and the surroundings and the monotonous architectural expression of the project resulting from the reliance on repetition and standardization suggested by the brief as the primary means of reducing construction costs. They felt the concept required change, yet they understood that any improvements to it would have to meet government expectations set for this specific site and be approved by the construction company, which had already committed to completing construction within the specified budget. Design and build contracts are not unusual in the construction industry anywhere in the world, nor is it uncommon that architects must meet standards and deal with budget constraints in their line of work. In this project, dealing with the described limitations was met by design innovation across extents not explicitly covered by early cost plans. The following paragraphs will discuss the project according to three topics and scales: spaces between buildings, spaces between dwellings, and, finally, dwellings themselves. Several less-defined extents of the project brief turned into design opportunities will be observed in relation to each of the three topics.

Between Buildings

The project is for an approximately 30-meter-wide and 240-meter-long lot sitting parallel to operating rail tracks. The surrounding fabric has a suburban character, with low-rise built fabric composed of individual homes and a regular grid of streets interrupted by the rail line. The development comprised seven multi-unit residential buildings with retail spaces on the ground floor, two on-site car parking zones, and landscaped areas. Three higher structures of seven floors mark the two ends and the middle of the elongated site. Two almost identical pairs of lower buildings are positioned between them. The presented floor plans and perspectives show one of the lower buildings to enable comparison by size with other projects included in this book.

The lower buildings are more than 60 meters long and 8 meters wide. They are positioned in pairs to form two communal outdoor areas. Bounded by buildings and wire mesh fences along the two shorter edges, these spaces are only 10 meters wide. They are accessible exclusively to residents and include only basic amenities and landscape areas. Buildings are dually oriented for better daylighting and ventilation of dwellings. The two buildings constituting a pair are of different heights. The taller one has three floors and twenty-four units, and the lower one has two floors and eighteen units. Rather than having a single point of access, these elongated buildings are subdivided into four clusters of units accessed from the same stairwell and with their own entry from the street.

Between Dwellings

The subdivision of the long buildings into smaller entities is the first of the design decisions that went against the grain of the initial scheme. The initial cost plan was based on access galleries and a single entry point to the buildings.[3] The proposed amendment and the shift from the gallery to core access typology provided multiple entrances to the building. Eight, rather than two, entrances have created a better interface between the building and the street. It has contributed to the activation of spaces between the buildings.

Furthermore, a large community of residents living in the two buildings with forty-two units with a jointly owned outdoor area was subdivided into smaller communities structured around the shared stairwells. These stairwells are spacious, filled with light and air, architecturally sculpted, and visible from the street. Architects had to ensure this design maneuver did not generate additional construction costs and did not reduce the number of units specified by the initial brief.

The architects describe these stairwells as empty spaces, equivalent to unbuilt areas between dwellings.[4] The architectural treatment of shared stairwells, including the selection of building materials, is one of an exterior

2. Fernando Brunel and Tomás Balparda, "Social Housing in Granadero Baigorria," research symposium, the Housing Assembly: Creating Socially Valuable Housing, Architecture vs. Housing: Four Case Studies, Melbourne School of Design, November 5, 2021, https://edsc.unimelb.edu.au/studio-epsilon/lecture-repository/bboa.
3. Brunel and Balparda, "Social Housing in Granadero Baigorria."
4. Brunel and Balparda, "Social Housing in Granadero Baigorria."

rather than the interior. These spaces appear as a part of the building, although they remain the outdoor environment. The temperate climate helped omit thermal barriers. The exterior walls and parts of the roof are reduced to galvanized steel mesh held by steel frames attached to the solid walls of the building. Single-flight steel stairs run in different directions to connect floors. However, landings are turned into more extensive areas, providing an addition to dwellings rather than serving for access only.

Between Rooms

Another critical design decision challenging this project's brief while complying with the stringent cost plan was introducing spatial variance and diversity visible in plans, sections, and elevations. The brief and the initial schematic design defined the number of units, demanded a standardization of building elements such as windows and doors, prescribed room dimensions, and suggested an optimal unit layout.4 From the interview with architects presented in the following section, we learn more about the design thinking in responding to the discrepancy in the project brief, which acknowledged the needs of households of different sizes and structures but suggested that a generic two-bedroom layout would be an optimal approach to allow for standardization in building construction.

The design proposition for the lower buildings was based on a catalog of six variants of two-bedroom units. Architects have conceptually divided the generic unit of 64 square meters into two halves, one containing the living area with the kitchen and the other containing two bedrooms and a bathroom. Then they assembled it in six different ways. A simplistic reference to Lego-like building blocks, too frequently used in architecture, may be helpful to illustrate how the two halves, as modules, are stacked one on top of the other and one by the other to form different single or double-floor dwelling configurations. Furthermore, the modules are rotated and differently oriented. As a result of this formal operation, the unit typology met spatial requirements and the necessary degree of standardization. Still, the overall architectural expression benefited from the differentiation, bringing diversity and distinction to a multiunit residential development of significant size. To illustrate, a single window dimension is used throughout the project, but as different unit configurations are interchangeably applied, openings occur irregularly on the building facades. The same applies to larger openings accommodating private outdoor areas. The overall fenestration strategy of this project is central to the perception of the building. The interchangeable arrangement of units of different configurations through simple stacking and rotating also defines spaces between dwellings. In turn, these spaces bind individual dwellings into clusters, sharing access routes and stairwells, as discussed in the previous paragraph.

Dwelling clusters are comprised of six units in the taller building, while the number of units forming a cluster in the lower building varies between three and six. The volumes of dwellings and how they are assembled determine the space between them. In each building, such spaces occur four times and in two different definitions. As previously discussed, they are central to how this multiunit residential development relates to its surroundings and how areas adjacent to buildings are structured. They appear as large openings in the brick wall of the building facades. Together with openings belonging to private dwellings, these gaps contribute to the diversity of the architectural expression of the building, which presents itself as a composite of individual homes and communities.

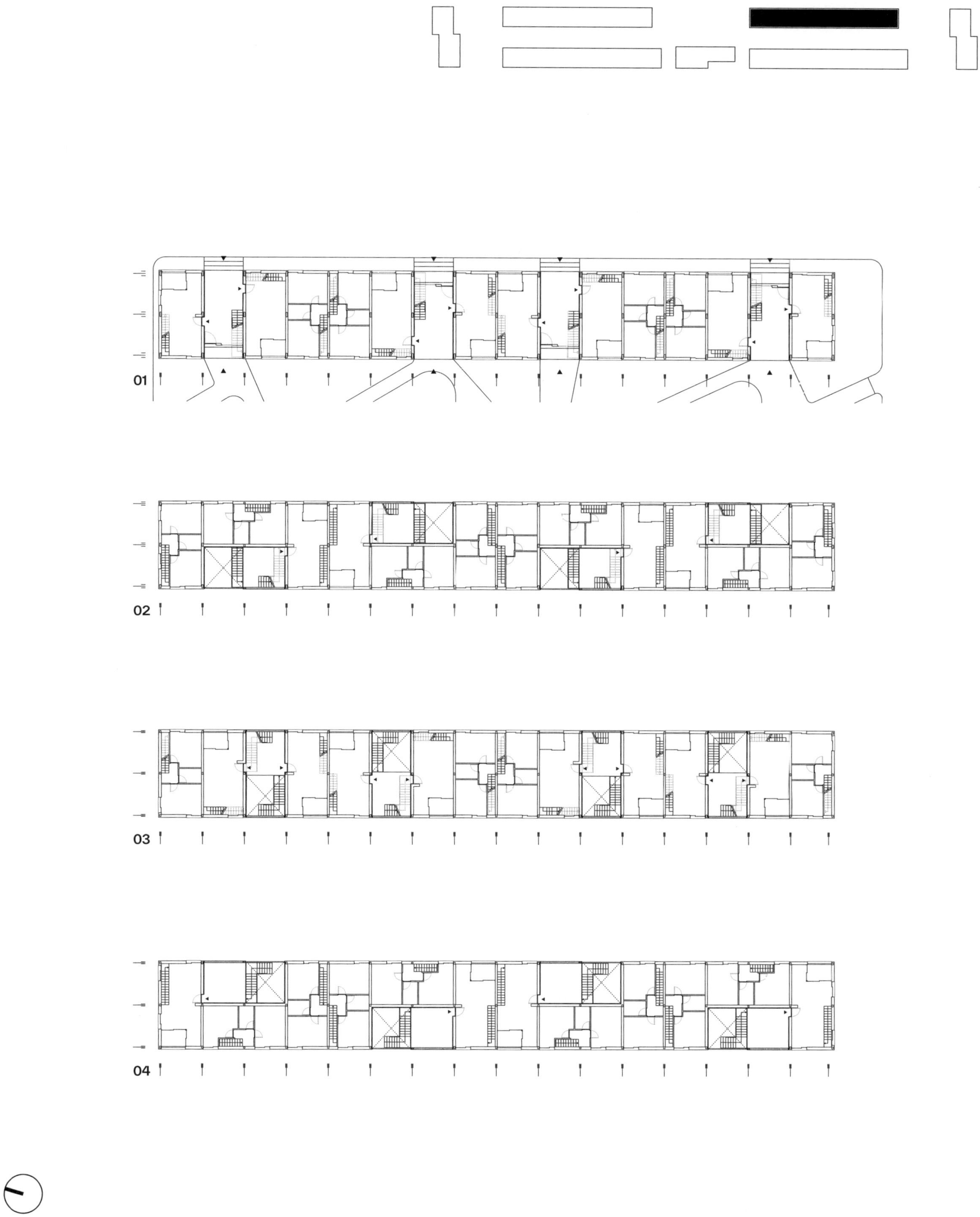

Figure 2
Levels 1–4 floor plans, drawing scale 1:500

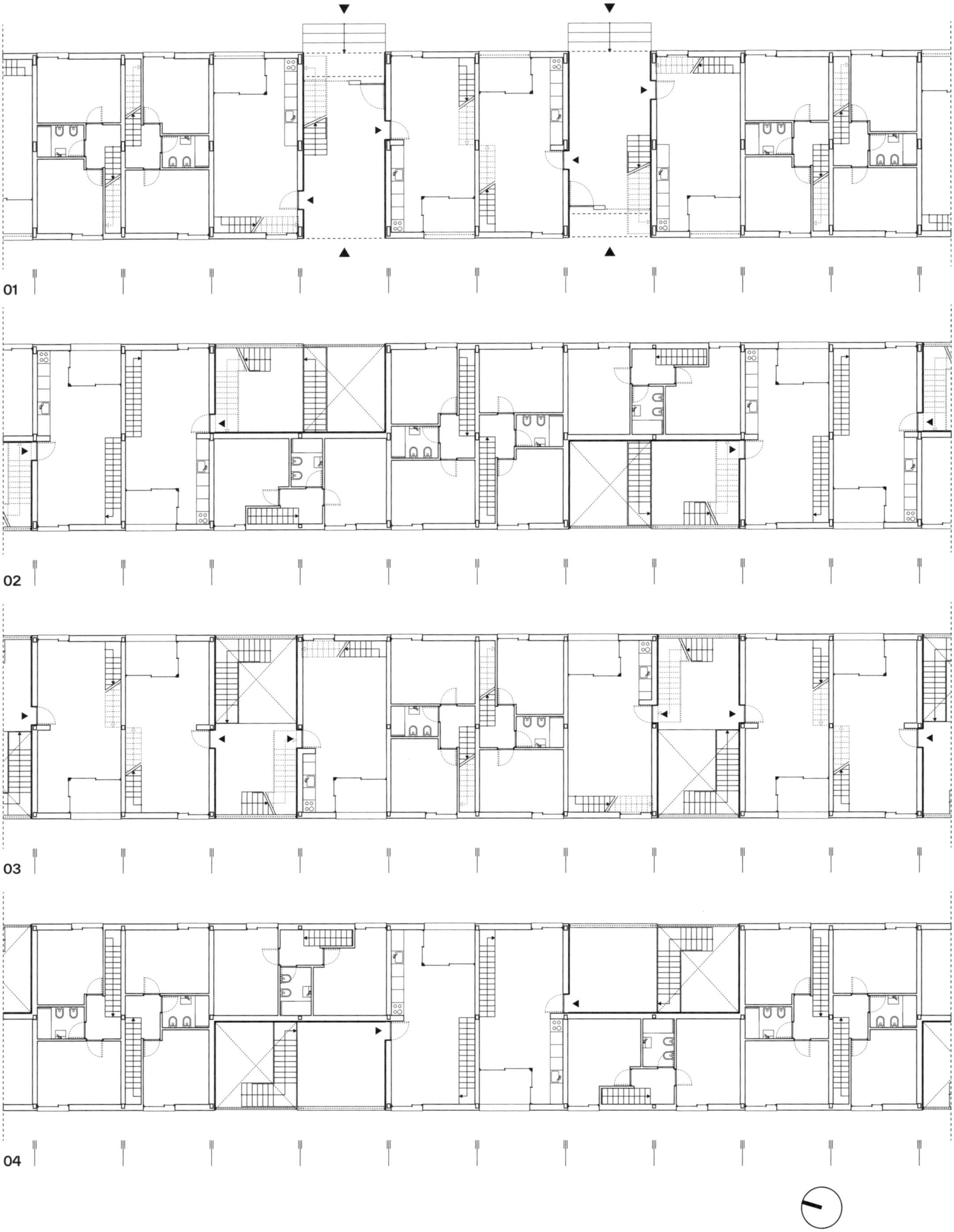

Figure 3
Levels 1–4 floor plans, drawing scale 1:250

In conversation

The following section, an edited interview with Fernando Brunel and Tomás Balparda, recorded on June 23, 2023, provides further information about the project from the architects' perspective.

DS This project was delivered as part of an extensive housing program led by the government. What was the main objective of the program?

FB The program was named PRO.CRE.AR. It was the government's response to the lack of financial mechanisms supporting affordable housing provision. It was an ambitious plan to build a vast number of dwellings over a few years. Unlike in many other countries, for a long time in Argentina, due to economic turmoil, one could not get a loan from the bank to buy a place to live in. As you could not make the borrowing, the only way to buy was if you had the entire amount, which was difficult for most people.

DS How did you get engaged with such a program?

TB We were fortunate that one of the invited construction companies wanted to work with us, even though we did not have much experience then. It is fair to say that the government program and circumstances we have described may not have been an ideal setup from the architect's point of view, but it created an opportunity for us. We participated in competitions for six sites organized in the same program. We won five. Three were built. In the first two, we could not get the way we wanted. It wasn't easy to accept, but it was a learning curve for us. The third one was the project at Granadero Baigorria, for which we were ready, having learned how to maintain the design intent throughout this specific procurement process. To illustrate, we learned what needs to be included in the project documentation at a scale of 1:100 due at a particular stage. By including the right amount of detail, not too much or too little, we could ensure the design intent would not be compromised further down the process.

Across the rail tracks, not far from our project, is another project concurrently completed as part of the same housing program. It was designed and built according to the same budget and brief, with the same dwelling specifications and the positioning of buildings. However, the outcome is very different.

DS Could you describe the procurement route envisaged by the program to establish context for the discussion about the design outcomes?

FB The government did a few things to make the program possible. First, they identified suitable land already belonging to its agencies and bodies, such as the National Rail and the military. Then they created a legal framework and agreed with banks to provide long-term loans to purchase dwellings built as part of the program. The government had to conduct feasibility studies and produce schematic drawings to strike a deal with the banks. They did that internally after they conducted economic analyses to determine the demand and the borrowing power, which gave them an understanding of dwelling sizes and typologies to pursue, in addition to planning constraints for each site. Consequently, these schematic plans became binding documents and the basis for the project cost calculations. They invited construction companies to a competitive tender process. The design was part of it, but the construction cost and assurances that only large companies could provide were put in the first place. Some companies had in-house architects, while others sought to collaborate with established architectural practices.

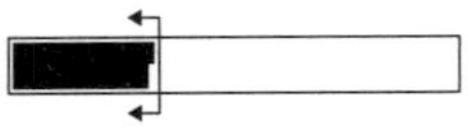

Figure 4
Section, drawing scale 1:100

DS What were the limitations of the brief that you were given?

FB A part of the brief we were given was rhetorical in addressing social issues, the changing family structures, and diversity. At the same time, the drawings, which were also part of the brief, demanded repetition and for all the units to be the same. They specified the unit size and even gave us the dimensions of individual rooms. As all units were to be sold at the same price, there was pressure to make them identical. The brief emphasized the need to create a community among residents and to integrate outdoor areas, but at the same time, it suggested that an 80-meter-long building has one entrance only. We structured our arguments for the introduction of empty spaces to break the building into smaller communities, as we believed that it would help people assume the duty of care for the communal areas associated with a smaller number of units. At the time when we were working on the project, a local newspaper reported on the state of social housing estates in the area. They found an old Fiat Topolino in an unused elevator shaft in one of them. We laughed, but it made us think about the relationship between the residents and the building and what makes people behave in a certain way.

DS What design decisions have helped reduce the construction cost?

TB We worked within the given constraints and had to address multiple issues simultaneously. We wanted to create an identity and a sense of belonging in a project with almost 150 identical units. Yet we were working according to the brief that specified many details. For example, it specified the number of windows that must be the same. We understood the imperative of staying on budget and made all the windows the same. We also made them square, with 1.5-meter sides, to avoid any waste using aluminum profiles produced in 6-meter-long bars. However, we arranged units so their windows do not appear uniformly on the building facade. Similarly, steel staircases in communal access areas are standardized but employed differently. We relied on traditional construction methods and standardized elements without negatively impacting spatial origination or perception of the building. The building has a concrete skeleton, and the walls are masonry. We used locally sourced brick.

DS What opportunities did you identify in the project brief?

TB The brief did not specify areas for circulation. It contradicted a very detailed breakdown of dwelling areas that Fernando just described. It created an opportunity to explore the role of access spaces in the project. The spaces we have created between dwellings, we call them empty spaces. This is not to be confused with a theoretical concept of a void. It is a practical thing, mainly to do the cost calculation. Such space does not feature in a spreadsheet with the schedule of areas. So, that helped construct the argument, but it must be said that our employer, the construction company, was willing to put in extra effort to work with us to improve the initial design scheme. We earned their trust working on previous projects, part of the same program. They were also aware that design improvements would be looked at favorably by the government and would improve their chances of getting the job.

Social Housing in Granadero Baigorria, Rosario

DS During your lecture at the Melbourne School of Design, you emphasized the building as a composite of individual homes rather than impersonal units.[5] You have translated this into a fenestration strategy. In different ways, the relationship between part and whole in large residential developments attracts interest across various research fields. I want to know more about how you see it from the designer's perspective.

FB Some time ago, I saw a Nordic movie that satirically addressed the impersonal character of residential buildings. It starts with a usual boy-meets-girl situation. Then they go to her place. They talk, and they feel hungry. The boy goes out to get a pizza, but on his way back, he cannot find the girl's apartment because it is part of a large social housing building composed of identical units. The entire movie is about them getting together. That's the movie, but, indeed, social housing is often characterized by seamless repetition. When you approach social housing estates in metropolitan areas in Argentina from a distance, you see endless water tanks on the roofs of buildings, all identical. When you get closer, you see the facade and can tell the living room windows from the bathroom windows. It opens a separate issue, not just about an impersonal expression of buildings but of the intimacy, too. Perhaps we don't need to know if someone is taking a shower.

DS Have you explored these topics in any other projects?

TB We have designed a group of seven single-family homes in the Fisherton area of Rosario. These homes are identical but arranged on the given site at different angles to create diverse spaces between them. They appear differently, yet they are the same and still belong to an ensemble of buildings.

"Some time ago, I saw a Nordic movie that satirically addressed the impersonal character of residential buildings. It starts with a usual boy-meets-girl situation. Then they go to her place. They talk, and they feel hungry. The boy goes out to get a pizza, but on his way back, he cannot find the girl's apartment because it is part of a large social housing building composed of identical units. The entire movie is about them getting together. That's the movie, but, indeed, social housing is often characterized by seamless repetition."

DS How would you describe the relationship between interior and exterior spaces in this project?

TB The outdoor area between buildings is closed off and used by residents only. There is a gate at each building entrance; once you pass it, you are in the communal area. Apartments are small, and this secured area is a vital extension where children can play. Now, a few years after residents have moved in, they have created and cultivated smaller gardens within that area. We did not have a significant budget for landscaping, and it was great to see residents starting to care for that space and doing it on their own.

5. Brunel and Balparda, "Social Housing in Granadero Baigorria."

DS Do residents exercise good care for the communal access areas, the empty spaces as you call them?

FB Residents have also appropriated communal access areas. On each floor, there are one or two entrances to dwellings, so there is a slightly different dynamic if this space is used individually or shared between the two units, but it works very well.

DS Do you have any feedback from residents?

TB We didn't take photos when the project was completed. Instead, we did it two years later. When we went there with the photographer, we met some residents curious about what we were doing. We learned from one of them that they are happy. They told us they lived in one of the strange dwellings. They called it odd because the entrance to their unit was from the upper level of their duplex. There are more than a few units where you must climb a flight of stairs to get to their dwelling, even if they are on the ground floor.

FB One of the best compliments we have received for this project is from people who are not architects, telling us that it does not look like social housing.

In conversation

The following section, an edited interview with one of the residents, recorded on July 1, 2023, provides further information about the project.

DS I understand that you worked on the construction of this project before you knew that you would live in the building.

BF I work in the building construction industry and was working on the construction site for this project when I applied for a housing support program started by the government. I met the criteria and was included in the register. I was hoping to get a place in this development, as I was involved with the construction of the buildings. However, the way the system operates is that dwellings are allocated to people on the list. You cannot choose the dwelling or the development, but I was lucky to be given a unit in the development I wanted. I am very happy with my dwelling and the loan terms.

DS What communal spaces do you use in the building, and do you interact with other residents?

BF I moved in shortly after construction was completed, along with most residents. I met the other residents when the bank handed the units over to us. There are three units on our floor, and I regularly meet people living on my floor in the communal access area. We greet each other cordially, but we don't interact. I park my car in the communal car park and meet other people there. Parking spots are not allocated to units. They are shared and used on a first-come, first-serve basis. There are twice as many units as parking spots in the development. Most of us use cars regularly, and it can be tricky sometimes. We also park vehicles on the side of access roads.

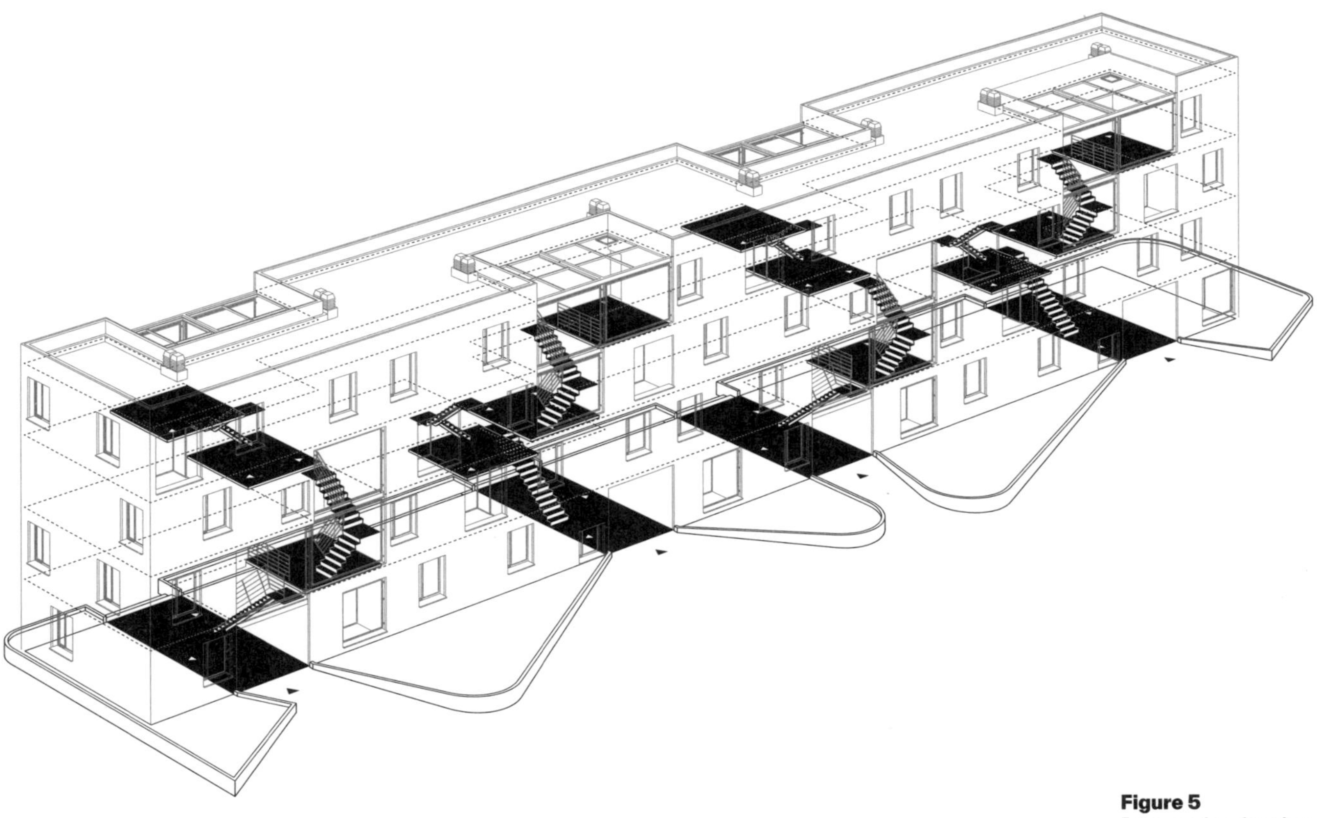

Figure 5
Perspective drawing indicating access and communal spaces.

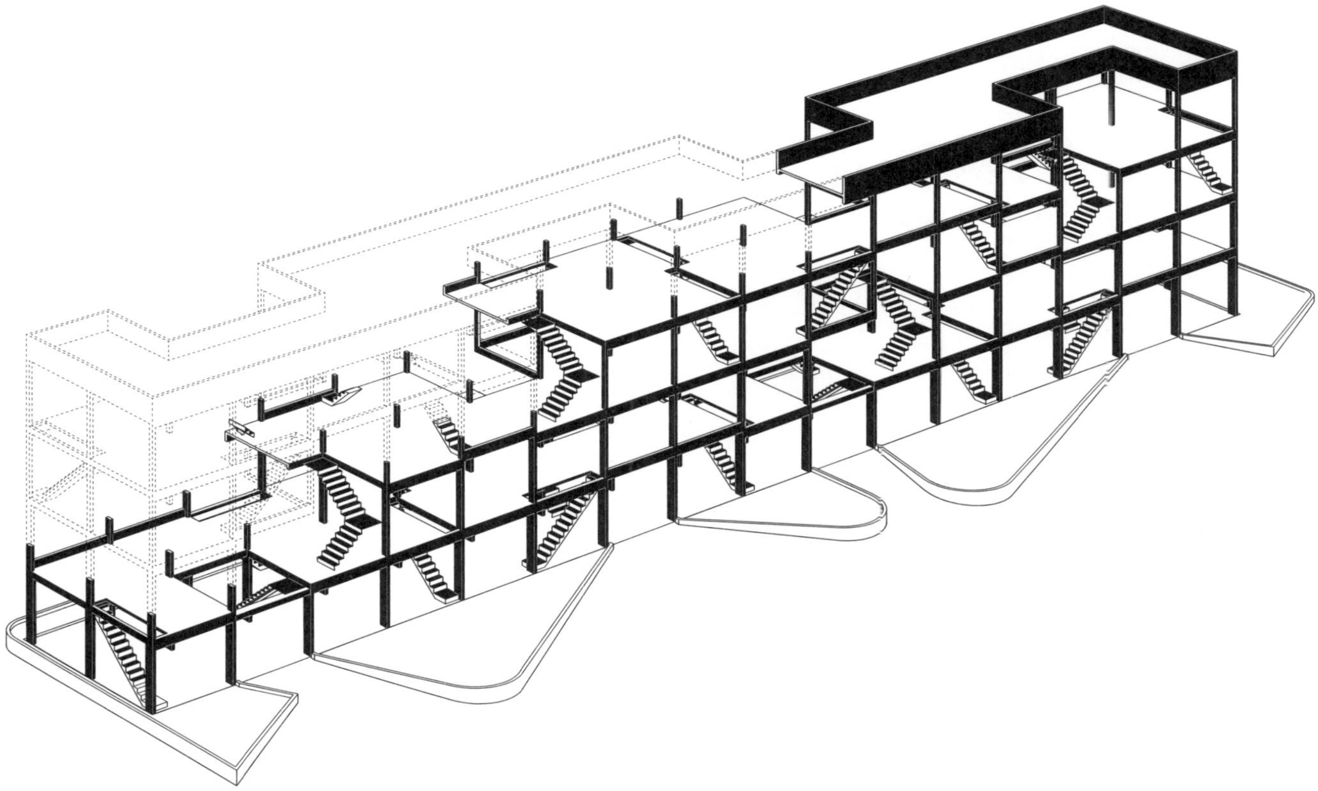

Figure 6
Perspective drawing indicating structural elements of the building.

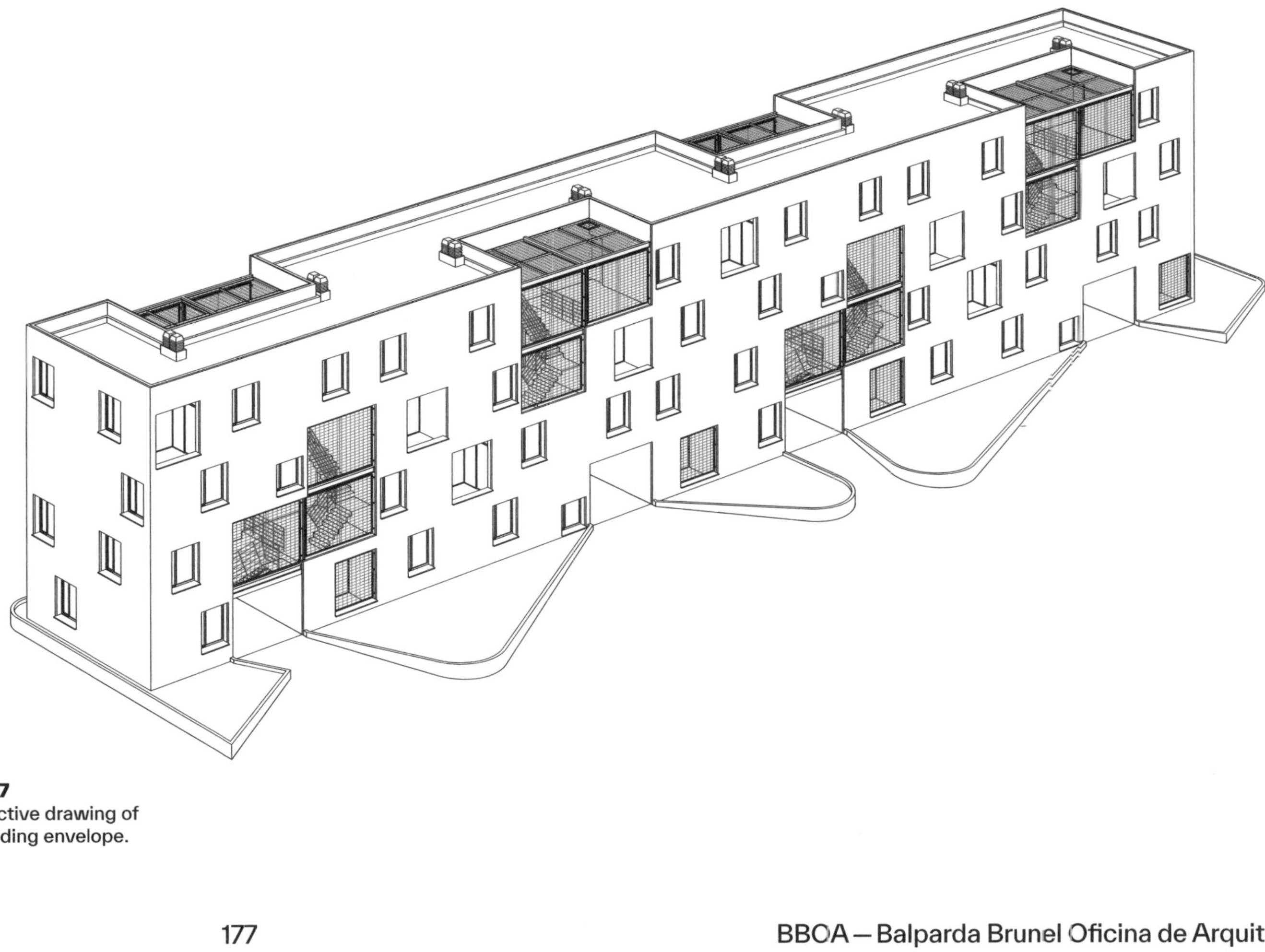

Figure 7
Perspective drawing of the building envelope.

DS Do you use any of the outdoor areas next to your building?

BF I have a colleague from work who lives in the same development, and we meet often. We like to spend time in the green area next to our building, between the road and the rail. This unused lot belongs to the National Railway System, maintained by the local municipality. It is a park with mature trees, lampposts, and gravel paths. The access to it is from the road built as part of the housing development. So hardly anyone can go there unnoticed, and only a few outsiders would come and use it anyway. It feels like residents appropriated it. It is frequently used. Our dwellings are small, and access to such a large open area is excellent. We like to have our tea there on Sundays. This is a local custom.

DS How do you have access to private outdoor areas?

BF I frequently use the private outdoor area in my unit. It is a good size, 2.4 meters wide and 1.8 meters deep. I like the kitchen is next to it. I added timber decking, and we have a small table with chairs. I have also added a rollable sunshade.

"Rail tracks are in operation, and a train passes roughly every hour, even at night. Our unit is facing that way. I am not bothered by the noise, but I know some residents are. I appreciate the view. I have an amateur interest in railways. I had train and track sets when I was a child."

DS How are the natural light and ventilation in your unit, and is it comfortable to live in?

BF We get plenty of daylight from the north. The dwelling was equipped with the basic gas heating devices commonly used in this part of Argentina. Like most residents, we have added air-conditioning devices and mainly use those now for both heating and cooling. I have also added shading devices to my windows, as this was not provided when we moved in.

DS Is there an issue with the noise from the rail?

BF Rail tracks are in operation, and a train passes roughly every hour, even at night. Our unit is facing that way. I am not bothered by the noise, but I know some residents are. I appreciate the view. I have an amateur interest in railways. I had train and track sets when I was a child.

DS Are you happy with the layout of your dwelling, and have you made any changes to it?

BF I live with my partner. The unit is a little small, but we have enough space for the two of us. We find it very functional. I know some residents have not made many changes to finishes and fittings, but we have changed almost everything. We have installed a wood floor over the original ceramic tiles, changed the kitchen fittings, and added built-in closets. We did not consider moving any of the internal walls. Windows are a good size, and I don't think we could change them even if we wanted to.

10 San Riemo, Munich

Summacumfemmer and Büro Juliane Greb

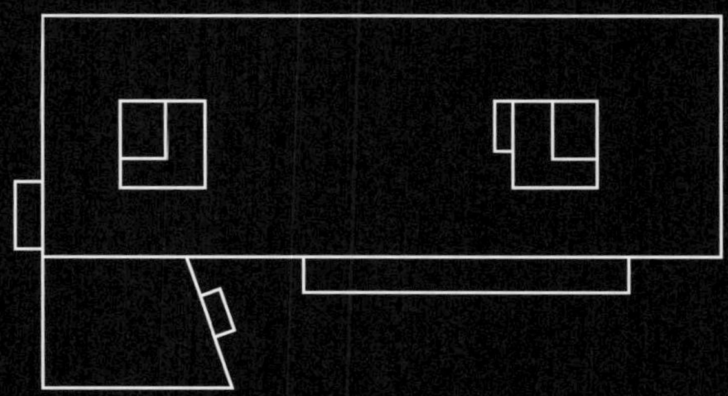

Figure 1
Site plan, drawing scale 1:2500

San Riemo, Munich

Summacumfemmer and Büro Juliane Greb

Year of completion: 2020
Number of units: 27

In this project, spatial adaptability embedded in the building's structure and layout enables dynamic thresholds between private and communal areas and permits dwellings to change size. The design addresses scales of individual households, small groups of adjacent dwellings, and the entire resident community. Central to this project is an expanded understanding of domesticity and residents' engagement in creating and modifying spaces.

Kooperative Großstadt initiated the project through an open architectural competition in 2017. A team combining two architectural offices, Büro Juliane Greb and Summacumfemmer, was selected to develop their competition entry into the project built three years later. The building provides homes for approximately 100 residents and is in a new residential neighborhood located in the metropolitan area of Munich. It occupies a lot measuring approximately 30 by 40 meters at the corner of two streets and forms a street front on the outer edges of the block and a courtyard on the inner side.

Envelope

Polycarbonate panels supported by slender steel profiles attached to concrete slabs cover the entire west facade above the ground floor. This outer layer of that building facade is a cost-efficient solution designed and prototyped by the architects. Behind it, at a 1.5-meter distance, is a thermal barrier, a solid wall with a grid of floor-to-ceiling openings. Between the outer layers and the solid wall is a narrow space that serves as a winter garden. The remaining facades of the building are simpler. They do not have such two layers but have equally industrial character. They are covered in corrugated steel cladding. Long window strips dominate the east facade on the inner side of the block. The carefully designed main entrance to the building, incorporating a doorway, a fire hydrant, and a distinctive triangular window, is on the south facade, facing a wide sidewalk and on-street parking.

Next to the entrance is a large, glazed surface and a colorful brise soleil protecting it from the southern sun.

Communal Spaces

The ground floor is divided into two parts. Along the west facade is a space currently occupied by a nonprofit society for youth welfare. This facility is accessible from the street and operates independently from the residential part of the building. Along the east facade, a 5-meter-wide space, paved with similar stone tiles as the sidewalk surrounding the building, is a communal area belonging to residents. This communal area is connected to the courtyard by a wall composed of large glass doors. It includes a shared laundry. A small workshop and a communal kitchen are also on the ground floor. A productive garden is on the building's roof. These amenities are accessible to the entire resident community.

Levels above the ground floor contain several smaller communal spaces used jointly by groups of residents from adjacent units. These spaces serve as access routes but also double as extensions of individual dwellings. Floor plans produced at early design stages show that the built structure harbors the potential to create more shared spaces throughout the building, enabling households to negotiate and develop symbiotic relationships by sharing space.[1,2] The complex nature of joint domestic spaces will be unpacked gradually in the following paragraphs, addressing several interrelated aspects of this project.

Spatial Adaptability

The building has a concrete skeleton structure. Vertical loads are met by columns concealed in facade walls and cores positioned in the central zone of the buildings, including two containing elevators and stairs and four wet cores. The central zone of the building is also reserved for kitchens, while rooms are positioned along the two facades. The structural grid has three equal spans across the width of the main building volume. Decent-sized concrete beams are employed to avoid columns in the interior of the building. The routing of building services, including heating and electrical, is accordingly planned. Double, instead of single doors, are often employed, and partition walls are omitted whenever possible to create openness in the unit layout and spaciousness, which is rarely associated with affordable housing.

The previously outlined structural scheme allows for more choices in connecting individual rooms. In turn, it gives more flexibility in planning unit layouts in response to individual needs and lifestyles. As presented floor plan drawings show, a dwelling can be composed of up to ten rooms. The building provides a range of unit sizes and types, including those for group living and nuclear families with shared spaces, allowing work-form options. There are four units on the first level, seven on the second, six on the third, and five more on each of the last two.

There are very few circulation-only spaces, such as corridors, in the building. Conceptually, the building may be understood as a composite of rooms of roughly the same size. The achieved floor area of 14 square meters per room exceeds the minimal spatial standards and allows the same room to be furnished and used in multiple ways.

Growing and Shrinking Dwellings

The project envisages a form of tenure and provides a spatial framework allowing a change of size for some dwellings in the building. A room can be added or subtracted from a unit. To illustrate this, during her lecture at the Melbourne School of Design on August 17, 2022, Anne Femmer described how one of the rooms was swapped between the two adjacent units one year after residents moved in.[3] The right-of-use for the room was exchanged between a household of four and a couple living next to each other. In the process, that room initially used as a bedroom became a living room. The couple also turned their former living room into a workspace in the process. The spatial flexibility requirement was an important part of the project brief developed by the housing cooperative, which sought to create ways to "grow and shrink dwellings" with as little technical effort as possible and within a tight budget.[4]

1. Summacumfemmer, "San Riemo," accessed August 8, 2023, https://www.summacumfemmer.com/sanriemo_027.html.
2. Büro Juliane Greb, "San Riemo," accessed August 8, 2023, https://julianegreb.com/.
3. Anne Femmer, "non-finito," guest lecture, Melbourne School of Design, August 17, 2022, https://edsc.unimelb.edu.au/studio-epsilon/lecture-repository/summacumfemmer.
4. Florian Fischer, "Summacumfemmer, Büro Juliane Greb, San Riemo," *Divisare*, accessed March 22, 2023, https://divisare.com/projects/445152-summacumfemmer-buro-juliane-greb-san-riemo.

Joint Domestic Spaces

It is essential to clarify the distinction between communal spaces, such as a large multifunctional room on the ground floor accessible to all residents, and smaller spaces used jointly by groups of residents and serving as an extension of their units, such as additional living room space, workplace, or guest room. On levels two, three, and four of this building, space equal to three rooms and to four rooms on level five is allocated for joint use. The project offers possibilities for other rooms to be used in rotation by different households. However, it is left to residents to negotiate and initiate spatial modifications. Related practical and social benefits, as well as challenges, will be discussed with architects and one of the residents in the following segments of this chapter.

Access

One of the critical design decisions in this project was to utilize jointly occupied rooms for access to individual units. It means that some residents must go through them to get to their dwellings. However, this decision improved floor area usage and contributed to lowering development costs by eliminating the need for access-only spaces. A building of this size and number of units would usually have one more vertical core with stairs and elevators or dedicated horizontal access in the form of corridors or galleries.

Moreover, almost by the rule, individual dwellings are entered via kitchens occupying the central zone of the building. One arrives at the kitchen from vertical cores or jointly used areas and, from there, has access to other rooms. Kitchens serve as entrance lobbies and spaces toward which household members gravitate, as it is where most movement trajectories intersect. However, their roles differ according to the nature of the unit they belong to. For the group living units on the first floor, the kitchen area acts as a binding space connecting individual rooms. On the second floor, kitchens serve as intermediate spaces between private bedrooms and shared living rooms. In most dwellings on floors three and above, kitchens are part of the open plan layout and integrated with private living areas and workplaces. As they are placed away from the building facade, the kitchen premises have less favorable daylighting. The priority is given to rooms in this regard. This is offset by kitchens with living rooms or workspaces with double doors to introduce daylight from two sides and enable cross ventilation.

Non-finito

During a public lecture hosted by the Melbourne School of Design, Anne Femmer presented that the building was designed as a uniform structure to meet diverse requirements and to enable spatial adaptability.[5] She describes their architectural approach as "non-finito," signifying a deliberate and conscious effort to make the project unfinished and allow residents to modify the building. Such an intent is fundamentally different from designing a finite number of unit types. It is about providing a system that complies with building regulations and standards and yet enables residents to engage in the design process and change the size and layout of their dwellings in the future. Like several other projects in this book, San Riemo may have lineage in Herman Hertzberger's work on polyvalence and the inherent potential of buildings to be reinterpreted and used differently, and John Habraken's supports-and-infill concept, whereby the architect's role is in empowering residents to take control over their dwelling space.

The conversations with architects and residents presented in the subsequent part of this chapter provide more information about workshops held throughout the design process. In some of the workshops, residents were provided with printed shell and core floor plans and cutout furniture blocks to explore dwelling layouts and negotiate the use of shared spaces, access rights, and boundaries between individual units. The contribution from the housing cooperative in supporting the collaborative design process and driving the project with innovative and practical ideas was as important to outcomes as the architectural design is.

5. Femmer, "non-finito."

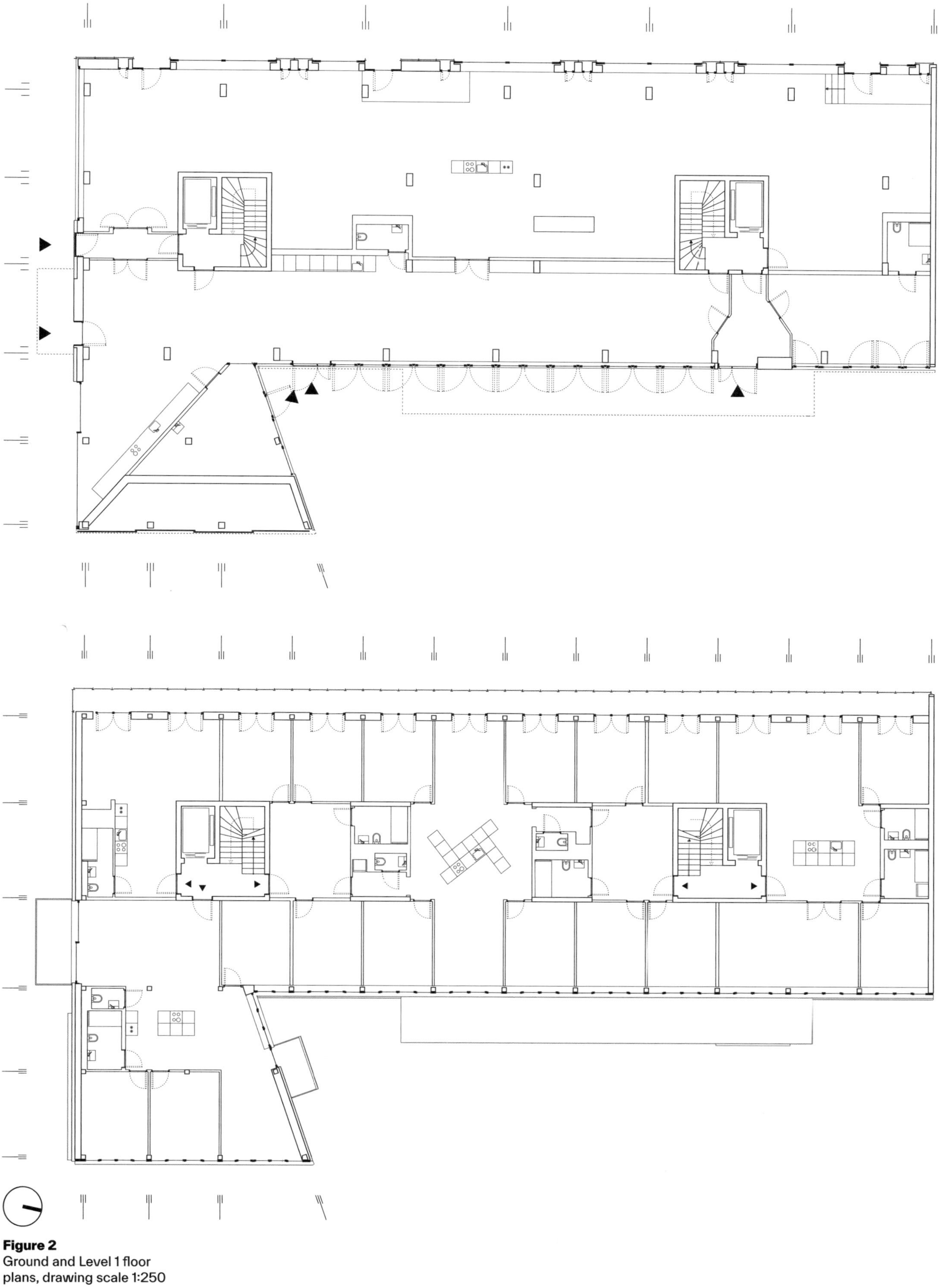

Figure 2
Ground and Level 1 floor plans, drawing scale 1:250

Figure 3
Levels 2 and 3 floor plans, drawing scale 1:250

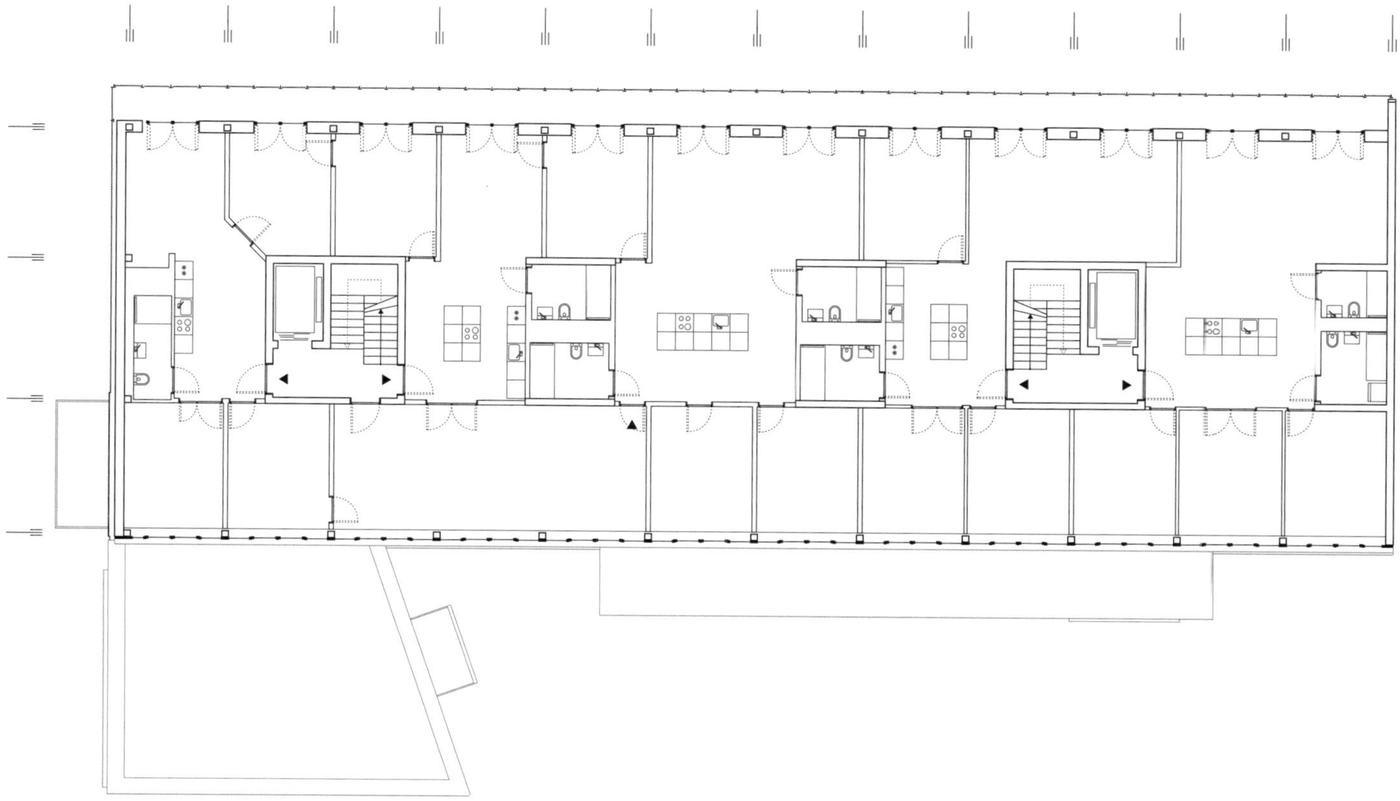

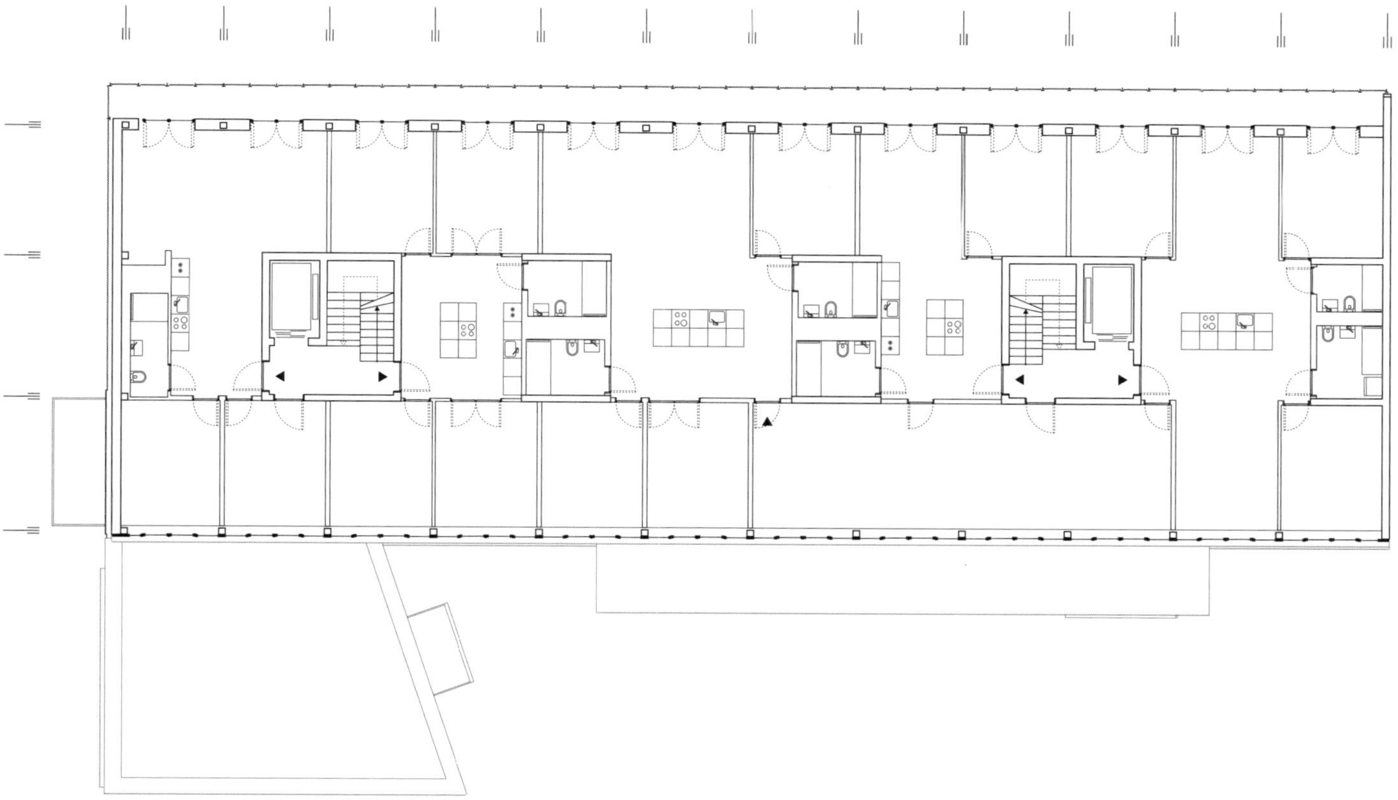

Figure 4
Levels 4 and 5 floor plans,
drawing scale 1:250

In conversation

The following section, the edited interview with Juliane Greb and Petter Krag, recorded on February 8, 2023, provides further information about the project from the architects' perspective.

DS What are the key communal spaces in the building?

JG There are collective spaces across all levels of the building. There is a difference between them, as there are different kinds of collectiveness. A large, shared space on the ground floor serves as an entrance hall and a multifunctional space. That space provides access to two vertical cores of the building. So, you first enter this space that occupies almost half of the building's ground floor on your way to your dwelling. Shared laundry and a small kitchen are part of the communal area on the ground floor. A guest room and a small workshop are on the ground floor, too. The roof garden, another crucial communal area of the building, has the same character. It is accessible to all residents. However, different kinds of collective space can be found on all other building floors where dwelling units are. Dwelling units are closed entities, but borders between them are made fluent so that spaces between dwellings can be shared. For example, three of four units can share an additional living space that is adjacent and physically connected to them. It is important to emphasize that such spatial connections are made explicit in the project.

DS Access spaces, typically associated with multi-unit buildings, are replaced with rooms jointly or alternately used by several adjacent units in your project. Is this decision driven by usage efficiency, that is, the ratio between usable and overall built area, or by the social value of shared spaces in a residential building, or something else?

PK We aimed to use space efficiently and tested multiple layout options. In this project, that did not mean making spaces smaller or as prescribed by housing guidelines but instead giving most spaces more than one use. For example, if you take a corridor of a residential building and make it slightly wider, it is not a corridor anymore. It can be a jointly used space. In San Riemo, some spaces provide access; people can go through them, but they are not corridors.

JG You can say that we have avoided using corridors in San Riemo altogether. You find yourself in the dwelling space when you exit vertical cores. You enter dwellings via the kitchens or spaces jointly used by two or more units. Now, you could say this configuration compromises privacy, but it is also true that it reinforces the possibility of an informal encounter between residents, which is equally important. There are practical values, too. These shared areas are great for childcare. For example, kids from different families can interact in the space between private dwellings or move safely between them.

DS What architectural means did you use to establish boundaries and facilitate a transition between communal and individual spaces in the building?

PK In some dwellings, double doors allow residents to open and connect their private space to space used by residents from several other units. When double doors are open, the boundary between the two rooms is removed, and the personal dwelling space extends into the shared area.

JG It was challenging to comply with building regulations and housing guidelines while maintaining fluent boundaries between individual spaces and shared areas, which also provide access. There were technical and practical things we had to consider. We wanted the double doors to stay open or give residents an option to keep them open. Still, firefighting regulations would not allow that, so we had to introduce an automated system that shuts the doors in case of an emergency.

DS What conventions or standards did you challenge in the project?

JG We have avoided conventional buffer zones in the project. In architectural projects, these spaces are usually introduced to safeguard the privacy of individual dwellings. There are certain stereotypes of what architects want people to see or not see. In San Riemo, you can see washing machines. The communal laundry is a socially relevant place. It does not matter if you see machines or not. You can also see individual dishwashers, as some kitchens are central spaces where people move freely. We do not see this as a disadvantage but a gain. Another unconventional but deliberate design decision concerning the layout of dwellings is that bathrooms, including toilets, are accessed from the kitchen. We have discussed and agreed on this with residents throughout the design process. After proposing it, we have yet to receive an indication that it would be a problem, and we continue receiving positive feedback from residents to date.

Of course, there were discussions about the acoustics and how to minimize any noise impacts arising from the layout we were proposing, and we had to convince everyone that the openness, connectivity, and flexibility could work.

DS Can you explain how you interacted with the residents during the design process and how you incorporated their feedback into the final architectural project?

JG We met with the representatives of the housing cooperative in the second round of the architectural competition and continued communication throughout the process. It was a collaborative process. There were some key meetings along the way. First was when we settled on a grid to facilitate the allocation of individual units, enabling residents to have a say on the position and boundaries of dwellings and their relationship to shared spaces. There were many current residents at that meeting. We discussed different options until one was agreed upon. The second pivotal moment of the participative process was a meeting when we started discussing the layout of the dwellings. Residents had a blank plan of their unit and cutouts of furniture blocks so they could puzzle together a home layout. By positioning drywall partitions, furniture, and doors, inhabitants were deciding to what extent their unit's layout should be open or how it should be connected to the shared space. We, as architects, have prepared a large physical model to help residents better understand the implications of their decisions. We followed up to help some residents with their units' layouts.

DS Can you describe your collaboration with the housing cooperative during the design process?

JG It is essential to say that the Kooperative Großstadt provided important input during the design process, including their views of how they want to live together. We started the project through an architectural competition. The brief, developed by Kooperative Großstad, specified that in addition to conventional (basic) units, a certain number of dwellings would be for shared or group living. They also emphasized the need for spatial adaptability to allow units to change their configuration and grow or shrink over time. We, too, felt that design should not cater to nuclear families only and have tried to extend principles of openness. In our view, housing needs continue to evolve, and the emerging ways of living can benefit from openness and careful consideration of both private and shared spaces jointly used by two or more units.

PK We understand that we can achieve much more if inhabitants are not just the building users but a part of the project. We believe in a definition of architecture that absorbs both the building and the people.

"We have avoided conventional buffer zones in the project. In architectural projects, these spaces are usually introduced to safeguard the privacy of individual dwellings. There are certain stereotypes of what architects want people to see or not see. In San Riemo, you can see washing machines."

DS Can you explain how the indoor and outdoor spaces of the building are related?

JG Almost the entire wall that divides the interior multifunctional space and the exterior courtyard is comprised of floor-to-ceiling windows. A canopy, attached to that facade just above those windows, is also important to the relationship between indoors and outdoors. San Riemo's courtyard merges with the courtyard of the adjacent building belonging to another cooperative. There is no fence, and residents often walk through this space on their way to the train station. The courtyard is paved and sometimes used as a workspace in connection to the workshop on the ground floor. People often repair their bikes there or use that space to assemble shelves and furniture pieces. We think of it as the building's equivalent of a backyard of an individual detached house. Another significant outdoor area belonging to all residents is the productive garden on the roof of the building. It includes a basic outdoor kitchen, which people mostly use in summer.

DS Should we consider the winter gardens attached to dwellings, part of the west facade, as the private or communal outdoor environment?

PK This space is minimal and not designed for gatherings. It is not subdivided by partitions but with potted plants or private items put there by residents. There is a clear sense of ownership and belonging to individual units. It is a space where one is aware of their neighbors.

DS What are the key design decisions concerning the building envelope?

JG We opted for polycarbonate material for the outer layer because it was affordable. It unifies the building facade and the appearance while allowing inhabitants to appropriate the space behind it in the way they like. Behind that first skin is a second one, composed of light wooden frame prefabricated panels with thermal insulation and a simple plaster finish, into which double glass doors are inserted. These floor-to-ceiling doors proved to be a very pragmatic choice that reduced the number of prefabricated modules and allowed deeper penetration of daylight into the interior of the building. The east facade has the same amount of glass, but the openings are horizontal strips, and the outer finish is corrugated metal.

DS What is the relationship between the building and the neighborhood?

JG The building's connection to the street and the public domain is also important. The combination of the wide sidewalks, the sliding window, the canopy, and people bringing out chairs and tables from the communal kitchen in summer activates the neighborhood in the best possible way.

DS How does the relationship between the inside and outside affect the layout of the units?

JG Kitchens and bathrooms, as we have mentioned before, are placed in the central zone, which gives more flexibility in planning the unit layout and spatial adaptability when the building is in use. Bathrooms are the only spaces of the building that depend on mechanical ventilation; all other rooms have direct access to daylight and are naturally ventilated.

DS Can you explain how the project incorporates spatial adaptability?

JG All rooms have roughly the same dimensions. Their large size means they can be used as living rooms, bedrooms, dining rooms, and home offices. The architectural project is neutral in that sense, and inhabitants can decide if they prefer to have their bedrooms along the east or west facade, have a large open living room, or split it with a home office. Our take on spatial adaptability is based on a nonhierarchical plan that can be reprogrammed.

DS What are the advantages of a nonhierarchical floor plan and the steps needed to implement it effectively?

JG A nonhierarchical layout, where all rooms are the same, allows a space to be switched or exchanged between units, effectively enabling dwellings to grow and shrink. This concept is supported by the building's structure and the strategic positioning of double doors. But other aspects are worth noting, too. For example, electrical installations are channeled inside prefabricated concrete beams to ease layout changes and positioning of drywall. For the same reason, the heating system has only vertical supply lines, and at least one heater is in every room.

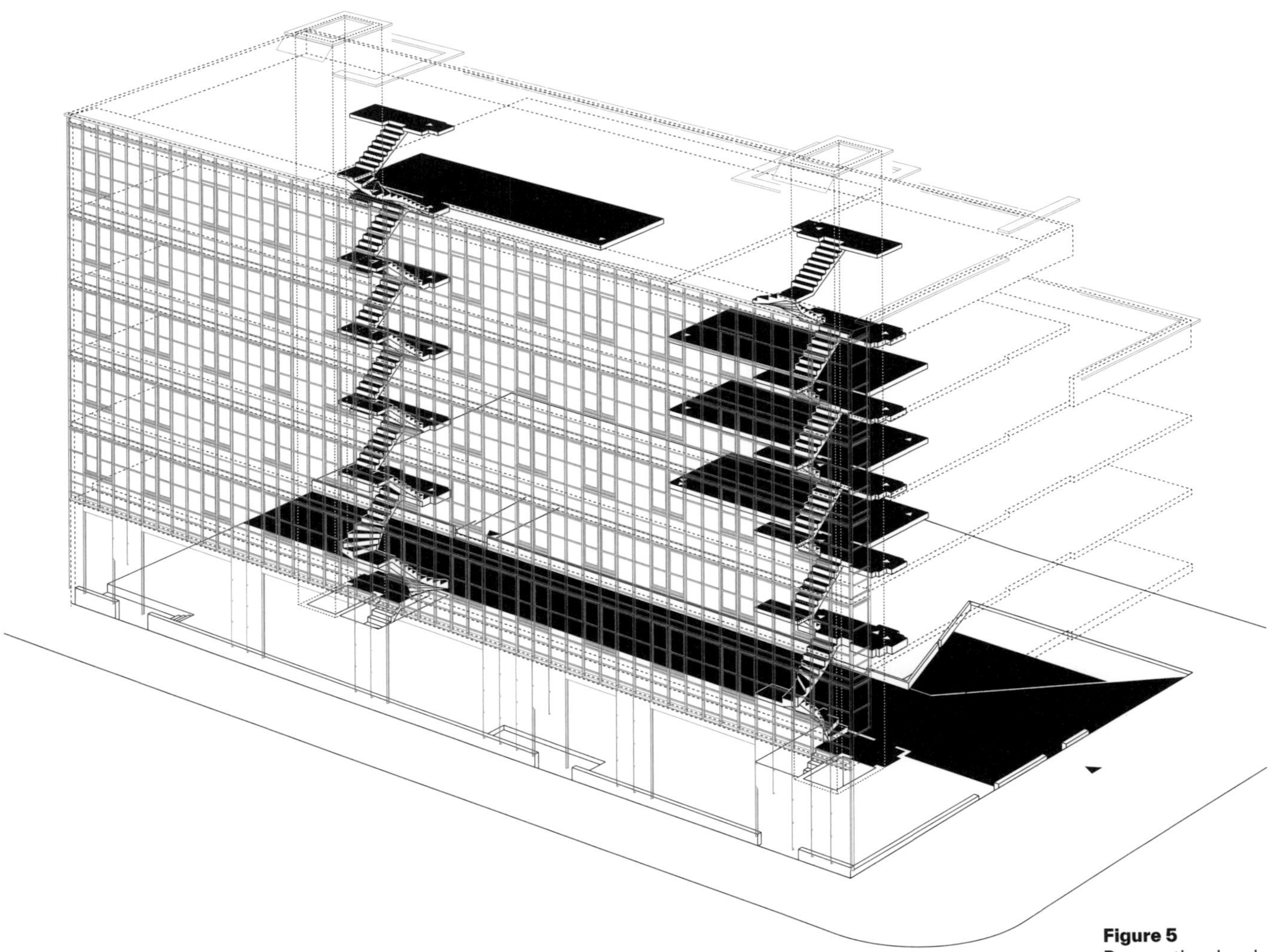

Figure 5
Perspective drawing indicating access and communal spaces in the building.

DS Were there any ideas related to the spatial adaptability requirements that did not make it through in this project but could be used in the next one?

JG We have considered designing reusable partitions that could be used instead of drywall, which is not the most suitable solution from an environmental point of view. The idea was that residents would assemble and disassemble these partitions by themselves. They could be made from wood and include channels for electrical installations. We also considered sliding walls and have gone quite far in developing the idea with manufacturers, but there were cost limitations.

DS What design decisions have contributed to lowering construction costs?

JG We accepted that a concrete skeleton may have been the most optimal solution for this project. We would have chosen a wooden structure if it had been economically feasible. We managed to incorporate the use of prefabricated panels with a timber frame structure for facade walls in the budget we have. Many design decisions were made with affordability in mind. However, we believe the most significant contributor to reducing the development cost in our architectural project is the layout and how shared spaces are utilized.

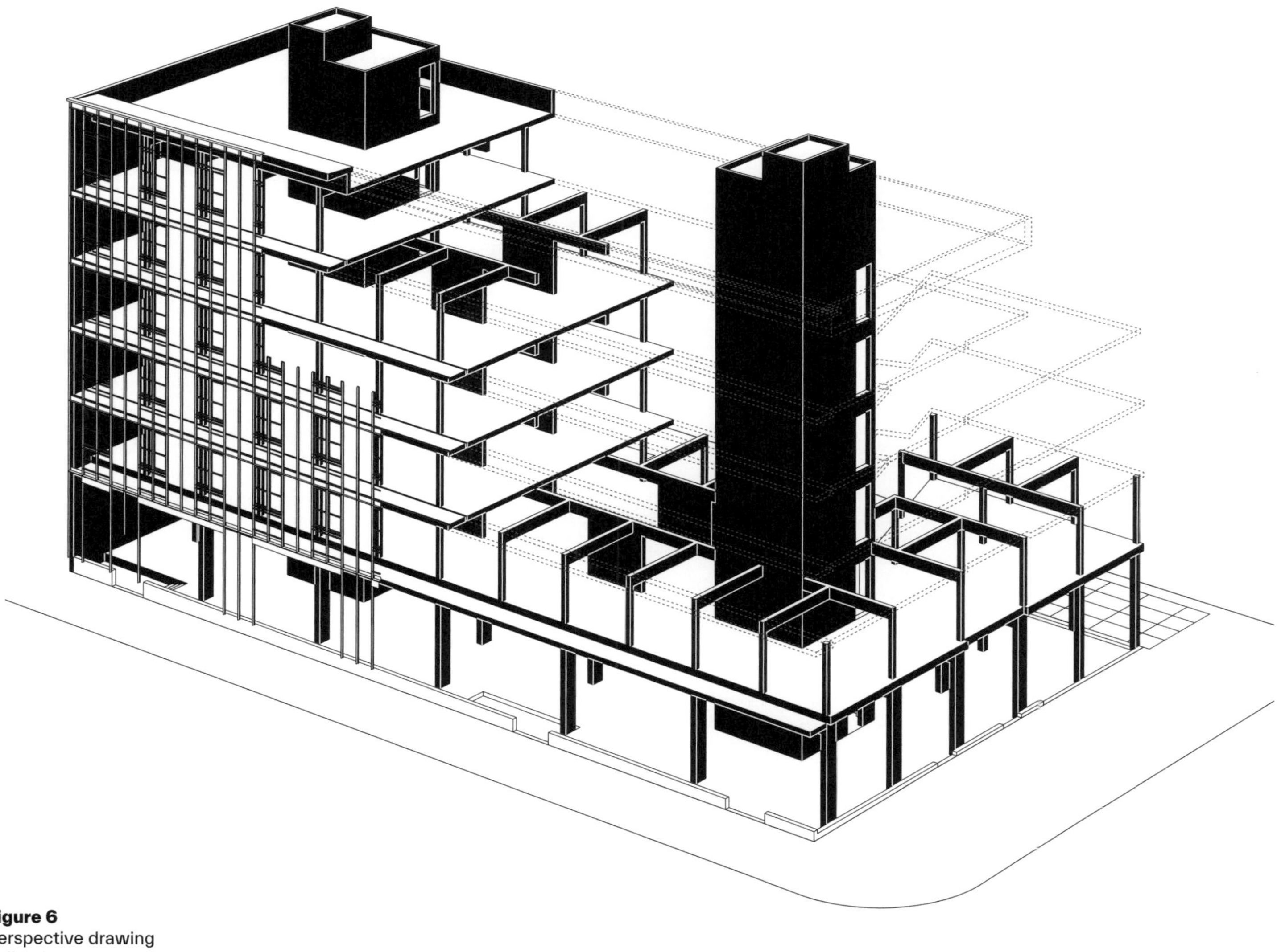

Figure 6
Perspective drawing indicating structural elements of the building.

In conversation

The following section is an edited interview recorded with one of the residents on September 20, 2023. They live on the fifth floor with their family of four.

DS How do you use communal areas on the ground floor?

MS Ground floor is a multipurpose space. We residents use it regularly and hold our monthly meetings there. We have different work groups, and they meet there. We use it more in the winter. The rooftop provides an alternative in the summer. We have a small kitchen on the ground floor, and on Fridays, it can work as an open bar. It can be as little as two people, but sometimes it is a much bigger Friday gathering. Sometimes there are parties. It is also convenient for children's birthday parties. We have a projector, and people watch movies or football games there, too. Some residents play table tennis there. Occasionally, I do yoga there. There are curtains that we can use to separate the space. However, everyone understands it is a communal space. It provides access to vertical cores leading to the dwellings above. We have communal washing machines there, and people go through that space to collect mail from their letterboxes or take their waste out. Also, a glass wall separates this space from the courtyard, which adds to its communal character.

DS There is a small workshop, too.

MS The workshop is not that small—it is very nice. It is equipped with tools, and you can do quite a lot with them. If I had more time, I would use it more to make things. There is a bike repair stand, which is very handy. I use it more regularly. We all have bicycles in our family.

DS Can you tell us more about the resident community?

MS The size of the community is very important. There are one hundred residents in the building who all know each other. I know that residents often do not create bonds with all other members in larger housing cooperatives. At the same time, our community is big enough so we can find those we want to be closer to and with whom we can form a community within the community. My family shares a common living room with two other households. It was essential that we had an opportunity to choose and decide with whom we wanted to share it. The cooperative was very helpful in that process.

DS How do you use the kitchen on the ground floor?

MS We had some initiatives, such as a communal baking session, but we don't use the kitchen for cooking that much. It is mainly for events and gatherings. There is a fridge in the kitchen, which is convenient. We have a guest apartment on the ground floor, which does not have a kitchen. So guests can use it, but more often they eat with their hosts and don't use the kitchen on the ground floor.

DS Are those facilities, which are accessible to the entire resident community, important socially?

MS I think space on the ground floor is key to community building. We also have a communal roof terrace, but people do not have to pass through that space. People meet on the ground floor randomly and start small conversations, which is important, in my view. You don't have to make formal arrangements to meet someone. The building belongs to a housing cooperative, and we, the cooperative's members, knew each other for two or three years before we moved in. But that's not always the case, which is why having such space on the ground floor makes sense.

DS Besides the communal space on the ground floor accessible to all residents, the building contains spaces used jointly by smaller groups of residents and serving as an extension of their units. How do you use such a shared space next to your unit?

MS We live on the fifth floor. We share a living room with two other households, another family of four, and a single person living on their own. We all have our autonomous units, but we share this additional space. Two households must go through it to get to their units. This space is a bonus, a luxury, and it is great to have it. There is freedom and a choice we can make if we want to use the shared living room. Sometimes, we open the doors of our units to connect them with this space.

DS How does it work at the practical level?

MS The key is that we all have our own kitchens, making it possible to balance individual and communal. When you are in the shared space, you understand that other residents may be there, too. We have rules and a general understanding of each other. For example, if doors are closed, you knock. If I am doing yoga, neighbors will not come and say hi, but if I do something else, we will greet each other. Every second Friday, we have dinners or stay together after we put the kids to sleep. For kids, it is excellent. They play together and move freely between dwellings with their toys.

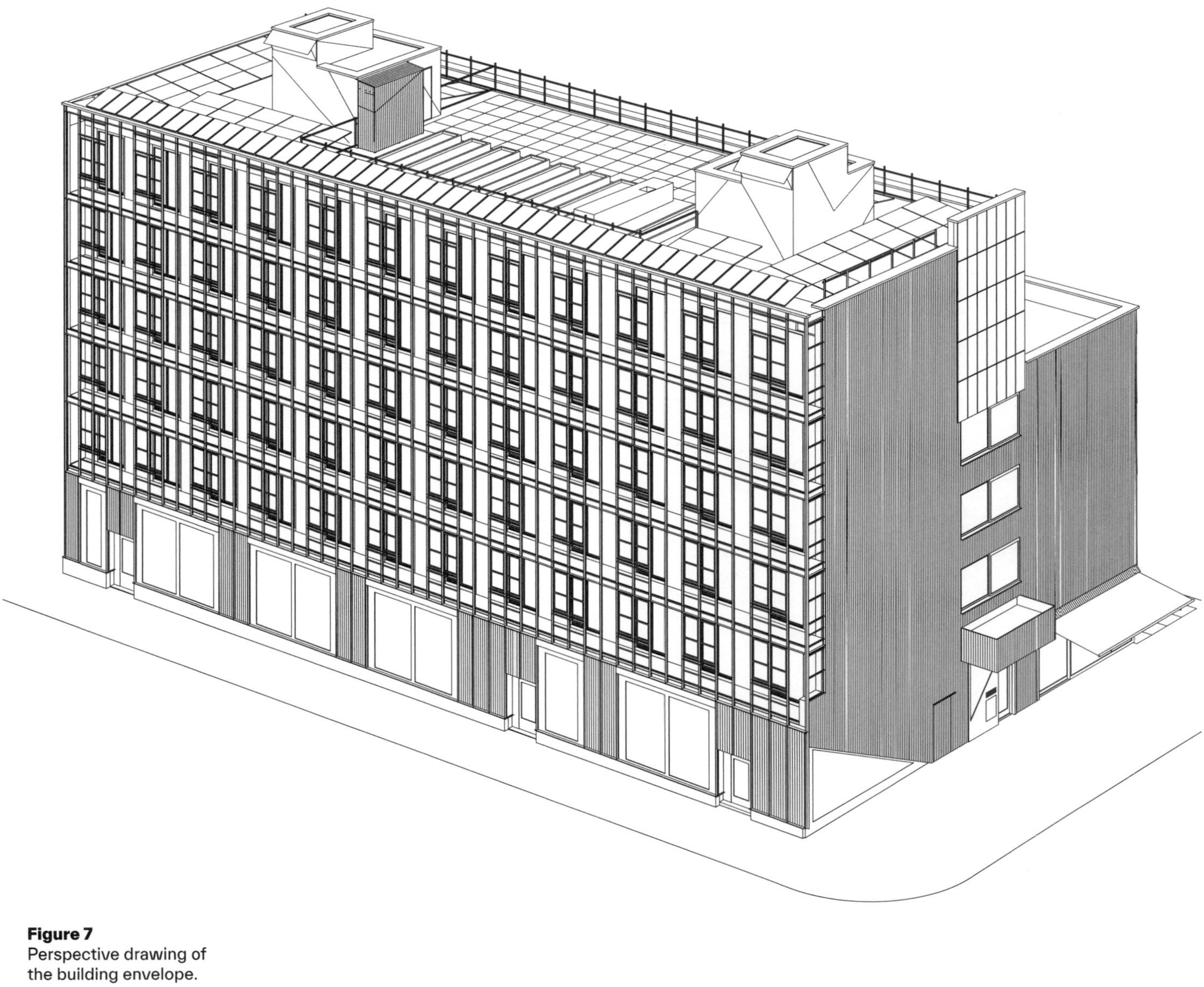

Figure 7
Perspective drawing of the building envelope.

San Riemo, Munich

DS Is there a difference in how individual dwellings relate to shared spaces across the building?

MS There are three kinds of dwellings in the building. Units for "basic living," as we call them, with no space shared. Units for "nucleus living," as we call them, can grow and shrink according to residents' needs. And then there are dwellings with a shared space, as ours is, that we call "filiale."

DS How do you find the layout of your dwelling?

MS We enter our dwelling through the spacious kitchen centrally positioned in our unit. The layout of our dwellings is very open. Our living room combines two rooms and a kitchen. We had an option to leave out walls, which creates openness. I like the fact that all the rooms are the same size.

DS How do you use the winter garden on the west facade of the building?

MS Winter garden looks nice but may not necessarily be the most practical. The polycarbonate panels are not aging well. They are less and less see-through. I feel we need just 20 centimeters more, so we can comfortably put chairs there. It gets hot in the summer and cold in the winter, but it is lovely in summer evenings. We have a lovely rooftop, but it is not as convenient as having access to outdoor areas directly from the dwelling. The winter garden is not split with barriers between units, but there is an agreement this space is used individually. We pass things to each other via winter gardens but do not use them for access.

DS I believe there was a requirement to provide noise protection from the street.

MS The street is relatively quiet, but further on that side, there is a convention center, which can be busy. Our windows are very good. They are floor-to-ceiling, triple-glazed, providing thermal and sound insulation. There was a cost associated with that. However, other things, such as floor finish, have helped bring the cost down. There is a divided opinion among residents about screed floors. It works okay for us, and I like the look of it. We have put carpets in the kids' bedroom.

"We share a living room with two other households, another family of four, and a single person living on their own. We all have our autonomous units, but we share this additional space. Two households must go through it to get to their units. This space is a bonus, a luxury, and it is great to have it."

DS Did you interact with architects during the design process?

MS There was an architectural competition to select an architect, and it was followed by direct communication between the housing cooperative and architects throughout the design process, and information was disseminated to members regularly. Architects joined our monthly meetings a few times to present and discuss with us. They had some very clear ideas they followed through. For example, they proposed an exposed concrete ceiling, and some residents were skeptical, but in the end, it came out very good.

11 Yokohama Apartment, Yokohama

ON design partners
(Osamu Nishida
and Erika Nakagawa)

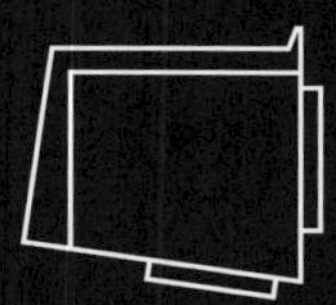

Flowing Noodles

Figure 1
Site plan, drawing scale 1:2500

Yokohama Apartment, Yokohama
ON design partners (Osamu Nishida and Erika Nakagawa)

Year of completion: 2009
Number of units: 4

This project may be closer to an individual house than a multiunit residential building by size and typology. Yet it supports communal living, interfaces with the public domain, and applies some design principles characteristic of much larger residential projects.

The building is in Nishi Ward, Yokohama City, Kanagawa Prefecture, in Japan. Its surrounding is a densely populated neighborhood with hilly topography, narrow streets, and low-rise private houses. It has only four rental units on level one and a shared space on the ground floor. The project was borne out of the intent to support young artists. The space on the ground floor is designed to serve as a communal living room and an extension of the private units but also a space where artists can create and display their work. The developer working with

ON design partners wanted to create a space where residents can interact but also a space that is a part of the neighborhood and occasionally open for public events, such as exhibitions, concerts, and gatherings.[1]

Communal and Individual

The building's footprint is almost rectangular, with sides of 8 and 10 meters. The communal area on the ground floor has an open plan configuration. There are no partitions. However, four storage rooms of the triangular base occupy its corners. Their sides loosely divide the space and allow its segments to be used autonomously, although they remain part of the same room. It means that within one communal space, smaller spaces can be used individually with a degree of privacy. As much as this space is left open to facilitate interaction, gatherings, and events, it is equally intended for individual creative work and usual domestic activities, such as cooking, eating, resting, and playing. It has a bench, several chairs, a large dining table, and a heater. A few potted plants are scattered around the room. A communal cooking area is established between the table with a gas stove and kitchen sink, fridge, and a small shelf for pots and utensils leaning on one of the walls.

Inside and Outside

Storage rooms where artists can keep their works, materials, and tools stand as four distinct buildings and define the space of the communal area, similar to how, on a different scale, buildings create the city's public spaces between them. The use of the same cladding material for the facade and interior walls on the ground floor further reinforces the architectural expression of the four buildings. The choice of aluminum lining for the interior walls could make ground-floor occupants wonder if they are inside or outside. What they see between the building walls could make them wonder even further. Clear views of the street and adjacent buildings from the shared space on the ground floor are made possible through large openings between walls to make occupants feel they are in the city rather than the private living room. Equally, anyone looking from the street has unobstructed interior views, making that shared space accessible and suitable for public events.

There are no windows and doors separating the interior from the exterior but only see-through vinyl curtains used in industrial premises. The air temperature in the shared living room cannot be too dissimilar from the outside air temperature, which can make ground-floor occupants again feel unsure if they are in the interior or exterior. Curtains are attached to the rail on the underside of the slab, and heating incorporated into the polished concrete floor suggests that the communal living room on the ground floor aspires to be an indoor space and a thermally controlled environment. It also suggests that these premises are less used in winter, as Yokohama is in the humid subtropical climate zone where the temperature drops close to zero degrees Celsius.

In the absence of windows, doors, and fences, the boundaries between the interior and exterior and between the neighborhood and the building are truly blurred. The subtle borders are established only by the 15-centimeter floor level difference between the shared living room and the surrounding terrain and by the floor finishes. The narrow area around the building, determined by setback regulations, is covered in gravel to divide the street's sidewalk from the communal living area.

Stairs

The ceiling height of the ground floor is five meters, the maximum allowed by the relevant building and planning regulations. It makes the shared space more suitable for different forms of creative work, gatherings, and exhibitions. Light, steel staircases wrapped around the four storage rooms provide access to the private dwellings on level one. Each staircase is associated with a single dwelling and defines a threshold between the communal space and that private dwelling. The first flight of stairs is indoors and offers itself as a piece of furniture where people can sit during events, creating an amphitheater-like configuration in the communal area. The landings pierce through the storage volumes. The second flight of stairs, which leads to the entrances of the dwellings, is outdoors. Units are, therefore, entered from the exterior, and such passage from the interior to the exterior establishes a boundary between the private and communal.

Units

Entrances to the four dwelling units are placed on four different facades. The units are small. Each occupies a quarter of level one and an area of 20 square meters. In contrast to the generous height of the ground floor, the distance between the floor and the ceiling is only 2.1 meters. All units have private kitchens and bathrooms and minimal outdoor space. The building volume containing the four dwellings is pushed back further from the street. It appears as if it is sitting on the platform, carried by previously described four storage volumes, acting as four distinct buildings. This formal gesture divides the building in two and contributes to establishing the boundary between the shared and the individual.

1. ON design partners, "Yokohama apartment," accessed May 30, 2023, http://www.ondesign.co.jp/city/housing/1/.

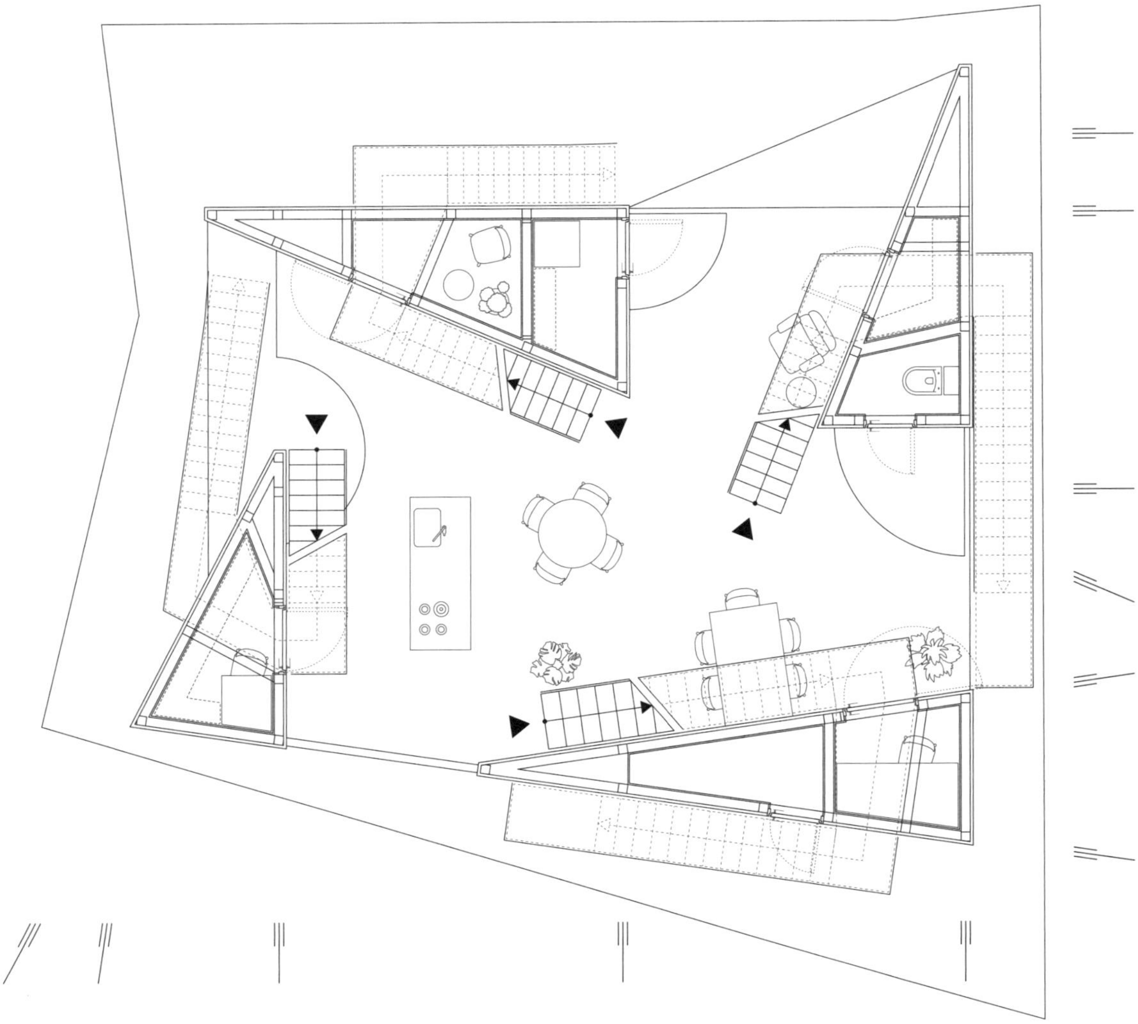

Flowing Noodles

During his lecture hosted by the Melbourne School of Design on March 9, 2021, Osamu Nishida explained his interest in designing small buildings and structures that can facilitate public programs and socially relevant events, which has led to his involvement with this project after its completion.[2] In this project, it means regular meetings and contributions to various events that have taken place in the communal space of the building. Such events include social gatherings, exhibitions, and events. In 2016, one such event was based on a robust architectural installation of copper gutters suspended in midair. It was dubbed the world's most difficult Nagashi-somen and made to accommodate a Japanese summer tradition, whereby people use chopsticks to catch and eat thin noodles carried by the ice-cold water in a waterslide, typically made of bamboo and placed across the room.[3]

2. Osamu Nishida, "Interactive Architecture: The Inherent Potential of Bringing People Together," guest lecture, Melbourne School of Design, March 9, 2021. https://edsc.unimelb.edu.au/studio-epsilon/lecture-repository/ondesign.
3. Hiroko Kawaguchi and Osamu Nishida, "Future Apartments, Future Areas, Part 2," *Beyond Architecture*, accessed May 30, 2023, https://beyondarchitecture.jp/magazine/kenchikuunchiku/nisida-kawaguchi02/.

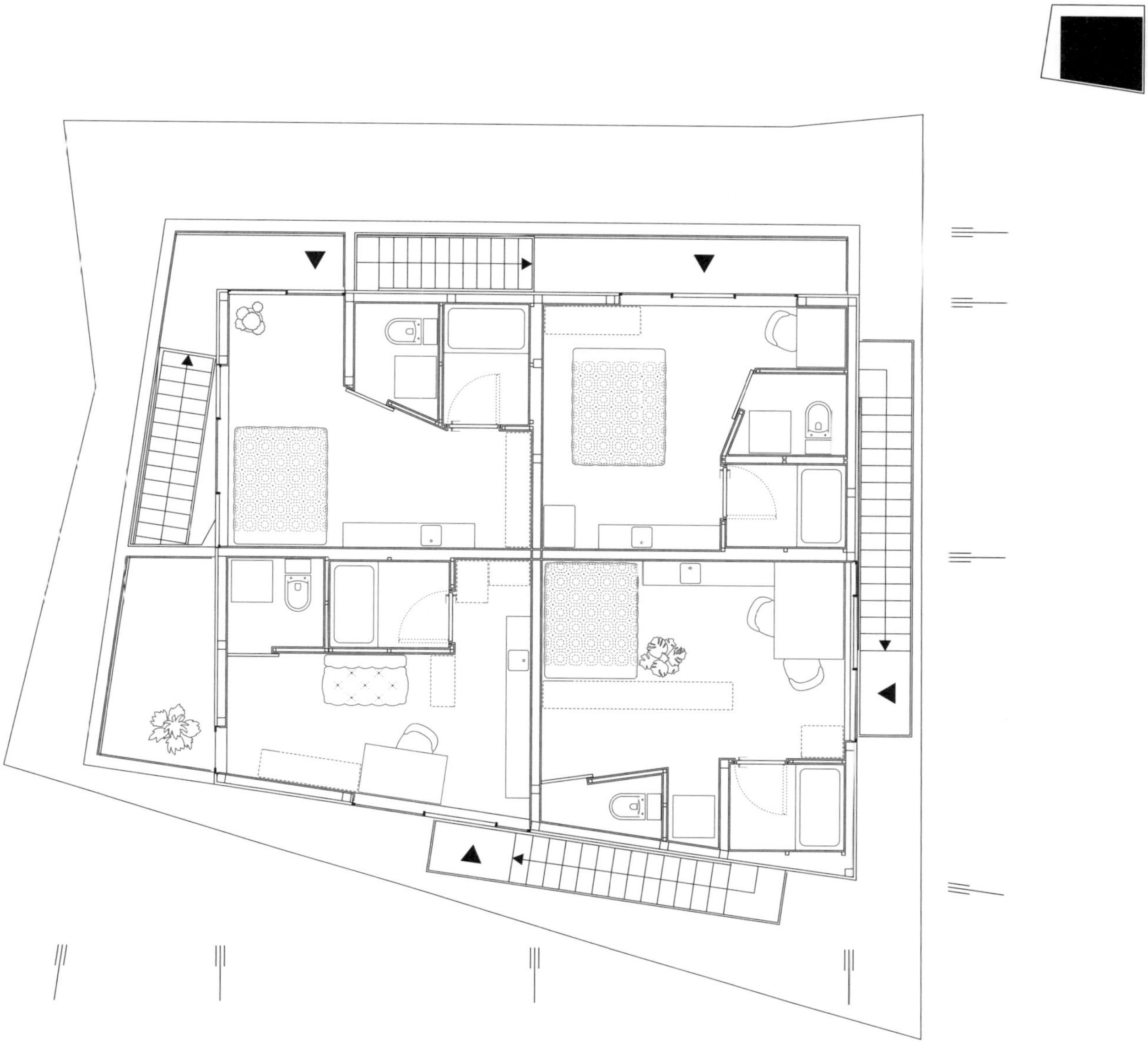

Figure 2
Ground floor plan,
drawing scale 1:100

Figure 3
Level 1 floor plan,
drawing scale 1:100

In conversation

The following text, an edited interview with Osamu Nishida, recorded on May 11, 2023, provides further information about the project from the architect's perspective.

DS I finished the project description by writing about your involvement with the building, which transcends its construction. I want to ask more about your views on the architect's role after completion. Can you tell us how that works in practice on this specific project?

ON It is almost fourteen years since the construction was completed and since the first residents moved in, but ON design partners are still engaged with the use of the building. We participate in meetings that take place every month with the owner and residents to discuss the use of the communal space on the building's ground floor. Sometimes, we help organize events there. For example, in December last year, we helped organize a themed party, bringing a group of people together to exchange small Christmas presents. Some maintenance work on the building facade has been done previously, and we wanted to celebrate that with residents, the building owner, their friends, and our friends. Other events, including tea ceremonies, mothers' group meetings, dinners, and welcome parties for the new residents, have occurred on the ground floor since 2009. There were various public exhibitions there. We watched the football World Cup games there. I feel that architecture and community building are connected and mutually dependent. It is why I am interested in how buildings are used and how architecture becomes the background of what happens In buildings.

DS It is not uncommon that multiunit residential buildings contain shared spaces in addition to individual dwellings. However, it is less common that these shared spaces are publicly accessible. Intriguingly, the space on the ground floor can host events that include residents and people who live elsewhere. Can you speak more about the interface between public and private in this project?

ON Ms. Hiroko Kawaguchi, the developer and the owner of the Yokohama Apartment, wanted to create a residential building like our office. At that time, when we met, ON design partners were sharing office space with many architects and artists, some of whom lived in that space. She was enticed by the atmosphere, and we, too, were keen to design a building that opened new possibilities for living. These possibilities, as we call them, are related to blurring the distinction between spaces for living and working, facilitating the interaction between residents, and the relationship between the resident community, the neighborhood, and the public through the events we just mentioned.

DS What exactly are those possibilities?

ON I lived in this building with my partner and our two-year-old daughter for almost two years, soon after it was completed. One of the residents was an artist who often worked on her paintings in the communal area on the ground floor. She allowed my daughter, much to her amusement, to interfere with a large canvas she was working on at the time. I also remember once I woke up one morning and walked into a yoga class held by another resident on the ground floor. The possibilities I was referring to are in the interaction between residents and creating daily routines that are not necessarily conventional.

"Once I woke up one morning and walked into a yoga class held by another resident on the ground floor. The possibilities I was referring to are in the interaction between residents and creating daily routines that are not necessarily conventional."

DS What is the relationship between the building and the neighborhood?

ON In my working experience with communities, developing an understanding can take two years. We had some success in creating a relationship with the neighborhood community straight away. One of the first public events in the building was an installation by the artist Junko Maruyama.[4] It generated soap bubbles. You can imagine children from the neighborhood were thrilled by it and immediately attracted. It took a little longer to create a relationship with older neighbors. They tended to be more skeptical of the extrovert nature of the communal space on the ground floor and unhappy with the noise that some events generated. The relationship with the neighborhood is more settled now. We have had musicians and drama theater groups performing there. There were some unusual events, too. For example, artist Mineki Murata washed books in the communal kitchen sink as part of his performance. Another artist working with live roosters in an art performance held them in a cage on the ground floor for a while.

The streets of the neighborhood are so tight that you can see what TV shows people watch when you pass by. At the same time, there is almost no interaction between people from adjacent buildings. Some residents work all day and come to their homes only to sleep. Our aim was to provide a housing solution that opposed all that.

4. Junko Maruyama, *The Beginning of ZZ.*

DS What architectural means did you employ, and what design decisions did you make to structure a three-way relationship between private, communal, and public that you describe?

ON We relish the opportunity to design unconventional buildings specific to individual requirements. However, in this project, we have also employed some of the principles and values of vernacular Japanese architecture. Traditionally, private and communal spaces in Japanese architecture are linked, and very often, there is no clear boundary where one stops and the other begins. We have designed the communal room on the ground floor as an outdoor public space, *hiroba*. We tried to facilitate a dynamic transition between the individual and communal within that space. In Japanese architecture, edge spaces of a private home, such as *engawa*, an outdoor deck, and *nokishita*, the space under the overhang of roof eaves, are private, but if people are there, the nature of the space changes, and it becomes public. In this project, we have employed irregular forms to subdivide a large open space without creating physical barriers to allow occupants to establish private spheres within that public space. We see the public space as a composite of private spheres.

DS The spatial complexity is such in this project that one is not entirely sure if they are indoors or outdoors when using the communal space on the ground floor. Was it your intention to reduce the distinction between interior and exterior?

ON We intended to avoid the distinction between interior and exterior. If we had closed off the ground floor with doors and windows, the space on the ground floor would be far less part of the neighborhood and more of the building. Instead, we established only subtle boundaries between the two, which can be read through the floor treatment. Floor heating and vinyl curtains are part of the project to ensure this space is not entirely outdoors. It means it can be comfortably used throughout most of the year.

DS It may be important to emphasize that this is achieved in a small-scale project.

ON Yes, we wanted to explore the potential of small buildings to facilitate gatherings and social events. We could have created four autonomous units of 36 square meters each. Instead, we decided to make smaller dwelling units of 20 square meters and one larger and shared working space of 75 square meters that also caters to exhibitions and gatherings.

DS The distinction between private dwellings and the communally used ground floor is made explicit in the project.

ON We wanted to make the ground floor as tall as possible to ensure it is suitable for public gatherings and artists working with different formats and scales. At the same time, we wanted the individual units to have views over the roofs of neighboring houses and enjoy more privacy. It is important to emphasize that the intimacy of one's home is intact in this project. Residents can use the shared space, eat, and cook together when they want, but their units are equipped with bathrooms and kitchens. They are fully independent. Moreover, dwelling units are entered from the exterior and not directly from the shared space. Stairs leading from the communal space to individual dwellings take you outside before you can enter the dwellings. That way, we have created a deliberate boundary between the two domains. You must exit communal space before you enter private dwellings. Having entrances on the outside helps minimize noise impact. It protects the intimacy of dwellings when gatherings and events occur on the ground floor.

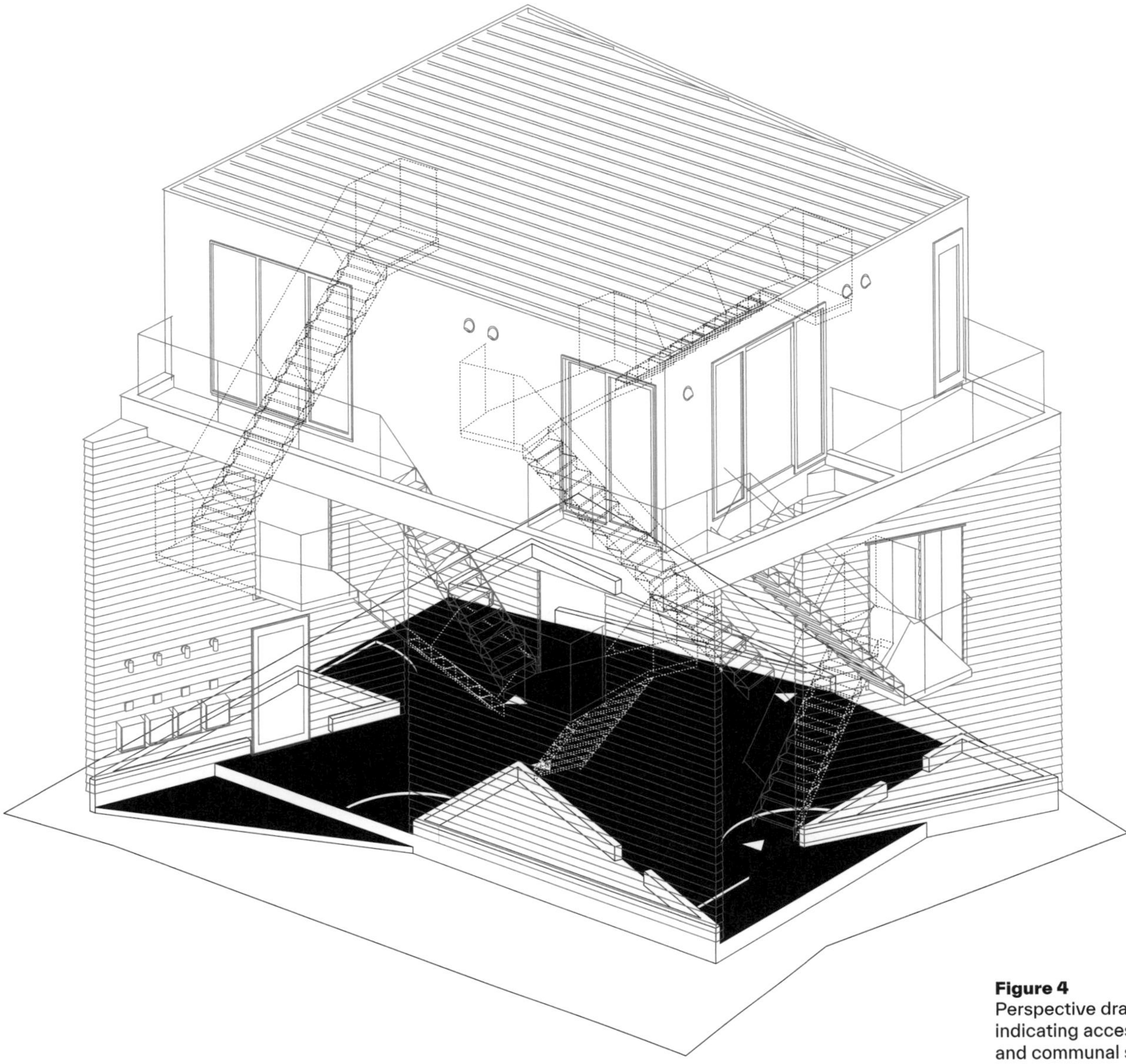

Figure 4
Perspective drawing indicating access and communal spaces in the building.

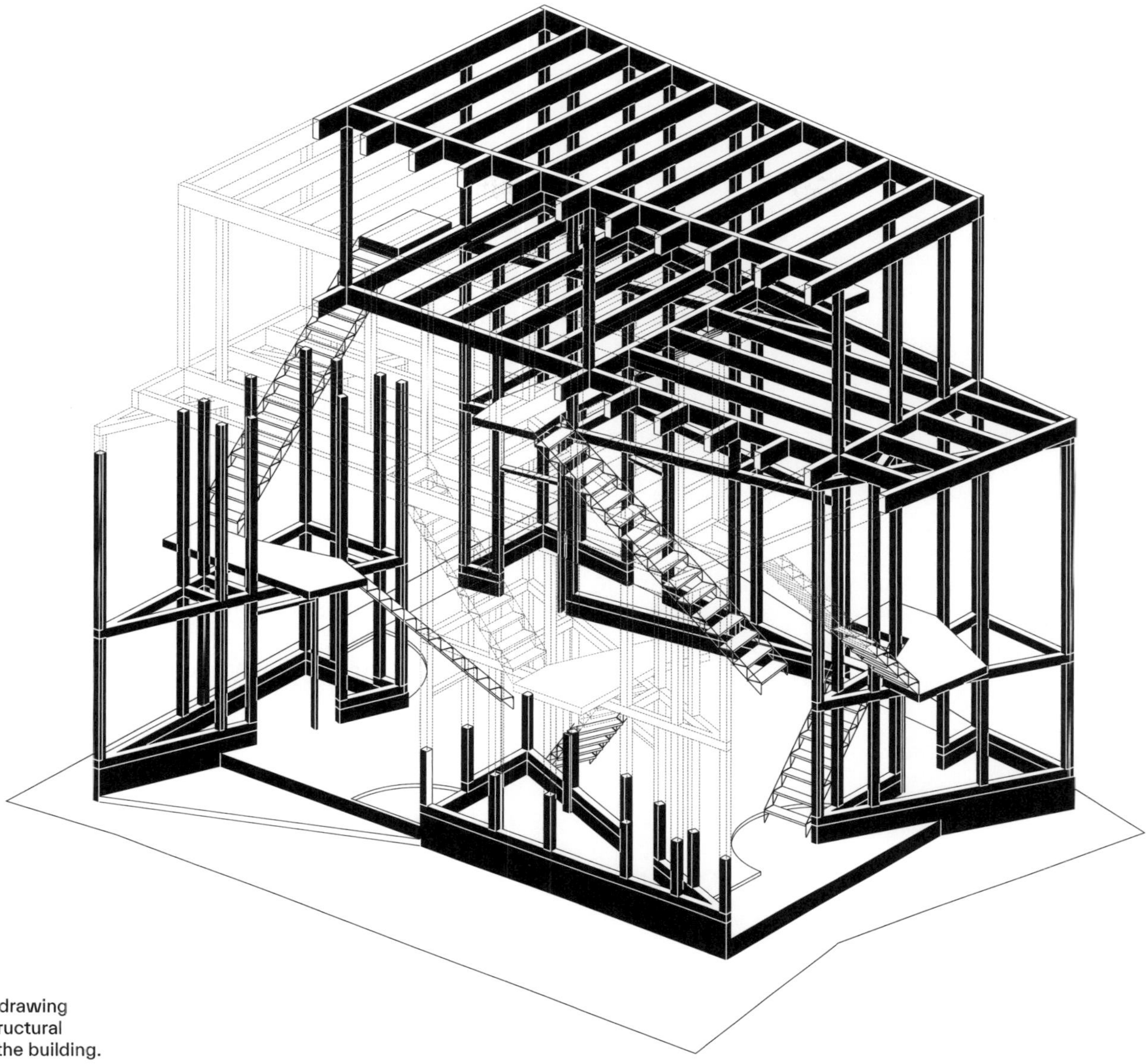

Figure 5
Perspective drawing indicating structural elements of the building.

DS **I understand that securing the intimacy of private dwellings is achieved in the project. Yet it feels as if this project does not want to provide a long-term housing solution. Does it foster specific lifestyles only?**

ON The building is for rental tenure rather than a place to stay for a long time. Initially, rental agreements are for two years, but sometimes they are extended. The owner's intention was to help young artists by providing a place where they could work and live. She interacts with residents through meetings and events I have mentioned. Interestingly, more than a few architects were among the residents over time. If you look at it from the developers' and facility managers' sides, having a longer tenancy agreement is probably better. This building's life span is thirty years or a bit more. It is a timber structure. It was calculated that eleven years of rent would pay off the investment. Moreover, it has allowed the owner to start another similar development.

In conversation

The following section is an edited interview recorded on June 27, 2023, with one of the residents.

DS How would you describe the resident community at Yokohama apartment?

AS I spent two years at the Yokohama apartment. I moved out just a month ago. I am an architect, and I knew of the building from before. While living there, I shared the facilities with a photographer, dancer, and stage designer. Shared facilities were not too busy most of the time. At one point, only me and one other resident lived there. That happens from time to time, as vacancies are not advertised. Instead, the new tenants come in by recommendations, as friends or friends of friends of current and past tenants. The owner also requests that all residents participate in monthly meetings and events organized by the residents' community, architects, and her. Not everyone wants to do that.

DS How did you interact with other residents?

AS Sometimes, we would meet to play board games such as Catan or Ticket to Ride and another game one of the residents designed. Once, the owner of the building joined us with her grandchild. We would often cook and eat together on these occasions. We had larger gatherings on special occasions, such as Christmas, but there was not much of that. My first year at the Yokohama apartment was during the pandemic lockdown, when public gatherings were not permitted. The other public events were at the time of traditional Japanese events such as Hanami, celebrating the cherry blossoms, and Kakizome, which takes place at the beginning of the new year when people write their resolutions using traditional calligraphy. We also interacted through the Zendo messaging app regarding practical matters.

DS How did you and other residents use storage space on the ground floor?

AS The storage belonging to my unit was full of objects used in past communal events; there have been quite a few of these events since 2008, when the building was completed, and much stuff was left there. I never used it personally. That was not the case with other storerooms. One of the residents had her fridge in there, and she used the storage as an extension of the communal kitchen on the ground floor.

DS How did you use the shared space on the ground floor?

AS My routine is different during the weekdays and on the weekends. On a typical weekday, I would wake up around 8 a.m. and leave by 9 a.m. without spending time in the communal area. I would return around 10 p.m. and stay on the ground floor for a bit. I like to spend some time on my phone to wind down and not always interact with other residents. During the weekdays, I would see other residents in the evenings, but most often, everyone would be doing their things. During the weekend, I would move a lot more between the ground floor and my dwelling. For example, I would spend time on the ground floor while doing my laundry in a store around the corner and see other residents running similar errands.

DS How is the shared space on the ground floor equipped?

AS Architect Erika Nakagawa was personally involved with the selection of furniture and the design of fittings in the communal living room on the ground floor. It includes a salvaged church choir chair and furniture from the workshop in Ishinomaki established as part of the aid program after the Tohoku tsunami disaster in 2011. There is also a gas stove and a communal fridge. There is an expandable dining table, which can accommodate up to eight people. We have been using it for table tennis occasionally. We have one shared electric bicycle. It comes very handy as the building is twenty minutes on foot from the nearest train station.

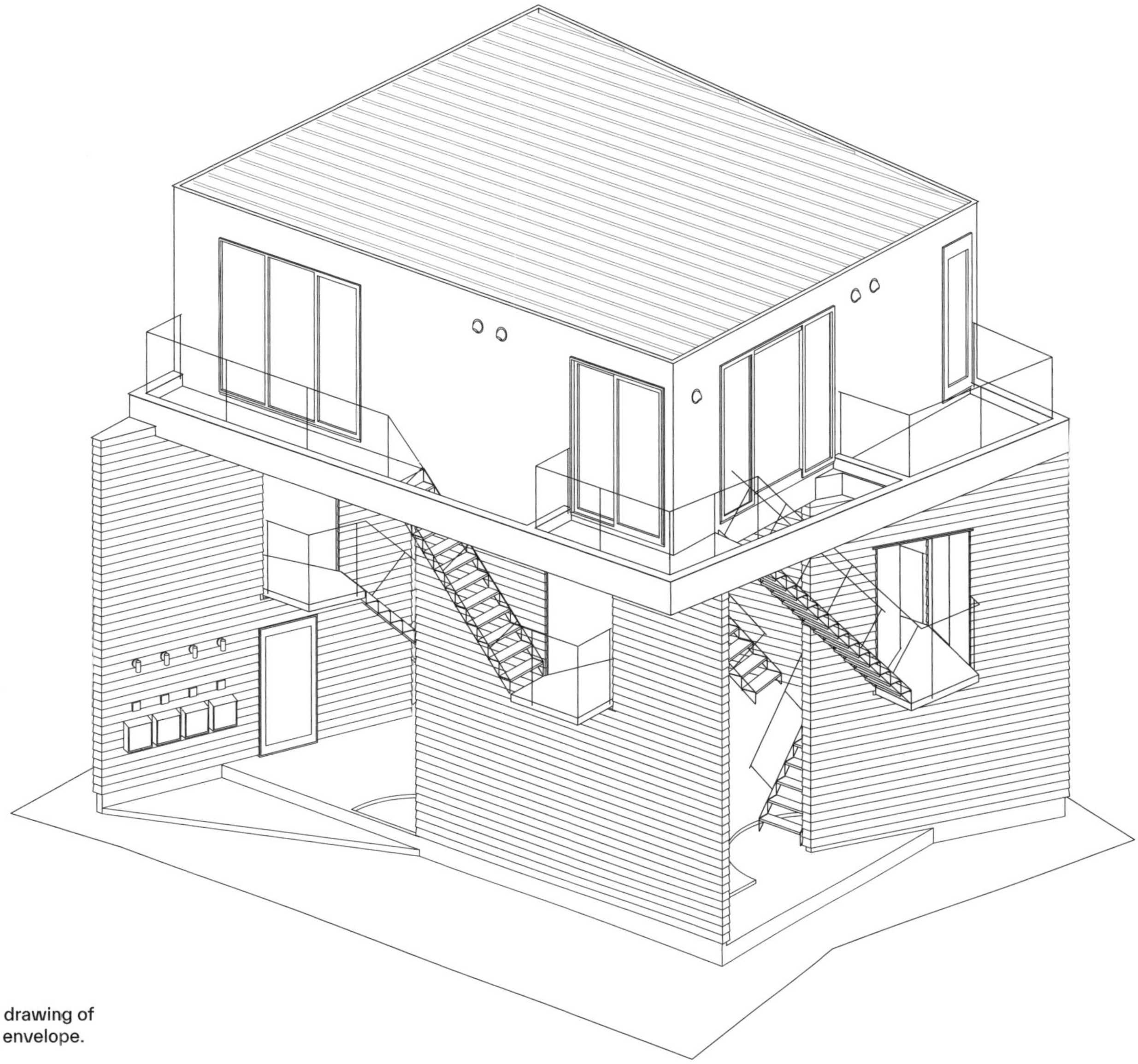

Figure 6
Perspective drawing of the building envelope.

DS The shared space on the ground floor is neither interior nor exterior. How comfortable is it?

AS In winter, it is cold, and this space is used much less. We did use floor heating, an additional heater, and vinyl curtains when planned events were taking place. In summer, the microclimate on the ground floor is great. There is shadow and a breeze as air moves naturally through large openings. The space is used much more. The only problem is mosquitos, as there is nothing to keep them out.

DS How is the shared space maintained?

AS The shared space is cleaned by residents spontaneously, and everyone makes some contribution to maintenance. Usually, there is an annual cleaning in September or October, followed by a social event. The owner and residents advertise the event on Facebook, inviting people to join the cleaning party and repay everyone with a dinner at the end. We had around ten people helping us last year.

DS The privacy of individual dwellings can be compromised in group living, an increasingly popular tenancy model in Japan. How do you find the balance between private and communal in the building?

AS The distinction between the communal and individual, across the two levels, is essential in my view. In most shared households, only a door separates the private dwelling from the communal living room. In this building, stairs that belong to the dwelling give more of a distance between the two. From your staircase, you can see what is happening in the living room and decide if you want to engage with other residents or if the space or facility you need is available. Soundproofing is excellent, and when you are in your apartment, you can't hear the noise from the ground floor, which also contributes to the intimacy.

"The distinction between the communal and individual, across the two levels, is essential in my view. In most shared households, only a door separates the private dwelling from the communal living room. In this building, stairs that belong to the dwelling give more of a distance between the two."

DS Overall, how would you rate your experience of living at the building?

AS I was initially unsure if I wanted to live in a building with shared facilities. As an architect, I was interested in the model, but as a resident, I was more concerned about privacy. Overall, it has been an excellent experience for me. I enjoyed meeting people who lived in adjacent buildings. I met a family who lived across the street and whose young child regularly visited us on the ground floor. I enjoyed spending time with other residents. I did not expect I would be immersed in playing board games.

12 R50, Berlin

ifau und Jesko Fezer, Heide & von Beckerath

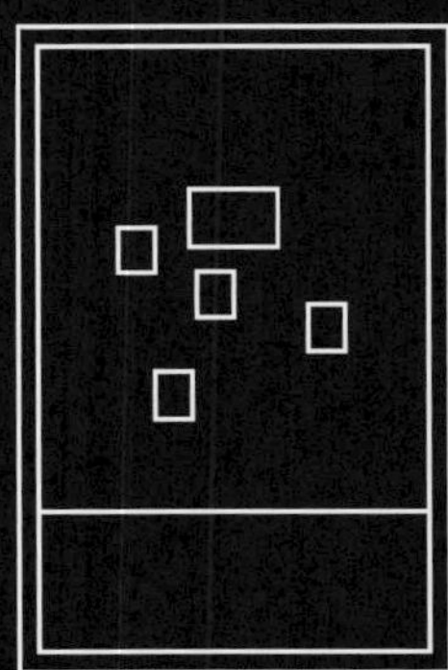

Rotation

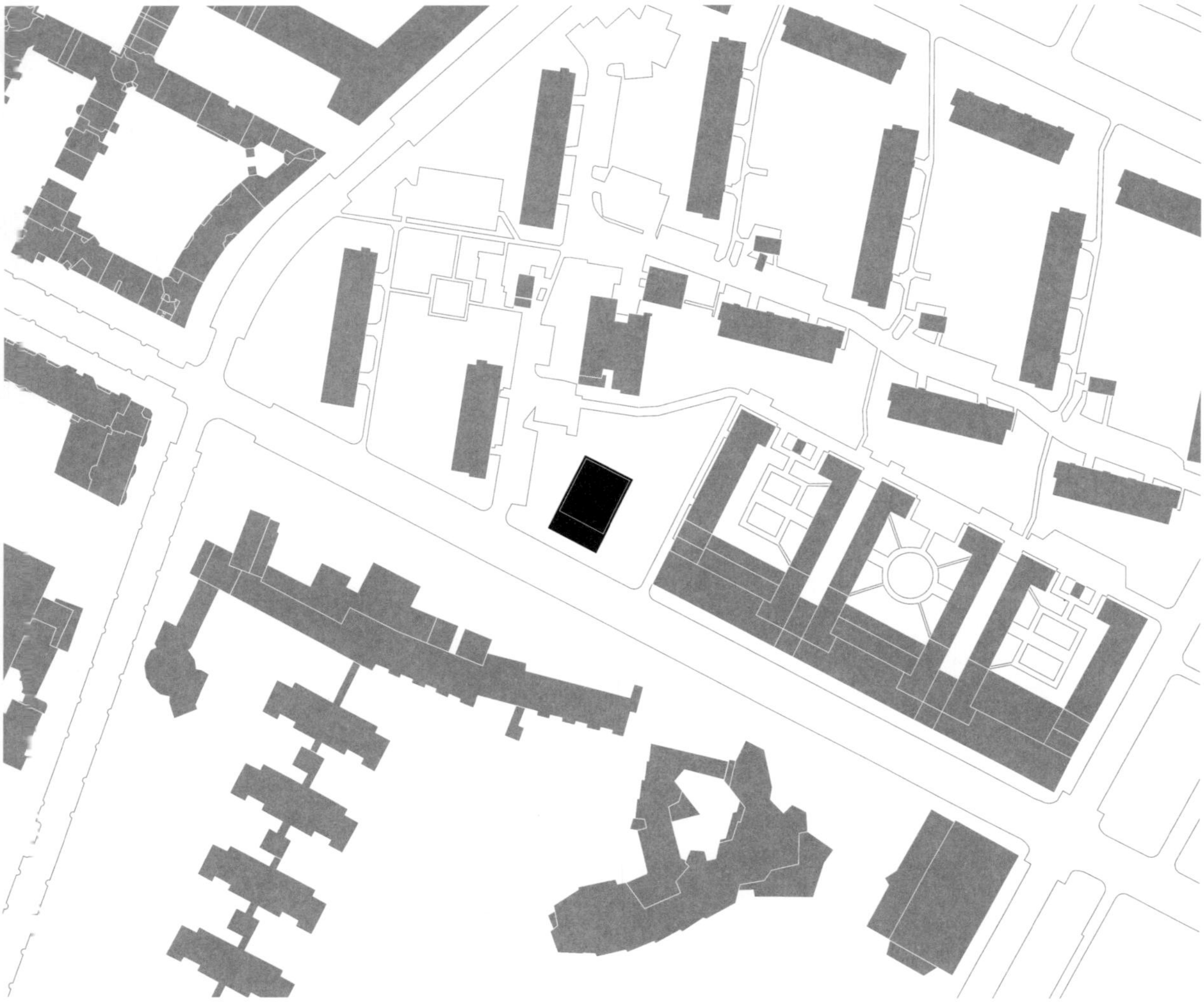

Figure 1
Site plan, drawing scale 1:2500

R50, Berlin
ifau und Jesko Fezer,
Heide & von Beckerath

Year of completion: 2013
Number of units: 19

This project exemplifies how design knowledge helped create a community, respond to individual needs, and reduce construction costs as part of the Baugruppe housing provision model. This self-organized model, driven by the shortage of affordable options, increasing rental prices, and a growing preference for home ownership, gained momentum in Berlin before a more recent policy shift toward subsidized housing.[1-4]

This project came off the back of the initiative started in 2010 by the Berlin Senate Department for Urban Development and Environment to increase the inner-city density to make better use of land by selling it to self-organized housing groups. A lot, formerly a designated traffic zone, was acquired through the fixed price bidding procedure by a group of thirty-two members with a proposal of the highest

1. Peter Ache and Micha Fedrowitz, "The Development of Co-Housing Initiatives in Germany: Co-Housing in the Making," *Built Environment* 38, no. 3 (2012): 365–83, https://doi.org/10.2148/benv.38.3.395.
2. Christiane Droste, "German Co-Housing: An Opportunity for Municipalities to Foster Socially Inclusive Urban Development?" *Urban Research & Practice* 8, no. 1 (2015): 79–92, https://doi.org/10.1080/17535069.2015.1011428.

merit and assurances of their financial capability to deliver the project. The resulting R50 building, named after its address, Ritterstraße 50, in the Kreuzberg district of Berlin, with nineteen dwelling units, has seven floors and a rectangular footprint with sides measuring 18 and 28 meters. It is positioned along the street at an equal distance from the surrounding multiunit residential buildings.

Communal Spaces

The outdoor area around the building extends into the network of publicly accessible spaces. The ground floor datum is below the street level. A ramp leads down from the street to the building entrance. Next to it is a double-height room occupying a large part of the ground floor, which serves as a communal space for gatherings. Neighborhood organizations occasionally use it in addition to the residents. The remaining space on the ground floor is for storage rooms, bicycle parking, and a communal laundry. A roof terrace with an open-air kitchen is equally accessible to all residents. Vertical circulation core and narrow balconies wrapped around the building on each floor are also part of the communal areas of the building. During a public lecture hosted by the Melbourne School of Design on August 18, 2020, Verena von Beckerath suggested that the building's character may be well understood through a photo by Andrew Alberts, showing the exterior of the building and surrounding trees.[5] In that image, one can identify the entrance ramp, the communal room on the ground floor, a cohesive facade that simultaneously allows for diverse and individualized dwelling layouts, and the steel floor grate incorporated into the building facade serving as an extension of indoor dwelling space.

The inclusion of communal spaces in the project, consuming approximately a quarter of the construction budget, had been extensively discussed between residents and architects throughout the design process.[6] In an interview published seven years after the building was completed, one of the residents provides an account of how the use of communal areas of the building evolved to become a more natural extension of the dwellings. They tell how the children who once played in the garden now tend to use the roof garden as they have become teenagers.[7] The role of communal spaces providing social and practical benefits will be discussed from different perspectives in the further text.

Visual Graphs and Meetings

A short documentary produced when construction works were nearly finished contains excerpts from interviews with the architects capturing some of the driving ideas behind the project.[8] They emphasize the group's intent to live together and form a community, to build as cost-efficiently as possible but robustly enough to allow inhabitants to assert control over their unit layout. Throughout the design process, architects organized regular meetings with residents to discuss their individual preferences for the unit layouts and how they could be supported by the construction system, positioning of building services, and the building facade.[9] The architects working with residents used visual graphs and network diagrams to capture quantitative and qualitative aspects of individual needs for the sequencing and dimensioning of domestic spaces. A catalog of diagrams corresponding to each dwelling in the building is available from the architects' websites and was published by *ARCH+* magazine.[10] The floor plans generated after these diagrams show diverse and innovative unit layouts. During her lecture, Verena von Beckerath discussed some of the unit layouts, permitting one to move along the facade and enabling rooms to expand into the access area, such as those on levels two and six.[11]

This building has a concrete skeleton spanning up to 7.8 meters. The vertical access core, with an elevator and stairs, and grouped building service installations are positioned in the central zone of the building. There are three dwellings per floor, apart from the first and top floors, where there are two. Walls separating individual units, made of sand-lime bricks, have a role in stiffening the building structure. Internal partitions are all drywall. Concrete ceilings are exposed, and the floor finish is a cement screed, contributing to the lower construction cost and easing the installation of drywall partitions and their potential repositioning. The project has benefited from the homogenous predispositions within the group and an agreement on construction standards, including building materials and the dimensioning of spaces. On the one side, such understanding between the residents has helped reduce construction costs and, on the other, it has helped consolidate the architectural expression of the building.

Balcony

The building's outer walls comprise thermally insulated solid parts with a pine wood finish and floor-to-ceiling glass panels and doors. In the short interviews recorded during the building's construction and incorporated into a documentary film, the architects explain the challenge of reconciling two objectives: a diversity of layouts for individual dwellings and a cohesive building facade.[12] The solution was a unitized system, including fixed and operable elements, whereby standardization of components was essential for cost reduction.

3. Iqbal Hamiduddin and Nick Gallent, "Self-Build Communities: The Rationale and Experiences of Group-Build (Baugruppen) Housing Development in Germany," *Housing Studies* 31, no. 4 (2016): 365–83, https://doi.org/10.1080/02673037.2015.1091920.
4. Jessics Bridger, "Don't Call It a Commune: Inside Berlin's Radical Cohousing Project," *Metropolis*, accessed August 8, 2023. https://metropolismag.com/projects/dont-call-it-a-commune-inside-berlin-radical-cohousing-project/.
5. Verena von Beckerath, "Housing Narratives," guest lecture, Melbourne School of Design, August 18, 2020, https://edsc.unimelb.edu.au/studio-epsilon/lecture-repository/heide-and-von-beckerath.
6. Christoph Schmidit, "R50," *Future Homes for London: Global Precedents of Community-led and Owned Housing*, Royal College of Art, April 13, 2018. https://vimeo.com/266503920.
7. Sophie Rzepecky, "Artist Ruth Buchanan on Living Life Collectively at R50 in Berlin," *Assemble Papers*, accessed August 8, 2023, https://assemblepapers.com.au/2020/07/29/collective-living-artist-ruth-buchanan-on-r50/.
8. Fred Plassmann, "R50," 2012, accessed December 10, 2023, https://www.architekturclips.de/r50/.
9. The architects on this project are two entities: ifau und Jesko Fezer; and Heide & von Beckerath. It is important to clarify that architects at ifau und Jesko Fezer are also residents.
10. ifau und Jesko Fezer, Heide & von Beckerath, "R50," *ARCH+* (March 2011).
11. von Beckerath, "Housing Narratives."
12. Plassmann, "R50."
13. Schmidit, "R50."

Floor-to-ceiling, single pivoting, or multiple foldable panels provide access from units to an 80-centimeter-wide balcony encircling the building on every floor. A light structure of galvanized steel forms the building's perimeter, including brackets attached to the concrete skeleton, the floor grate, and the outer frame with a mesh wire railing. This narrow grate, through which light and water can slip, serves as an outdoor extension of the dwellings. There are no partitions along the balcony to enable informal interaction between people living in units on the same floor. At the same time, the sheer length of approximately 100 meters per building floor containing only up to three units provides sufficient room for everyone to keep their privacy. Architects explain that balconies running around the entire building are designed as simply as possible, and that can be understood as permanent scaffolding needed for maintenance, including regular varnishing and oiling of the building's pine facade.[13]

In conversation

The following section, an edited interview with Verena von Beckerath, recorded on March 31, 2023, provides further information about the project from the perspective of one of the architects.

DS What is the relationship between communal and individual in this project?

VvB A short film was made by residents for the exhibition related to the project's shortlist for the European Union Prize for Contemporary Architecture, Mies van der Rohe Award.[14] The production was led by Maya Schweizer and Clemens von Wedemeyer, artists using film and other media to explore physical spaces and their social contexts. Their lead was important. However, residents made crucial contributions to the movie by jointly creating a narrative to show a day at the building. Some residents also appear in the film. The camera moves through both private dwellings and communal areas to provide an account of the spatial relationship between the two domains and their everyday use.

DS What means did you use to address the relationship between individual and communal needs during the design process?

VvB Twelve years ago, the communal aspects of housing were discussed less than today, but they were central to this project from the beginning. We used diagrams to facilitate the participative process. Jesko Fezer initiated using visual graphs to analyze residents' lifestyles and daily routines. These diagrams have helped with individual questions related to dwellings, and other graphic aids were used for communal issues about the provision and use of shared spaces, among other things. These joint decisions required voting and consensus to be reached, and there was a lot of negotiation in the process. Some ideas didn't make it through. For example, the architects proposed a small communal space on each level to be shared between three apartments, such as a guest room, home office, or some other extension of the individual dwelling space. We thought that would benefit the residents, but through discussions, the group agreed that it would be better to have one large communal space that can be used in different ways, such as gatherings and neighborhood activities. We ended up with a double-height room next to the entrance. That is now a multifunctional space that can be subdivided. That space is the most apparent communal area in the building, but other spaces are equally crucial for interaction between residents. There is a ramp that takes you from the street to the lower entrance door. Here, people meet while pushing their bikes into the storage room or entering the building. The garden is shared, too, and at the same time, open to the public. We have avoided fences not to separate the building's garden and surrounding green areas. There is a communal roof terrace, laundry, and a workshop. All of it required discussion and joint decisions.

14. Maya Schweizer, Clemens von Wedemeyer, and R50, "R50 Cohousing," 2015, accessed March 5, 2023. https://heidevonbeckerath.com/single/r50-cohousing-film.

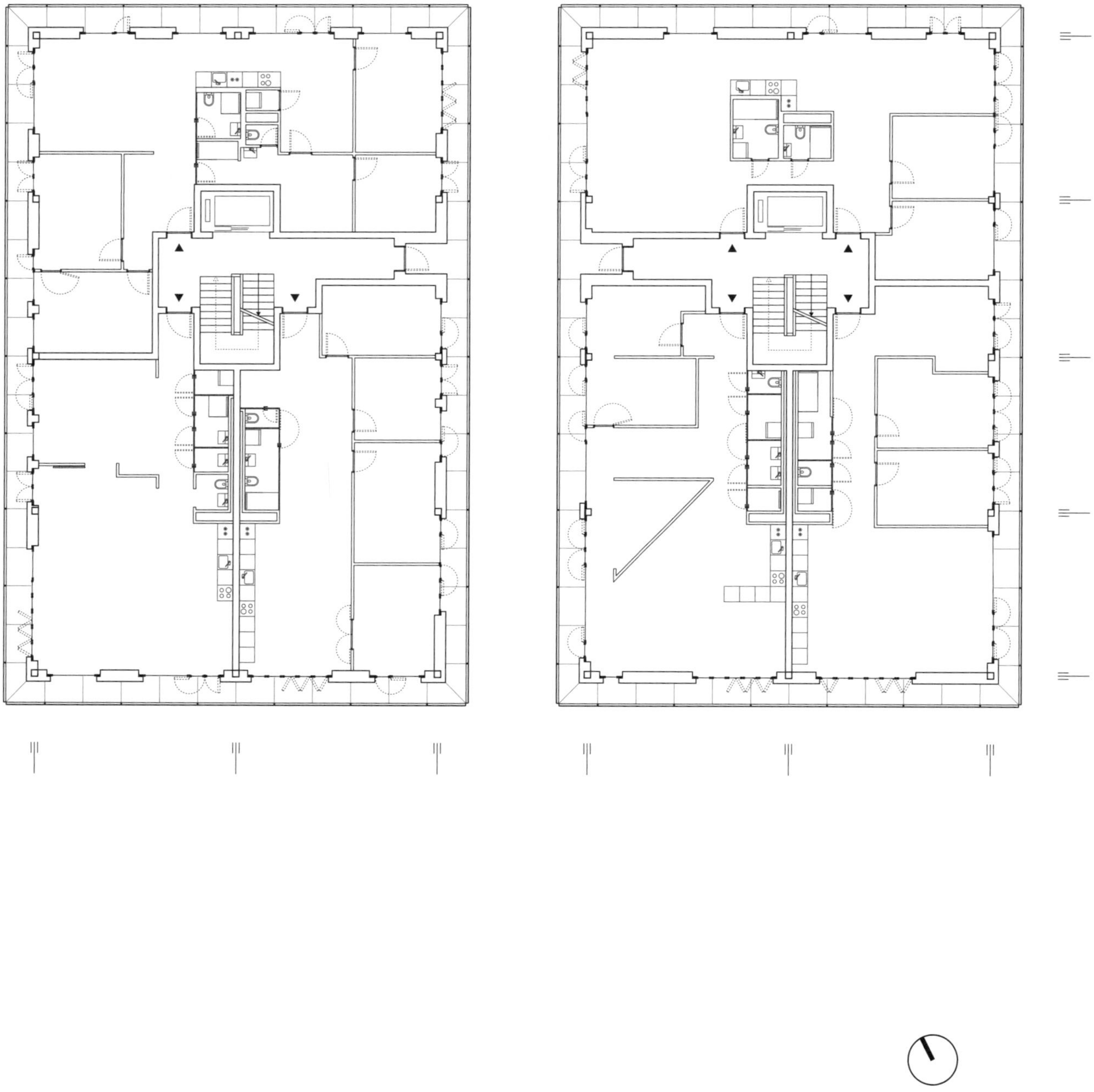

Figure 2
Levels 3 and 6 floor plans, drawing scale 1:250

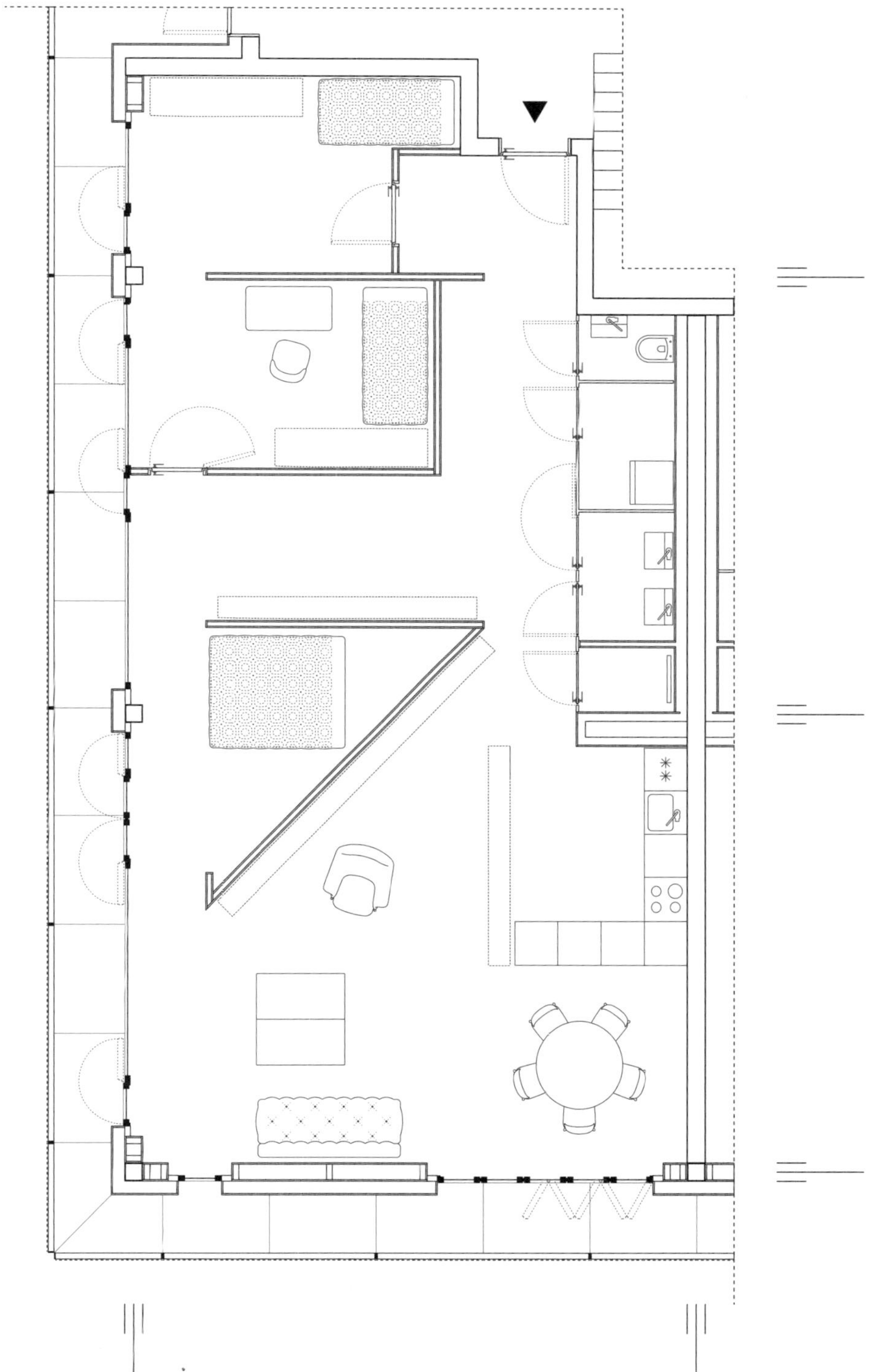

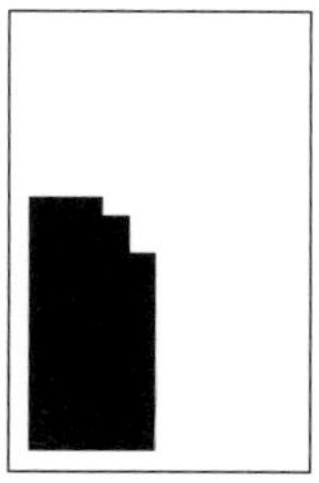

Figure 3
Unit layout, drawing scale 1:100

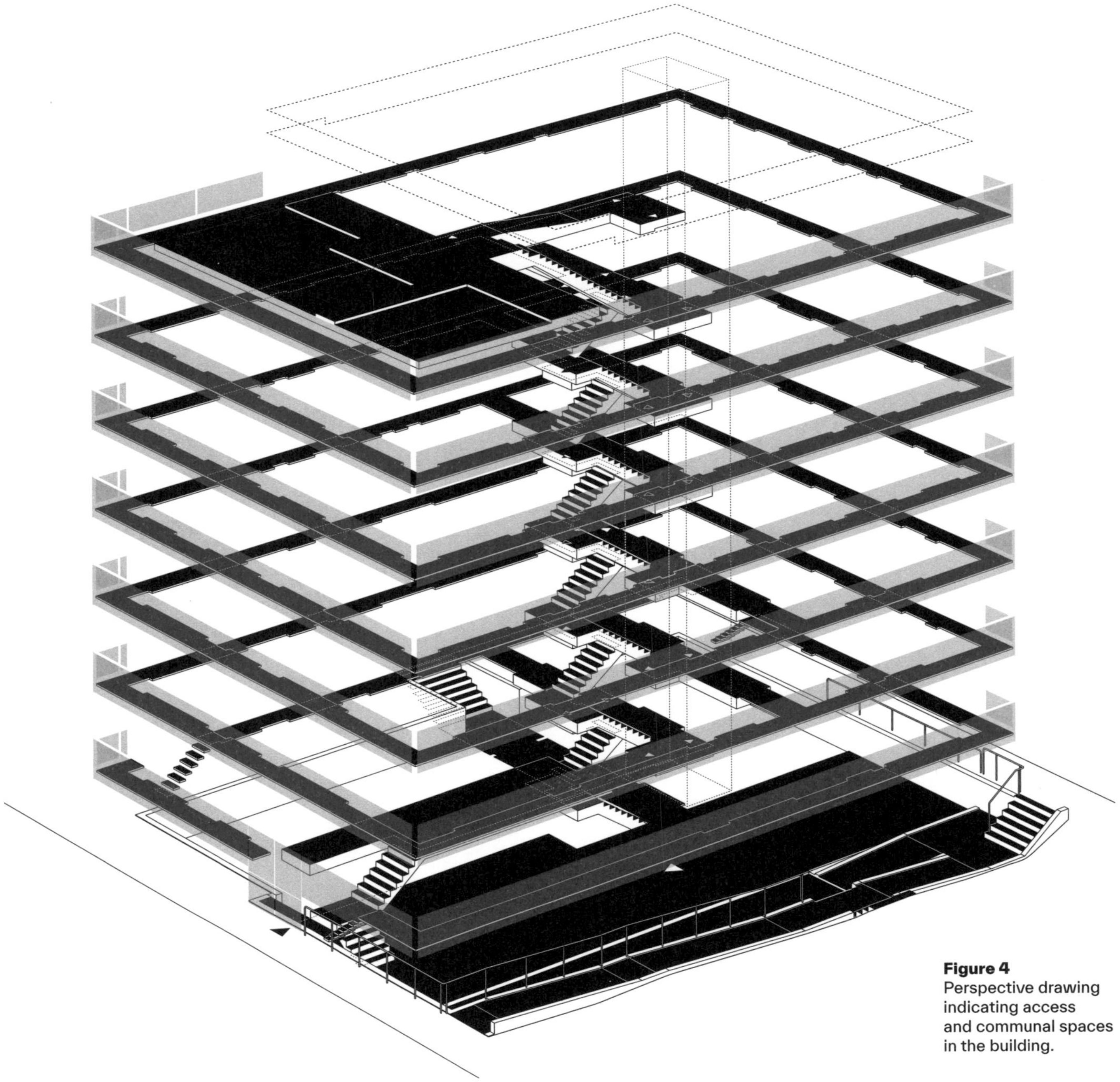

Figure 4
Perspective drawing indicating access and communal spaces in the building.

DS **The building has communal balconies, which are integrated into the facade and wrapped around the entire building on each floor. They connect the dwellings on the same floor and can be entered directly from the elevator lobby. Why did you create these connections?**

VvB They were helpful to a villain escaping the crime scene in *Homeland*, the television drama series filmed at the R50.[15] There are other reasons, of course. The glass door between the lobby and balcony brings daylight and natural ventilation to the staircase. Moreover, it is handy on some occasions, such as visits and gatherings, when people circulate in and out of the dwelling. Children find it helpful when they play. A second entrance to private dwellings via the balcony creates a spatial condition we are interested in. We see it as a latent spatial organization embedded in the floor plan and refer to it as "rotation." We find the concept relevant at different scales. If you look at the layout of level six, for example, there is circular communication around a triangular bedroom. The space between the room and the facade can be used as part of the room or as access between rooms. In the late 1990s, Tim Heide and I worked on a model for a single-family home in which we applied the very same principle.[16] In a way, that project was a critique of a conventional dwelling layout for the nuclear family, where you have a hierarchy between rooms. We did not accept that rooms should have only one function, and we integrated a series of neutral rooms and spaces for circulation. If we go back to R50, we could say that, at the conceptual level, having a balcony that wraps around the building allows for a similar form of rotation, also impacting the relationship between inside and outside.

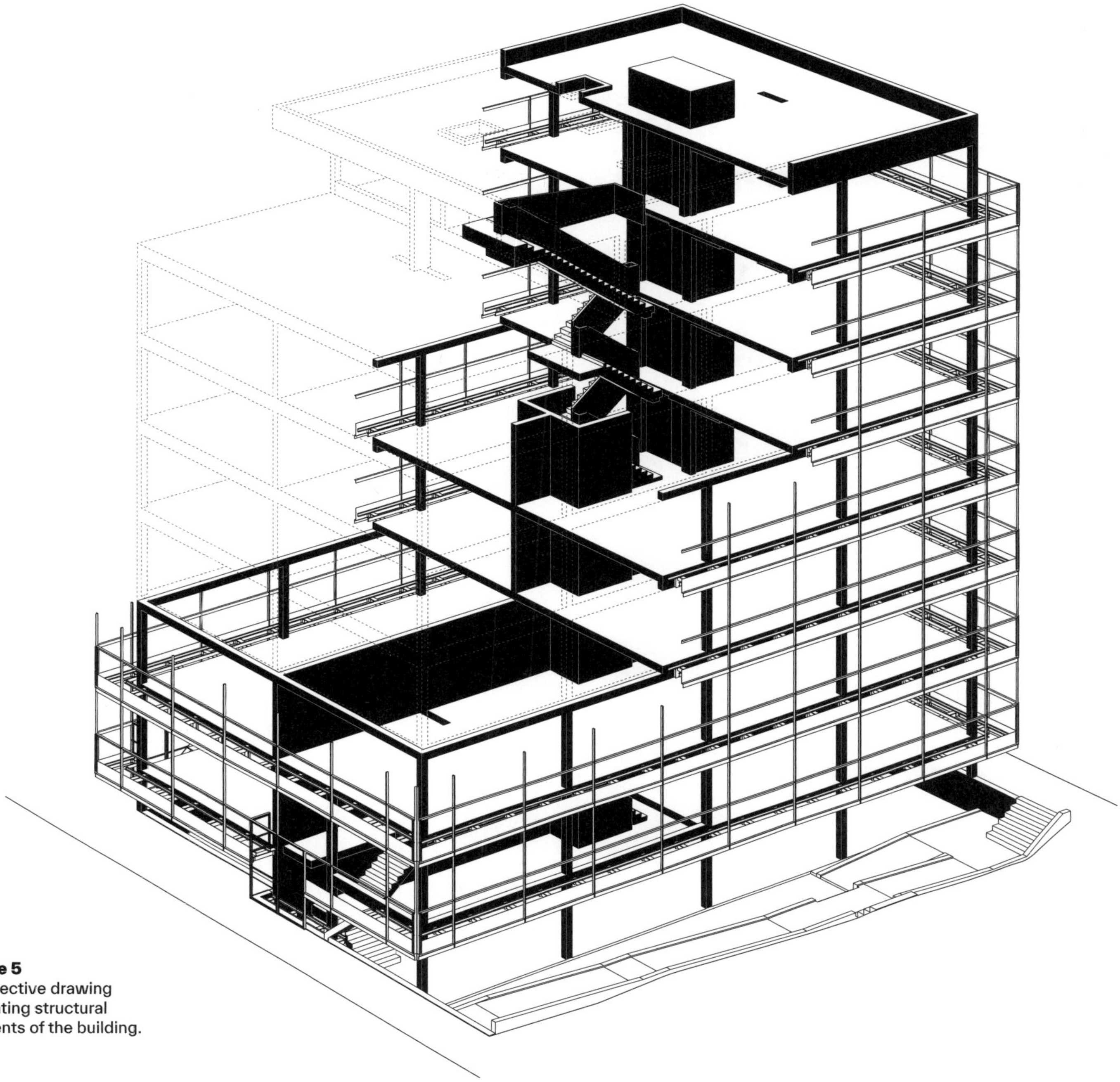

Figure 5
Perspective drawing indicating structural elements of the building.

DS Do the windows and foldable doors in dwellings open outward to allow movement along the facade?

VvB That is not the only reason. Panels open outward to create subtle barriers and divide a very long balcony, which helps a bit to provide privacy. It is important to emphasize that the balcony is not just a communal space. It is private, too. Since it is long enough, there is room for everyone, and because of that, we can rely on such subtle barriers to help differentiate between personal and communal. The other reason for windows at R50 to open outward is, as you suggest, the efficient use of interior space, so you do not have to move plants and furniture if you want to open windows. It also allows better use of the interior walls.

15. *Homeland*, the television drama series that premiered on October 4, 2015, on Showtime, filmed at the R50. See https://www.sho.com/homeland/.
16. Heide & von Beckerath, "Wunschhaus#1," accessed February 16, 2023, https://heidevonbeckerath.com/single/wunschhaus-1.

DS Two of this project's defining aspects are the residents' participation in the design process and empowering residents to assert control over their dwellings throughout the building's use. You already mentioned that visual graphs were instrumental in the participative design process. Can you tell us how spatial adaptability is embedded in the project?

VvB The project results from an intense dialogue between architects and residents, where we have professional knowledge on one side and everyday experiences and needs on the other. It is more complex and refined than having a skeleton and everyone doing what they want. There were decisions, starting with the positioning of the access core and service shafts, finding ways to stiffen the building structure without compromising the flexibility of the layout, and continuing with other finer details that were critical to the project. The building facade is also a result of an architectural strategy supporting diverse unit layouts and spatial adaptability. It comprises a range of floor-to-ceiling elements, including operable components such as foldable panels and pivoting doors, and fixed elements that are either glazed panels or solid insulated components with pinewood finish. Residents could choose elements they wanted in their dwellings, yet their choices added up to form an articulated building facade. Now that ten years have passed, it would be interesting to ask residents what they have changed in their dwellings and the building since one of the principal ideas behind the project was to enable residents to alter their homes and use shared spaces in different ways.

DS What challenges and opportunities do you foresee designing private outdoor areas in multiunit residential buildings?

VvB The provision of private outdoor areas is often a point of discussion when we work with private or public housing providers. Some want a place where people would have tables and chairs, but this differs from how we saw the private outdoor environment in this project. Take Lacaton and Vassal's work, Tour Bois le Prêtre, for example, and how they add winter gardens to the existing structure.[17] It is about adding space, not balconies, as we know them from the previous generation of multiunit residential buildings. There is a widespread illusion that the apartment should be a detached house that happens to be on level six of a large structure. We believe that it is more important to have the possibility to enlarge the apartment using the outdoor environment. That way, you can use the outdoor space in different ways. Is it not more practical if you have only one set of chairs and a table to move from the interior to the exterior? Our climate is warm-temperate. It is not exactly true that you can live outside. Still, there are many days when you can keep your windows open, which suggests both opportunities and challenges in resolving the relationship between inside and outside.

DS What design decisions had the most significant impact on the project's cost?

VvB We used durable and affordable materials throughout the project. At that time, using timber for the primary structure was not feasible. We had to do columns and slabs in concrete, but it was viable to have timber wall finishes, secondary structure, and window frames. The two materials work together as opposites. As part of the cost-efficiency plan, we used prefabricated and standardized building elements when we could. For example, bathroom walls are from a building system that is used for schools. Floor slabs are made of panels produced off-site, and stairs are prefabricated. Other design decisions, including the building's compact volume, were important to cost savings. Exposed concrete ceilings and screed floors responsible for the unfinished look of the building's interior contribute to reducing construction costs. We wanted to avoid unnecessary details and finishes. Screed floors were treated minimally, just so they could be cleaned and maintained, but we also made provisions so that residents could add timber flooring at any point.

17. Lacaton & Vassal, "Transformation of the Tour Bois le Prêtre – Paris 17 Druot, Lacaton & Vassal," accessed March 5, 2023, https://www.lacatonvassal.com/index.php?idp=56.

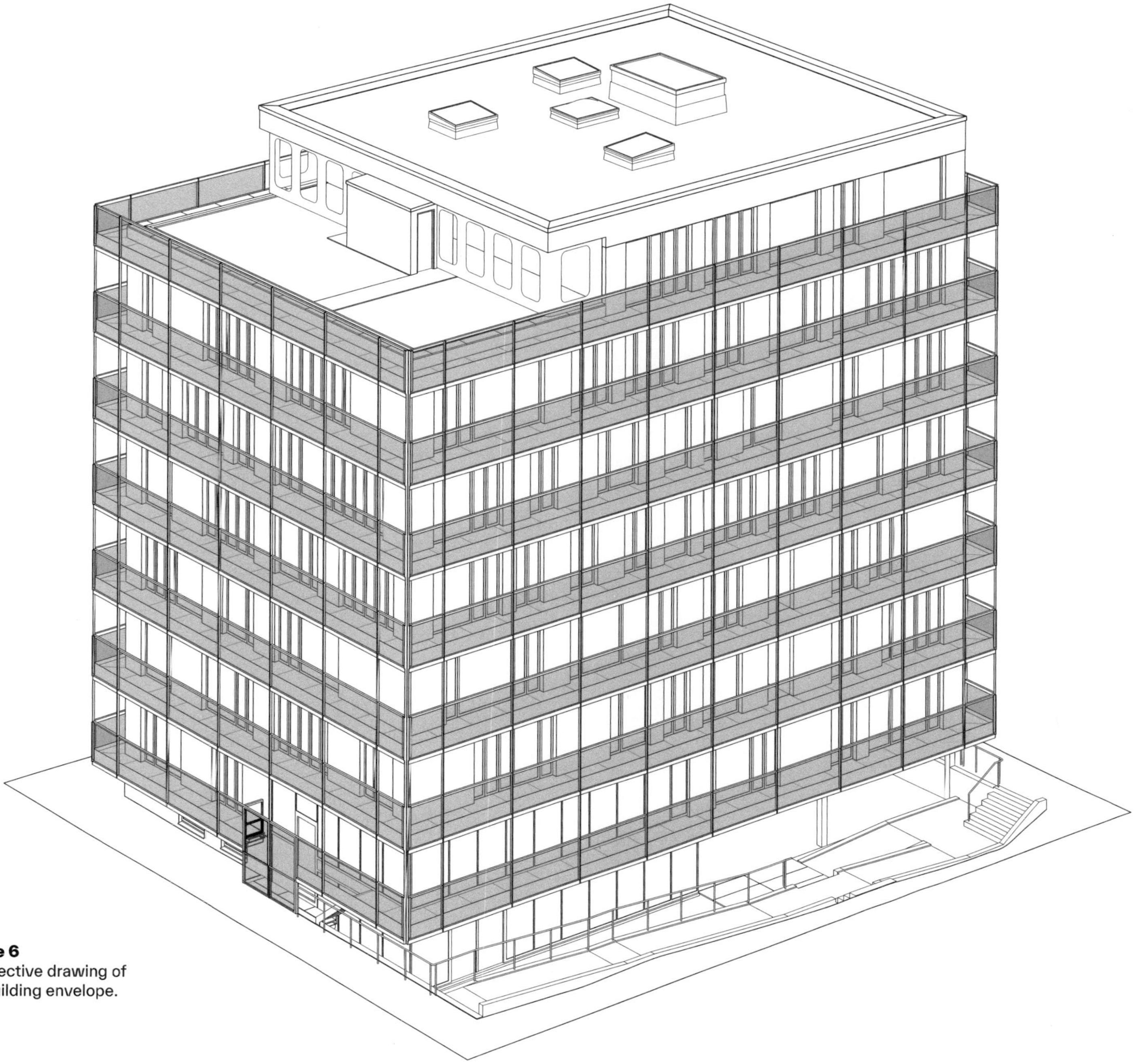

Figure 6
Perspective drawing of the building envelope.

"...the balcony is not just a communal space. It is private, too. Since it is long enough, there is room for everyone, and because of that, we can rely on such subtle barriers to help differentiate between personal and communal."

DS How do you see the project now, ten years after residents have moved in?

VvB With the benefit of hindsight, you could say R50 was developed by and for a group of people, of whom many are architects and artists with precarious employment, and that the agency about it and how it is done may be valuable to other settings. The experience of people who have lived in the building for a decade is relevant to understanding how we can live together and how important community building is in housing provision.

There still is a lasting public interest in the project, and it can be discussed from different angles and viewpoints. The experience of working with our collaborators ifau und Jesko Fezer and the group has enriched our practice and has laid the ground for other projects such as the residential and studio building at the former Berlin flower market IBeB[18] and the project Spiegelfabrik in Fürth.[19] We were just recently invited to participate in the *Mass Support: Flexibility and Resident Agency in Housing* exhibition at the Spitzer School of Architecture, City College, New York, and to speak about R50 in an accompanying symposium.[20] R50 is important for our practice, and I see it as a model project from which ideas and knowledge can be distilled, even at the larger scale associated with public housing.

18. Heide & von Beckerath, "IBeB," accessed August 8, 2023, https://heidevonbeckerath.com/single/ibeb?search=ibeb.
19. Heide & von Beckerath, "Spiegelfabrik," accessed August 8, 2023, https://heidevonbeckerath.com/single/spiegelfabrik.
20. Bernard and Anne Spitzer School of Architecture at The City College of New York, *Mass Support: Flexibility and Resident Agency in Housing*, exhibition, March 26–May 7, 2023; symposium, April 26, https://ssa.ccny.cuny.edu/events/exhibition-symposium/.

DS Is there a shift from self-organized housing provision based on private ownership in Berlin and Germany, and is your practice impacted by such changes?

VvB R50 was made possible through a concept-based bidding process. The IBeB project, which I briefly mentioned before, on which we worked together with ifau, is a larger multiunit residential building at a central location in Kreuzberg, Berlin. The building combines rental and owner tenancy, includes live and work options, and is a little bit different from R50. There is a larger and more heterogeneous group of residents and artists. It was a logical progression from R50. However, in that project, the lot was also acquired through concept-based bidding. One of the criteria in the process was that the project would positively impact the surrounding, but essentially, it was a sale of public land to a private group of people. Today, Berlin and many other cities are more aware of their responsibility for public housing, and they now understand that it is not sustainable to sell the land and to encourage short-term profit. The Senate of Berlin does not sell land anymore. At the same time, the Baugruppe concept is based on the availability of land, as well as the ability of groups of people to purchase the land and commission an architecture practice. This shift of public interest has made it almost impossible to initiate and realize a project like R50 today. Our work has followed that transition. We are now working more with housing cooperatives and public housing providers. The focus of innovative housing projects in Germany has shifted to land lease models, which suit housing cooperatives in particular. There is a programmatic lineage to R50, as present-day housing cooperatives are often intentional single-building undertakings based on different forms of communal living.

In conversation

The following section is an edited interview recorded on June 27, 2023, with Jesko Fezer, who lives in the building with his family and is one of the architects behind the project.[21]

DS What was the group's primary motivation for undertaking this project?

JF We, the group behind the project, wanted to live together, not isolated from other residents in the same building or neighborhood. That was our primary intent. However, the real estate market changed in Berlin at that time, and rental costs escalated. We did not want to be pushed out of the city center, where most of us faced rising rents. Therefore, ownership or autonomy became central to the project. We were looking for a model that would combine ownership with rental tenure, and what we have in R50 is individual ownership of our dwellings and the collective title of shared spaces and the lot. Initially, we wanted to take on a project as a housing cooperative, which at that time was not opportune. Today, we are starting to see a greater diversity of alternative housing models in Germany.

We wanted to make R50 a collective building. From the very start of the project, we planned for a lot of communal spaces, including a garden, workshop facilities, laundry, guest room, a big, shared space on the ground floor, balconies, a roof garden, and, of course, all the access spaces. We have created an unconventional building where the dwellings are connected by balconies and depend on the shared spaces.

It begs the question of what happens if someone wants to sell their apartment at a price significantly higher than the investment because of the market conditions and how that affects the community. Until today, none of the units have been sold. New tenants have moved into two units. One of the dwellings is inherited by the children of the initial group members. It shows that the project was not driven by profit but by housing needs.

DS Can you tell us more about why the group wanted to live together?

JF Living together was a practical idea for most of us. Some of the families involved with the project were experiencing the need to socialize with other families because of their children. We all did have contact with our neighbors in the multiunit residential buildings we lived in before moving to R50. The advantages of enabling interaction between children without making formal appointments and complicated childcare arrangements were evident to us. The same logic applies to having a communal roof garden, a workshop, a place for a piano, guests, or washing machines. We understood social and practical benefits and agreed we could reduce costs by sharing facilities we do not use daily. It allowed us to make individual units smaller and, therefore, cheaper.

DS The group of people behind the project appears to be homogenous. Was it a deliberate decision, or what contributed to it?

JF We did not go into the project as a group of friends who work in creative industries. Our approach was open. We advertised the initiative online and published the project on a website focusing on alternative collective housing in Berlin. We had a good response. Many were interested, but in the end, mainly people from our personal environment, friends, and colleagues stuck with the project and formed a homogenous group. There are many reasons for that. Part of it has to do with the planning process, which was experimental, long, and demanding. There needed to be trust. People responding to the online call were unsure where such a collective decision-making process would lead. It was much easier to commit to the project for those who knew each other. Finally, not everyone was convinced by our architectural intent.

21. Jesko Fezer's book *Controversial Methods: Architectural Discourses of Scientification, Politicization and Participation in the Environment of the Design Methods Movement of the 1960s* was published in 2022.

DS How important was housing affordability to this project?

JF At that time, there was no pressure, to the same extent as it is today, to build cost-efficiently. However, for a group like ours, with many working in professions with precarious jobs, the construction cost needed to be kept as low as possible. At the same time, we believed that housing should be affordable. That way, affordability in this project was political as much as it was practical. Once we agreed that affordability is one of our main objectives, all decisions were assessed through that lens. It meant we did not have to get into unnecessary discussions if someone said that one of the options would be unaffordable to them.

DS I understand that creating a large communal space on the ground floor was a subject of debate.

JF The group agreed to have a large, shared space on the ground floor, but it was not straightforward. Firstly, we suggested having smaller shared spaces on each level that could be shared between the three apartments and serve as their extension. After lengthy discussions, we settled on the ground-floor option. It meant that this space could be open to the public and connected to the street. It is designed as a winter garden with different heating systems and thermal comfort standards from what we have in the dwellings, which also helped reduce construction costs. The ground-floor space was left unfinished when residents moved in, and it was gradually fitted and equipped over time. That is also an example of postponing that I spoke about earlier.

22. Hochschule für Gestaltung Ulm, HfG.

DS Another important characteristic of this project is the participatory design process. Can you tell me more about how the decision-making during the design process unfolded?

JF There were two layers of participation. There was cooperation concerning individual layouts of the nineteen dwellings, and there was an intense collective debate on the design of the shared spaces. It took work to agree on everything. We are a big group, after all. We established some principles at the outset, and that was helpful. Another critical component of the decision-making process was postponing decisions when it was needed and feasible. We avoided making decisions if we could not agree on something and if that did not cause any foreseeable problems. The idea was to do what was necessary, use the budget we had in the best possible way, and allow inhabitants to make decisions after they moved in.

DS Regarding the individual dwellings, how important was the use of visual graphs to the design process?

JF The entire design process was based on participation. It involved negotiation and collective decision-making even when we discussed individual dwellings. We wanted to empower people who are not architects to communicate their preferences about the layout of their units. My colleagues and I wanted to start this conversation on abstract terms. We know that people expressing their spatial needs often fall into the trap of trying to reproduce what they experience, such as something from their childhood or something they have absorbed from various media. So, rather than jumping into floor plans, we wanted to support the decision-making process and postpone determining dwelling layouts. We used visual graphs, a method developed by Anthony Froshaug, a British graphic designer who, in the late 1950s, taught at the Ulm School of Design.[22] The method provided a way to capture complex spatial properties and mediate between science and design in a way that applied to our project. Today, many online tools make the use of visual graphs even more accessible. For our project, such a tool served to mediate between individual needs and architectural drawings and as a proxy to facilitate discussion.

DS How do you feel about the layout of your dwelling?

JF In the entire building, we have two nonrectangular walls. One is in our unit to maximize book storage and minimize the bedroom floor area. I learned to live and work with it. I must credit my partner for it. She only forgot to put a door in there; this was what I added. Another less common feature of our unit's layout is that it includes three parallel corridors. It gives possibilities, and these corridors are used differently. The entrance lobby is the most obvious one. It is used as a circulation space but often gets blocked as the small bathroom, conceptualized as three cells, expands into it. Separate access to the shower, bathroom sinks, and toilet is convenient for a household of four. The balcony is also corridor-like. It is used to connect with neighbors, and our children used to play there with other children. The third corridor, which runs along the facade, once connected three small bedrooms. When our children were younger, it was working perfectly fine. However, things become different now that they are older. They have convinced us that there needs to be a wall between their two rooms, and we closed that entryway five years after we moved in.

DS Was there much retrofitting in other units to meet the changing lifestyles similar to what you have just described in yours?

JF I know that in another unit, they did the opposite of what we did. They combined two rooms into one after some time. And I know that two dwellings took much longer to fix their layouts after we moved in. One bathroom was refitted, and a few partition walls have been moved to accommodate the usual household cycles. Overall, there were no significant changes.

"The advantages of enabling interaction between children without making formal appointments and complicated childcare arrangements were evident to us. The same logic applies to having a communal roof garden, a workshop, a place for a piano, guests, or washing machines. We understood social and practical benefits and agreed we could reduce costs by sharing facilities we do not use daily."

DS How do you interact with other residents?

JF The social dynamics and interaction between residents change throughout the day. It also depends on the day of the week and the time of the year. It depends if someone is working or looking after their kids. We meet informally in small groups to hang out and have a larger gathering regularly when we do the gardening and other things. It is also okay to stay in to watch a movie or work. We individually decide if and how we want to socialize. The building only provides good opportunities for it.

DS The communal balcony, a steel floor grate wrapped around the building and incorporated into the facade, often attracts attention when the project is discussed. How do you use it, and does it compromise the privacy of your dwelling?

JF Like everyone in the building, we have only two neighbors on our floor. One of them we would only meet with arranging it because of our unit layouts. Their kitchen and living areas are on the opposite side of the building. However, we interact much more with the second neighbor. Their kitchen and living room are adjacent to ours, and we can see and hear them when they are outdoors. Our daughters are friends, and many children often came over when they were younger. I know that some residents wanted partitions because of their pets or have placed potted plants in a certain way, and it can be regulated individually. For us, it works very well.

DS What are the other reasons for creating an 80-centimeter-wide, communally accessible balcony wrapped around the building on every level?

JF As we envisaged that unit layout would change over time and that residents would want to have diverse configurations, we didn't want to impose any limitations by placing private outdoor spaces anywhere specific. Instead, we decided to have them everywhere so they did not impact the unit layouts. It allowed inhabitants to develop their own arrangements during the design processes more freely and to change them as their needs changed. There were some practical aspects to it as well. It allowed doors to open outward and thus make better use of the interior. It created a little extension to each room.

DS Is it also to do with the architectural expression of the building?

JF The facade reflects the overall design strategy, which has to do with how the building is used and cared for or maintained and not how it can be sold. If we did not have a balcony that works like permanent scaffolding, we would not be able to use timber cladding and fixed glass panels for the facade, which reduces construction costs but requires varnishing and cleaning. Timber needs to be oiled every two years, and fixed glass panels must be cleaned from the outside. We wanted to make a statement with the building facade by opposing the use of costly building materials and unnecessary architectural surface treatments in housing projects, which was prevalent at the time in Berlin. The facade is not the main feature of the project. We just wanted to make it simple and not stand out from the surrounding social housing buildings. Today, it still confuses people in exciting ways. Judging by the exterior, some have asked if the building is still unfinished.

13 La Borda, Barcelona

Lacol

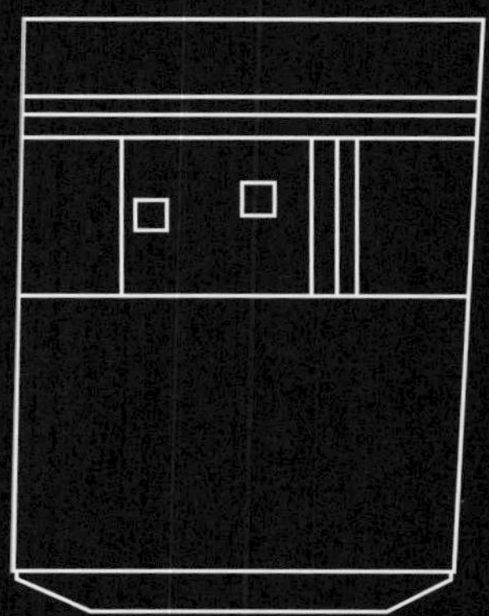

Community Infrastructure

Figure 1
Site plan, drawing scale 1:2500

La Borda, Barcelona
Lacol

Year of completion: 2018
Number of units: 28

This project provides affordable housing, and it is driven by the intent of a self-organized group to live in a community while maintaining the privacy of individual dwellings. It was initiated and led to completion by the housing cooperative La Borda, which owns the building, while residents, as its members, rent their dwellings. The local government supported this self-organized undertaking by providing a long-term lease for the land on which the building stands. Not all housing cooperatives are set in the same way, and this project's context includes its own specific economic, social, and regulatory aspects.[1] Central to the scope of this book is the architectural outcome of this project, which is internationally acclaimed and widely published. However, the following project description will focus on the links between architectural

1. Eduard Cabré and Andrés Arnau, "La Borda: A Case Study on the Implementation of Cooperative Housing in Catalonia," *International Journal of Housing Policy* 18, no. 3 (2018): 412–32, https://doi.org/10.1080/19491247.2017.1331591.

accomplishment and collaborative or participative design processes involving the resident community.

Background

The building is in La Bordeta, a neighborhood in Barcelona that includes a sizable Can Batlló textile factory, which was shut in the 1960s. The land use was requalified shortly after.[2] Still, because of the impasse between the owners and planners, the industrial premises were underutilized for almost fifty years until various community-driven initiatives established a joint platform for their conversion into cultural and social facilities.[3] La Borda housing cooperative was born in such a context along with other bottom-up initiatives. However, it was also distinctive in focusing on affordable housing provision. The housing cooperative, working with Lacol architects and incorporating some group members, argued that housing would complete the urban renewal and, along with cultural and social amenities, would help make the neighborhood an integral part of the city tissue.

Designing for Communities

In the public lecture hosted by the Melbourne School of Design on August 26, 2020, Cristina Gamboa presented how information collected from the housing cooperative members has led to the formulation of design objectives.[4] The survey conducted by Lacol revealed that most participants were experiencing housing stress by paying more than half of their gross income toward rent. It showed some were experiencing energy poverty through cost-prohibitive access to modern services and products. The survey also showed that participants preferred alternatives to cars because of the environmental impact, vehicle ownership and maintenance cost, and the development cost associated with the provision of parking. These findings were used to establish the project's priorities. In parallel, the design means to achieve such priorities were identified.

Shared Facilities

Reducing the cost of development and supporting a sense of community were among the leading design drivers of this project. The inclusion of shared and communal facilities in the building, in addition to private dwellings, was one of the primary means of achieving these objectives. The building has approximately 280 square meters of shared areas, including a kitchen and dining area, co-working and commercial area, multipurpose space, guest rooms, laundry, bicycle parking, and storage rooms. In this project, shared amenities improve housing conditions and, in return, allow for private dwellings to be relatively small. Simplistically put, as there are 28 units, each was designed smaller by 10 square meters so that the building could accommodate the listed communal areas. Finding the balance between the size of shared spaces and private dwellings may be unique for each project. However, the inclusion of jointly used spaces in this project, as architects will clarify in the interview in the further part of this chapter, was part of the strategy to build less and make cost savings. In addition, shared rather than individual use of spaces was seen as a way of reducing energy consumption and thus improving the building's environmental impact.

The rationale for sharing facilities while maintaining the privacy of individual dwellings is manifold. Jointly used facilities in residential buildings can provide infrastructure for social cohesion and support heterogeneous and intergenerational communities such as the one at La Borda. The communal laundry replacing a washing machine in each dwelling exemplifies how a shared facility saves space, reduces cost, potentially contributes to lower energy consumption, and creates space where residents can interact informally. A communal kitchen is also a place where people can meet. At La Borda, joint preparation of meals is seen as an equitable share of household tasks and a way of addressing gender-based inequalities.[5] Car parking is omitted altogether in this project. The planning requirements mandated the inclusion of car parking, and its omission had to be negotiated between architects and the municipality with the consensus of the residential community as a way of improving housing affordability. The heating system is another shared facility provided because of the housing cooperative's economic and environmental awareness.

Participative Design

In their lecture hosted by the Melbourne School of Design, Lacol architects suggested that the participative process is essential to challenging social stereotypes and housing typologies.[6] At the same time, they emphasize their efforts in establishing what is best for each community, as no single housing model would work for all resident communities. Regular meetings and design workshops between architects and housing cooperative members were central to the design development. Lacol suggested that understanding individual daily practices and routines was essential to finding ways a building could support social transformation.[6] They pointed out that including communal facilities, such as a laundry or kitchen, even though these have been historically part of many progressive buildings, may only be adequate for some communities. In their view, the collaborative process

2. The land use was requalified in the Barcelona General Metropolitan Plan of 1976.
3. Platforma Recuperem Can Batlló was established by various community-driven initiatives.
4. Christina Gamboa, "Infrastructures for Sustainable Living: Modes of Housing," guest lecture, Melbourne School of Design, August 26, 2020, https://edsc.unimelb.edu.au/studio-epsilon/lecture-repository/lacol.
5. Gamboa, "Infrastructures for Sustainable Living."
6. Gamboa, "Infrastructures for Sustainable Living."

is critical to addressing diverse ways of living and enabling more flexible use of the dwelling and communal spaces.

Courtyard

Communal spaces are structured around the courtyard. Shared facilities, such as the kitchen on the ground floor, the multipurpose room with a double height on level one, and a large outdoor area on level five, are linked with the courtyard. This space has a social and environmental role. The built volume surrounds the courtyard on the ground floor and levels three and four. Translucent polycarbonate panels provide enclosure on other levels but let daylight into this semioutdoor space. Large operable panels on levels five and six permit natural ventilation and help control the microclimate of the courtyard. Dwellings are ventilated via the courtyard. When panels are closed in winter, the sun preheats the air in the courtyard. In summer, panels open to draw in cooler air from the outside. The air from the courtyard is used to improve thermal comfort in dwellings and thus help reduce energy consumption for the heating and cooling of the building.

The building forms the street frontage by closing the space between two structures of different heights on the north. To the south, the building looks to the inner area of a large city block planned for public use. A passage from the street connects to the block's inner side. Most dwellings have private outdoor areas facing south.

Dwellings

Dwelling variants have a different number of 15-square-meter rooms and a single wet core containing a bathroom and a kitchen. As a rule, rooms are positioned along the facade for daylight and natural ventilation, while wet cores are placed in the central zone of the building.

The load-bearing elements above the ground floor are made of cross-laminated timber. The structural walls define six strips of space. In the southern part of the building, where most units are, four strips host what architects call "basic dwelling configurations," composed of two rooms and a wet core. The two remaining strips contain rooms called "satellites," as they are not stand-alone modules and can only be part of the basic dwelling configuration.[7] A pair of satellites are strategically positioned between basic dwellings so they can be attached or detached. Concealed double door openings are incorporated into cross-laminated timber panels to allow residents to negotiate unit boundaries during the design process and potentially after the building is in use.

The project envisages three dwelling sizes: small, medium, and large. However, there are many more layout variants. Small-size units of approximately 40 square meters are equivalent to a basic configuration module that can be either open plan or have two separate rooms. Medium-size units of roughly 55 square meters have one additional room, and large-size units of approximately 70 square meters have two more rooms.

The differences between dwellings of the same size range from minimal, driven by the slightly irregular shape of the building lot, to significant, generated by the differently connected satellites and basic dwelling configurations. Currently, there are twenty-eight units, including five small, sixteen medium, and seven large size variants. Forty-nine adults and thirteen children live at La Borda, while only two households are nuclear families of four.[8] The spacious rooms and the possibility to make dwellings from different numbers of rooms enable spatial adaptability and provide a way of meeting the needs of households of different sizes and structures. The building was handed over to residents after the basic construction works had been completed. The project envisaged that residents would complete the finishes and fittings themselves as part of the cost-saving strategy and the plan to let inhabitants assert control over their dwelling spaces. Floor plans published on the architect's website utilize black linework for fixed elements, such as structural walls and wet cores, while red linework indicates furniture and fittings added by residents.[9]

7. Lacol, "La Borda Cooperative Housing," accessed February 16, 2023, https://www.lacol.coop/projectes/laborda/.
8. Lacol, "La Borda Cooperative Housing."
9. Lacol, "La Borda Cooperative Housing."

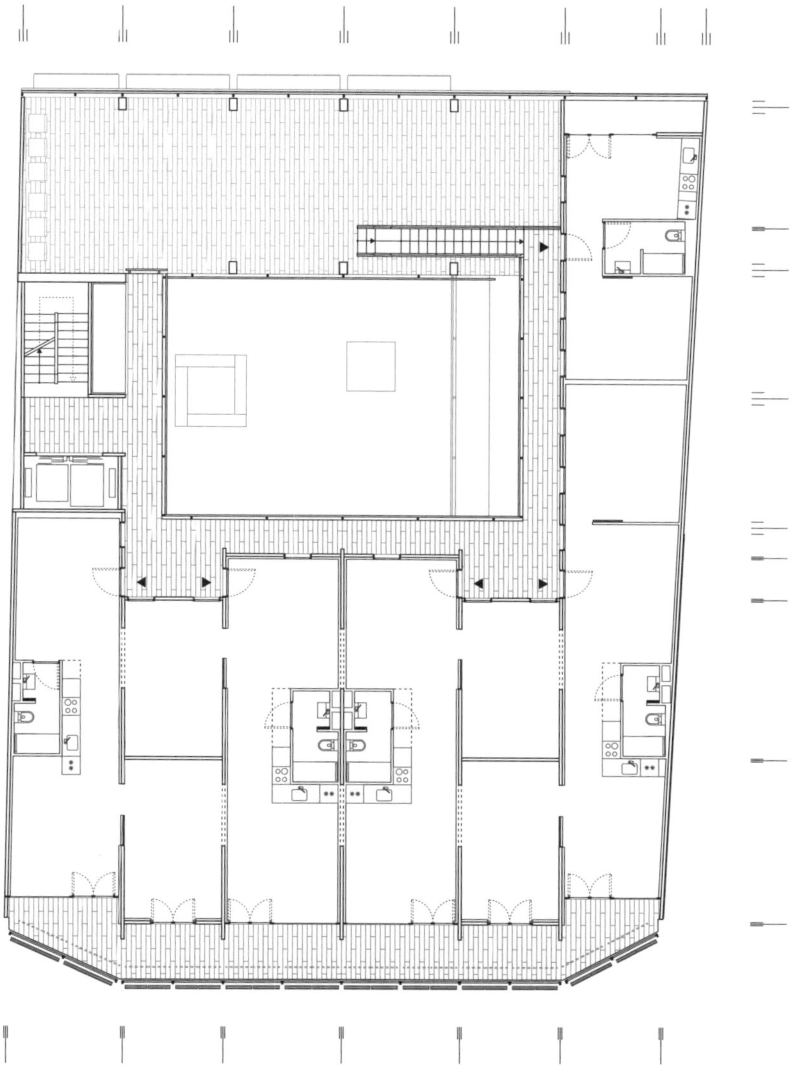

Figure 2
Typical floor plan, drawing scale 1:250

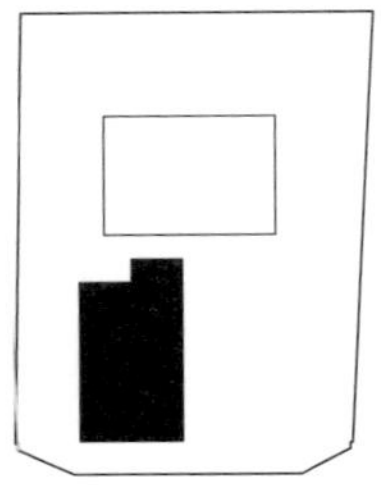

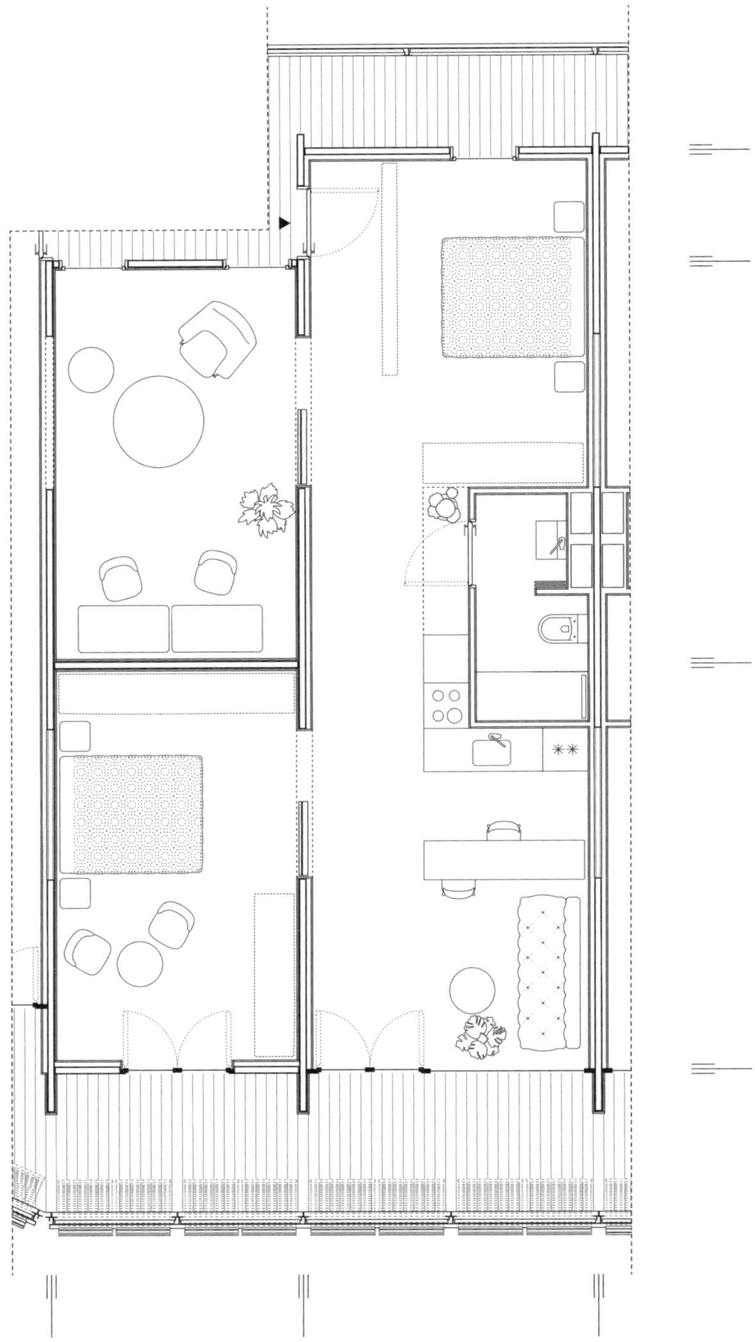

Figure 3
Sample unit layout, drawing scale 1:100

In conversation

The following section, an edited interview with Lacol members Cristina Gamboa Masdevall and Carles Baiges Camprubí recorded on January 23, 2023, provides further information about the project from the architects' perspective.

DS The inclusion of shared or communal facilities is one of the defining aspects of the project. What are the main values of the communal spaces in the building?

CG The project results from an understanding that some facilities can be taken out of the individual units and made communal to reduce the cost of construction and operation and efficiently use space and energy. So the practical side of the communal is important to the project, but there are other things, such as the social benefits of living in the community and how people interact. The communal spaces are organized around the courtyard. You enter the building via the courtyard, and from there, galleries and stairs take you throughout the building, linking communal spaces on different floors. Those shared facilities have a practical and social role, as this is where residents interact. A route to the shared laundry on the second floor generates the possibility of meeting someone and speaking with them. In addition to the social, there are economic and environmental reasons for shared laundry.

DS Is there a clear divide between individual and communal in the building?

CB Within the La Borda community, residents speak about the building as a house. There is a level of intimacy whereby people in their pajamas and flip-flops circulate throughout the building, to give an example. I think residents feel at home, even in communal areas, such as the kitchen on the ground floor. At the same time, there is a different kind of intimacy within the private units. But it is not a simple divide between individual and communal. The boundary between the two is blurred in many ways in the building.

DS What architectural means do you use to negotiate the boundary between individual and communal?

CG For example, we have floor-to-ceiling windows separating units from the access gallery. And you know, people were saying that's funny. But it was a conscious decision. Having glass there enables interaction between people. For example, during the recent pandemic, it helped people connect. People kept a physical distance in compliance with requirements but could see each other. In more ordinary times, these openings permit a visual connection between parents staying inside the units and kids who might be playing in the communal areas of the building. It enables communal areas to operate as a true extension of private dwellings.

There is a sequence of thresholds between private and communal in which floor-to-ceiling windows play a part. There is a gradual transition between the interior of the dwelling, the exterior area just in front of the window where the entrance to the unit is, which we call the "square," and finally, there is the remaining part of the galleries and stairs that enable circulation throughout the building and access to units. The gradient transition extends further into the unit layout and how we think of the relationship between rooms in the unit. We try to connect kitchens, which we see as the most open part of the private dwellings, and the communal spaces in the buildings, considering other functional and regulatory requirements. We place rooms for living and sleeping next to the facades of the building to benefit from daylighting and natural ventilation. But with floor-to-ceiling windows and the configuration of internal partitions, we permit a visual connection between the kitchen and communal areas via rooms.

CB That works very well in practice. For example, if you are in the apartment with your child and see someone in the multipurpose space with their kid, you can join them without having to arrange it. Spontaneous meetings are something that only happens sometimes in more conventional multiunit residential buildings.

CG There are different ways of using shared spaces in the building, which is central to considering the relationship between private and communal. One can individually use communal spaces of the building, effectively extending the private dwelling space into the communal areas.

DS You have already identified the importance of the courtyard for the relationship between individual and communal, but the courtyard is also essential for the relationship between inside and outside, having a central role in the heating and ventilation of the building. Can you speak more about the overlap between social and environmental strategies in the project?

CG As the lot is deep, we thought the courtyard would be a good way to introduce daylight into dwellings and help natural ventilation. It is also a reference to *corrala* buildings and vernacular architecture.[10] The building's courtyard has a social value, but we also see it as an energy-saving device. It combines architectural form and several mechanisms for the efficient use of energy. Having an enclosed courtyard increased the construction cost, but its role in the building's heating and ventilation has justified it. The automated openings in the courtyard control air circulation. The air from the courtyard is used in cooling or heating of dwellings. However, as all units take air from the courtyard as well as from the outside, we have developed protocols for operating windows and sunshades belonging to individual units to respond collectively to both warm and cold weather. There is a personal responsibility and collective action in that.

The joint use of some facilities is also key to the environmental impact of the building. For example, instead of twenty-eight washing machines, one for each unit, we have two high-end shared ones. On Wednesdays, when we cook together, only one stove is running. We get the supplies from the shop on the ground floor. All of this reduces the environmental impact of living.

DS Are there any private outdoor areas in the building, or are all outdoor areas shared?

CB In the south, we have outdoor areas associated with dwellings. These terraces are mainly used individually, but no fences divide the space. Boundaries are loose and established by pots with plants placed there by residents. Neighbors can meet there. During the recent pandemic-related lockdowns, this was particularly valuable in combating loneliness.

CG Otherwise, a toddler or pet can make their way across occasionally. We did not design any physical dividers and have assumed that the space in front of the units on the south facade, which is either 3.6 meters wide or twice that, would be an extension of that unit.

DS What other architectural decisions have contributed to the environmental impact of the building?

CG The environmental impact is central to the project. Regarding space planning, it is important to underline that all units have dual orientation and that twenty-four out of twenty-eight units have southern exposure to minimize reliance on heating and ventilation systems.

CB The weather has been freezing in the past few days in Barcelona, with the temperature dropping to 3 degrees Celsius at night, and most of the south-facing units have not used the heating system, while the temperature in the dwellings remains around 20 degrees. Interestingly, when residents moved in, the first impression we heard was not how nice but how warm their units were. The community is making further improvements to how energy is consumed. Compared to the first year, biomass used for heating, including hot water, has dropped by one-fifth.

10. *Corrala* are historical multiunit residential buildings with a central courtyard and outdoor access galleries built throughout Spain.

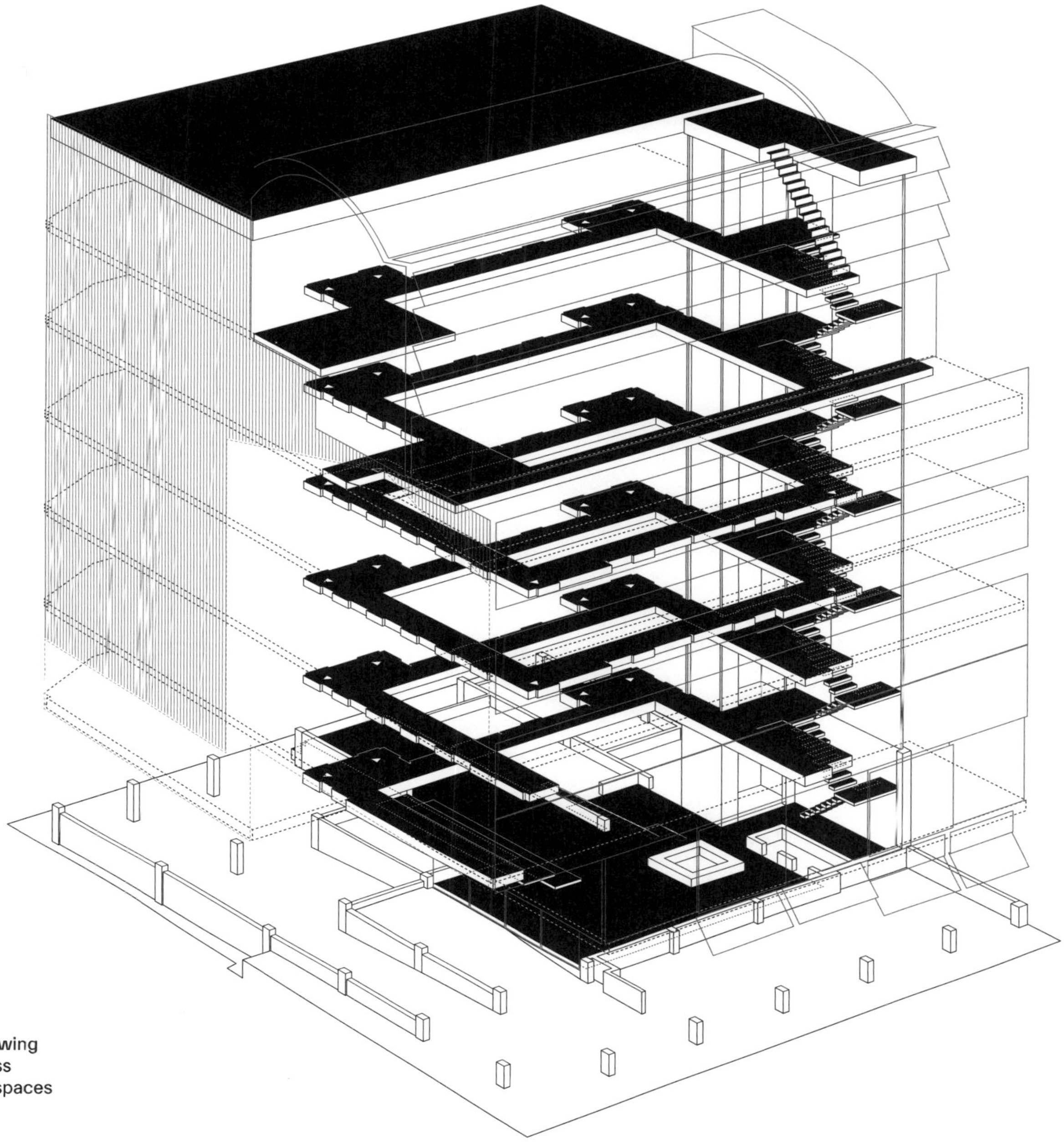

Figure 4
Perspective drawing indicating access and communal spaces in the building.

DS What are the main drivers for the design of the building's envelope?

CB Our strategies for the two building facades, one facing north and the other south, were very different. The outer layer of the south facade is made of simple rollable sunshades. On the north side, we have less sun and a noisy street. Therefore, the building envelope is less permeable on that side and dominated by polycarbonate panel cladding. We only have housing units on the two upper floors on the northern side. There is a communal outdoor area on top of it. The space below is a semioutdoor environment intended for joint use and designed as a multipurpose space. It is separated with polycarbonate panels from the busy street. There is no thermal insulation. In winter, it gets cold, and it is mainly used by children as a playground. The communal kitchen and living room, located on the ground floor and facing south, are used more regularly.

DS Why did you use polycarbonate panels?

CG We chose polycarbonate panels to enclose the semioutdoor environment of the courtyard because they are cost-effective. We could not afford glass. Working with a limited budget, we decided to use the funds for other parts of the building. Polycarbonate provides some protection from noise and is a lightweight material, not requiring an expensive support structure. It is used in agriculture and produced by a company near Barcelona.

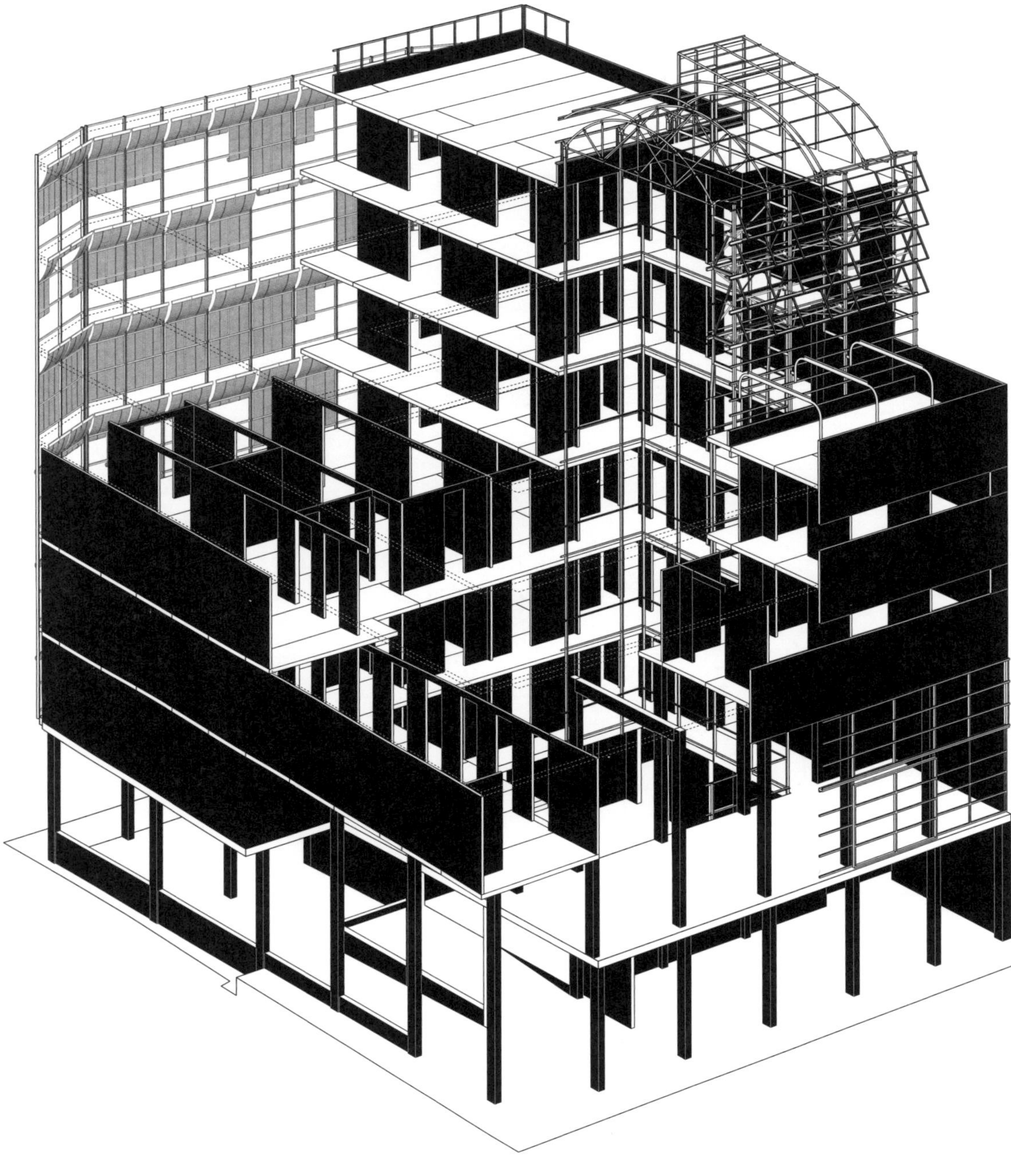

Figure 5
Perspective drawing indicating structural elements of the building.

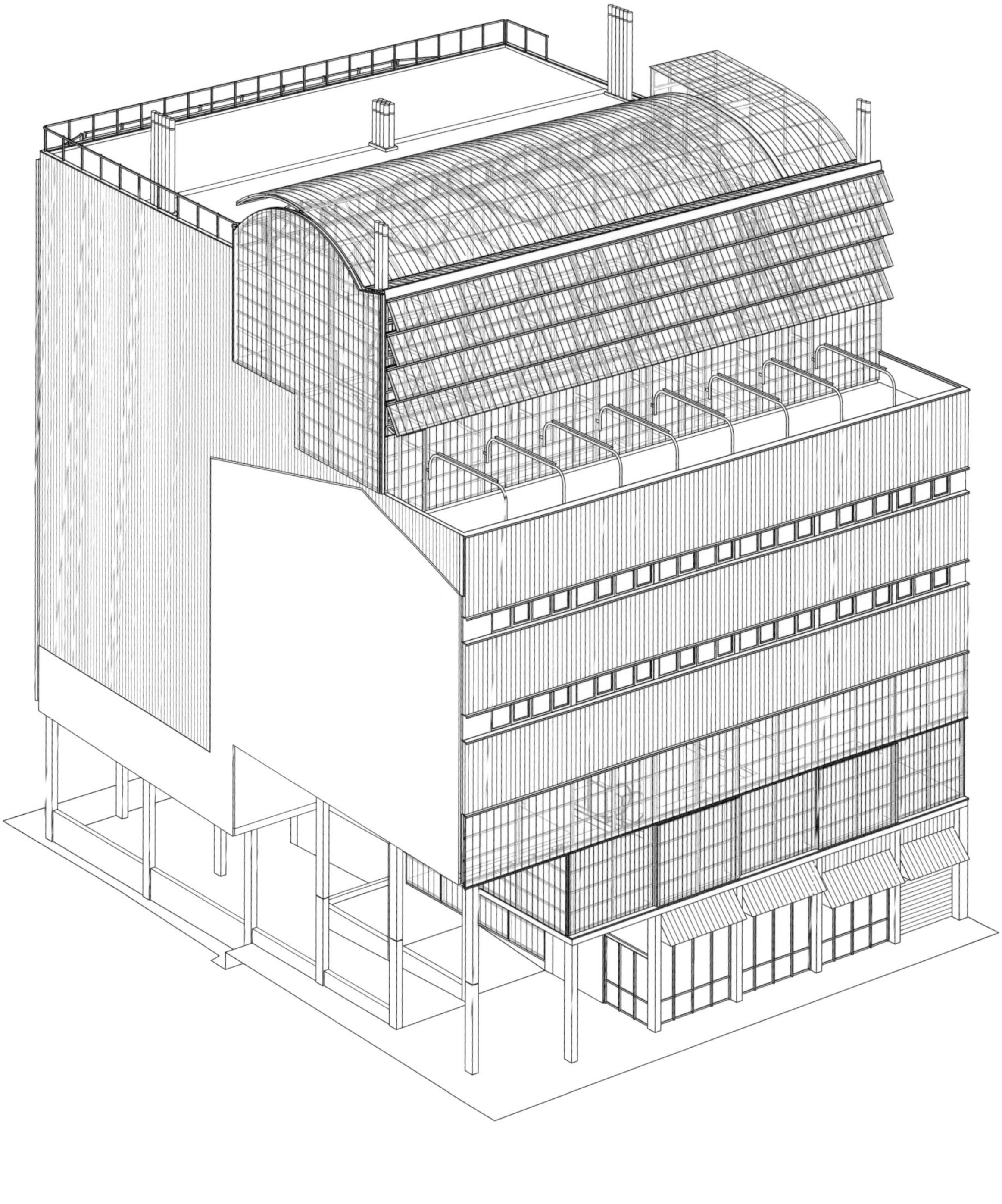

Figure 6
Perspective drawing of
the building envelope.

DS How did you address spatial adaptability in this project, and how does it work in practice?

CG We have developed unit layouts using basic dwelling configurations and satellite modules to respond to residents' needs and to facilitate changes that may be required in the future. The positioning of cross-laminated timber walls impacts the flexibility of the plan and how satellite modules can be exchanged between units. We have included door-size openings in the structural walls precisely to enable more spatial adaptability for the future use of the building. These openings are concealed with drywall. We also envisaged that kitchens could be differently customized according to individual preferences but staying roughly in the same position because of the services. The architectural project for the building and construction works have stopped at a stage that is in line with building regulations, such as that the kitchen is operational, but at the same time allows residents to complete their dwelling according to their choice. Some residents have done the second phase works themselves; some wanted an open plan configuration, and some wanted professional builders to complete the interior. We have conducted workshops to help with different layouts. Like the communal areas, they, too, were gradually finished. Guest rooms, kitchen, and dining area are complete, but there is always more work in other areas.

DS Do you feel that residents could assert control and modify their dwellings according to their preferences?

CB It is exciting to see how the twenty-eight units designed according to the same principles become very different. It includes minor changes but also more significant ones. Some units that started as open plan configurations now have rooms for kids born in the meantime. Recently, one of the households has decided to move out. It is the very first relocation in the building. However, another current resident wants to move into their unit, which triggers some changes in the two units. We have yet to have an instance where a satellite module was exchanged between units, although that would be feasible. We have also learned that some layouts have a better capacity for change, even though they appear similar. For example, the positioning of windows impacts the possibility of subdividing rooms.

DS What are the main challenges in empowering residents to customize their dwellings?

CG When the building project stops at the level of minimal definition of dwelling to allow for appropriation, to let residents make dwellings their own, as we want, a cost is associated with it. It is often the case that residents moving in may not be financially capable, nor have the knowledge, to undertake construction work and complete fittings and finishes of the interior. It is not easy for everyone to design a unit layout, and we try to help with workshops and manuals. We are now considering if it is better to do more, in terms of the building works, to ensure specific benchmarks are met.

CB There is a bit of a discrepancy between individual and communal needs in this regard. For example, a family leaving one unit and moving into another may feel they are losing what they have invested in adapting their old home. Our experience is that this is an issue for bigger projects more so than for the smaller ones, where residents come and go more frequently. The architect needs to consider different aspects, ranging from electrical services, including the layout of power lines, to those related to legal and contractual matters. For example, we are now considering whether basic dwelling configurations and satellite rooms should be leased under separate contracts to facilitate a potential future exchange.

CG The construction budgets we are currently involved with are higher. We are working toward higher standards of finishes, and there is an expectation that the interior of the dwelling would require less investment from residents after they move in. We undertook much risk in La Borda by making it an experimental project, contributing to addressing some of the big issues of affordable housing supply and community building.

La Borda, Barcelona

In conversation

The following section is an edited interview recorded on March 7, 2023, with one of the residents at La Borda, who lives in the building with their partner and two children. They live on the sixth floor.

DS How do you find the relationship between communal and individual life at the building?

SG The building has a good balance between the individual and communal. I know this may not always be the case with housing cooperatives—I have friends living elsewhere in bigger communities, and I understand this balance is not always achieved. For me, this is an essential quality of La Borda. We have plenty of communal spaces, but we also have our dwellings where we have privacy. That is why I say the balance is good.

DS What communal areas do you use the most?

SG I use the communal kitchen and the dining room to invite my friends and have communal weekly dinners with people living in the cooperative. Meetings often take place here. For example, when we meet with other cooperatives, it is in the communal dining room. I also use the laundry very often, like everyone else. I use guest rooms often when my father comes to visit us. It is very convenient.

DS Can you say more about the benefits of living in the community for children and how relevant is access to communal spaces for them?

SG Yes, shared spaces are important to children. During the recent pandemic, we were under lockdown for three months and could not go out as much as we wanted to. Living in a community and accessing spaces outside your apartment within the building was very important. My daughter was one year old at the time, just starting to walk, and she enjoyed communal spaces in the building, such as the courtyard, the terrace, and the galleries. Children like to play in the courtyard, where we keep our bicycles. I think the space is important so children can be safe and well there. But equally important to them are the relationships created between residents. My daughter, now four years old, knows other children and adults in the community. Children have an understanding of the community and the relationship between neighbors in the building. The benefits are primarily social and, to some extent, practical. My daughter is still too young to be left unattended. So I can't stay in my apartment and do my work while she plays alone in the communal areas. But she meets other children in communal areas, and they play together, giving you those moments during communal dinners or other times. When I do the laundry, she can play and meet other children.

DS What do you think of the decision to use glass panels to separate private dwellings from the access gallery and communal areas in the courtyard? There could be smaller windows, but there are floor-to-ceiling glass panels instead.

SG It is not as common in Spain as it may be in Northern Europe, so residents were surprised a bit when it was proposed and even when we moved in. We have curtains on our bedroom windows, but it is nice to have an opportunity to see into the courtyard and more daylight from two different sides. It does make you feel more connected to your neighbors.

DS How do you share tasks and organize communal activities?

SG Maybe I can focus on communal dinners to explain more. We take responsibility for organizing the dinners in teams, each having their turn every six weeks. Teams go shopping, do the cooking, and decide what to prepare. It is always vegetarian, and we use fresh produce from the shop in our building. The team washes the cookware, but everyone else washes their dishes. These dinners are a critical social moment, nice for everyone. Children love them and sometimes take part in cooking and play together in the courtyard.

DS Do you feel comfortable in your dwelling regarding thermal comfort, daylight, and ventilation?

SG In that regard, our dwellings are wonderful. I spend a lot of time in my apartment and often work from home. Daylight and natural ventilation are great. The indoor temperature is excellent. In winter, we are warm and do not have to put the heating on. It is very different from other Barcelona apartments I lived in, which were more expensive and less comfortable. In summer, we keep windows toward the courtyard open to ventilate our units. As you know, summers in Barcelona can be very hot.

DS Do you use outdoor areas of the building?

SG We use the terrace in front of the apartment a lot. We have a table with chairs and a hammock there. There are some plants. In winter, we like gardening with the children. We use it the most in spring and summer. We have a small inflatable pool for the children in the summer. We meet people living in adjacent flats, and sometimes, not very often, we have dinners there. We have created the sixth-floor community. We have dinners together, using the communal terrace located on the other side of the courtyard or in our apartments, more often than on the deck in front. No other children are on the same floor, so our children interact with children from other building floors.

"Children like to play in the courtyard, where we keep our bicycles. I think the space is important so children can be safe and well there. But equally important to them are the relationships created between residents. My daughter, now four years old, knows other children and adults in the community. Children have an understanding of the community and the relationship between neighbors in the building."

DS How do you find the layout of your dwelling?

SG We have one of the most spacious apartments in the building. It is not huge, but there is enough space for us. We have two bedrooms and one open area comprising the kitchen, dining room, and living space. We have sufficient storage space, including the built-in overhead storage space in the apartment, and we also use one of the small communal storages we have on each floor of the building. We modified the entry zone of our apartment to create space to leave your coats, bags, and umbrellas. We have a shoe bench outside and keep prams in the access gallery by the entrance to our unit.

DS Can you talk more about any changes you made to your dwelling since you moved in, or if there were any recent building works?

SG We moved into our dwelling right after the main construction works were complete. We did some of the work on finishings and fittings ourselves. Our unit was all an open space, and we installed partitions to create rooms we needed for the children and us. It would have been nice to have it all open, but we organized the space as we wanted. We did the painting ourselves. My partner is a carpenter and did most of the finishes and fittings in our apartment. When residents moved into the building, a group of people with some experience helped everyone with work in their apartments. In this process, lasting several months, we have informally consulted architects who are also part of the community. More recently, last week, we had a community workshop to help one of the residents to refurbish a unit. They are moving from one unit to another, and some renovation is needed.

DS Would you like to add anything specific about the building from your point of view?

SG The building and the cooperative I am part of are connected to the neighborhood with a rich history of self-organized movements. It made a difference in making the project happen, especially at the beginning. The people involved were part of the collaborative culture. They had the knowledge necessary to realize the project, to enable participation and dialogue, but not to take too much of everyone's time.

14

85 Social Dwellings in Cornellà, Barcelona

Peris+Toral Arquitectes

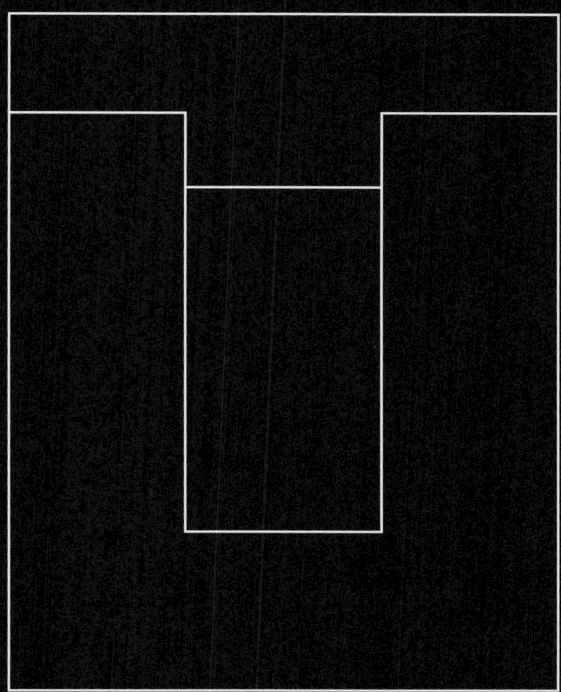

Rooms

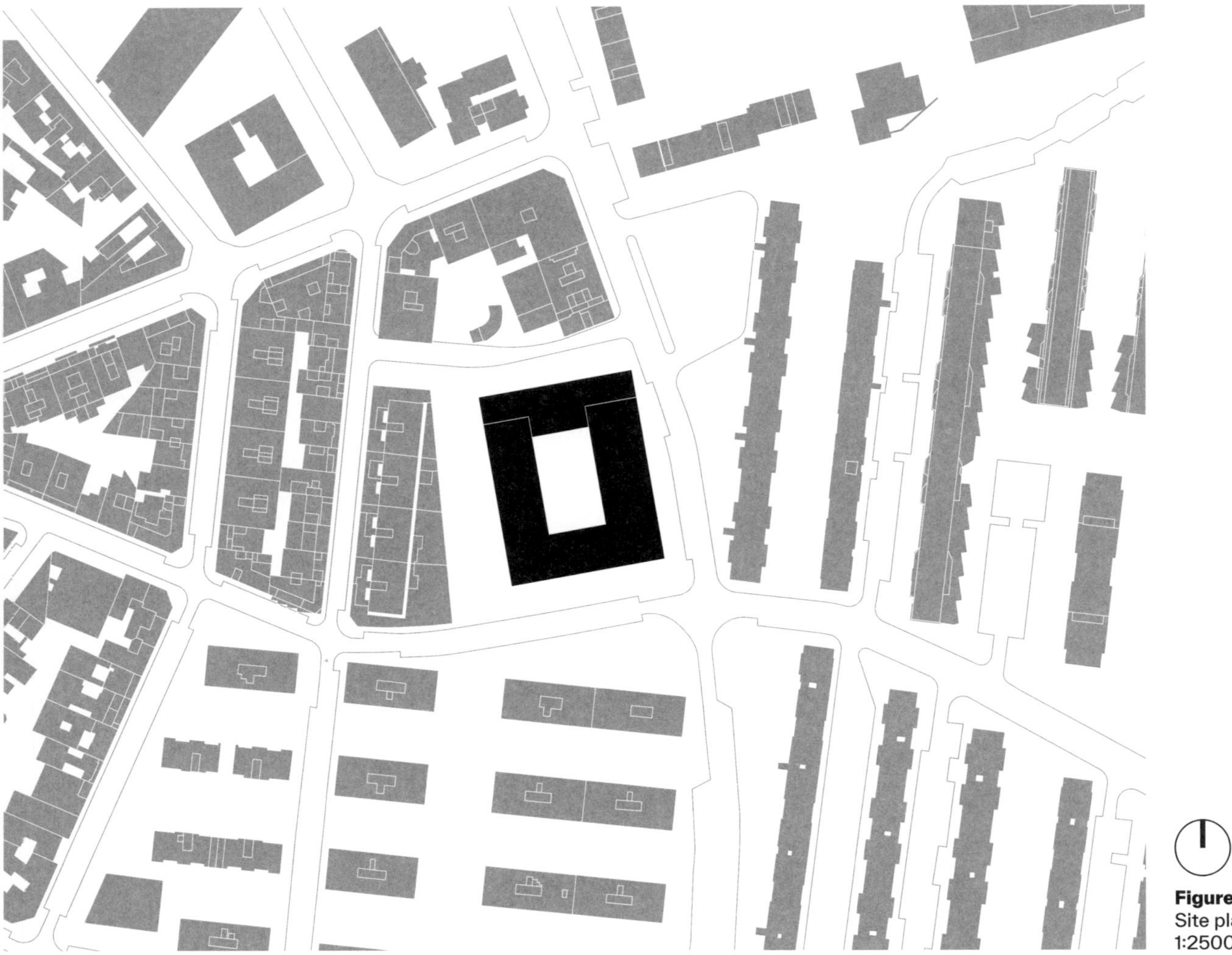

Figure 1
Site plan, drawing scale 1:2500

85 Social Dwellings in Cornellà, Barcelona

Peris+Toral Arquitectes

Year of completion: 2021
Number of units: 85

This building is conceptualized as a composite of rooms of the same dimension. Among the main characteristics of this project are the spatial adaptability of the dwelling layout, the primary timber structure, and a layered envelope designed as an interface between indoor and outdoor environments.

Peris+Toral Arquitectes won the architectural competition in 2017 after the social housing provider, L'Institut Metropolità de Promoció de Sòl i Gestió Patrimonial (IMPSOL), initiated the project.[1] The site is in Cornellà de Llobregat municipality, Barcelona's southwestern metropolitan area, on the lot formerly occupied by a cinema in a densely built residential neighborhood. The planning requirements and the competition brief determined that the building have five floors, a rectangular base of 50 by

1. The project is part of the Vivienda con Protección Oficial (VPO) program. The developer is L'Institut Metropolità de Promoció de Sòl i Gestió Patrimonial (IMPSOL) (Metropolitan Institute for Land Promotion and Property Management).

40 meters, and a courtyard measuring 24 by 14 meters in footprint.

Universal Room

During the public lecture hosted by the Melbourne School of Design on August 10, 2022, José Toral explained that their intent was to create an entire building of identical rooms.[2] They started the project by focusing on spatial organization and dwelling layouts as the building volume was determined. They wanted to depart from a conventional unit layout and the hierarchical order of rooms in a dwelling, explaining that traditional dwelling layouts include rooms of different sizes dictated by their use. Usually, living rooms are the biggest. The parents' bedrooms are smaller, and the gradation continues via children's rooms and other spaces. However, José Toral and several more architects whose work is presented in this book point out that such hierarchy limits the flexibility and the possibility of using dwelling spaces according to diverse needs and lifestyles. Instead, he suggests that all rooms could be dimensioned to be used in multiple ways. Since recommendations for the dimensioning of such universal rooms are not part of most multiunit residential design guidelines, José Toral referred to three architectural precedents relevant to their work.[2] The first is a traditional Japanese concept of domestic space, whereby rooms have multiple purposes and are not named after their use but by their size based on tatami modules, a type of floor mat measuring 1.8 by 0.9 meters. The second reference is a kitchen designed in several versions by Margarete Schütte-Lihotzky, which found application in thousands of residential units delivered through the housing program New Frankfurt in the 1920s.[3] These kitchens were acclaimed for their functional clarity, incorporating contemporary thinking about hygiene and workflow and based on detailed time-motion studies and interviews with women's groups.[4] The third and final precedent is Le Corbusier's Cabanon, designed after anthropometric analysis and the Modular system as a basic accommodation unit.[5] The square bases of the eight-tatami room, a version of the Frankfurt Kitchen, Le Corbusier's Cabanon, and the rooms in the project by Peris+Toral coincide almost to a centimeter. Dimensions tested for a habitable room in vernacular architecture, a kitchen, and a self-contained unit in modernist architecture have found application in accommodating spatial adaptability in the multiunit residential building in Cornellà. The benefits of dwellings composed of universal rooms, dimensioned above subsidized housing standards, including suitability for the diversity of contemporary lifestyles, will be further discussed with the architect in the following segment of this chapter.

The matrix of 543 almost identical rooms, with a square base of 3.6 meters side, makes an underlying concept of this project.[6] It works well with the lot dimensions and the given planning constraints and has allowed architects to articulate a three-room-wide volume wrapped around the courtyard. The strategy enables all units to have dual orientation and private outdoor areas. The positioning of building services and access routes aligns with the matrix logic. Wet cores, including kitchens and bathrooms, are placed in the central zone so that habitable rooms have better daylight and outlook prospects. The ratio between the overall and the usable built area is very efficient. The four vertical circulation cores, with elevators and stairs, are placed at the corners of the courtyard. Each core provides access to four or five dwelling units per floor level. The access area connecting vertical cores and units is minimal.

Courtyard

The courtyard, enclosed by the building volume and entered from the street, provides a way to all four vertical cores. It is visually connected with the street via a wide opening. The courtyard is designed as a transient space without amenities that would attract people to spend more time there. There is some vegetation contributing to the microclimate conditions. The air circulation through the courtyard is aided by the mentioned large opening at the ground level. The air moves between the cooler base, benefiting from shade and vegetation, and the warmer upper part. Breeze path in residential units, which are dually oriented for better air and light intake, is essentially based on the continuous air circulation through the courtyard.

A communal roof terrace is planned on the northern side. There are plans to introduce a movie library and a cinema on the ground floor that would be accessible from the street and operate independently from the housing.

Envelope

The building envelope has two layers made of durable and cost-efficient building materials. The outer layer provides solar protection. It incorporates rollable wooden shades, fixed fabric, a galvanized steel structure, and railings. Light colors dominate to reduce heat gain. Only the minimum of building material is used. To illustrate, a thin steel mesh used for railing is folded to gain stiffness without additional supporting structure. The inner layer of the building envelope is a thermal barrier. It is the wall of cross-laminated panels, protected with paint-coated steel cladding, often used in industrial buildings. Floor-to-ceiling openings in this wall connect the interior to private outdoor areas sitting between the two layers of the building

2. José Toral, "Building and Housing," guest lecture, Melbourne School of Design, August 3, 2022, https://msd.unimelb.edu.au/events/msd-public-lecture-building-and-housing.
3. The Frankfurt Kitchen was designed by Margarete Schütte-Lihotzky for the Ginnheim-Höhenblick Housing Estate, Frankfurt am Main, Germany, 1926–27.
4. The Museum of Modern Art, "The Frankfurt Kitchen," *Counter Space*, accessed March 12, 2023, https://www.moma.org/interactives/exhibitions/2010/counter_space/the_frankfurt_kitchen/.
5. Cabanon, designed and built by Le Corbusier in 1951 at Roquebrune-Cap-Martin in France, is now a UNESCO World Heritage Site.
6. Peris+Toral, "85 Viviendas Sociales en Cornellà, Cornellà 2021," accessed March 12, 2023, https://peristoral.com/proyectos/modulus-matrix-85-social-housing-cornella.

envelope, providing an extension to individual dwellings. As they are only partially enclosed by the outer layer, private outdoor areas offer a gradient transition between indoors and outdoors. Architectural means are used to create a microclimate in this intermediate space, which can be a few degrees Celsius cooler than the outside in summer.

Structure

The underlying architectural concept, the matrix of identical rooms, is reflected in the structural grid of the project. Consistent with the original proposal, the building has a concrete base, including foundations and an underground level, and a locally sourced timber structure, starting from the ceiling of the ground floor. The architects' intention, developed during the competition stage, was that a system of intersecting cross-laminated timber walls would be visible in the interior, further reinforcing the architectural conception of the building as a composite of universal rooms. However, during the project development phase, partially driven by fire safety regulations imposing an additional 30 millimeters of thickness for each exposed side of the structure, cross-laminated timber walls in the interior of the building were replaced with a structural system of glue-laminated beams and columns. The change reduced the use of timber by more than half, from 0.5 to 0.24 cubic meters of wood per square meter of floor area, helping to optimize the project's construction cost and environmental impact.[7]

Dwellings

The dwelling interior is dominated by white wall surfaces, hardwood flooring, and exposed cross-lamented timber ceilings. Plasterboard lines the interior side of cross-laminated timber facade walls, and all partitions are drywall. There are five different unit layouts that vary in size between four-and-a half and six rooms. The benefits of the universal room concept are apparent in the flexibility and efficiency of the unit layout. No dwelling space is consumed by corridors. Seamless transition between rooms has qualities of an open plan layout, including good cross ventilation and daylight, yet all rooms remain well-defined. It is easy to envisage how households of varied structures could use the dwellings differently. In his lecture hosted by the Melbourne School of Design, José Toral pointed out two principles of the unit layout in this project.[8] One is the sequencing of spaces. When looking longitudinally through the dwelling, rooms connected with large openings between cross walls create a rich visual experience and make the subjective perception of dwellings more spacious and larger than expected. The second point, also related to the cross-like configuration of partition walls apparent in floor plans, is about the customization of dwellings. Corner areas created by the walls can be understood as smaller and distinct parts of the rooms, which can be personalized and differently populated with furniture.

7. Peris+Troal, "85 Viviendas Sociales en Cornellà, Cornellà 2021."
8. Toral, "Building and Housing."

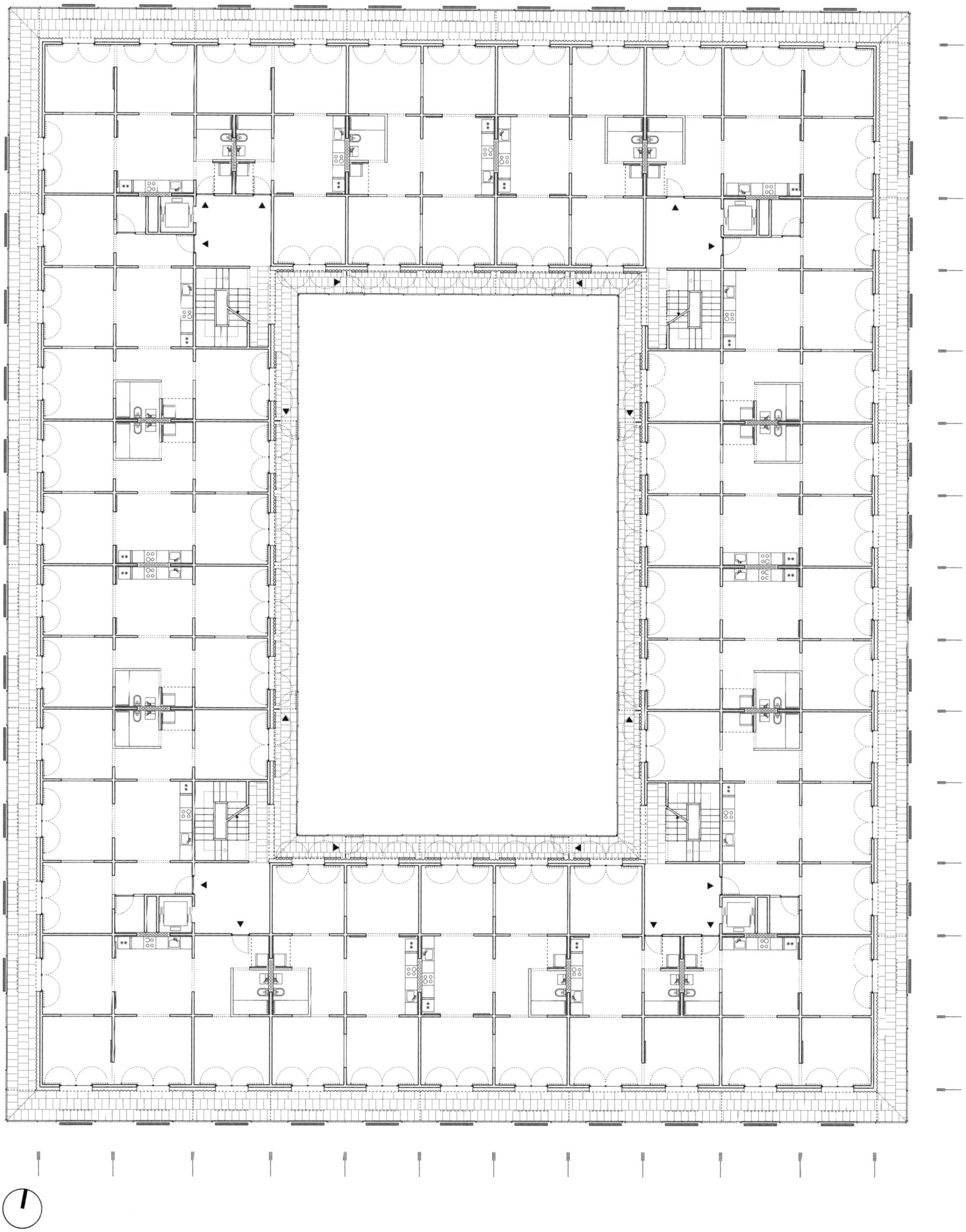

Figure 2
Typical floor plan, drawing scale 1:250

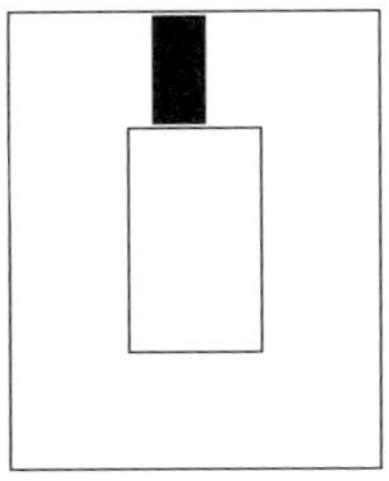

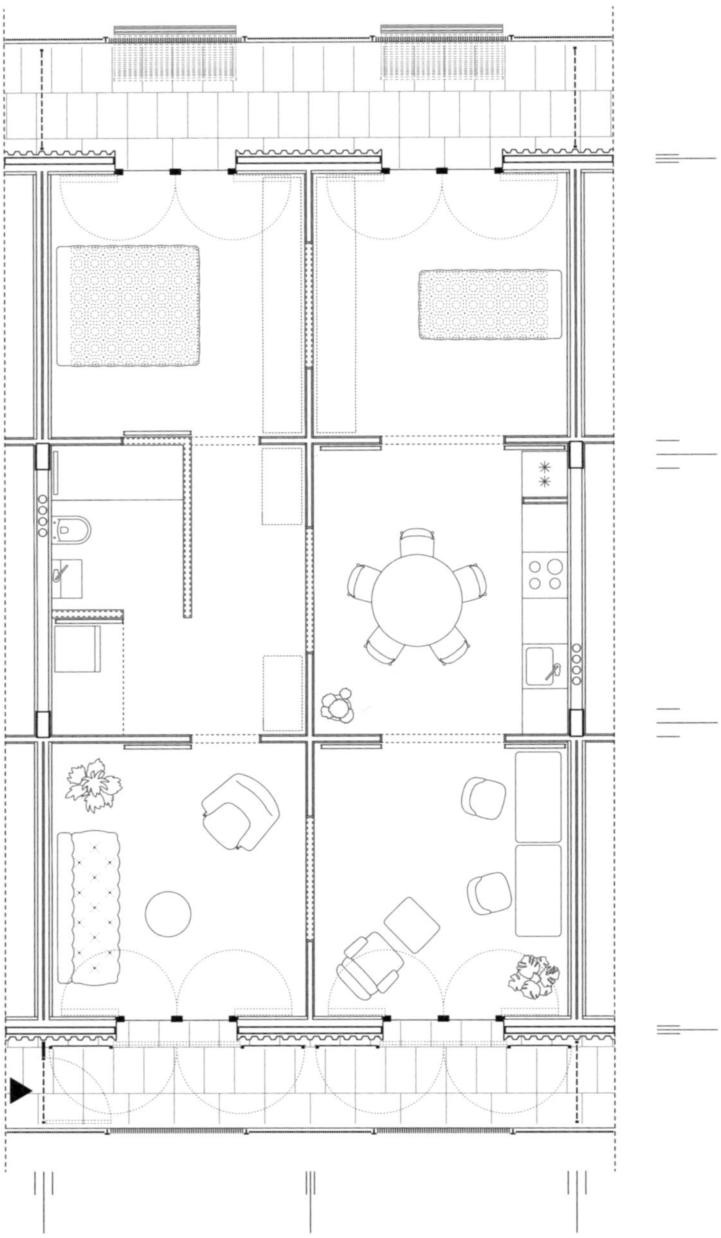

Figure 3
Sample unit layout, drawing scale 1:100

In conversation

The following section, an edited interview with José Toral recorded on January 17, 2023, provides further information from the architect's perspective.

DS My questions are about social, environmental, and economic values supported by the architectural project for Social Housing in Cornellà. How do you see the relationship between these three aspects in your work?

JT We often begin our lectures with a diagram showing how architecture relates to these three topics, and try to explain how our work in architectural design is situated between them to create integrated sustainability, combining social, economic, and environmental aspects into one. In our view, architecture deals with these challenges simultaneously and not any one of them separately. We aim to create buildings that are socially and environmentally adept at the same time. For example, in Cornellà, residents enter the building from the street via the courtyard before they choose one of the four vertical cores. We see the courtyard as a communal space with social value where people can meet and interact. At the same time, the courtyard has a role in air circulation. The shade and vegetation in the courtyard create a microclimate that is a bit cooler than the outdoor spaces exposed to the sun. It helps air movement and natural ventilation of the units. That is how architecture provides two answers, social and environmental, with the same gesture. As architects, we are interested in intermediate spaces, such as atriums and patios that we have created in several buildings to date, precisely for their dual roles, impacting social aspects and thermal comfort. Moreover, we aim to use the minimum building material needed for environmental and economic reasons. And finally, we are interested in the shared use of spaces, a concept that includes financial and social drivers and is central to collective housing.

DS What is the relationship between individual and communal spaces in the building?

JT Communal access areas are kept to a minimum. It is partly driven by efficiency, as this is a social housing project with a limited budget. We had a choice between creating access galleries and individually owned outdoor areas. We thought individual use was better than access. So, we have private outdoor areas overlooking the courtyard, which is the main communal space in the building. The overlooking improves safety. We were aware that it also created a condition that we know from *Rear Window*, a Hitchcock movie, whereby one can see a bit of what is happening in other apartments.[9] It concerns the relationship between individual and communal. In Spain, the privacy of the individual home is important. In some other cultures, there are different perceptions of privacy, and it may be more acceptable to have a visual connection between the communal space and the interior of the unit. Therefore, we introduce an intermediate space, a narrow and compressed space, to act as a buffer, protecting the intimacy of dwellings and providing an interface between interior and exterior.

9. *Rear Window* (1954, dir. Alfred Hitchcock) is based on Cornell Woolrich's 1942 short story.

DS That was another evidence of the overlap between the social and environmental values you mentioned earlier. The transition between the individual or private and communal is linked to the transition between inside and outside in the project. Can you say more about architectural means addressing the threshold between inside and outside?

JT A significant fraction of our construction budget was dedicated to the building envelope with two layers. We employ two building materials in the outer layer, a fixed galvanized steel mesh and rollable wooden blinds, to provide solar protection. Both materials are porous, allowing for natural ventilation of the intermediate space between the two layers of the facade, the inner layer being the insulated facade, combining solid parts with floor-to-ceiling windows. That outer layer is what one sees from the outside when looking from the street or across the courtyard. It creates a filter so one can understand what is happening but cannot or does not have to see what is inside. It safeguards the intimacy of private units. The appearance of the outer layer and one's ability to see through changes throughout the day because of the porosity of the steel mesh and its exposure to the sun. We started experimenting with this when we designed a temporary pavilion in a public space at Glories in Barcelona.[10] We continue our interest in how the transparency of the envelope changes from almost opaque to fully transparent throughout the day. Now that the building is in use and residents are bringing their plants and leaving bicycles out, we see that the transparency of the outer envelope works well with the personalization of private outdoor spaces in the building. It may be important to add that residents operate rollable shades and thus further impact the transparency levels and how the appearance of the building changes throughout the day.

DS What other architectural design decisions have impacted indoor air quality, thermal comfort, and residents' well-being?

JT Here in Barcelona, we have a humid climate. Air humidity levels spike to 80 percent in the summer, well above the ideal threshold of 50 percent. We know that high air humidity impacts thermal comfort and is suitable for propagating bacteria and fungi. In contrast, low humidity dries our airways and thus reduces our capacity to resist viruses and infections. To balance humidity levels in residential units, we use wood, a highly hygroscopic material, and have exposed the ceiling and underside of cross-laminated timber slabs throughout the interior. So, this large wood surface absorbs moisture from the interior in the summer and releases it in winter when indoor air is dry. That works quite well, although we had to explain to concerned residents that the sound of fine cracks in the wood during the process is not to worry about. Air movement is critical, and we ensured all residential units in Cornellà are cross-ventilated. Still, dehumidification is equally important for thermal comfort and for reducing/avoiding the need for mechanical air-conditioning. We know that thermal comfort can be adequate even if the air temperature is high, but humidity is kept in check, and the choice of clothing is right. In addition to hygroscopic, we employ building materials with high thermal inertia to reduce and avoid the need for mechanical air-conditioning. For example, for the flooring of outdoor areas, we use a form of concrete-based tiles, a material that attracts heat during the day and releases it at night when the air temperature is lower.

10. Peris+Toral, "Punto de Información En Glòries, Barcelona 2013," accessed March 15, 2023, https://peristoral.com/proyectos/punto-de-informacion-en-glories.

DS Can you explain your decision at the start of the design process to conceptualize the building as a composite of identical rooms?

JT We understand that family structure is changing. It is not about nuclear families only anymore. People live differently, households are of different structures, and some conventions concerning the unit layout may be outdated. In Cornellà, there is no usual hierarchy between rooms. All rooms are the same. We also made them big for Spanish standards so that they can be more than just bedrooms and be used in many ways. We understand that present-day households do not watch TV together in the living rooms, but their members use their own devices and spend more time individually. So, as we know it from the second part of the twentieth century, the living room may not be adequate for modern lifestyles. The role of a bedroom has also changed, as it is not only for sleeping anymore. Now, I am not saying that we are designing for less interaction between household members but that our design allows for flexibility and change. Most of the exchange today happens in the kitchen, where domestic work is done, where everyone passes through, and you have a table with a central role in the communal life of a household. This is how it was in the first part of the twentieth century when there was no TV. The drawings and analysis of Alexander Klein, known for his early work on the rationalization of building typologies, show that there were no living rooms in that period. Consequently, the dining table and the space around it took the central role in a household's communal life. I think this is relevant today since the importance of television is diminished.

"From the second part of the twentieth century, the living room may not be adequate for modern lifestyles. The role of a bedroom has also changed, as it is not only for sleeping anymore. Now, I am not saying that we are designing for less interaction between household members but that our design allows for flexibility and change. Most of the exchange today happens in the kitchen, where domestic work is done, where everyone passes through, and you have a table with a central role in the communal life of a household."

DS To conclude, I would like to ask one more question about your views of the economic side of housing provision. What design decisions have helped reduce the construction cost of this project?

JT The construction cost increases when you combine the involvement of different manufacturers in the same process. As an architect, a way to reduce the cost of a multiunit residential project is to consider the implications of using certain building materials and minimize the labor needed for manufacturing and construction. For example, we try to reduce the number of joints for any building element we design. To us, the key is understanding the constraints of building materials and construction techniques when considering forms. Consistency between design, building material, and construction process is essential. Different forms in our work result from using different materials, and we aim to get the most out of each building material. The key is understanding the process leading up to the realization of the specific element of the building and, eventually, the entire building.

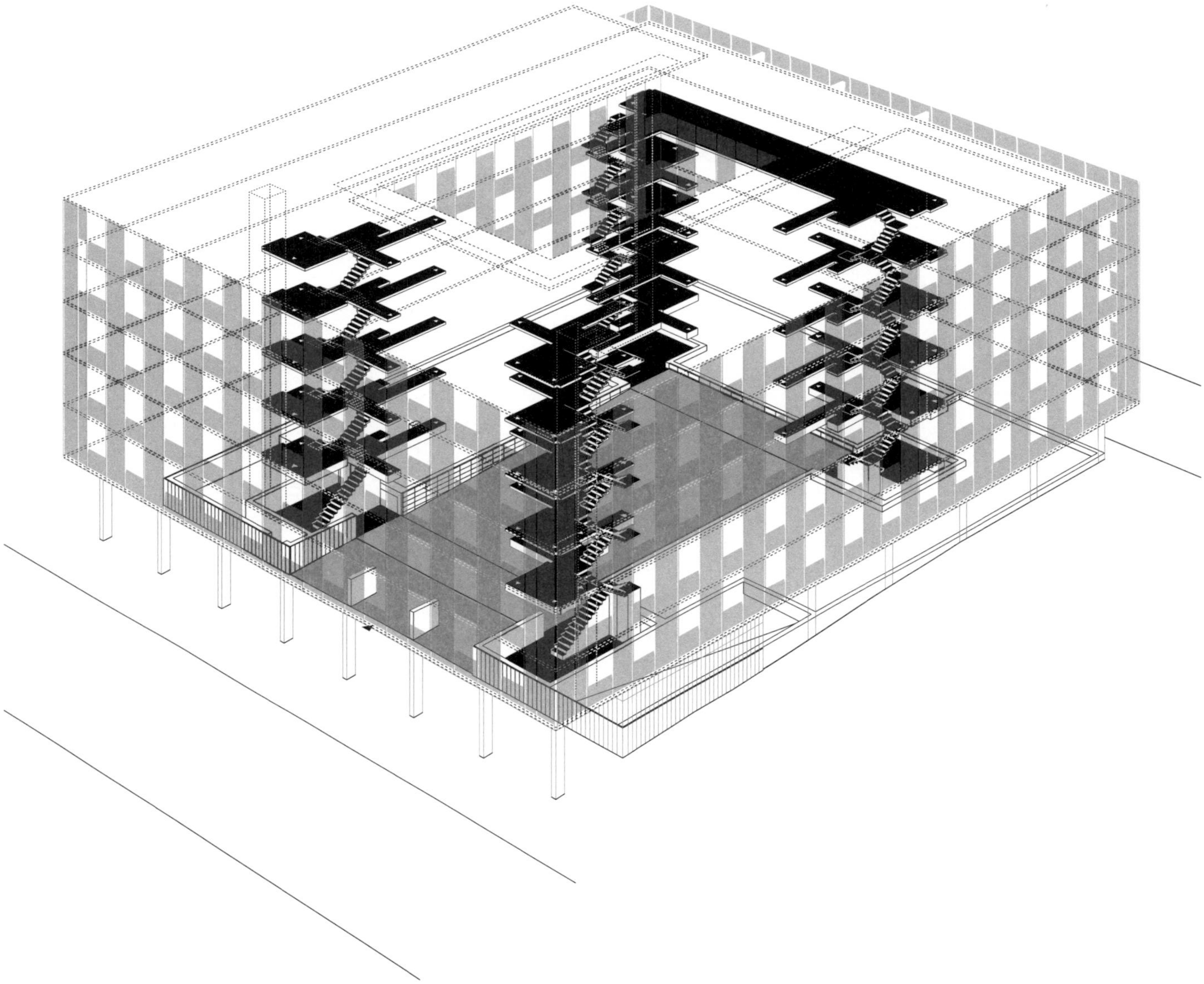

Figure 4
Perspective drawing indicating access and communal spaces in the building.

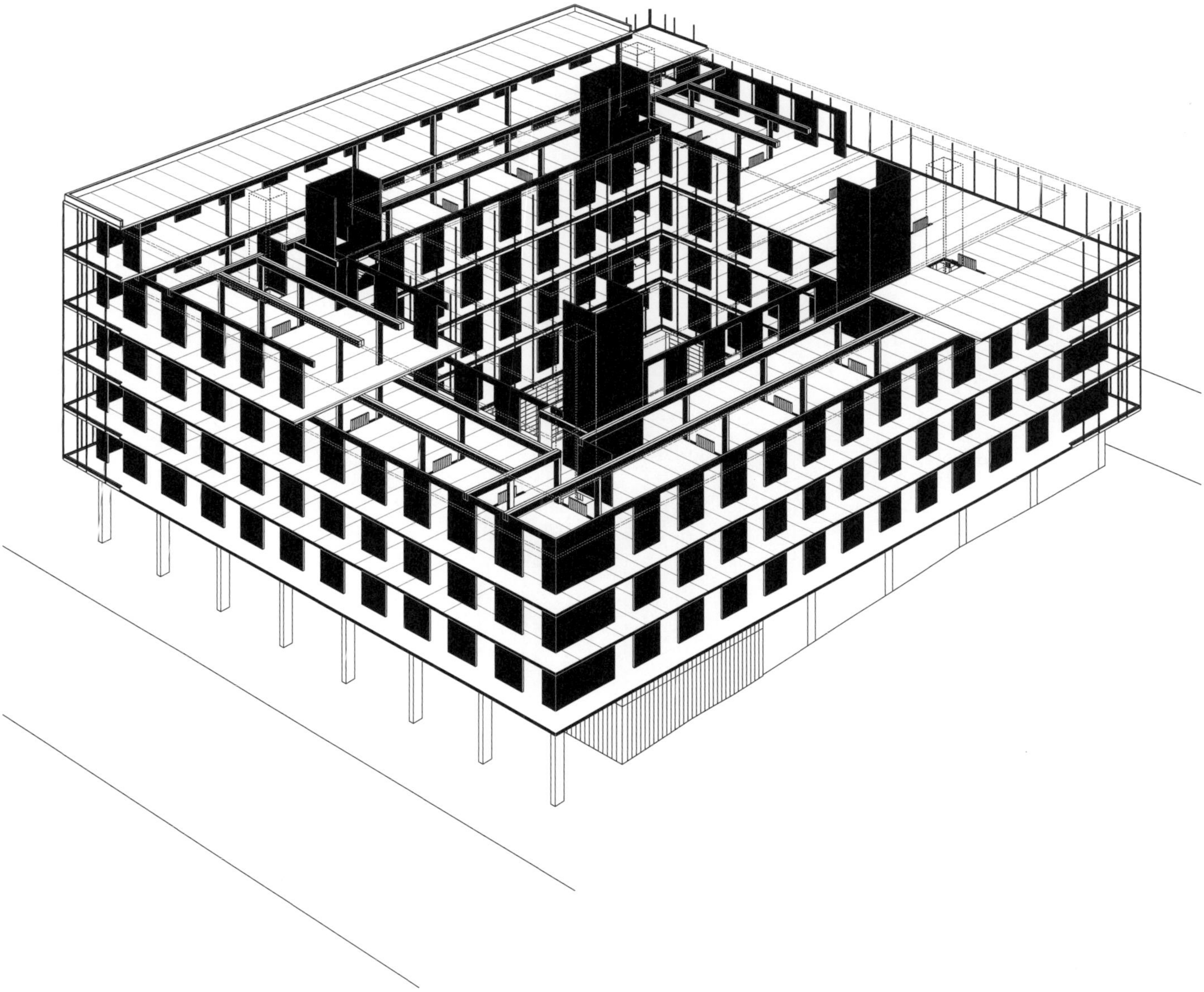

Figure 5
Perspective drawing indicating structural elements of the building.

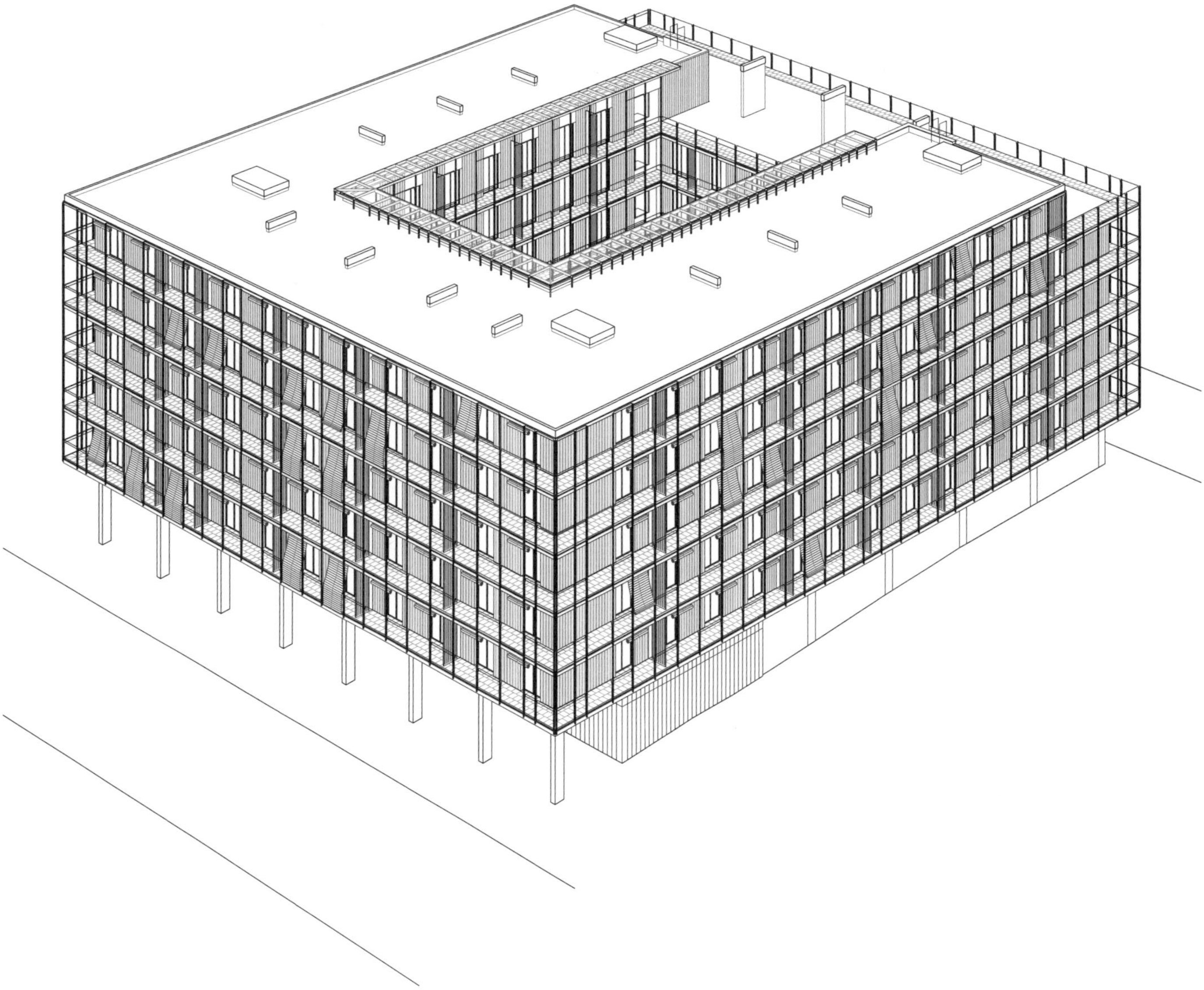

Figure 6
Perspective drawing of the building envelope.

In conversation

The following section is the edited interview with one of the residents, recorded on March 2, 2023. They live with their partner in the unit on the fifth floor.

DS How do you use the communal spaces of the building?

JV We don't have many communal spaces in our building, almost none indoors. We have a central courtyard, which is big. Residents' meetings or assemblies, as we call them, take place there. It is when all residents get together to discuss and vote on issues affecting the building management and maintenance. For example, we have recently discussed using the rooftop on level five, which is exactly next to my unit, and have voted as a group not to proceed with some building works.

DS Why is that?

JV The rooftop has not been used since the building was handed over to residents. I believe gravel would have to be replaced with some other finish on the roof surface. So, there is an economic side, but I also felt that people were not that keen on the communal use of the roof terrace. I hope that changes in the future. For now, the courtyard remains the main communal area. But this is not the place where people spend time. Everyone passes through it, and we meet there for assemblies that I mentioned, which take place only once or twice a year. That place is quiet, and the noise has never been an issue. If you shout, perhaps people would hear that in their apartments, but it does not happen. I wondered about it when we were moving here, not so much about the noise from the courtyard but from the noise coming from other apartments across it, but it proved not to be a problem. We all keep our windows open in summer, and it is okay. There is more of an issue with noise from the street side; there is a music bar across the street. But if you close your windows, it is okay. I can see children in the building, but they don't play in the courtyard. There is a kids' playground just next to the building.

DS Did you get the chance to meet your neighbors?

JV No, I don't know people living in the building well. We meet on our way in or out of the building. We exchange hellos, but not more than that. We have a WhatsApp group for practical things where you can report the defect of the entrance door, for example. The WhatsApp group is for residents using the same elevator and stairs. The building has four cores labeled A, B, C, and E, and each operates as if it were an independent building. There are four units on each floor per core, but only two are on the last floor where I am. Our neighbors from the fifth floor enter their unit directly from the vertical core while we use the gallery to enter our apartment. I suppose people run into each other more often on different floors.

DS Is privacy an issue?

JV I suppose privacy could be an issue for someone, but not for me on the fifth floor. You can see people on their terraces, eating dinner, or watering plants. At night, you can see a bit of the interior of other apartments, too, but only a little because we have perforated screens that help and provide a visual barrier. There are also built-in blinds that all units have, and some have added curtains.

DS How do you find daylighting and natural ventilation in your unit, and is your dwelling comfortable?

JV Daylight is one of the best things in our apartment. The room where I work, even though it faces west, still gets plenty of daylight in the early mornings from the other facade. Because of the dual orientation, the entire apartment, including the central zone quite far from the windows, is well lit throughout the day. It is the same with ventilation. We rely on natural ventilation, which works well with the windows opening with the tilt mechanism. I would love energy-efficient ventilation with a heat exchange system, which is now more common in residential buildings. However, we are never cold, nor have we had to use additional heaters. The central hydronic heating system which all units have is more than enough. I love the building materials used in the apartment's interior, such as timber ceiling, and throughout the building, such as the almost industrial treatment of handrails and building facade without paint. There are no defects. It feels like the details are well thought through and executed.

DS How do you use the private outdoor areas?

JV Like most other units in the building, our apartment has two outdoor areas. We use them both throughout the year, a bit less in the winter. We sunbathe, have lunch or breakfast, or read a book there. We have tables and chairs on both. It is great to have two options, one looking east and one looking west, as we can choose which one to use and when we want sun or shadow.

"You can see people on their terraces, eating dinner, or watering plants. At night, you can see a bit of the interior of other apartments, too, but only a little because we have perforated screens that help and provide a visual barrier."

DS Can you describe your unit's layout and how it fits your needs?

JV I am pleased with the unit layout, too. We have four rooms, and we feel they can be used in many ways. We almost always keep open the double doors between the living room facing the courtyard and kitchen and a room facing the street, which we use as a home office, so they are all combined into one large open space with plenty of light coming from two sides. The other two rooms we use as bedrooms, one for us and one for guests. We are a couple, and we need only one bedroom. We have decided to sleep in the room facing the courtyard, along the east facade where we have the morning sun. The size of the rooms is generous, above the usual standard, I would say. We have modified the central zone of the unit where the kitchen and bathroom are. We have removed the two small walls that were creating a buffer between the two to extend the kitchen and have a larger dining table for more people. I feel good in this unit and want to stay here for many years.

Photo Credits

Page 20
La Borda – Barcelona, Lacol
Lluc Miralles

Page 28
6×6 Block – Girona, bosch.capdeferro arquitectura
José Hevia

Page 37
Bonpland – Buenos Aires, adamo-faiden
Javier Agustín Rojas

Pages: 52, 55
New Housing on Briesestraße – Berlin, EM2N
Andrew Alberts

Pages: 67, 69
Buildings R and S in Pierre Loti Residential Area – Aytré, Guinée*Potin with Alterlab Architects
Sergio Grazia

Pages: 83, 85
Wildgarten / Sonnenblumenhäuser – Vienna, arenas basabe palacios arquitectos with M&S Architekten / Buschina & Partner
Kurt Hörbst

Pages: 100, 101
Iroko Housing – London, Haworth Tompkins
Morley von Sternberg

Pages: 111, 116, 117
La Vecindad Plaza Mafalda – Buenos Aires, adamo-faiden
Javier Agustín Rojas

Pages: 126, 127, 129
Wohnregal – Berlin FAR, frohn&rojas
David von Becker

Pages: 141, 148, 149
6×6 Block – Girona, bosch.capdeferro arquitectura
José Hevia

Page: 161
Residential Building in Straßgang – Graz, Riegler Riewe Architects
Bas Princen

Pages: 172, 174
Social Housing in Granadero Baigorria – Rosario, BBOA
Javier Agustín Rojas

Pages: 175
Social Housing in Granadero Baigorria – Rosario, BBOA
Manuel Pablo Cucurell

Pages: 186, 195 (up)
San Riemo – Munich, Summacumfemmer and Büro Juliane Greb
Petter Krag

Pages: 194, 195 (down)
San Riemo – Munich, Summacumfemmer and Büro Juliane Greb
Florian Summa

Pages: 203, 205
Yokohama Apartment – Yokohama, ON design partners
Koichi Torimura

Pages: 214, 222, 227
R50 – Berlin, ifau und Jesko Fezer, Heide & von Beckerath
Andrew Alberts

Page: 241
La Borda – Barcelona, Lacol
Baku Akazawa

Page: 242
La Borda – Barcelona, Lacol
Lluc Miralles

Pages: 258, 259, 261
85 Social Dwellings in Cornellà – Barcelona, Peris+Toral Arquitectes
José Hevia

Acknowledgments

Author
Dr Djordje Stojanović is a senior lecturer at the University of Melbourne, Faculty of Architecture, Building and Planning and a registered architect in the UK.

Acknowledgments
Drawings in this book were created by Milan Katic and Djordje Stojanović based on the concept design stage drawings produced by the architects whose work is presented.

The book follows a series of now publicly available online talks hosted by the Melbourne School of Design, organized between August 2020 and April 2023 in conjunction with the curriculum and as part of the ongoing debate on the role of architectural design practice in improving housing outcomes in urban environments. The book also springs from the research started in 2020 under Affordable Homes, Hallmark Research Initiative of the University of Melbourne.

Thanks
Thank you, José Toral (Peris+Toral Arquitectes), Verena von Beckerath (Heide & von Beckerath), Osamu Nishida (ON design partners), Marcelo Faiden (adamo-faiden), Graham Haworth (Haworth Tompkins), Fernando Brunel and Tomás Balparda (BBOA), Marc Frohn (FAR frohn& rojas); Ramon Bosch and Bet Capdeferro (bosch.capdeferro arquitectura), Hervé Potin (Guinée*Potin), Roger Riewe (Riegler Riewe Architects), Juliane Greb and Petter Krag (Büro Juliane Greb), Verena Lindenmayer (EM2N), Luis Basabe (arenas basabe palacios arquitectos), and Cristina Gamboa Masdevall and Carles Baiges Camprubí (Lacol) for providing most valuable insights into your architectural design practice.

Thank you, Katharina Kirsch-Soriano da Silva, Leonhard Schilling, Iain Tuckett, Jesko Fezer, Dörte Böschemeyer, Diego Silberberg, Paul Pistorius, Maria Sisternas Tusell, Franco Butteri, Maria Steyer, Atsuhiko Sano, Shin Yokoo, Sandra Girbés and Jan Vidal for your contributions.

Thank you, Andrew Alberts, José Hevia, Javier Agustín Rojas, Sergio Grazia, Kurt Hörbst, Morley von Sternberg, David von Becker, Bas Princen, Manuel Pablo Cucurell, Florian Summa, Petter Krag, Koichi Torimura, Baku Akazawa and Lluc Miralles for your wonderful photos.

Dedication
To Kristina and Sima, my family, for inspiration and support.

Imprint

Copy editing: Keonaona Peterson

Project management: Baharak Tajbakhsh, Regina Herr

Production: Anja Haering

Layout, cover design and typesetting: Ronald Adolf/Roman Heinrich; HE&AD Büro für Gestaltung Stuttgart—Basel

Paper: 120 g/m² Amber Graphic
Printing: Grafisches Centrum Cuno GmbH & Co. KG, Calbe
Image Editing: Repromayer GmbH, Reutlingen

Library of Congress Control Number: 2024901192

Bibliographic information published by the German National Library
The German National Library lists this publication in the Deutsche Nationalbibliografie; detailed bibliographic data are available on the Internet at http://dnb.dnb.de.

ISBN 978-3-0356-2761-9
e-ISBN (PDF) 978-3-0356-2763-3

Im Westfeld 8, 4055 Basel, Switzerland
Part of Walter de Gruyter GmbH, Berlin/Boston

9 8 7 6 5 4 3 2 1
www.birkhauser.com

MIX
Paper from responsible sources
FSC® C043106
FSC www.fsc.org